W9-BOF-175

Taking SIDES

Clashing Views on Controversial Moral Issues

Sixth Edition

Edited, Selected, and with Introductions by

Stephen Satris
Clemson University

Dushkin/McGraw-Hill
A Division of The McGraw-Hill Companies

To my father and the memory of my mother

Cover Art Acknowledgment

Charles Vitelli

Library of Congress Cataloging-in-Publication Data

Main entry under title:
    Taking sides: clashing views on controversial moral issues/edited, selected, and with introductions by Stephen Satris.—6th ed.
    Includes bibliographical references and index.
    1. Ethics. 2. Social ethics. I. Satris, Stephen, *comp.*

170'.22

0-697-39106-X   ISSN: 1094-7604

Printed on Recycled Paper

PREFACE

This text contains 34 essays, arranged in pro and con pairs, that address 17 controversial issues in morality and moral philosophy. Each of the issues is expressed in terms of a single question in order to draw the lines of debate more clearly.

Some of the questions that are included here have been in the mainstream of moral philosophy for hundreds of years and are central to the discipline. I have not shied away from abstract questions about moral knowledge, relativism, and the relationship between morality and religion. Other questions relate to specific topics of contemporary concern, such as euthanasia, abortion, affirmative action, and drug legalization.

The authors of the selections included here take a strong stand on a given issue and provide their own best defenses of a pro or con position. The selections were chosen for their usefulness in defending a position and for their accessibility to students. The authors are philosophers, scientists, and social critics from a wide variety of backgrounds. Each presents us with a determinant answer on an issue—even if we ultimately cannot accept the answer as our own.

Each issue is accompanied by an *introduction*, which sets the stage for the debate, and each issue concludes with a *postscript* that summarizes the debate, considers other views on the issue, and suggests additional readings. The introductions and postscripts do not preempt what is the reader's own task: to achieve a critical and informed view of the issue at stake. I have also provided relevant Internet site addresses (URLs) on the *On the Internet* page that accompanies each part opener.

Taking Sides: Clashing Views on Controversial Moral Issues is a tool to encourage critical thought on important moral issues. Readers should not feel confined to the views expressed in the selections. Some readers may see important points on both sides of an issue and may construct for themselves a new and creative approach, which may incorporate the best of both sides or provide an entirely new vantage point for understanding.

Changes to this edition   This new edition is significantly different from the fifth edition. There are two completely new issues: *Will the Information Revolution Benefit Society?* (Issue 5) and *Should Welfare Benefits Be Unconditional?* (Issue 7). In addition, for five of the issues retained from the previous edition, the issue question has been significantly modified and one or both selections have been replaced in order to focus the debate more sharply and to bring it up to date: Issue 1 on ethics, Issue 3 on morality and religion, Issue 4 on feminism, Issue 13 on the death penalty, and Issue 15 on affirmative action. For the issues on morality and culture (Issue 2), animal liberation (Issue 6), "hate speech" (Issue 8), homosexuality (Issue 9), and rich nations helping poor nations (Issue 17), one of the selections has been replaced to provide a new point of view. In all, there are 15 new readings in this edition. I have also revised and updated the issue introductions and postscripts where necessary.

A word to the instructor   An *Instructor's Manual With Test Questions* (multiple-choice and essay) is available through the publisher for the instructor using *Taking Sides* in the classroom. A general guidebook, *Using Taking Sides in the Classroom,* which discusses methods and techniques for using the pro-con approach in any classroom setting, is also available. An online version of *Using Taking Sides in the Classroom* and a correspondence service for *Taking Sides* adopters can be found at www.cybsol.com/usingtakingsides/. For students, we offer a field guide to analyzing argumentative essays, *Analyzing Controversy: An Introductory Guide,* with exercises and techniques to help them to decipher genuine controversies.

Taking Sides: Clashing Views on Controversial Moral Issues is only one title in the Taking Sides series. If you are interested in seeing the table of contents for any of the other titles, please visit the Taking Sides Web site at http://www.dushkin.com/takingsides/.

Acknowledgments   I would like to thank David Dean, list manager for the Taking Sides series at Dushkin/McGraw-Hill for his valuable editorial assistance and sound advice. In working on this revision, I also received useful suggestions from many of the users of the fifth edition, and I was able to incorporate several of their recommendations in this edition. I particularly wish to thank the following:

Sharron Cutbirth
Baylor University

James E. Doan
Nova Southeastern
    University

Douglas K. Erlandson
Southeast Community
    College

Guy P. Fenger
Barry University

Timothy C. Fout
University of Louisville

Thomas Halkett
University of Maine–Machias

Andrew Hamilton
University of Illinois at
    Chicago

Chris Jakway
Kellogg Community College

Robert M. Johnson
Community College of
    Vermont

Andrew Kampiziones
Florence Darlington Technical
   College

Sam Schlageter
Rowan Cabarrus Community
   College

Peter R. Loving
St. Francis College

Richard Werner
Hamilton College

Paul Rowgo
Barry University

Finally, a special debt of thanks is owed to those who tolerated my strange hours and the time spent away from them as this book was being prepared and revised: Kim, Angela, and Michelle.

Stephen Satris
Clemson University

CONTENTS IN BRIEF

CONTENTS

Philosopher James Rachels argues that there is indeed such a thing as moral knowledge and that it can be attained through careful attention to facts, logic, and argument. In particular moral cases, the right course of action is the one that is backed by the best reasons. British philosopher Bertrand Russell (1872–1970) argues that there is no such thing as moral knowledge. He maintains that morality is subjective—it is outside the realm of truth and falsehood.

American anthropologist Melville J. Herskovits (1895–1963) takes the position that morality has no absolute identity and that it is a social and cultural phenomenon that varies according to the customs and beliefs of different cultural groups. In his view, the great enemy of relativism is ethnocentrism. Professor of philosophy Louis P. Pojman holds that ethnocentrism is a prejudice like racism or sexism. He agrees that moral beliefs and practices vary greatly across cultures and from one person to another, but he finds very serious problems in the contention that moral principles derive their validity from dependence on society or individual choice.

Philosopher C. Stephen Layman argues that morality makes the most sense from a theistic perspective and that a purely secular perspective is insufficient. The secular perspective, Layman asserts, does not adequately deal with secret violations, and it does not allow for the possibility of fulfillment of people's deepest needs in an afterlife. Philosopher John Arthur argues that morality is logically independent of religion, although there are historical connections. Religion, he believes, is not necessary for moral guidance or moral answers; morality is social.

Author and social scientist Ruth Sidel argues that although feminism has made some progress, it holds the promise of even greater progress in the future toward a more caring society. Author and educator Elizabeth Powers argues that feminism naturally leads to strong governmental enforcement; a devaluing of housework, childrearing, and the family; and a struggle against the biology that links women with childbirth.

John S. Mayo, president emeritus of Lucent Technologies Bell Laboratories, formerly AT&T Bell Laboratories, argues that many benefits will follow from the information superhighway. One primary benefit will be that, since there will be less need to be in an urban location, people will be able to choose to live and work in rural or small-town environments and still have access to many of the resources that were previously available only in large cities. Political scientist James H. Snider argues that the very benefits brought by the information revolution also have tremendous environmental impacts, as the population is concentrated less in metropolises, spreads out more evenly across the country, and is drawn to currently rural areas.

Australian philosopher Peter Singer argues that since animals can suffer pain, and since pain is a bad experience for whatever being has that experience, human beings need to take the suffering of animals into consideration. British philosopher Michael P. T. Leahy argues that although it may be necessary to be more humane to animals, drastic changes in human behavior toward animals are not called for.

Canadian philosopher Trudy Govier argues that society does have an obligation to care for the less well off and that welfare benefits should be provided without being made contingent upon something (a willingness to work, for example). Tom Bethell, a contributing editor to the *National Review,* argues that the incentives of a generous welfare program encourage welfare dependency and discourage work and family life.

Writer and social commentator Jonathan Rauch argues that since it is impossible to eliminate bigotry from society completely, intellectual pluralism, which permits the verbal expression of various forms of bigotry, should be promoted. Philosopher Thomas W. Peard argues that some forms of hate speech—especially racist hate speech in the form of "fighting words"—are rightfully regulated. He maintains that such language causes serious harm and that this harm outweighs any interest on the part of the speaker.

Attorney Michael Nava and history teacher Robert Dawidoff argue that basic constitutional freedoms and liberties require the social acceptance of homosexuality. Carl F. Horowitz, a policy analyst at the Heritage Foundation, argues that legal acceptance of homosexuality has gone too far. He maintains that open displays of homosexual affection, the homosexualization of entire neighborhoods, and gay mannerisms are deeply offensive to heterosexuals.

Philosopher Helen E. Longino argues that pornography defames women, endorses the degradation of women, and contributes to a sexist culture that fosters psychological and physical violence against women. Philosopher Alan Soble contends that portrayals of degradation do not necessarily endorse it and that pornography is not responsible for violence against women.

Professor of philosophy Don Marquis argues that abortion is generally wrong because it deprives the individual of a future that he or she would otherwise have. Philosopher Jane English (1947–1978) argues that there is no well-defined line dividing persons from nonpersons and that some abortions are morally justifiable.

Ethan A. Nadelmann, an assistant professor of politics and public affairs, argues that drug prohibition is costly, ineffective, and immoral. Professor of history David T. Courtwright maintains that controlled legalization of drugs will lead to an increase in drug abuse and drug addiction.

Professor of law Ernest van den Haag argues that although studies of its deterrent effect are inconclusive, the death penalty is morally justified and should be retained. Professor of philosophy Hugo Adam Bedau argues that the death penalty should be abolished because it is unconstitutionally applied, fails to have a deterrent effect, and is not morally justified.

J. Gay-Williams believes that euthanasia is immoral because it violates one's natural personal will to survive. Moral philosopher Richard Brandt argues that in cases of euthanasia the killing could be allowable.

Professor of philosophy Albert G. Mosley argues that affirmative action is
a continuation of the history of black progress since the *Brown v. Board of
Education* desegregation decision of 1954 and the Civil Rights Bill of 1964. He
defends affirmative action as a "benign use of race." Professor of philosophy
Nicholas Capaldi argues that affirmative action is a vague notion but when
suitably defined, it is illegal and without moral justification.

Rhoda E. Howard, a Canadian sociologist, argues that universal human rights
are so basic that sometimes cultures have to change in order to accommodate
them. Vinay Lal, a professor of humanities, argues that the idea of human
rights is fundamentally a Western concept that is alien to most cultural traditions in the Third World.

Professor of philosophy Peter Singer argues that citizens of rich nations can
help those in poor nations without great harm to themselves and that, therefore, they *should* help. Biologist Garrett Hardin argues that since birthrates in
poorer nations are high and the earth can provide only finite resources, future
generations of all nations will be hurt if wealthy nations help poor nations.

INTRODUCTION

Thinking About Moral Issues

Stephen Satris

GETTING STARTED

If you were asked in your biology class to give the exact number of bones in the average human foot, you could consult your textbook, or you could go to the library and have the librarian track down the answer, or you could ask your friend who always gets A's in biology. Most likely you have not previously had any reason to consider this question, but you do know for certain that it has one right answer, which you will be expected to provide for the final exam.

What do you do, however, when faced with a moral question like one of the ones raised in this text? Where do you begin when asked, for example, Should welfare benefits be unconditional? Maybe this is something you have already thought about, particularly if you have ever been stopped by a streetperson and asked for money. You may already have formed some opinions or made some assumptions—or maybe you even have conflicting opinions. Whereas it is a relatively straightforward matter to find out how many bones there are in the human foot, in addressing moral issues, understanding cannot be acquired as easily. Someone cannot report back to you on the right answer. You will have to discuss the ideas raised by these moral questions and determine the answers for yourself. And you will have to arrive at an answer through reason and careful thought; you cannot just rely on your *feelings* to answer these questions. Keep in mind, too, that these are questions you will be facing your entire life—understanding will not end with the final exam.

In approaching the issues in this book, you should maintain an open mind toward both sides of the question. Many readers will already have positions on many of the issues raised in this book. But if you are committed to one side of an issue, it will be more difficult for you to see, appreciate, and, most important, learn from the opposing position. Therefore, you first ought to ask yourself what your own assumptions about an issue are; become aware of any preconceived notions you may have. And then, after such reflection, you ought to assume the posture of an impartial judge. If you have a strong prior attachment to one side, that should not prevent you from giving a sympathetic ear to the opposing side.

Once the arguments have been laid out and you have given them careful consideration, you do not want to remain suspended in the middle. *Now* is the time for informed judgment.

A natural dramatic sequence is played out for each of the 17 issues discussed in *Taking Sides: Clashing Views on Controversial Moral Issues*. A question is posed, and you must open yourself to hear each author's arguments, reasons, and examples, which are meant to persuade you to take the author's viewpoint. But then comes the second part of the drama. Having heard and considered both sides of an issue, what will *you* say? What understanding of the issue can *you* achieve?

You can choose aspects of the "yes" answer and aspects of the "no" answer and weave them together to construct a coherent whole. You can accept one answer and build some qualifications or limitations into it. Or you might be stimulated to think of a completely new angle on the issue.

Be aware of two dangers. The first is a premature judgment or fixed opinion that rules out a fair hearing of the opposing side. The second danger is to lack a judgment after having considered the issue. In this case, two contrary positions simply cannot both be right, and it is up to the reader to make an effort to distinguish what is acceptable from what is unacceptable in the arguments and positions that have been defended.

FUNDAMENTAL QUESTIONS

The 17 issues in this book are divided into five sections, or parts. The first section deals with fundamental questions about morality considered as a whole. It is in this context that one might be told that there is no such thing as moral knowledge, or that "it's all relative." The issues in the first part do not directly confront specific moral problems; they question the nature of morality itself.

Already in Part 1 we see something that is a recurring feature of moral thought and of this book: moral issues are interrelated. Suppose, for example, that you answer the question, Is morality relative to culture? in the affirmative and also answer the question, Does morality need religion? in the affirmative. How can these two answers fit together? A positive answer to the second question is generally thought to involve a source for morality that is beyond the customs and traditions of any one particular social group. (It may be possible to maintain affirmative answers to both of these questions, but a person who does so owes us an explanation as to how these two ideas fit together.) Many other issues that at first sight might seem distinct have connections between one another.

A further point, and one that applies not only to the issues in Part 1 but to controversial issues in general, is this: In evaluating any position, you should do so on the merits (or lack of merit) of the specific case that is made. Do not accept or reject a position on the basis of what the position (supposedly) tells you about the author, and do not criticize or defend a position by reducing it to simplistic slogans. The loss of articulation and sophistication that occurs when a complex position is boiled down to a simple slogan is significant and real. For example, a no answer to the question, Does morality need religion? might be superficially labeled as "antireligion" and a yes answer as "proreligion." Yet Saint Thomas Aquinas, who has always been regarded as the foremost theologian of the Christian tradition, would respond with a no to that question. Moral questions are complex, and the reduction of answers to superficial slogans will not be helpful. The questions and issues that are raised here require careful analysis, examination, and argumentation.

MORALITY AND CONTEMPORARY SOCIAL THOUGHT

Part 2 includes several questions that have to do with ways of looking at society and the world, turning a critical eye to social arrangements, and considering possible changes. In many ways the issues raised in this section are basic to an understanding of our own place within society and our relationships both to other people and to animals. Issues considered in Part 2 are: Does feminism provide a positive direction for society? Will the information revolution benefit society? Should animals be liberated? Should welfare benefits be unconditional? and, Should "hate speech" be tolerated?

The question of whether or not feminism provides a positive direction for society is one that relates to contemporary society. That is, even if we can agree that in the past feminism has provided much-needed benefit in addressing problems of second-class citizenship for women, does feminism also contain some disagreeable elements that are now coming to light? Has feminism already run its course, so that continued reliance upon it would be unhelpful? Or is there a positive view of society—some future ideal that we can aspire to—that feminism can enable us to envision and pursue?

The question of whether or not the information revolution will benefit society is worth raising partly because so much in the way of social benefits has been promised. How believable are these promises for future good? The optimistic view says that if the information revolution is successful and is able to deliver on its promises (for example, that we will be able to do so much more from our home computers), there will be less need for people to congregate in large metropolitan areas (near jobs). However, if people are spread out much more over the land, there will be massive environmental damage. Ironically, this objection does not stem from pessimism about achieving the results that information technology aspires to; rather, it stems from the idea of the very success of the information revolution.

Should animals be liberated? is a question that challenges much that has been taken for granted in our culture and that underlies the ways in which animals are currently treated. Is there such a thing as cruelty to animals and mistreatment of animals? Can animals suffer wrongfully at the hands of human beings? It is difficult to claim exemption from society's attitude toward animals—an attitude that tends to regard animals as *things* that people may use for their own purposes. Since most of us eat animals and participate in a system of raising animals for food, and since most of us use consumer items (such as shampoo) that have been tested on animals, are we (as Peter Singer and others would say) *speciesists*? Do we regard other animals as things that we may use for our own purposes? Is the call for animal liberation valid, or is it perhaps an expression of sentimentality or hazy thinking? Can a serious defense of the *status quo* be given, or is such a defense really just a rationalization or an expression of self-interest?

Should welfare benefits be unconditional? Those who answer no to this question usually want to make welfare payments conditional upon the recipient's being willing and able to work. Supporters of conditional welfare anticipate that as the recipients move into jobs they will move off welfare. Welfare is thus envisioned as temporary help, useful until the recipient gets back on his or her feet. On the other hand, many of those who support unconditional welfare see the idea of attaching conditions to welfare as involving unwelcome government intrusion into the lives of individuals. If conditions are imposed, government workers will have to check to determine whether or not the conditions are met.

The question about the toleration of "hate speech" is one about what kind of society we judge to be the best. We can anticipate that there will be individuals who hate and that some people will hate others because of their race, gender, ethnic origin, etc. The question is whether or not society—or some part of it, such as college campuses—should tolerate the open expression of this hatred in the form of speech. For our purposes, whether or not society should tolerate "hate speech" is more than simply a legal question, answerable by reference to the Constitution or prior court cases; it is a moral one.

MORALITY, SEX, AND REPRODUCTION

Part 3 introduces questions about particular moral issues that relate specifically to individuals as sexual and reproductive beings. The questions here are: Should society be more accepting of homosexuality? Is pornography degrading to women? and, Is abortion immoral?

Only in the last 20 years or so has a movement for "gay rights" and "gay liberation" in the United States even dared to be active and visible. Prior to that, public pressure with regard to homosexuality had been consistently negative. It is still largely negative, but there is also a strong belief that what consenting adults do in private is their own business (and not society's business). Homosexuality does not just involve private acts, however. Sexual orientation has at least as much to do with perceptions—with how one views one's own sexual identity and how one sees others—as it does with private acts. This issue is worth exploring not only for possible insights into homosexuality but also for possible insights into wider social arrangements and institutions.

A similar recommendation can be made about the question, Is pornography degrading to women? An exploration of this question, and associated social observations, might lead not only to insight into pornography itself but also to insight into larger social phenomena. Feminist criticism of pornography, represented by Helen Longino's selection, must be recognized as quite different from more traditional complaints about such things as "dirty pictures." Longino and others invite us to consider the matter in a new light; and when we do, that light may be turned onto other social phenomena too.

The question, Is abortion immoral? is not at all a new one. It threatens to polarize people into pro-life and pro-choice camps, but it is best to leave such labels and superficial slogans behind. Whenever an issue seems to demand answers very quickly, as this one might, it is better to go slowly and to first consider the arguments, examples, and rationale of each position before making up your mind.

MORALITY, LAW, AND SOCIETY

This section considers the questions, Should drugs be legalized? Should the death penalty be retained? Is euthanasia immoral? and, Is affirmative action fair?

Asking whether or not drugs should be legalized raises a number of points that require consideration. Here we are asking about the future and about what kind of society we think is worth aiming for. Should we strive for a society in which certain substances are available on the open market, with full legal status and quality control, or one in which certain substances are not allowed and violators are dealt with by the law? As the authors of the readings in this issue indicate, whatever the legal status of drugs, there will always be social costs.

Many subsidiary questions enter into the issue about the death penalty. Does the death penalty deter crime? Is it the only way to give some criminals what they deserve? Does it fall unfairly on minorities? Is there a worldwide contemporary movement away from capital punishment? And, finally, even if we had the answers to all these questions, is there a way of using those answers to address the overarching question of whether or not the death penalty should be retained?

Is euthanasia immoral? is another question of life and death. In addressing this question, it might be useful to keep in mind the distinction between voluntary euthanasia (where the person who is killed has specifically requested this) and involuntary euthanasia (where no such request has been made). Another important factor is the physical, mental, and emotional condition of the person who makes this request. Could it be that euthanasia is called for in some cases but not in others? Or is euthanasia always wrong?

The final topic discussed in this section is affirmative action, a policy that is intended to address problems arising from the history and the current state of race relations in the United States. Most arguments in favor of affirmative action can be seen as either backward-looking or forward-looking. Arguments that regard affirmative action as a form of compensation or as a response to previous injustices are backward-looking because they focus on prior events. Arguments that regard affirmative action as a means of achieving integration or diversity or as a means of providing minority role models are forward-looking because they point to the future. Critics of programs of affirmative action, however, have charged that such programs lead to reverse discrimination and unfairly focus on "group rights," whereas the only actual rights are rights of individuals.

MORALITY AND THE INTERNATIONAL SCENE

Since many legal matters only extend as far as a country's boundaries, and since morality is often associated with legality, moral concerns might be thought to be confined within one country's boundaries. But this would be a mistaken view. In the absence of any special theory to the contrary, it seems that moral issues do not radically change—as the law might well change—when we cross international borders.

The issues considered in Part 5 are by no means the only issues that involve the world outside one's own country, but they do raise questions that specifically address matters of government and international relations. The questions are: Are human rights basic to justice? and, Do rich nations have an obligation to help poor nations?

The question, Are human rights basic to justice? asks whether or not there are limits to what anyone—even a government or country—can demand of people. If there are basic human rights, then whatever system of law and justice is established by a given country must be a system that recognizes these human rights. But a contrary view would assert that the idea of human rights is only a Western idea that is not necessarily applicable on a universal basis.

The last issue, which asks whether or not rich nations have an obligation to help poor nations, can be considered in terms of a global village or a community of nations. Catastrophic natural disasters and political turmoil bring suffering and even starvation to the people of some nations. Is there an obligation on the part of more financially stable nations to assist in such cases? Or is reference to a global village or a community of nations inappropriate here? What responsibility does our own nation have toward the people of distant nations?

On the Internet . . .

Philosophy Associations
This site contains a listing of 15 diverse philosophical organizations that will provide students of philosophy with opportunities for greater involvement in the study of their subject matter and possible future career options.
http://www.rpi.edu/~cearls/pa.htm

The Internet Encyclopedia of Philosophy
This site is a very useful reference tool for the serious philosophy student. It contains an excellent collection of readings from classic philosophy texts and original contributions by professional philosophers around the Internet.
http://www.utm.edu/research/iep/

Internet Resources on Moral Relativism
This site, sponsored by *Ethics Updates,* contains discussion questions and Internet resources devoted to moral, cultural, and ethical relativism.
http://ethics.acusd.edu/relativism.html

Ethics Updates
Ethics Updates is an online journal edited by ethicist Lawrence M. Hinman of San Diego State University. The site organization proceeds from simple concept definitions to complex analyses, original treatises, and sophisticated search engines. There is a wide variety of subject matter, running from ethical theory to applied ethics, and the site offers frequent opportunities for user input.
http://ethics.acusd.edu/index.html

PART 1

Fundamental Issues In Morality

Even before confronting particular moral issues, we find that there are several conflicting claims that have been made about morality considered as a whole. Some people claim that there is no such thing as moral knowledge and that morality can provide no answers. Among them, subjectivists claim that all moral talk is simply the expression of subjective feelings, which vary from person to person. Cultural relativists, on the other hand, claim that morality is different for different cultural groups: one culture determines what is right or wrong for that culture, and another culture determines what is right or wrong for itself. Still other people claim that morality does not have a source in purely human experience and interaction. Religion, they say, is the ground of morality. These and other ideas are discussed in this section.

■ Can Ethics Provide Answers?

■ Is Morality Relative to Culture?

■ Does Morality Need Religion?

ISSUE 1

Can Ethics Provide Answers?

YES: James Rachels, from "Can Ethics Provide Answers?" *Hastings Center Report* (June 1980)

NO: Bertrand Russell, from *Religion and Science* (Oxford University Press, 1935)

ISSUE SUMMARY

YES: Philosopher James Rachels argues that there is indeed such a thing as moral knowledge and that it can be attained through careful attention to facts, logic, and argument. In particular moral cases, the right course of action is the one that is backed by the best reasons.

NO: British philosopher Bertrand Russell (1872–1970) argues that there is no such thing as moral knowledge. He maintains that morality is subjective—it is outside the realm of truth and falsehood. Differences in moral and value judgments are due to differences in taste.

One of the strange things about the question of whether or not moral knowledge exists is that many people feel attracted to both an affirmative and a negative answer. In support of the positive answer, it might be thought that there must be such a thing as moral knowledge because moral knowledge is something that a good upbringing is supposed to supply us with. A newborn baby doesn't know right from wrong, but the parents are supposed to raise the child so that she or he eventually does know right from wrong. In the law, a criminal defendant who is unable to distinguish right from wrong could plead insanity. Guilt itself seems to require the guilty party to have moral knowledge.

On the other hand, in support of the negative answer is the argument that although there are specialists in many branches of knowledge (e.g., geology and physics), there are no specialists in moral knowledge. Some religious people and members of the clergy have been deemed specialists in moral knowledge. But these "specialists"—unlike geologists and physicists —derive their "moral knowledge" from very different points of view and disagree greatly with each other about the so-called knowledge that they are supposed to have.

One of the obstacles to belief in moral knowledge stems from the difficulty of convincing people of the validity of a moral view that they are unwilling to accept. Naturally, it is extremely difficult to convince other people of *anything* that they are unwilling to accept! But this shouldn't be an obstacle. Think about what it is like for you to change your own mind about a moral matter. Suppose that at one time you believed that marriage between people of different races was morally wrong, but that you now believe that it is morally acceptable—in fact, assume that you think people of different races who want to marry each other have a *right* to do so. You would then think that your earlier view was wrong. Contrast this with your coming to dislike a certain type of food that you had previously enjoyed. Unlike the case about interracial marriage, you would not think that you used to have a wrong view, only that you used to like something that you no longer like.

As people pass through adolescence and into adulthood, they change in many ways. Some things that used to be liked are no longer liked; some things that used to be thought wrong are no longer thought wrong; and some things that used to be thought right are now thought wrong. Just as new likes and dislikes develop, new moral beliefs are formed. Old likes and dislikes are merely discarded, but old moral beliefs are not only discarded but thought wrong. All this suggests that there is indeed such a thing as moral knowledge.

Yet there are numerous challenges from science. One challenge comes from the physical sciences, where scientific knowledge can be achieved through experimentation and interaction with the physical world. The validity of the knowledge gained in this way can be demonstrated, and it can be demonstrated so strongly that scientists sometimes have to accept new beliefs and admit that they were previously wrong. The scientific challenge is that so-called moral knowledge has no solid connection with reality.

In the selections that follow, James Rachels argues that the idea of moral knowledge is valid. He does not expect moral knowledge to come from science—or at least not from science alone—but from careful attention to facts, logic, and argument. Moral knowledge, Rachels says, must of course be answerable to the facts, but it must also be answerable to reason. It is of no use to pretend to solve moral questions on the basis of your "intuitions" or your immediate responses to these questions. Such intuitions may have nothing to do with knowledge. In any particular moral case, the right answer is the one that is backed by the best reasons and arguments. It is *these* that must be examined by anyone whose goal is moral knowledge.

Bertrand Russell argues that knowledge must be grounded in science. Moral knowledge (if there were such a thing) would therefore have to be grounded in science. If two people agree in their values, science can help them by determining the best means of realizing those values. But if those people disagree, Russell concludes, there is no intellectual way of resolving their disagreement.

YES
James Rachels

CAN ETHICS PROVIDE ANSWERS?

THE DIFFERENCE SCIENCE MAKES

Somehow it seems *natural*, at the end of the twentieth century, to be skeptical about ethics. . . . Moral skepticism seems to be our lot. The explanation of why this should be so goes deep into our history and into our understanding of the world and our place in it. The most salient part of this history concerns the rise of modern science. Before modern science, people could reasonably believe that their moral judgments were warranted by the facts of nature. The prevailing view of what the world was like supported such a belief. Today this is no longer true.

Understanding What the World Is Like

The Greeks conceived the world to be an orderly system in which everything has its proper place. A central feature of this conception was the idea that *everything in nature exists for a purpose.* Aristotle incorporated this idea into his system of thought when he said that in order to understand anything, we must ask four questions: What is it? What is it made of? How did it come to exist? And what is it for? (The answers might be: this is a knife, it is made of steel, it was made by a craftsman, and it is used for cutting.) Aristotle assumed that the last question—What is it for?—could sensibly be asked of anything whatever. "Nature," he said, "belongs to the class of causes which act for the sake of something."[1]

It seems obvious that artifacts such as knives have purposes, because we have a purpose in mind when we make them. But what about natural objects that we do not make? Do they have purposes too? Aristotle thought so. One of his examples was that we have teeth so that we can chew. Such biological examples can be quite persuasive; the parts of bodies do seem, intuitively, to have particular purposes—eyes are for seeing, the heart is for pumping blood, and so on. But Aristotle's thesis was not limited to organic beings. He also thought, to take a different sort of example, that rain falls so that plants can grow. As odd as it may seem to a modern reader, Aristotle was perfectly serious about this. He considered other alternatives, such as that the rain falls "of necessity" and that this helps the plants only be "coincidence," and rejected them. He even considered a hypothesis strikingly like Darwinian natural selection: "Wherever then all the parts [of plants and animals] came about just what they would have been if they had come to be for an end, such things survived, being organized spontaneously in a fitting way; whereas those which grew otherwise perished and continue to perish[2].... But Aristotle rejects this, too. His considered view was that plants and animals are what they are and that the rain falls as it does "because it is better so."

The world, therefore, is an orderly, rational system, with each thing having its own proper place and serving its own special purpose. There is a neat hierarchy: the rain exists for the sake of the plants, the plants exist for the sake of the animals, and the animals exist—of course—for the sake of people, whose well-being is the point of the whole arrangement:

> [W]e must believe, first that plants exist for the sake of animals, second that all other animals exist for the sake of man, tame animals for the use he can make of them as well as for the food they provide; and as for wild animals, most though not all of these can be used for food or are useful in other ways; clothing and instruments can be made out of them. If then we are right in believing that nature makes nothing without some end in view, nothing to no purpose, it must be that nature has made all things specifically for the sake of man.[3]

It was a stunning anthropocentric view. Aristotle may be forgiven, however, when we consider that virtually every important thinker in our history has entertained some such thought. Humans are a remarkably vain species.

The Christian thinkers who came later found this view of the world to be perfectly congenial. Only one thing was missing: God was needed to make the picture complete.... Thus, the Christian thinkers said that rain falls to help the plants *because that is what the Creator intended* and the animals are for human use *because that is what God made them for*. Values and purposes were, therefore, conceived to be a fundamental part of the nature of things, because the world was believed to have been created according to a divine plan.

The Aristotelian-Christian view of the world had a number of consequences for ethics. On the most general level, it affirmed the supreme value of human life, and it explained why humans are entitled to do whatever they please with the rest of nature. The basic moral arrangement —human beings, whose lives are sacred, dominating a world made for their benefit—was enshrined as the Natural Order of Things.

At a more detailed level, a corollary of this outlook was that the "laws of nature" specify how things ought to be as well as describing how things are. In turn, knowing how things ought to be enables us to evaluate states of affairs as objectively good or bad. Things are as they ought to be when they are serving their natural purposes; when they do not or cannot serve those purposes, things have gone wrong. Thus, teeth that have decayed and cannot be used for chewing are defective; and drought, which deprives plants of the rain they need, is a natural objective evil.

There were also implications for human action. Moral rules could be viewed as one type of law of nature. A leading idea was that some forms of human behavior are "natural," while others are not; and "unnatural" acts are said to be wrong. Beneficence, for example, is natural for us because God has made us social creatures. We want and need the friendship of other people and we have natural affections for them; hence, behaving brutishly toward them is unnatural. Or, to take a different sort of example, the purpose of the sex organs is procreation. Thus the use of them for other purposes is "contrary to nature"—that is why the Christian church has traditionally regarded as impermissible any form of sexual activity that does not result in procreation, such as masturbation, gay sex, or the use of contraceptives.

The Aristotelian worldview began to break up in the sixteenth century when it was discovered that the earth orbits the sun, rather than the other way around. This was an alarming development, because the earth's being at the center of things was an important symbol of mankind's central place in the divine plan. But the heliocentric solar system was by no means the most subversive aspect of the emerging new science. Galileo, Newton, and others developed ways of understanding natural phenomena that made no use of evaluative notions. To their way of thinking, the rain has no purpose. It does not fall in order to help the plants grow. Instead, it falls as a result of physical causes....

This style of explanation—appealing only to physical laws devoid of any evaluative content—was developed in such great and persuasive detail, in connection with so many natural phenomena, that educated people universally gravitated to it. With its superior predictive and explanatory power, this way of thinking transformed people's view of what the world is like. But part of the transformation, inseparable from the rest, was an altered view of the nature of ethics. Right and wrong could no longer be deduced from the nature of things in themselves, for on the new view, the natural world does not, in and of itself, manifest value and purpose. The inhabitants of the world may have needs and desires that generate values special to them, but that is all. The world apart from those inhabitants knows and cares nothing for their values, and it has no values of its own. A hundred and fifty years before Nietzsche declared, "There are no moral facts," David Hume had reached the same conclusion. Hume summed up the moral implications of the new worldview when he wrote: "Take any action allow'd to be vicious: Willful murder, for instance. Examine it in all lights, and see if you can find that matter of fact, or real existence, which you call *vice*. In whichever way you take it, you find only certain passions, motives, volitions and thoughts. There is no other matter of fact in the case."[4] And what of the old idea that "nature has made all things for the sake of man?" In his great essay on suicide, published posthumously in 1783, Hume replied: "The life of a man is of no greater importance to the universe than that of any oyster."[5]

Emotivism and the Eclipse of Ethics

Hume considered belief in an objectively correct ethical system to be part of the old "superstition and false religion." Stripped of false theology, Hume said, we should come to see our morality as nothing more than the expression of our feelings. "When you pronounce any action or character to be vicious," he wrote, "you mean nothing, but that from the constitution of your nature you have a feeling or sentiment of blame from the contemplation of it."[6]

In the twentieth century Hume's thoughts were adapted to support a theory known as *emotivism*. The development of emotivism was one of the great achievements of twentieth-century philosophy....

To its supporters, emotivism seemed in keeping with a properly scientific outlook. Science describes the facts in an exhaustive way: any state of affairs, any "fact" that is part of the objective world, must be discoverable by scientific methods and describable in the language of science, broadly speaking. The emotivists denied that there are moral facts. One way of putting their argument is this: Facts are the counterparts of true statements; the fact that Buster Keaton made movies is what makes the statement "Buster Keaton made movies" true. We might think there are moral facts because we mistakenly assume that moral "statements" are the kinds of utterances that could be true. Thus, if in saying that Hitler is wicked we are saying something true, there must be a corresponding fact, Hitler's being wicked, that makes it true. However, once we understand that moral "statements" are not really statements at all and, indeed, are not even the sorts of utterances that could be true, the temptation to think there are moral facts disappears. Thus, the belief in moral facts could now be seen not only as the legacy of discarded scientific and religious views but as the symptom of a mistaken assumption about moral language as well.

With the arrival of emotivism as the dominant theory of ethics, many philosophers believed that the final truth about morality had at last been discovered. We can now understand, they said, why ethical disputes go on endlessly, with neither side being able to convert the other. In an ethical dispute, neither side is "correct," because ethical utterances are not the kinds of utterances that are correct or incorrect. Moreover, there are no "proofs" in ethics, because matters of fact and matters of attitude are logically distinct. Two people can agree on all the facts about a situation and yet have utterly different attitudes toward it. Ethical disagreement is like disagreeing about the choice of a restaurant: people might agree on all the facts about restaurants and yet disagree about where to eat, because some prefer Chinese food while others prefer Italian. That's the way ethics is, and that's all there is to it....

Eventually, however, emotivism fell out of favor, and today it has few adherents. The theory's demise was partly a matter of intellectual fashion. Before his death in 1979, Charles Stevenson, whose book *Ethics and Language* was the definitive statement of emotivism,[7] remarked that while philosophers had abandoned the theory, no one had actually refuted it. But emotivism had failed because it did not do one of the main things that a theory of ethics must do: it did not provide a satisfactory account of the place of reason in ethics. It is a point of logic that moral judgments, if they are to be acceptable, must be founded on good reasons. If I tell you that such-and-such action is wrong, you are entitled to ask why it is wrong; and if I have no adequate reply, you may reject my advice as unfounded. This is what separates moral judgment from mere statements of preference. If I only say "I like so-and-so," I do not need to have a reason; it may just be a brute fact about me that I happen to like it. In making a moral judgment, however, one is at least implicitly claiming that there is some reason for or against what is being recommended or rejected....

ETHICS AND RATIONALITY

Ultimately the case against ethics can be answered only by demonstrating how moral problems are solvable by rational methods.... But what can be said of a ... general nature? How does one go about establishing what is the right thing to do? If there are answers in ethics, how are they to be found? Considered abstractly, these may seem to be impossibly difficult questions. But they are not so hard as one might think.

We have already alluded to the key idea: In any particular case, the right course of action is the one that is backed by the best reasons. Solving moral problems, then, is largely a matter of weighing the reasons, or arguments, that can be given for or against the various alternatives....

But how are arguments to be tested? What distinguishes strong arguments from weak ones? The first and most obvious way that a moral argument can go wrong is by misrepresenting the facts. A rational case for or against a course of conduct must rest on some understanding of the facts of the case—minimally, facts about the nature of the action, the circumstances in which it would be done, and its likely consequences. If the facts are misrepresented, the argument is no good. Even the most skeptical thinkers agree that reason has this role to play in moral judgment.

Unfortunately, however, attaining a clear view of the facts is not always a simple matter. In the first place, we often need to know what the consequences of a course of action will be, and this may be impossible to determine with any precision or certainty....

Moreover, it is often difficult to determine the facts because the facts are distressingly complex....

Suppose, though, that we have a clear view of the relevant facts, and so our arguments cannot be faulted on that ground. Is there any other test of rationality the arguments must pass? Hume's official view was that, at this point, reason has done all it can do, and the rest is up to our "sentiments." Reason sets out the facts; then sentiment takes over and the choice is made. This is a tempting idea, but it only illustrates a common trap into which people may fall. Philosophical theses may seduce with their beautiful simplicity. An idea may be accepted because of its appeal at a high level of generality, even though it does not conform to what we know to be the case at a lower level.

In fact, when Hume was considering actual ethical issues and not busy overemphasizing the role of sentiment, he knew very well that appeals to reason are often decisive in other ways. In the essay on suicide, he produced a number of powerful arguments in support of his view that a person has the right to take his own life when he is suffering without hope from a painful illness. Hume specifically opposed the traditional religious view that since life is a gift from God, only God may decide when it shall end. About this he made the simple but devastating observation that we "play God" as much when we save life as when we take it. Each time a doctor treats an illness and thereby prolongs a life, he decrees that this life should not end *now*. Thus if we take seriously that only God may determine the length of a life, we have to renounce not only killing but saving life as well.

Hume's point has force because of the general requirement that our arguments be consistent, and consistency, of course, is the prime requirement of rationality. Hume... was pointing out that we may appeal to a general principle ("Only God has the right to decide when a life shall end") only if we are willing to accept its consequences. If we accept some of them (the prohibition of suicide and euthanasia) but not others (the abandonment of medicine), then we are inconsistent....

There are other ways an ethical view may fail to pass the test of consistency. An ethical view may be based on one's "intuitions"—prereflective hunches about what is right or wrong in particular cases—and, on examination, these may turn out to be incompatible with one another. Consider the difference between killing someone and "merely" allowing someone to die. Many people feel intuitively that there is a big moral difference between these two. The thought of actively killing someone has a kind of visceral repulsiveness about it that is missing from the more passive (but still unpleasant) act of standing by and doing nothing while someone dies. Thus it may be held that although euthanasia is wrong, since it involves direct killing, nevertheless it is sometimes permissible to allow death by refraining from life-prolonging treatment.

To be sure, if we do nothing more than consult our intuitions, there seems to be an important difference here. However, it is easy to describe cases of killing and letting die in which there does *not* seem to be such a difference. Suppose a patient is brought into an emergency room and turned over to a doctor who recognizes him as a man against whom he has a grudge. A quick diagnosis reveals that the patient is about to die but can be saved by a simple procedure—say, an appendectomy. The doctor, seeing his chance, deliberately stalls until it is too late to perform the life-saving procedure, and the patient dies. Now, most of us would think, intuitively, that the doctor is no better than a murderer and that the fact that he did not directly kill the patient, but merely let him die, makes no difference whatever.

In the euthanasia case, the difference between killing and letting die seems important. In the grudge case, the difference seems unimportant. But what is the truth? Is the difference important, or isn't it? Such cases show that unexamined intuitions cannot be trusted. That is not surprising. Our intuitions may be nothing more than the product of prejudice, selfishness, or cultural conditioning; we have no guarantee that they are perceptions of the truth. And when they are not compatible with one another, we can be sure that one or the other of them is mistaken....

THE LIMITS OF RATIONALITY

This discussion will not have dispelled all the nagging doubts about ethics. Rational methods can be used to construct arguments and to expose factual error and inconsistency in the ways we have described, but is that enough to save ethics from the charge that, at bottom, there is no "truth" in its domain? Couldn't two people who are equally rational—who have all the relevant facts, whose principles are consistent, and so on—still agree? And if "reason" were inadequate to resolve the disagreement, wouldn't this show that, in the end, ethics really is only a matter of opinion? These questions will not go away.

There is a limit to what rational methods can achieve, which Hume described in the first appendix to his *Inquiry Concerning the Principles of Morals:*

> Ask a man *why he uses exercise;* he will answer, *because he desires to keep his health.* If you then inquire *why he desires health,* he will readily reply, *Because sickness is painful.* If you push your inquires further and desire a reason *why he hates pain,* it is impossible he can ever give any. This is an ultimate end, and is never referred to any other object.
>
> Perhaps to your second question, *why he desires* health, he may also reply that *it is necessary for the exercise of his calling.* If you ask *why he is anxious on that head,* he will answer, *because he desires to get money.* If you demand, *Why? It is the instrument of pleasure,* says he. And beyond this, it is an absurdity to ask for a reason. It is impossible there can be a progress *in infinitum,* and that one thing can always be a reason why another is desired. Something must be desirable on its own account, and because of its immediate accord or agreement with human sentiment and affection.[8]

The impossibility of an infinite regress of reasons is not peculiar to ethics; the point applies in all areas. Mathematical reasoning eventually ends with axioms that are not themselves justified, and reasoning in science ultimately depends on assumptions that are not proved. It could not be otherwise. At some point, reasoning must always come to an end, no matter what one is reasoning about.

But there is a difference between ethics and other subjects, and that difference is in the involvement of the emotions. As Hume observed, when we come to the last reason, we must mention something we care about. Thus, even though "the right thing to do" always depends on what there are the best reasons for doing, *what counts as a reason* itself depends on our emotions. Nothing can count as an ultimate reason for or against a course of conduct unless we care about that thing in some way. In the absence of any emotional involvement, there are no reasons for action. On this point the emotivists were right, whatever defects their overall theory might have had. And it is the possibility that people might care about different things, and so accept different ultimate principles between which reason cannot adjudicate, that continues to undermine confidence in ethics.

I believe this possibility cannot ever be ruled out entirely and that it will always be the source of a kind of nervousness about ethics. The nervousness cannot be eliminated; we have to live with it. There is, however, one further point to be considered—a point that goes some way toward minimizing the worry.[9]

What people care about is itself sensitive to pressure from the deliberative process and can change as a result of thought. This applies as much to people's "ultimate" cares and desires as to their more passing fancies. Someone might not care very much about something before he thinks it through but come to feel differently once he has thought it over. This has been considered extremely important by some of the major philosophers. Aristotle, Butler, and others emphasized that responsible moral judgment must be based on a full understanding of the facts; but, they added, after the facts are established, a separate cognitive process is required for the agent to understand fully the import of what he or she knows. It is necessary not merely to know the facts but also to rehearse them carefully in one's mind, in an impartial, nonevasive way. Only then will one have the kind of knowledge on which moral judgment may be based.

Aristotle even suggested that there are two distinct species of knowledge: first, the sort of knowledge had by one who is able to recite facts, "like the drunkard reciting the verses of Empedocles," but without understanding their meaning; and, second, the sort of knowledge had when one has thought carefully about what one knows. An example might make this clearer. We all know, in an abstract sort of way, that many children in the world are starving; yet for most of us this makes little difference to our conduct. We will spend money on trivial things for ourselves, rather than allowing it to be spent on food for them. How are we to explain this? The Aristotelian explanation is that we "know" the children are starving only in the sense in which the drunkard knows Empedocles' verses—we simply recite the fact.[10] Suppose, though, that we thought carefully about what it must be like to be a starving orphan. Our attitudes, our conduct, and the moral judgments we are willing to make might be substantially altered.

Some years ago, during the Vietnamese War, a wire-service photograph of two Vietnamese orphans appeared in American newspapers. They were sleeping on a Saigon street; the younger boy, who seemed to be about four, was inside a tattered cardboard box, while his slightly older brother was curled up around the box. The explanation beneath the photograph said that while they begged for food during the day, the older boy would drag the box with them, because he didn't want his brother to have to sleep on the sidewalk at night.

After this photograph appeared, a large number of people wrote to relief agencies offering help. What difference did the picture make? It was not a matter of people's being presented with new information—it wasn't as though they did not know that starving orphans have miserable lives. Rather, the picture brought home to them in a vivid way things they already knew. It is easy to think of starving children in an abstract, statistical way; the picture forced people to think of them concretely, and it made a difference to people's attitudes.

In moral discussion we often recognize that thinking through what one knows is a separate matter from merely knowing; and we exploit this in a certain strategy of argument. It is the strategy that begins "Think what it is like . . ."

- Those who favor voluntary euthanasia ask us to consider what it is like, from the point of view of the dying patient, to suffer horribly. If we did, they imply, we would feel more favorably disposed toward mercy killing.

- Albert Camus, in his essay on capital punishment, "Reflections on the Guillotine," argued that people tolerate the death penalty only because they think of it in euphemistic terms ("Pierre paid his debt to society") rather than attending to the sound of the head falling into the basket.[11] If we thought about it nonevasively, he says, we could not avoid detesting it.

- Opponents of abortion show pictures of fetuses to force us to pay attention to what it is that is killed. The assumption is that if we did, we could not approve of killing it.

Often this method of argument is dismissed as nothing more than a demagogic appeal to emotion. Sometimes the charge is true. But this type of argument may also serve as an antidote for the self-deception that Bishop Butler saw as corrupting moral thought. When we do not want to reach a certain conclusion about what is to be done—perhaps we would rather spend money on ourselves than give it for famine relief—we may refuse to face up in a clear-minded way to what we know. Facts that would have the power to move us are put out of mind or are thought of only bloodlessly and abstractly. Rehearsing the facts in a vivid and imaginative way is the needed corrective.

Now let us return to the question of ethical disagreement. When disagreement occurs, two explanations are possible. First, we might disagree because there has been some failure of rationality on the part of one of us. Or, second, the people who disagree might simply be different kinds of people, who care but different things. In principle, either explanation may be correct. But, in practice, when important matters are at issue, we always proceed on the first hypothesis. We present arguments to those who disagree with us on the assumption (in the hope?) that they have missed something: they are ignorant of relevant facts, they have not thought through what they know, they are inconsistent, and so on. We do not, as a practical matter, credit the idea that we are simply and irreconcilably "different."

Is this assumption reasonable? Isn't it possible that sometimes people just care about different things? It is possible; but if such cases do exist, they are notoriously hard to find. The familiar examples of the cultural anthropologists turn out upon analysis to have other explanations. The Eskimos who allow their firstborn daughters to die of exposure and who abandon feeble old people to a similar fate do not have less concern for life than peoples who reject such practices. They live in different circumstances, under threat of starvation in a hostile environment, and the survival of the community requires policies that otherwise they would happily renounce. Or consider the Ik, a tribe of Africans who during the 1970s were observed to be indifferent even to the welfare of their own children. They would not share food with their children and they laughed when others were sick. Surely, one might think, the Ik are radically different from us. But not so: they took on those characteristics only after a prolonged period of near-starvation that virtually destroyed their tribal culture. Of course human behavior will be modified by calamity; but before their calamity, the Ik were much too "normal" to attract attention. To be sure, there may be some disagreements that reflect cultural variables ... but, beyond that, and barring the kind of disaster that reduced the Ik, it is plausible to think that people are enough alike to make ethical agreement possible, if only full rationality were possible.

The fact that rationality has limits does not subvert the objectivity of ethics, but it does suggest the need for a certain modesty in what can be claimed for it. Ethics provides answers about what we ought to do, given that we are the kinds of creatures we are, caring about the things we will care about when we are as reasonable as we can be, living in the sort of circumstances in which we live. This is not as much as we might want, but it is a lot. And it is as much as we can hope for in a subject that must incorporate not only our beliefs but our ideals.

NOTES

1. Aristotle, *Physics*, in *The Basic Works of Aristotle*, ed. Richard McKeon (New York: Random House, 1941), 249.

2. Aristotle, *Physics*, 249.

3. Aristotle, *Politics*, trans. T. A. Sinclair (Harmondsworth, England: Penguin Books, 1962), 40.

4. David Hume, *A Treatise of Human Nature* (Oxford: Oxford University Press, 1888), 468. Originally published in 1739.

5. David Hume, *Essays Moral, Political, and Literary* (Oxford: Oxford University Press, 1963), 590. Originally published in 1741–42.

6. Hume, *Treatise*, 469.

7. C. L. Stevenson, *Ethics and Language* (New Haven: Yale University Press, 1944).

8. David Hume, *An Inquiry Concerning the Principles of Morals* (Indianapolis: Bobbs-Merrill, 1957), 111. Originally published in 1752.

9. Among contemporary moral philosophers, W. D. Falk has made this point most forcefully; see, for example, his essay "Action-Guiding Reasons," *Journal of Philosophy* 60 (1963): 702–18.

10. Aristotle, *Nicomachean Ethics* 1147b.

11. Albert Camus, "Reflections on the Guillotine," in *Resistance, Rebellion, and Death* (New York: Knopf, 1961), 175–234.

NO   Bertrand Russell

SCIENCE AND ETHICS

Those who maintain the insufficiency of science:... appeal to the fact that science has nothing to say about "values." This I admit; but when it is inferred that ethics contains truths which cannot be proved or disproved by science, I disagree. The matter is one on which it is not altogether easy to think clearly, and my own views on it are quite different from what they were thirty years ago. But it is necessary to be clear about it if we are to appraise such arguments as those in support of Cosmic Purpose. As there is no consensus of opinion about ethics, it must be understood that what follows is my personal belief, not the dictum of science....

Different philosophers have formed different conceptions of the Good. Some hold that it consists in the knowledge and love of God; others in universal love; others in the enjoyment of beauty; and yet others in pleasure. The Good once defined, the rest of ethics follows: we ought to act in the way we believe most likely to create as much good as possible, and as little as possible of its correlative evil. The framing of moral rules, so long as the ultimate Good is supposed known, is matter for science. For example: should capital punishment be inflicted for theft, or only for murder, or not at all? Jeremy Bentham, who considered pleasure to be the Good, devoted himself to working out what criminal code would most promote pleasure, and concluded that it ought to be much less severe than that prevailing in his day. All this, except the proposition that pleasure is the Good, comes within the sphere of science.

But when we try to be definite as to what we mean when we say that this or that is "the Good," we find ourselves involved in very great difficulties. Bentham's creed that pleasure is the Good roused furious opposition, and was said to be a pig's philosophy. Neither he nor his opponents could advance any argument. In a scientific question, evidence can be adduced on both sides, and in the end one side is seen to have the better case—or, if this does not happen, the question is left undecided. But in a question as to whether this or that is the ultimate Good, there is no evidence either way; each disputant can only appeal to his own emotions, and employ such rhetorical devices as shall rouse similar emotions in others.

Reprinted from *Religion and Science* by Bertrand Russell (1935) by permission of Oxford University Press.

Take, for example, a question which has come to be important in practical politics. Bentham held that one man's pleasure has the same ethical importance as another man's, provided the quantities are equal; and on this ground he was led to advocate democracy. Nietzsche, on the contrary, held that only the great man can be regarded as important on his own account, and that the bulk of mankind are only means to his well-being. He viewed ordinary men as many people view animals: he thought it justifiable to make use of them, not for their own good, but for that of the superman, and this view has since been adopted to justify the abandonment of democracy. We have here a sharp disagreement of great practical importance, but we have absolutely no means, of a scientific or intellectual kind, by which to persuade either party that the other is in the right. There are, it is true, ways of altering men's opinions on such subjects, but they are all emotional, not intellectual.

Questions as to "values"—that is to say, as to what is good or bad on its own account, independently of its effects —lie outside the domain of science, as the defenders of religion emphatically assert. I think that in this they are right, but I draw the further conclusion, which they do not draw, that questions as to "values" lie wholly outside the domain of knowledge. That is to say, when we assert that this or that has "value," we are giving expression to our own emotions, not to a fact which would still be true if our personal feelings were different. To make this clear, we must try to analyse the conception of the Good.

It is obvious, to begin with, that the whole idea of good and bad has some connection with *desire*. *Prima facie*, anything that we all desire is "good," and anything that we all dread is "bad." If we all agreed in our desires, the matter could be left there, but unfortunately our desires conflict. If I say "what I want is good," my neighbour will say "No, what *I* want." Ethics is an attempt—though not, I think, a successful one—to escape from this subjectivity. I shall naturally try to show, in my dispute with my neighbour, that my desires have some quality which makes them more worthy of respect than his. If I want to preserve a right of way, I shall appeal to the landless inhabitants of the district; but he, on his side, will appeal to the landowners. I shall say: "What use is the beauty of the countryside if no one sees it?" He will retort: "What beauty will be left if trippers are allowed to spread devastation?" Each tries to enlist allies by showing that his own desires harmonize with those of other people. When this is obviously impossible, as in the case of a burglar, the man is condemned by public opinion, and his ethical status is that of a sinner.

Ethics is thus closely related to politics: it is an attempt to bring the collective desires of a group to bear upon individuals; or, conversely, it is an attempt by an individual to cause his desires to become those of his group. This latter is, of course, only possible if his desires are not too obviously opposed to the general interest: the burglar will hardly attempt to persuade people that he is doing them good, though plutocrats make similar attempts, and often succeed. When our desires are for things which all can enjoy in common, it seems not unreasonable to hope that others may concur; thus the philosopher who values Truth, Goodness and Beauty seems, to himself, to be not merely expressing his own desires, but pointing the way to the welfare of all mankind. Unlike the burglar, he is able to believe that his desires are for something that has value in an impersonal sense.

Ethics is an attempt to give universal, and not merely personal, importance to certain of our desires. I say "certain" of our desires, because in regard to some of them this is obviously impossible, as we saw in the case of the burglar. The man who makes money on the Stock Exchange by means of some secret knowledge does not wish others to be equally well informed: Truth (in so far as he values it) is for him a private possession, not the general human good that it is for the philosopher. The philosopher may, it is true, sink to the level of the stock-jobber, as when he claims priority for a discovery. But this is a lapse: in his purely philosophic capacity, he wants only to enjoy the contemplation of Truth, in doing which he in no way interferes with others who wish to do likewise.

To seem to give universal importance to our desires—which is the business of ethics—may be attempted from two points of view, that of the legislator, and that of the preacher. Let us take the legislator first.

I will assume, for the sake of argument, that the legislator is personally disinterested. That is to say, when he recognizes one of his desires as being concerned only with his own welfare, he does not let it influence him in framing the laws; for example, his code is not designed to increase his personal fortune. But he has other desires which seem to him impersonal. He may believe in an ordered hierarchy from king to peasant, or from mine-owner to black indentured labourer. He may believe that women should be submissive to men. He may hold that the spread of knowledge in the lower classes is dangerous. And so on and so on. He will then, if he can, so construct his code

that conduct promoting the ends which he values shall, as far as possible, be in accordance with individual self-interest; and he will establish a system of moral instruction which will, where it succeeds, make men feel wicked if they pursue other purposes than his.[1] Thus "virtue" will come to be in fact, though not in subjective estimation, subservience to the desires of the legislator, in so far as he himself considers these desires worthy to be universalized.

The standpoint and method of the preacher are necessarily somewhat different, because he does not control the machinery of the State, and therefore cannot produce an artificial harmony between his desires and those of others. His only method is to try to rouse in others the same desires that he feels himself, and for this purpose his appeal must be to the emotions. Thus Ruskin caused people to like Gothic architecture, not by argument, but by the moving effect of rhythmical prose. *Uncle Tom's Cabin* helped to make people think slavery an evil by causing them to imagine themselves as slaves. Every attempt to persuade people that something is good (or bad) in itself, and not merely in its effects, depends upon the art of rousing feelings, not upon an appeal to evidence. In every case the preacher's skill consists in creating in others emotions similar to his own—or dissimilar, if he is a hypocrite. I am not saying this as a criticism of the preacher, but as an analysis of the essential character of his activity.

When a man says "this is good in itself," he *seems* to be making a statement, just as much as if he said "this is square" or "this is sweet." I believe this to be a mistake. I think that what the man really means is: "I wish everybody to desire this," or rather "Would that everybody desired this." If what he says is interpreted as a statement, it is merely an affirmation of his own personal wish; if, on the other hand, it is interpreted in a general way, it states nothing, but merely desires something. The wish, as an occurrence, is personal, but what it desires is universal. It is, I think, this curious interlocking of the particular and the universal which has caused so much confusion in ethics.

The matter may perhaps become clearer by contrasting an ethical sentence with one which makes a statement. If I say "all Chinese are Buddhists," I can be refuted by the production of a Chinese Christian or Mohammedan. If I say "I believe that all Chinese are Buddhists," I cannot be refuted by any evidence from China, but only by evidence that I do not believe what I say; for what I am asserting is only something about my own state of mind. If, now, a philosopher says "Beauty is good," I may interpret him as meaning either "Would that everybody loved the beautiful" (which corresponds to "all Chinese are Buddhists") or "I wish that everybody loved the beautiful" (which corresponds to "I believe that all Chinese are Buddhists"). The first of these makes no assertion, but expresses a wish; since it affirms nothing, it is logically impossible that there should be evidence for or against it, or for it to possess either truth or falsehood. The second sentence, instead of being merely optative, does make a statement, but it is one about the philosopher's state of mind, and it could only be refuted by evidence that he does not have the wish that he says he has. This second sentence does not belong to ethics, but to psychology or biography. The first sentence, which does belong to ethics, expresses a desire for something, but asserts nothing.

Ethics, if the above analysis is correct, contains no statements, whether true or false, but consists of desires of a certain general kind, namely such as are concerned with the desires of mankind in general—and of gods, angels, and devils, if they exist. Science can discuss the causes of desires, and the means for realizing them, but it cannot contain any genuinely ethical sentences, because it is concerned with what is true or false.

The theory which I have been advocating is a form of the doctrine which is called the "subjectivity" of values. This doctrine consists in maintaining that, if two men differ about values, there is not a disagreement as to any kind of truth, but a difference of taste. If one man says "oysters are good" and another says "I think they are bad," we recognize that there is nothing to argue about. The theory in question holds that all differences as to values are of this sort, although we do not naturally think them so when we are dealing with matters that seem to us more exalted than oysters. The chief ground for adopting this view is the complete impossibility of finding any arguments to prove that this or that has intrinsic value. If we all agreed, we might hold that we know values by intuition. We cannot *prove*, to a colour-blind man, that grass is green and not red. But there are various ways of proving to him that he lacks a power of discrimination which most men possess, whereas in the case of values there are no such ways, and disagreements are much more frequent than in the case of colours. Since no way can be even imagined for deciding a difference as to values, the conclusion is forced upon us that the difference is one of tastes, not one as to any objective truth.

The consequences of this doctrine are considerable. In the first place, there can be no such thing as "sin" in any absolute sense; what one man calls "sin" another may call "virtue," and though they may dislike each other on account of this difference, neither can convict the other of intellectual error. Punishment cannot be justified on the ground that the criminal is "wicked," but only on the ground that he has behaved in a way which others wish to discourage. Hell, as a place of punishment for sinners, becomes quite irrational.

In the second place, it is impossible to uphold the way of speaking about values which is common among those who believe in Cosmic Purpose. Their argument is that certain things which have been evolved are "good," and therefore the world must have had a purpose which was ethically admirable. In the language of subjective values, this argument becomes: "Some things in the world are to our liking, and therefore they must have been created by a Being with our tastes, Whom, therefore, we also like, and Who, consequently, is good." Now it seems fairly evident that, if creatures having likes and dislikes were to exist at all, they were pretty sure to like *some* things in their environment, since otherwise they would find life intolerable. Our values have been evolved along with the rest of our constitution, and nothing as to any original purpose can be inferred from the fact that they are what they are.

Those who believe in "objective" values often contend that the view which I have been advocating has immoral consequences. This seems to me to be due to faulty reasoning. There are, as has already been said, certain ethical consequences of the doctrine of subjective values, of which the most important is the rejection of vindictive punishment and the notion of "sin." But the more general consequences which are feared, such as the decay of all sense of moral obligation, are not to be logically deduced. Moral obligation, if it is to influence conduct, must consist not merely of a belief, but of a desire. The desire, I may be told, is the desire to be "good" in a sense which I no longer allow. But when we analyse the desire to be "good" it generally resolves itself into a desire to be approved, or, alternatively, to act so as to bring about certain general consequences which we desire. We have wishes which are not purely personal, and, if we had not, no amount of ethical teaching would influence our conduct except through fear of disapproval. The sort of life that most of us admire is one which is guided by large impersonal desires; now such desires can, no doubt, be encouraged by example, education, and knowledge, but they can hardly be created by the mere abstract belief that they are good, nor discouraged by an analysis of what is meant by the word "good."

When we contemplate the human race, we may desire that it should be happy, or healthy, or intelligent, or warlike, and so on. Any one of these desires, if it is strong, will produce its own morality; but if we have no such general desires, our conduct, whatever our ethic may be, will only serve social purposes in so far as self-interest and the interests of society are in harmony. It is the business of wise institutions to create such harmony as far as possible, and for the rest, whatever may be our theoretical definition of value, we must depend upon the existence of impersonal desires. When you meet a man with whom you have a fundamental ethical disagreement—for example, if you think that all men count equally, while he selects a class as alone important—you will find yourself no better able to cope with him if you believe in objective values than if you do not. In either case, you can only influence his conduct through influencing his desires: if you succeed in that, his ethic will change, and if not, not.

Some people feel that if a general desire, say for the happiness of mankind, has not the sanction of absolute good, it is in some way irrational. This is due to a lingering belief in objective values. A desire cannot, in itself, be either rational or irrational. It may conflict with other desires, and therefore lead to unhappiness; it may rouse opposition in others, and therefore be incapable of gratification. But it cannot be considered "irrational" merely because no reason can be given for feeling it. We may desire A because it is a means to B, but in the end, when we have done with mere means, we must come to something which we desire for no reason, but not on that account "irrationally." All systems of ethics embody the desires of those who advocate them, but this fact is concealed in a mist of words. Our desires are, in fact, more general and less purely selfish than many moralists imagine; if it were not so, no theory of ethics would make moral improvement possible. It is, in fact, not by ethical theory, but by the cultivation of large and generous desires through intelligence, happiness, and freedom from fear, that men can be brought to act more than they do at present in a manner that is consistent with the general happiness of mankind. Whatever our definition of the "Good," and whether we believe it to be subjective or objective, those who do not desire the happiness of mankind will not endeavour to further it, while those who do desire it will do what they can to bring it about.

I conclude that, while it is true that science cannot decide questions of value, that is because they cannot be intellectually decided at all, and lie outside the realm of truth and falsehood. Whatever knowledge is attainable, must be attained by scientific methods; and what science cannot discover, mankind cannot know.

NOTES

1. Compare the following advice by a contemporary of Aristotle (Chinese, not Greek): "A ruler should not listen to those who believe in people having opinions of their own and in the importance of the individual. Such teachings cause men to withdraw to quiet places and hide away in caves or on mountains, there to rail at the prevailing government, sneer at those in authority, belittle the importance of rank and emoluments, and despise all who hold official posts." Waley, *The Way and its Power*, p. 37.

POSTSCRIPT

Can Ethics Provide Answers?

Rachels argues that moral knowledge can be achieved if one carefully attends to facts, logic, and argument. It is important not to exaggerate his position. He does not claim that *all* moral disputes can be solved or answered by this method or that moral knowledge can *always* be attained. But, Rachels argues, there is indeed such a thing as moral knowledge, and there are indeed definite answers in ethics.

Rachels states that in a particular moral dispute, it is important to be faithful to facts and to not be carried away by intuitions or hunches. Logical consistency is required in reasoning, and sometimes careful analysis of concepts is necessary. When two people have a moral disagreement, there is *much* work for reason.

Rachels admits that at some point reasoning must come to an end. But this, he says, is true of all reasoning, including reasoning in mathematics and reasoning in science. Mathematics, for example, has its axioms—self-evident truths or maxims taken as true based on their intrinsic merit—that must simply be accepted if any mathematical reasoning is to take place. And scientific disputes always take place against a background of assumptions that are taken for granted.

Perhaps some of the resistance to Rachels's ideas comes from the image of knowledge as a building built upon a solid foundation. Where is the solid foundation for moral knowledge? But another image is that of a pier, whose surface is solid enough to walk on, but whose strength comes from pilings sunk deep in the water and in the ground below the water. The result is a solid structure with partially hidden but solid supports, although the pilings, like reasoning, must come to an end somewhere.

Russell—and many other people—maintain that science provides knowledge because it is grounded in the external world. Since ethical matters are not similarly grounded, there is no such thing as moral knowledge. One question to ask those who champion science is whether or not their own views about the presence or absence of knowledge in morality is a scientific one. Does science tell us that only what science tells us is knowledge? This seems to be a circular argument. People who say "Only what science tells us is true" are caught in a dilemma. Either their statement is itself a scientific one and thus a case of arguing in a circle, or it is not a scientific one, in which case (since science is not telling us this) the statement is false by its own lights.

Sources that are relevant to this issue are J. L. Mackie, *Ethics: Inventing Right and Wrong* (Penguin, 1977); Renford Bambrough, *Moral Skepticism and Moral Knowledge* (Humanities Press, 1979); Ronald Dworkin, "Objectivity and

Truth: You'd Better Believe It," *Philosophy and Public Affairs* (vol. 25, 1996); and the essays collected in Walter Sinnott-Armstrong and Mark Timmons, eds., *Moral Knowledge? New Readings in Moral Epistemology* (Oxford University Press, 1996).

ISSUE 2

Is Morality Relative to Culture?

YES: Melville J. Herskovits, from "Cultural Relativism and Cultural Values," in Frances Herskovits, ed., *Cultural Relativism: Perspectives in Cultural Pluralism* (Random House, 1972)

NO: Louis P. Pojman, from *Ethics: Discovering Right and Wrong,* 2d ed. (Wadsworth, 1995)

ISSUE SUMMARY

YES: American anthropologist Melville J. Herskovits (1895–1963) takes the position that morality has no absolute identity and that it is a social and cultural phenomenon that varies according to the customs and beliefs of different cultural groups. In his view, the great enemy of relativism is ethnocentrism, especially as expressed by European colonialism.

NO: Professor of philosophy Louis P. Pojman holds that ethnocentrism is a prejudice like racism or sexism. He agrees that moral beliefs and practices vary greatly across cultures and from one person to another, but he finds very serious problems in the contention that moral principles derive their validity from dependence on society or individual choice.

As the social sciences began to be recognized in the nineteenth century, many thinkers developed a particular interest in the customs and morals of other groups of people. In 1865 (six years after naturalist Charles Darwin's *Origin of Species* and six years before his *Descent of Man*), Sir Edward Tylor (1832–1917), one of the great leaders in the scientific study of human beings, published his *Researches into the Early History of Mankind.* Tylor believed that the study of ancient pagans and the study of uncivilized people and various heathen groups that lived outside the scope of civilized Victorian culture would throw light on English culture itself. It was Tylor's view that all people shared the same human capacities and mental potentialities and that there had been a progression, or positive development, from ignorant savagery to civilized culture. This was a daring view at the time. Many people (especially defenders of religious orthodoxy) believed both that Darwin was seriously wrong to affirm a development or evolution of human beings from animals and that Tylor was seriously wrong to affirm a development or evolution of intelligent civilized Christians from ignorant uncivilized pagan savages. The conventional view held by many was that God had created human beings in his image as rational and moral beings; any savages who existed in the nineteenth century must have fallen into that state through a neglect of reason, a lack of morality, and an absence of faith. Surely, this view continued, human beings were not initially created as ignorant savages who wore beads (if anything at all) and followed a pagan life of promiscuity and superstition.

Sir James Frazer (1854–1941) was greatly stimulated by his reading of Tylor. He too wrote extensively about the customs of primitive people, and he believed that such people exhibited "the rudimentary phases, the infancy and childhood, of human society." To the question of whether or not he had actually seen any of the savages that he had written so much about, Frazer is said to have replied, "God forbid!" Frazer and most social scientists of the late nineteenth century studied books, read the diaries of travelers, and corresponded with those in distant lands. Field study had not yet established itself as a necessary social scientific technique. The armchair studies of Frazer are by no means manifestations of laziness or lack of commitment; Frazer devoted his life to the scientific study of humankind and is said to have spent 12 hours a day for over 50 years reading, taking notes, and writing.

During this century several well-known social scientists have endorsed a sophisticated type of cultural relativism. The armchair studies have been replaced by years of field studies that include a sympathetic involvement with the lives of the people one is studying. Gone is the view that so-called primitive people are standing on the lower rungs of the same ladder that leads to modern Western culture. There is no separation of the "civilized" and the "uncivilized." There are *various* civilizations and *various* cultures, and our own culture is only one of many.

Melville J. Herskovits was a champion of cultural relativism, which he saw as an antidote to European colonial attitudes and the ethnocentrism that they express. Herskovits was, in particular, a student of African societies and of the experience of blacks in the New World. He regarded it as a great mistake and a great tragedy that Europeans thought that they were the civilized ones and that the Africans were not. It was by force, not by civilization, that Europeans imposed themselves upon African cultures. According to cultural relativism, it is false to think that, in matters of morality, our own Western culture is uniquely in a position to make absolute moral judgments. The fact is that different cultures simply have different moralities. The moral precepts of a given culture might appear as absolute to the individual who is enculturated in that culture, but this is a common error. Such is the view that Herskovits expresses in the following selection.

Louis P. Pojman responds critically to cultural relativism. He agrees with Herskovits on the wrongfulness of ethnocentrism, but he argues that cultural relativism, at least with respect to morality, has several highly implausible consequences. And these consequences, when understood, should lead to the rejection of moral relativism.

YES

Melville J. Herskovits

CULTURAL RELATIVISM AND CULTURAL VALUES

All peoples form judgments about ways of life different from their own. Where systematic study is undertaken, comparison gives rise to classification, and scholars have devised many schemes for classifying ways of life. Moral judgments have been drawn regarding the ethical principles that guide the behavior and mold the value systems of different peoples. Their economic and political structures and their religious beliefs have been ranked in order of complexity, efficiency, desirability. Their art, music, and literary forms have been weighed.

It has become increasingly evident, however, that evaluations of this kind stand or fall with the acceptance of the premises from which they derive. In addition, many of the criteria on which judgment is based are in conflict, so that conclusions drawn from one definition of what is desirable will not agree with those based on another formulation.

A simple example will illustrate this. There are not many ways in which the primary family can be constituted. One man may live with one woman, one woman may have a number of husbands, one man may have a number of wives. But if we evaluate these forms according to their function of perpetuating the group, it is clear that they perform their essential tasks. Otherwise, the societies wherein they exist would not survive.

Such an answer will, however, not satisfy all those who have undertaken to study cultural evaluation. What of the moral questions inherent in the practice of monogamy as against polygamy, the adjustment of children raised in households where, for example, the mothers must compete on behalf of their offspring for the favors of a common husband? If monogamy is held to be the desired form of marriage, the responses to these questions are predetermined. But when we consider these questions from the point of view of those who live in polygamous societies, alternative answers, based on different conceptions of what is desirable, may be given.

Let us consider, for example, the life of a plural family in the West African culture of Dahomey.[1] Here, within a compound, live a man and his wives. The man has his own house, as has each of the women and her children, after the basic African principle that two wives cannot successfully inhabit the same quarters. Each wife in turn spends a native week of four days with the common husband, cooking his food, washing his clothes, sleeping in his house, and then making way for the next. Her children, however, remain in their mother's hut. With pregnancy, she drops out of this routine, and ideally, in the interest of her child's health and her own, does not again visit her husband until the child has been born and weaned. This means a period of from three to four years, since infants are nursed two years and longer.

The compound, made up of these households, is a cooperative unit. The women who sell goods in the market, or make pottery, or have their gardens, contribute to its support. This aspect, though of great economic importance, is secondary to the prestige that attaches to the larger unit. This is why one often finds a wife not only urging her husband to acquire a second spouse but even aiding him by loans or gifts to make this possible.

Tensions do arise between the women who inhabit a large compound. Thirteen different ways of getting married have been recorded in this society, and in a large household those wives who are married in the same category tend to unite against all others. Competition for the regard of the husband is also a factor, when several wives try to influence the choice of an heir in favor of their own sons. Yet all the children of the compound play together, and the strength of the emotional ties between the children of the same mother more than compensates for whatever stresses may arise between brothers and sisters who share the same father but are of different

mothers. Cooperation, moreover, is by no means a mere formality among the wives. Many common tasks are performed in friendly unison, and there is solidarity in the interest of women's prerogatives, or where the status of the common husband is threatened.

We may now return to the criteria to be applied in drawing judgments concerning polygamous as against monogamous families. The family structure of Dahomey is obviously a complex institution. If we but consider the possible lines of personal relations among the many individuals concerned, we see clearly how numerous are the ramifications of reciprocal right and obligation of the Dahomean family. The effectiveness of the Dahomean family is, however, patent. It has, for untold generations, performed its function of rearing the young; more than this, the very size of the group gives it economic resources and a resulting stability that might well be envied by those who live under different systems of family organization. Moral values are always difficult to establish, but at least in this society marriage is clearly distinguished from casual sex relations and from prostitution, in its supernatural sanctions and in the prestige it confers, to say nothing of the economic obligations toward spouse and prospective offspring explicitly accepted by one who enters into a marriage.

Numerous problems of adjustment do present themselves in an aggregate of this sort. It does not call for much speculation to understand the plaint of the head of one large compound when he said: "One must be something of a diplomat if one has many wives." Yet the sly digs in proverb and song, and the open quarreling, involve no greater stress than is found in any small rural community where people are also thrown closely together for long periods of time. Quarrels between co-wives are not greatly different from disputes over the back fence between neighbors. And Dahomeans who know European culture, when they argue for their system, stress the fact that it permits the individual wife to space her children in a way that is in accord with the best precepts of modern gynecology.

Thus polygamy, when looked at from the point of view of those who practice it, is seen to hold values that are not apparent from the outside. A similar case can be made for monogamy, however, when it is attacked by those who are enculturated to a different kind of family structure. And what is true of a particular phase of culture such as this, is also true of others. Evaluations are *relative* to the cultural background out of which they arise.

* * *

Cultural relativism is in essence an approach to the question of the nature and role of values in culture. It represents a scientific, inductive attack on an age-old philosophical problem, using fresh, cross-cultural data, hitherto not available to scholars, gained from the study of the underlying value-systems of societies having the most diverse customs. The principle of cultural relativism, briefly stated, is as follows: *Judgments are based on experience, and experience is interpreted by each individual in terms of his own enculturation.* Those who hold for the existence of fixed values will find materials in other societies that necessitate a reinvestigation of their assumptions. Are there absolute moral standards, or are moral standards effective only as far as they agree with the orientations of a given people at a given period of their history? We even approach the problem of the ultimate nature of reality itself. Cassirer[2] holds that reality can only be experienced through the symbolism of language. Is reality, then, not defined and redefined by the ever-varied symbolisms of the innumerable languages of mankind?

Answers to questions such as these represent one of the most profound contributions of anthropology to the analysis of man's place in the world. When we reflect that such intangibles as right and wrong, normal and abnormal, beautiful and plain are absorbed as a person learns the ways of the group into which he is born, we see that we are dealing here with a process of first importance. Even the facts of the physical world are discerned through the enculturative screen, so that the perception of time, distance, weight, size, and other "realities" is mediated by the conventions of any given group.

No culture, however, is a closed system of rigid molds to which the behavior of all members of a society must conform. In stressing the psychological reality of culture, it was made plain that a culture, as such, can *do* nothing. It is but the summation of the behavior and habitual modes of thought of the persons who make up a particular society. Though by learning and habit these individuals conform to the ways of the group into which they have been born, they nonetheless vary in their reactions to the situations of living they commonly meet. They vary, too, in the degree to which they desire change, as whole cultures vary. This is but another way in which we see that culture is flexible and holds many possibilities of choice within its framework, and that to recognize the values held by a given people in no wise implies that these values are a constant factor in the lives of succeeding generations of the same group....

[W]hile recognizing the role of both father and mother in procreation, many peoples have conventions of relationship that count descent on but one side of the family. In such societies, it is common for incest lines to be so arbitrarily defined that "first cousins," as we would say, on the mother's side call each other brother and sister and regard marriage with one another with horror. Yet marriage within the same degree of biological relationship on the father's side may be held not only desirable, but sometimes mandatory. This is because two persons related in this way are by definition not considered blood relatives.

The very definition of what is normal or abnormal is relative to the cultural frame of reference. As an example of this, we may take the phenomenon of possession as found among African and New World Negroes. The supreme expression of their religious experience, possession, is a psychological state wherein a displacement of personality occurs when the god "comes to the head" of the worshipper. The individual thereupon is held to be the deity himself. This phenomenon has been described in pathological terms by many students whose approach is nonanthropological, because of its surface resemblance to cases in the records of medical practitioners, psychological clinicians, psychiatrists, and others. The hysteria-like trances, where persons, their eyes tightly closed, move about excitedly and presumably without purpose or design, or roll on the ground, muttering meaningless syllables, or go into a state where their bodies achieve complete rigidity, are not difficult to equate with the neurotic and even psychotic manifestations of abnormality found in Euroamerican society.

Yet when we look beneath behavior to meaning, and place such apparently random acts in their cultural frame of reference, such conclusions become untenable. For *relative to the setting in which these possession experiences occur, they are not to be regarded as abnormal at all,* much less psychopathological. They are *culturally* patterned, and often induced by learning and discipline. The dancing or other acts of the possessed persons are so stylized that one who knows this religion can identify the god possessing a devotee by the behavior of the individual possessed. Furthermore, the possession experience does not seem to be confined to emotionally unstable persons. Those who "get the god" run the gamut of personality types found in the group. Observation of persons who frequent the cults, yet who, in the idiom of worship "have nothing in the head" and thus never experience possession, seems to show that they are far less adjusted than those who do get possessed. Finally, the nature of the possession experience in these cultures is so disciplined that it may only come to a given devotee under particular circumstances. In West Africa and Brazil the gods come only to those who have been designated in advance by the priest of their group, who lays his hands on their heads. In Haiti, for an initiate not a member of the family group giving a rite to become possessed at a ceremony is considered extremely "bad form" socially and a sign of spiritual weakness, evidence that the god is not under the control of his worshipper.

The terminology of psychopathology, employed solely for descriptive purposes, may be of some utility. But the connotation it carries of psychic instability, emotional imbalance, and departure from normality recommends the use of other words that do not invite such a distortion of cultural reality. For in these Negro societies, the meaning this experience holds for the people falls entirely in the realm of understandable, predictable, *normal* behavior. This behavior is known and recognized by all members as an experience that may come to any one of them, and is to be welcomed not only for the psychological security it affords, but also for the status, economic gain, aesthetic expression, and emotional release it vouchsafes the devotee.

* * *

The primary mechanism that directs the evaluation of culture is *ethnocentrism*. Ethnocentrism is the point of view that one's own way of life is to be preferred to all others. Flowing logically from the process of early enculturation, it characterizes the way most individuals feel about their own culture, whether or not they verbalize their feeling. Outside the stream of Euroamerican culture, particularly among nonliterate peoples, this is taken for granted and is to be viewed as a factor making for individual adjustment and social integration. For the strengthening of the ego, identification with one's own group, whose ways are implicitly accepted as best, is all-important. It is when, as in Euroamerican culture, ethnocentrism is rationalized and made the basis of programs of action detrimental to the well-being of other peoples that it gives rise to serious problems.

The ethnocentrism of nonliterate peoples is best illustrated in their myths, folk tales, proverbs, and linguistic habits. It is manifest in many tribal names whose meaning in their respective languages signifies "human beings." The inference that those to whom the name does not apply are outside this category is, however, rarely, if ever, explicitly made. When the Suriname Bush Negro, shown a flashlight, admires it and then quotes the proverb: "White man's magic isn't black man's magic," he is merely reaffirming his faith in his own culture. He is pointing out that the stranger, for all his mechanical devices, would be lost in the Guiana jungle without the aid of his Bush Negro friends.

A myth of the origin of human races, told by the Cherokee Indians of the Great Smoky Mountains, gives another instance of this kind of ethnocentrism. The Creator fashioned man by first making and firing an oven and then, from dough he had prepared, shaping three figures in human form. He placed the figures in the oven and waited for them to get done. But his impatience to see the result of this, his crowning experiment in the work of creation, was so great that he removed the first figure too soon. It was sadly underdone—pale, an unlovely color, and from it descended the white people. His second figure had fared well. The timing was accurate, the form, richly browned, that was to be the ancestor of the Indians, pleased him in every way. He so admired it, indeed, that he neglected to take out of the oven the third form, until he smelled it burning. He threw open the door, only to find this last one charred and black. It was regrettable, but there was nothing to be done; and this was the first Negro.[3]

This is the more usual form that ethnocentrism takes among many peoples—a gentle insistence on the good qualities of one's own group, without any drive to extend this attitude into the field of action. With such a point of view, the objectives, sanctioned modes of behavior, and value systems of peoples with whom one's own group comes into contact can be considered in terms of their desirability, then accepted or rejected without any reference to absolute standards. That differences in the manner of achieving commonly sought objectives may be permitted to exist without a judgment being entered on them involves a reorientation in thought for those in the Euroamerican tradition, because in this tradition, a difference in belief or behavior too often implies something is worse, or less desirable, and must be changed.

The assumption that the cultures of nonliterate peoples are of inferior quality is the end product of a long series of developments in our intellectual history. It is not often recalled that the concept of progress, that strikes so deep into our thinking, is relatively recent. It is, in fact, a unique product of our culture. It is a part of the same historic stream that developed the scientific tradition and that developed the machine, thus giving Europe and America the final word in debates about cultural superiority. "He who makes the gun-powder wields the power," runs a Dahomean proverb. There is no rebuttal to an argument, backed by cannon, advanced to a people who can defend their position with no more than spears, or bows and arrows, or at best a flint-lock gun.

With the possible exception of technological aspects of life, however, the proposition that one way of thought or action is better than another is exceedingly difficult to establish on the grounds of any universally acceptable criteria. Let us take food as an instance. Cultures are equipped differently for the production of food, so that some peoples eat more than others. However, even on the subsis-

tence level, there is no people who do not hold certain potential foodstuffs to be unfit for human consumption. Milk, which figures importantly in our diet, is rejected as food by the peoples of southeastern Asia. Beef, a valued element of the Euroamerican cuisine, is regarded with disgust by Hindus. Nor need compulsions be this strong. The thousands of cattle that range the East African highlands are primarily wealth to be preserved, and not a source of food. Only the cow that dies is eaten—a practice that, though abhorrent to us, has apparently done no harm to those who have been following it for generations.

Totemic and religious taboos set up further restrictions on available foodstuffs, while the refusal to consume many other edible and nourishing substances is simply based on the enculturative conditioning. So strong is this conditioning that prohibited food consumed unwittingly may induce such a physiological reaction as vomiting. All young animals provide succulent meat, but the religious abhorrence of the young pig by the Mohammedan is no stronger than the secular rejection of puppy steaks or colt chops by ourselves. Ant larvae, insect grubs, locusts—all of which have caloric values and vitamin content—when roasted or otherwise cooked, or even when raw, are regarded by many peoples as delicacies. We never eat them, however, though they are equally available to us. On the other hand, some of the same peoples who feed on these with gusto regard substances that come out of tin cans as unfit for human consumption....

* * *

Before we terminate our discussion of cultural relativism, it is important that we consider certain questions that are raised when the cultural-relativistic position is advanced. "It may be true," it is argued, "that human beings live in accordance with the ways they have learned. These ways may be regarded by them as best. A people may be so devoted to these ways that they are ready to fight and die for them. In terms of survival value, their effectiveness may be admitted, since the group that lives in accordance with them continues to exist. But does this mean that all systems of moral values, all concepts of right and wrong, are founded on such shifting sands that there is no need for morality, for proper behavior, for ethical codes? Does not a relativistic philosophy, indeed, imply a negation of these?"

To hold that values do not exist because they are relative to time and place is to fall prey to a fallacy that results from a failure to take into account the positive contribution of the relativistic position. For cultural relativism is a philosophy that recognizes the values set up by every society to guide its own life and that understands their worth to those who live by them, though they may differ from one's own. Instead of underscoring differences from absolute norms that, however objectively arrived at, are nonetheless the product of a given time or place, the relativistic point of view brings into relief the validity of every set of norms for the people who have them, and the values these represent.

It is essential, in considering cultural relativism, that we differentiate absolutes from universals. *Absolutes* are fixed, and, as far as convention is concerned, are not admitted to have variation, to differ from culture to culture, from epoch to epoch. *Universals,* on the other hand, are those least common denominators to be extracted from the range of variation that all phenomena of the natural or cultural world manifest. If we apply the distinction between these two concepts in drawing an answer to the points raised in our question, these criticisms are found to lose their force. To say that there is no absolute criterion of values or morals, or even, psychologically, of time or space, does not mean that such criteria, in differing *forms*, do not comprise universals in human culture. Morality is a universal, and so is enjoyment of beauty, and some standard for truth. The many forms these concepts take are but products of the particular historical experience of the societies that manifest them. In each, criteria are subject to continuous questioning, continuous change. But the basic conceptions remain, to channel thought and direct conduct, to give purpose to living.

In considering cultural relativism, also, we must recognize that it has three quite different aspects, which in most discussions of it tend to be disregarded. One of these is methodological, one philosophical, and one practical. As it has been put:

As method, relativism encompasses the principle of our science that, in studying a culture, one seeks to attain as great a degree of objectivity as possible; that one does not judge the modes of behavior one is describing, or seek to change them. Rather, one seeks to understand the sanctions of behavior in terms of the established relationships within the culture itself, and refrains from making interpretations that arise from a preconceived frame of reference. Relativism as philosophy concerns the nature of cultural values, and, beyond this, the implications of an epistemology that derives from a recognition of the force of enculturative conditioning in shaping thought and behavior. Its practical aspects involve the application—the practice—of the philosophical principles derived from this method, to the wider, cross-cultural scene.

We may follow this reasoning somewhat further.

In these terms, the three aspects of cultural relativism can be regarded as representing a logical sequence which, in a broad sense, the historical development of the idea has also followed. That is, the methodological aspect, whereby the data from which the epistemological propositions flow are gathered, ordered and assessed, came first. For it is difficult to conceive of a systematic theory of cultural relativism—as against a generalized idea of live-and-let-live—without the pre-existence of the massive ethnographic documentation gathered by anthropologists concerning the similarities and differences between cultures the world over. Out of these data came the philosophical position, and with the philosophical position came speculation as to its implications for conduct.[4]

Cultural relativism, in all cases, must be sharply distinguished from concepts of the relativity of individual behavior, which would negate all social controls over conduct. Conformity to the code of the group is a requirement for any regularity in life. Yet to say that we have a right to expect conformity to the code of our day for ourselves does not imply that we need expect, much less impose, conformity to our code on persons who live by other codes. The very core of cultural relativism is the social discipline that comes of respect for differences—of mutual respect. Emphasis on the worth of many ways of life, not one, is an affirmation of the values in each culture. Such emphasis seeks to understand and to harmonize goals, not to judge and destroy those that do not dovetail with our own. Cultural history teaches that, important as it is to discern and study the parallelisms in human civilizations, it is no less important to discern and study the different ways man has devised to fulfill his needs.

That it has been necessary to consider questions such as have been raised reflects an enculturative experience wherein the prevalent system of morals is not only consciously inculcated, but its exclusive claim to excellence emphasized. There are not many cultures, for example, where a rigid dichotomy between good and evil, such as we have set up, is insisted upon. Rather it is recognized that good and evil are but the extremes of a continuously varied scale between these poles that produces only different degrees of greyness. We thus return to the principle enunciated earlier, that "judgments are based on experience, and experience is interpreted by each individual in terms of his enculturation." In a culture where absolute values are stressed, the relativism of a world that encompasses many ways of living will be difficult to comprehend. Rather, it will offer a field day for value judgments based on the degree to which a given body of customs resembles or differs from those of Euroamerican culture.[5]

Once comprehended, however, and employing the field methods of the scientific student of man, together with an awareness of the satisfactions the most varied bodies of custom yield, this position gives us a leverage to lift us out of the ethnocentric morass in which our thinking about ultimate values has for so long bogged down. With a means of probing deeply into all manner of differing cultural orientations, of reaching into the significance of the ways of living of different peoples, we can turn again to our own culture with fresh perspective, and an objectivity that can be achieved in no other manner.

NOTES

1. Cf. M. J. Herskovits, 1938b, Vol. I, pp. 137–55, 300–51.

2. E. Cassirer, 1944, p. 25.

3. This unpublished myth was told to F. M. Olbrechts of Brussels, Belgium, in the course of field work among the Cherokee. His having made it available is gratefully acknowledged. A similar tale has been recorded from the Albany Cree, at Moose Factory, according to information received from F. Voget.

4. M. J. Herskovits, 1951, p. 24.

5. Instances of the rejection of relativism on philosophical grounds, by writers who attempt to reconcile the principle of absolute values with the diversity of known systems, are to be found in E. Vivas, 1950, pp. 27–42, and D. Bidney, 1953a, pp. 689–95, 1953b, pp. 423–9. Both of these discussions, also, afford examples of the confusion that results when a distinction is not drawn between the methodological, philosophical, and practical aspects of relativism. For a critical consideration of relativism that, by implication, recognizes these differences, see R. Redfield, 1953, pp. 144 ff.

NO   Louis P. Pojman

ETHICAL RELATIVISM: WHO'S TO JUDGE WHAT'S RIGHT AND WRONG?

Ethical relativism is the doctrine that the moral rightness and wrongness of actions varies from society to society and that there are no absolute universal moral standards binding on all men at all times. Accordingly, it holds that whether or not it is right for an individual to act in a certain way depends on or is relative to the society to which he belongs.

—John Ladd, *Ethical Relativism*

In the 19th century Christian missionaries sometimes used coercion to change the customs of pagan tribal people in parts of Africa and the Pacific Islands. Appalled by the customs of public nakedness, polygamy, working on the Sabbath, and infanticide, they paternalistically went about reforming the "poor pagans." They clothed them, separated wives from their husbands in order to create monogamous households, made the Sabbath a day of rest, and ended infanticide. In the process they sometimes created malaise, causing the estranged women to despair and their children to be orphaned. The natives often did not understand the new religion, but accepted it in deference to the white man's power. The white people had guns and medicine.

Since the 19th century we've made progress in understanding cultural diversity, and now realize that the social dissonance caused by "do-gooders" was a bad thing. In the last century or so, anthropology has exposed our penchant for *ethnocentrism*, the prejudicial view that interprets all of reality through the eyes of one's own cultural beliefs and values. We have come to see enormous variety in social practices throughout the world.

For instance, Eskimos allow their elderly to die by starvation, whereas we believe that this is morally wrong. The Spartans of ancient Greece and the Dobu of New Guinea believe that stealing is morally right; but we believe it is wrong. Many cultures, past and present, have practiced or still practice infanticide. A tribe in East Africa once threw deformed infants to the hippopotamus, but our society condemns such acts. Sexual practices vary over time and clime. Some cultures permit homosexual behavior, whereas others condemn it. Some cultures, including Moslem societies, practice polygamy,

From Louis P. Pojman, *Ethics: Discovering Right and Wrong*, 2d ed. (Wadsworth, 1995). Copyright © 1995 by Wadsworth Publishing Company. Reprinted by permission.

while Christian cultures view it as immoral. Anthropologist Ruth Benedict describes a tribe in Melanesia that views cooperation and kindness as vices, and anthropologist Colin Turnbull has documented that the Ik in Northern Uganda have no sense of duty toward their children or parents. There are societies that make it a duty for children to kill their aging parents (sometimes by strangling).

The ancient Greek historian Herodotus (485–430 B.C.) told the story of how Darius, the king of Persia, once brought together some Callatians (Asian tribal people) and some Greeks. He asked the Callatians how they disposed of their deceased parents. They explained that they ate the bodies. The Greeks, who cremate their parents, were horrified at such barbarous behavior. No amount of money could tempt them to do such an irreverent thing. Then Darius asked the Callatians, "What should I give you to burn the bodies of your fathers at their decease?" The Callatians were utterly horrified at such barbarous behavior and begged Darius to cease from such irreverent discourse. Herodotus concluded that "Custom is the king o'er all."[1]

Today we condemn ethnocentrism as a variety of prejudice tantamount to racism and sexism. What is right in one culture may be wrong in another, what is good east of the river may be bad west of the same river, what is a virtue in one nation may be seen as a vice in another, so it behooves us not to judge others but to be tolerant of diversity.

This rejection of ethnocentrism in the West has contributed to a general shift in public opinion about morality, so that for a growing number of Westerners, consciousness-raising about the validity of other ways of life has led to a grad-ual erosion of belief in moral objectivism, the view that there are universal moral principles, valid for all people at all times and climes. For example, in polls taken in my ethics and introduction to philosophy classes over the past several years (in three different universities in three areas of the country) students affirmed by a 2 to 1 ratio, a version of moral relativism over moral absolutism with barely 3 percent seeing something in between these two polar opposites. Of course, I'm not suggesting that all these students have a clear understanding of what relativism entails, for many of those who say they are ethical relativists also state on the same questionnaire that "abortion, except to save the mother's life, is always wrong," that "capital punishment is always morally wrong," or that "suicide is never morally premissible." The apparent contradictions signal some confusion on the matter.

[Here] we examine the central notions of ethical relativism and look at the implications that seem to follow from it. . . .

AN ANALYSIS OF RELATIVISM

Ethical relativism holds that there are no universally valid moral principles, but rather that all moral principles are valid relative to culture or individual choice. It is to be distinguished from *moral skepticism*—the view that there are no valid moral principles at all (or at least we cannot know whether there are any) —and from all forms of *moral objectivism* or *absolutism*. John Ladd's statement . . . is a typical characterization of the theory:

> Ethical relativism is the doctrine that the moral rightness and wrongness of actions varies from society to society

and that there are no absolute universal moral standards binding on all men at all times. Accordingly, it holds that whether or not it is right for an individual to act in a certain way depends on or is relative to the society to which he belongs.[2]

If we analyze this passage, we derive the following argument:

1. What is considered morally right and wrong varies from society to society, so that there are no universal moral standards held by all societies.
2. Whether or not it is right for an individual to act in a certain way depends on or is relative to the society to which he or she belongs.
3. Therefore, there are no *absolute* or objective moral standards that apply to all people everywhere and at all times.

The Diversity Thesis

The first thesis, which may be called the *diversity thesis* and identified with *cultural relativism*, is simply an anthropological thesis that acknowledges the fact that moral rules differ from society to society. As we illustrated earlier..., there is enormous variety in what may count as a moral principle in a given society. The human condition is malleable in the extreme, allowing any number of folkways or moral codes. As Ruth Benedict has written:

> The cultural pattern of any civilization makes use of a certain segment of the great arc of potential human purposes and motivations, just as we have seen... that any culture makes use of certain selected material techniques or cultural traits. The great arc along which all the possible human behaviors are distributed is far too immense and too full of contradictions for any one culture to

utilize even any considerable portion of it. Selection is the first requirement.[3]...

The Dependency Thesis

The second thesis, the *dependency thesis*, asserts that individual acts are right and wrong depending on the nature of the society in which they occur. Morality does not exist in a vacuum; rather, what is considered morally right or wrong must be seen in a context, depending on the goals, wants, beliefs, history, and environment of the society in question. As William Graham Sumner says,

> We learn the [morals] as unconsciously as we learn to walk and hear and breathe, and [we] never know any reason why the [morals] are what they are. The justification of them is that when we wake to consciousness of life we find them facts which already hold us in the bonds of tradition, custom, and habit.[4]

Trying to see things from an independent, noncultural point of view would be like taking out our eyes in order to examine their contours and qualities. We are simply culturally determined beings.

We could, of course, distinguish both a weak and a strong thesis of dependency. The nonrelativist can accept a certain relativity in the way moral principles are *applied* in various cultures, depending on beliefs, history, and environment. For example, Orientals show respect by covering the head and uncovering the feet, whereas Occidentals do the opposite. Though both adhere to a principle of respect for deserving people, they apply the principle differently. But the ethical relativist must maintain a stronger thesis, one that insists that the very validity of the principles is a product of the culture and that different cultures will invent different valid principles. The ethical relativist maintains that even beyond the environmental factors and differences in beliefs, there are fundamental disagreements among societies.

In a sense, we all live in radically different worlds. Each person has a different set of beliefs and experiences, a particular perspective that colors all of his or her perceptions. Do the farmer, the real estate dealer, and the artist looking at the same spatiotemporal field actually see the same thing? Not likely. Their different orientations, values, and expectations govern their perceptions, so that different aspects of the field are highlighted and some features are missed. Even as our individual values arise from personal experience, so social values are grounded in the peculiar history of the community. Morality, then, is just the set of common rules, habits, and customs that have won social approval over time, so that they seem part of the nature of things, like facts. There is nothing mysterious or transcendent about these codes of behavior. They are the outcomes of our social history.

There is something conventional about *any* morality, so that every morality really depends on a level of social acceptance. Not only do various societies adhere to different moral systems, but the very same society could (and often does) change its moral views over time and place. For example, in the southern United States slavery is now viewed as immoral, whereas just over 100 years ago, it was not. We have greatly altered our views on abortion, divorce, and sexuality as well.

The conclusion—that there are no absolute or objective moral standards binding on all people—follows from the first two propositions. Cultural relativism (the diversity thesis) plus the dependency the-

sis yields ethical relativism in its classic form. If there are different moral principles from culture to culture and if all morality is rooted in culture, then it follows that there are no universal moral principles valid for all cultures and all people at all times.

SUBJECTIVE ETHICAL RELATIVISM (SUBJECTIVISM)

Some people think that even the conclusion just stated is too tame. They maintain that morality is not dependent on the society but on the individual himself or herself. As students sometimes maintain, "Morality is in the eye of the beholder." Ernest Hemingway wrote:

> So far, about morals, I know only that what is moral is what you feel good after and what is immoral is what you feel bad after and judged by these moral standards, which I do not defend, the bullfight is very moral to me because I feel very fine while it is going on and have a feeling of life and death and mortality and immortality, and after it is over I feel very sad but very fine.[5]

The form of *moral subjectivism* has the sorry consequence that it makes morality a useless concept, for, on its premises, little or no interpersonal criticism or judgment is logically possible. Hemingway may feel good about the killing of bulls in a bullfight, whereas Albert Schweitzer or Mother Teresa would no doubt feel the opposite. No argument about the matter is possible. The only basis for judging Hemingway, or anyone else, wrong would be if he failed to live up to his own principles; however, one of Hemingway's principles could be that hypocrisy is morally permissible (he feels good about it), so that it would be impossible for him to do wrong. For Hemingway, hypocrisy and nonhypocrisy are both morally permissible. On the basis of subjectivism it could very easily turn out that Adolf Hitler was as moral as Mahatma Gandhi, as long as each believed he was living by his chosen principles. Notions of moral good and bad, right and wrong cease to have interpersonal evaluative meaning.

In the opening days of my philosophy classes, I often find students vehemently defending subjective relativism. I then give the students their first test. The next class period I return all the tests, marked F even though my comments show that most of them are of a very high quality. When the students express outrage at this injustice, I answer that I have accepted subjectivism for purposes of marking the exams, in which case the principle of justice has no objective validity.

Absurd consequences follow from subjective ethical relativism. If it is correct, then morality reduces to aesthetic tastes, over which there can be neither argument nor interpersonal judgment. Although many people say they hold this position, there seems to be a conflict between it and other of their moral views (e.g., that Hitler was really morally bad or that capital punishment is always wrong). There seems to be a contradiction between subjectivism and the very concept of morality, which it is supposed to characterize, for morality has to do with *proper* resolution of interpersonal conflict and the amelioration of the human predicament. Whatever else it does, morality has the minimal aim of preventing a state of chaos in which life is "solitary, poor, nasty, brutish, and short." But if so, subjectivism is no help at all in doing this, for it does not rest on social *agreement* of principle (as the conventionalist maintains) or on an objectively independent set of norms that bind all people for the common good.

Subjectivism treats individuals like billiard balls on a societal pool table where they meet only in radical collisions, each aimed at his or her own goal and striving to do in the others before they themselves are done in. This atomistic view of personality is belied by the facts that we develop in families and mutually dependent communities in which we share a common language, common institutions, and similar habits, and that we often feel one another's joys and sorrows. As John Donne said, "No man is an island, entire of itself; every man is a piece of the continent."

Radical individualistic relativism seems incoherent. If so, it follows that the only plausible view of ethical relativism must be one that grounds morality in the group or culture. This form of relativism is called *conventionalism*, which we looked at earlier and to which we now return.

CONVENTIONAL ETHICAL RELATIVISM (CONVENTIONALISM)

Conventional ethical relativism, the view that there are no objective moral principles but rather that all valid moral principles are justified by virtue of their cultural acceptance, recognizes the social nature of morality. That is precisely its power and virtue. It does not seem subject to the same absurd consequences that plague subjectivism. Recognizing the importance of our social environment in generating customs and beliefs, many people suppose that ethical relativism is the correct ethical theory. Furthermore, they are drawn to it for its liberal philosophical stance. It seems to be an enlightened response to the sin of ethnocentricity, and it seems to entail or strongly imply an attitude of tolerance toward other cultures. As Ruth Benedict says, in recognizing ethical relativity

> we shall arrive at a more realistic social faith, accepting as grounds of hope and as new bases for tolerance the coexisting and equally valid patterns of life which mankind has created for itself from the raw materials of existence.[6]

The most famous of those holding this position is the anthropologist Melville Herskovits, who argues even more explicitly than Benedict that ethical relativism entails intercultural tolerance:

1. Morality is relative to its culture.
2. There is no independent basis for criticizing the morality of any other culture.
3. Therefore we ought to be tolerant of the moralities of other cultures.[7]

Tolerance is certainly a virtue, but is this a good argument for it? I think not. If morality is simply relative to each culture, then if the culture does not have a principle of tolerance, its members have no obligation to be tolerant. Herskovits seems to be treating the principle of tolerance as the one exception to his relativism. But from a relativistic point of view there is no more reason to be tolerant than to be intolerant, and neither stance is objectively morally better than the other.

Not only do relativists fail to offer a basis for criticizing those who are intolerant, but they cannot rationally criticize anyone who espouses what they might regard as a heinous principle. If, as seems to be the case, valid criticism supposes an objective or impartial standard, relativists cannot morally criticize anyone outside their own culture. Adolf Hitler's genocidal actions, as long as they were culturally accepted, were as morally legitimate as Mother Teresa's works of mercy. If conventional relativism is accepted, then racism, genocide of unpopular minorities, oppression of the poor, slavery, and even the advocacy of war for its own sake are as equally moral as their opposites. And if a subculture decided that starting a nuclear war was somehow morally acceptable, we could not morally criticize those people, for any actual morality, whatever its content, is as valid as every other and more valid than ideal moralities, because the latter aren't adhered to by any culture.

There are other disturbing consequences of ethical relativism. It seems to entail that reformers are always (morally) wrong, since they go against the tide of cultural standards. William Wilberforce was wrong, in the 18th century, to oppose slavery; the British were immoral in opposing suttee in India (the burning of widows on their husbands' funeral pyres, which is now illegal in India); and missionaries were immoral in opposing clitorectomies in Central Africa. The early Christians were wrong in refusing to serve in the Roman army or to bow down to Caesar, since the majority in the Roman Empire believed these acts were moral duties. In fact, Jesus himself was immoral in advocating the beatitudes and principles of the Sermon on the Mount, since it is clear that few in his time (or in ours) accepted them.

Yet we normally believe just the opposite, that the reformer is the courageous innovator who is right, who has the truth, in the face of the mindless majority. Sometimes the individual must stand alone with the truth, risking social censure and persecution. As Dr. Stockman says in Ibsen's *Enemy of the People*, after he loses the battle to declare his town's profitable polluted tourist spa unsanitary, "The most dangerous enemy of the truth and freedom among us—is the compact majority. Yes, the damned... majority. The majority has *might*—unfortunately—but *right* it is not. Right—are I and a few others." Yet if relativism is correct, the opposite is necessarily the case. Truth is with the crowd and error with the individual.

Similarly, conventional ethical relativism entails disturbing judgments about the law. Our normal view is that we have a prima facie duty to obey the law, because law, in general, promotes the human Good. According to most objective systems, this obligation is not absolute but rather is conditional, depending on the particular law's relation to a wider moral order. Civil disobedience is warranted in some cases in which the law seems to be in serious conflict with morality. However, if moral relativism is true, then neither law nor civil disobedience has a firm foundation. On the one hand, for society at large, civil disobedience will be morally wrong, so long as the culture agrees with the law in question. On the other hand, if you belong to the relevant subculture that doesn't recognize the particular law in question, disobedience will be morally mandated. The Ku Klux Klan, which believes that Jews, Catholics, and Blacks are evil or undeserving of high regard, are, given conventionalism, morally permitted or required to break the laws that protect these endangered groups. Why should I obey a law that my group doesn't recognize as valid?

To sum up, unless we have an independent moral basis for law, it is hard to see why we have any general duty to obey it; and unless we recognize the priority of a universal moral law, we have no firm basis to justify our acts of civil disobedience against "unjust laws." Both the validity of law and morally motivated disobedience of unjust laws are annulled in favor of a power struggle.

There is an even more basic problem with the notion that morality is dependent on cultural acceptance for its validity. The problem is that the concepts of *culture* and *society* are notoriously difficult to define, especially in a pluralistic society such as our own, in which the concepts seem rather vague. One person may belong to several societies (subcultures) with different emphases on values and arrangements of principles. A person may belong to the nation as a single society with certain values of patriotism, honor, courage, laws (including some that are controversial but have majority acceptance, such as the law on abortion). But he or she may also belong to a church that opposes some of the laws of the state. The same individual may also be an integral member of a socially mixed community in which different principles hold sway, and additionally may belong to clubs and a family that adhere to still other rules. Relativism would seem to tell us that when a person is a member of societies with conflicting moralities, that person must be judged both wrong and not wrong, whatever he or she does. For example, if Mary is a U.S. citizen and a Roman Catholic, she is wrong (qua Catholic) if she chooses to have an abortion and not wrong (qua citizen of the United States) if she acts against the teaching of the church on abortion. As a member of a racist university fraternity, the Klu Klux Klan, John has no obligation to treat his fellow African American students as equals; but as a member of the university community itself (in which the principle of equal rights is accepted), he does have that obligation; but as a member of the surrounding community (which may reject the principle of equal rights), John again has no such obligation; but then again as a member of the nation at large (which accepts the principle), he is obligated to treat his fellow citizens with respect. What is the morally right thing for John to do? The question no longer makes much sense in this moral Babel; morality has lost its action-guiding function.

Perhaps the relativist would adhere to a principle that says in such cases the individual may choose which group to belong to as primary. If Mary chooses to have an abortion, she is choosing to belong to the general society relative to that principle. And John must likewise choose among groups. The trouble with this option is that it seems to lead back to counterintuitive results. If Mafia Mike feels like killing bank president Otis Ortcutt and wants to feel good about it, he identifies with the Mafia society rather than with the general public morality. Does this justify the killing? In fact, couldn't one justify anything simply by forming a small subculture that approved of it? Charles Manson would be morally pure in killing innocents simply by virtue of forming a little coterie. How large must the group be in order to be a legitimate subculture or society? Does it need 10 or 15 people? How about just 3? Come to think about it, why can't my burglary partner and I found our own society with a morality of its own? Of course, if my partner dies, I could still claim that I was acting from an originally social set of norms. But why can't I dispense with the interpersonal agreements altogether and invent my own morality? After all, morality, on this view, is only an invention any-

way. Conventionalist relativism seems to reduce to subjectivism. And subjectivism leads, as we have seen, to the demise of morality altogether....

However, though we may fear the demise of morality as we have known it, this in itself may not be a good reason for rejecting relativism (that is, for judging it as false). Alas, truth may not always be edifying. But the consequences of this position are sufficiently alarming to prompt us to look carefully for some weakness in the relativist's argument. So let us examine the premises and conclusion listed earlier... as the three theses of relativism.

1. *The Diversity Thesis.* What is considered morally right and wrong varies from society to society, so that there are no universal moral standards held by all societies.

2. *The Dependency Thesis.* Whether or not it is right for an individual to act in a certain way depends on or is relative to the society to which he or she belongs.

3. *Ethical Relativism.* Therefore, there are no absolute or objective moral standards that apply to all people everywhere and at all times.

Does any one of these seem problematic? Let us consider the first thesis, the diversity thesis, which we have also called cultural relativism. Perhaps there is not as much diversity as anthropologists like Sumner and Benedict suppose. We can also see great similarities between the moral codes of various cultures. E. O. Wilson has identified over a score of common features,[8] and before him Clyde

Kluckhohn noted some significant common ground:

> Every culture has a concept of murder, distinguishing this from execution, killing in war, and other "justifiable homicides." The notions of incest and other regulations upon sexual behavior, the prohibitions upon untruth under defined circumstances, of restitution and reciprocity, of mutual obligations between parents and children—these and many other moral concepts are altogether universal.[9]

And Colin Turnbull, whose description of the sadistic, semidisplaced Ik in Northern Uganda was seen as evidence of a people without principles of kindness and cooperation, has produced evidence that underneath the surface of this dying society is a deeper moral code, from a time when the tribe flourished, that occasionally surfaces and shows its nobler face.[10]

On the other hand, there is enormous cultural diversity, and many societies have radically different moral codes. Cultural relativism seems to be a fact; but even if it is, it does not by itself establish the truth of ethical relativism. Cultural diversity in itself is neutral relative to theories: The objectivist could concede complete cultural relativism but still defend a form of universalism, for he or she could argue that some cultures simply lack correct moral principles.

... [T]he first premise doesn't by itself, imply ethical relativism, and its denial doesn't disprove ethical relativism.

We turn to the crucial second thesis, the dependency thesis.... We distinguished between a weak and a strong thesis of dependency. The weak thesis says that the application of principles depends on the particular cultural predicament, whereas the strong thesis affirms that the principles themselves depend on that predicament. The nonrelativist can accept a certain relativity in the way moral principles are *applied* in various cultures, depending on beliefs, history, and environment. For example, a harsh environment with scarce natural resources may justify the Eskimos' brand of euthanasia to the objectivist, who in another environment would consistently reject that practice. One tribe in East Africa throws its deformed children into the river because it believes that such infants *belong* to the hippopotamus, the god of the river. We consider this a false belief, but the point is that the same principles of respect for property and for human life are operative in these contrary practices. These people differ with us only in belief, not in substantive moral principle. This is an illustration of how nonmoral beliefs (e.g., deformed children belong to the hippopotamus god), when applied to common moral principles (e.g., give to each his or her due), generate different actions in different cultures. In our own culture the difference in the nonmoral belief about the status of a fetus generates opposite moral prescriptions. So the fact that moral principles are weakly dependent doesn't show that ethical relativism is valid. In spite of this weak dependency on nonmoral factors, there could still be a set of general moral norms applicable to all cultures and even recognized in most, which are disregarded at a culture's own expense.

What the relativist needs is a strong thesis of dependency—that somehow all principles are essentially cultural inventions. But why should we choose to view morality this way? Is there anything to recommend the strong thesis over the weak thesis of dependency? The relativist may argue that in fact we lack an obvious impartial standard from which to judge. "Who's to say which culture is right and which is wrong?" But this seems to be dubious. We can reason and perform thought experiments in order to make a case for one system over another. We may not be able to *know* with certainty that our moral beliefs are closer to the truth than those of another culture or those of others within our own culture, but we may be *justified in believing* that they are. If we can be closer to the truth regarding factual or scientific matters, why can't we be closer to the truth on moral matters? Why can't a culture simply be confused or wrong about its moral perceptions? Why can't we say that a society like that of the Ik, which sees nothing wrong with enjoying watching its own children fall into fires, is less moral in that regard than the culture that cherishes children and grants them protection and equal rights? To take such a stand does not commit the fallacy of ethnocentrism, for in doing so we are seeking to derive principles through critical reason, not simply uncritical acceptance of or own mores.

CONCLUSION

Ethical relativism—the thesis that moral principles derive their validity from dependence on society or individual choice —seems plausible at first glance, but when scrutinized closely is seen to have some serious difficulties. Subjectivism seems to boil down to anarchistic individualism, and conventionalism fails to deal adequately with the problems of the reformer, the question of defining a culture, and the whole enterprise of moral criticism.

NOTES

1. *History of Herodotus*, trans. George Rawlinson (Appleton, 1859), Bk. 3, Ch. 38.

2. John Ladd, *Ethical Relativism* (Wadsworth, 1973), p. 1.

3. Ruth Benedict, *Patterns of Culture* (New American Library, 1934), p. 257.

4. W. G. Sumner, *Folkways* (Ginn & Co., 1906), section 80, p. 76. Ruth Benedict indicates the depth of our cultural conditioning this way: "The very eyes with which we see the problem are conditioned by the long traditional habits of our own society." ["Anthropology and the Abnormal," *The Journal of General Psychology* (1934): 59–82.]

5. Ernest Hemingway, *Death in the Afternoon* (Scribners, 1932), p. 4.

6. Benedict, *Patterns of Culture*, p. 257.

7. Melville Herskovits, *Cultural Relativism* (Random House, 1972).

8. E. O. Wilson, *On Human Nature* (Bantam Books, 1979), p. 22f.

9. Clyde Kluckhohn, "Ethical Relativity: Sic et Non," *Journal of Philosophy* LII (1955).

10. Colin Turnbull, *The Mountain People* (Simon & Schuster, 1972).

POSTSCRIPT

Is Morality Relative to Culture?

Ethical relativism can be a very difficult thesis to state. It is not the same as what Pojman calls the "diversity thesis"—the thesis that what is considered right and wrong varies from society to society so that there are no universal moral standards held by all societies. The key word in the diversity thesis is *considered*. Pojman concedes that what is considered moral at one time and place is not always what is considered moral at another time and place. A nonrelativist like Pojman, however, will insist that it does not follow from the fact that people or groups disagree about what is moral (or have different opinions about what is moral) that both opinions are equally correct. Nor does it follow from that fact of disagreement that there are no universally valid moral principles. All that follows is that there is disagreement.

A relativist like Herskovits will agree that there is disagreement—at least when the parties are brought together. But since moral principles are in every case the product of a certain time and place, Herskovits considers Pojman's so-called universal moral norms pure fantasy.

One problem for the relativist who maintains that the thesis that our own perceptions, beliefs, and opinions are bound by ethnocentrism and are therefore unable to achieve any truly "objective" point of view is that the thesis of relativism seems to require just such a point of view for itself. If, on the other hand, relativistic ideas are simply those that have arisen at a certain time and place, subject to their own ethnocentrism, then we might wonder why it is that a relativist claims special status for them.

Classic social scientific views in the relativistic tradition are Ruth Benedict, *Patterns of Culture* (Pelican, 1946) and Melville J. Herskovits, *Man and His Works* (Alfred A. Knopf, 1948). The relevance of the anthropological data to philosophical issues is discussed by Kai Nielsen in "Ethical Relativism and the Facts of Cultural Relativity," *Social Research* (1966). Ethics and cultural relativity are also discussed in May Edel and Abraham Edel, eds., *Anthropology and Ethics: The Quest for Moral Understanding* (Press of Case Western Reserve University, 1968). Gilbert Harman has provided a sophisticated defense of moral relativism in his "Moral Relativism Defended," *Philosophical Review* (1975).

Further sources are David Wong, *Ethical Relativity* (University of California Press, 1984); Michael Krausz, ed., *Relativism: Interpretation and Conflict* (University of Notre Dame Press, 1989); Hugh LaFollette, "The Truth in Ethical Relativism," *Journal of Social Philosophy* (1991); and Christopher Norris, *Reclaiming Truth: A Critique of Cultural Relativism* (Duke University Press, 1996).

ISSUE 3

Does Morality Need Religion?

YES: C. Stephen Layman, from *The Shape of the Good: Christian Reflections on the Foundations of Ethics* (University of Notre Dame Press, 1991)

NO: John Arthur, from "Religion, Morality, and Conscience," in John Arthur, ed., *Morality and Moral Controversies,* 4th ed. (Prentice Hall, 1996)

ISSUE SUMMARY

YES: Philosopher C. Stephen Layman argues that morality makes the most sense from a theistic perspective and that a purely secular perspective is insufficient. The secular perspective, Layman asserts, does not adequately deal with secret violations, and it does not allow for the possibility of fulfillment of people's deepest needs in an afterlife.

NO: Philosopher John Arthur argues that morality is logically independent of religion, although there are historical connections. Religion, he believes, is not necessary for moral guidance or moral answers; morality is social.

There is a widespread feeling that morality and religion are connected. One view is that religion provides a ground for morality, so without religion there is no morality. Thus, a falling away from religion implies a falling away from morality.

Such thoughts have troubled many people. The Russian novelist Dostoyevsky (1821–1881) wrote, "If there is no God, then everything is permitted." Many Americans today also believe that religious faith is important. They often believe that even if doctrines and dogmas cannot be known for certain, religion nevertheless leads to morality and good behavior. President Dwight D. Eisenhower is reputed to have said that everyone should have a religious faith but that it did not matter what that faith was. And many daily newspapers throughout the country advise their readers to attend the church or synagogue of their choice. Apparently, the main reason why people think it is important to subscribe to a religion is that only in this way will one be able to attain morality. If there is no God, then everything is permitted and there is moral chaos. Moral chaos can be played out in societies and, on a smaller scale, within the minds of individuals. Thus, if you do not believe in God, then you will confront moral chaos; you will be liable to permit (and permit yourself to do) anything, and you will have no moral bearings at all.

Such a view seems to face several problems, however. For example, what are we to say of the morally good atheist or of the morally good but completely nonreligious person? A true follower of the view that morality derives from religion might reply that we are simply begging the question if we believe that such people *could* be morally good. Such people might do things that are morally right and thus might *seem* good, the reply would go, but they would not be acting for the right reason (obedience to God). Such people would not have the same anchor or root for their seemingly moral attitudes that religious persons do.

Another problem for the view that links morality with religion comes from the following considerations: If you hold this view, what do you say of devoutly religious people who belong to religious traditions and who support moralities that are different from your own? If morality is indeed derived from religion, if different people are thus led to follow different moralities, and if the original religions are not themselves subject to judgment, then it is understandable how different people arrive at different moral views. But the views will still be different and perhaps even incompatible. If so, the claim that morality derives from religion must mean that one can derive *a* morality from *a* religion (and not that one derives morality itself from religion). The problem is that by allowing this variation among religions and moralities back into the picture, we seem to allow moral chaos back in too.

The view that what God commands is good, what God prohibits is evil, and without divine commands and prohibitions nothing is either good or bad in itself is called the *divine command theory,* or the *divine imperative view.* This view resists the recognition of any source of good or evil that is not tied to criteria or standards of God's own creation. Such a recognition is thought to go against the idea of God's omnipotence. A moral law that applied to God but was not of God's own creation would seem to limit God in a way in which he cannot be limited. But, on the other hand, this line of thought (that no moral law outside of God's own making should apply to him) seems contrary to the orthodox Christian view that God is good. For if good means something in accordance with God's will, then when we say that God is good, we are only saying that he acts in accordance with his own will—and this just does not seem to be enough.

In the following selections, C. Stephen Layman argues that a religious perspective makes better sense of moral commitment than a secular perspective. Indeed, in his view, it is not even clear that a secular individual who followed the dictates of morality would be rational. John Arthur asserts that morality does not need a religious foundation at all and that morality is social.

YES

C. Stephen Layman

ETHICS AND THE KINGDOM OF GOD

Why build a theory of ethics on the assumption that there is a God? Why not simply endorse a view of ethics along... secular lines...? I shall respond to these questions in [two] stages. First, I contrast the secular and religious perspectives on morality. Second, I explain why I think the moral life makes more sense from the point of view of theism [belief in God] than from that of atheism....

* * *

As I conceive it, the modern secular perspective on morality involves at least two elements. First, there is no afterlife; each individual human life ends at death. It follows that the only goods available to an individual are those he or she can obtain this side of death.[1]

Second, on the secular view, moral value is an *emergent* phenomenon. That is, moral value is "a feature of certain effects though it is not a feature of their causes" (as wetness is a feature of H_2O, but not of hydrogen or oxygen).[2] Thus, the typical contemporary secular view has it that moral value emerges only with the arrival of very complex nervous systems (viz., human brains), late in the evolutionary process. There is no Mind "behind the scenes" on the secular view, no intelligent Creator concerned with the affairs of human existence. As one advocate of the secular view puts it, "Ethics, though not consciously created [either by humans or by God], is a product of social life which has the function of promoting values common to the members of society."[3]

By way of contrast, the religious point of view (in my use of the phrase) includes a belief in God and in life after death. God is defined as an eternal being who is almighty and perfectly morally good. Thus, from the religious point of view, morality is not an emergent phenomenon, for God's goodness has always been in existence, and is not the product of nonmoral causes. Moreover, from the religious point of view, there are goods available after death. Specifically, there awaits the satisfaction of improved relations with God and with redeemed creatures.

From C. Stephen Layman, *The Shape of the Good: Christian Reflections on the Foundations of Ethics* (University of Notre Dame Press, 1991). Copyright © 1991 by University of Notre Dame Press. Reprinted by permission.

It is important to note that, from the religious perspective, *the existence of God and life after death* are not independent hypotheses. If God exists, then at least two lines of reasoning lend support to the idea that death is not final. While I cannot here scrutinize these lines of reasoning, I believe it will be useful to sketch them.[4] (1) It has often been noted that we humans seem unable to find complete fulfillment in the present life. Even those having abundant material possessions and living in the happiest of circumstances find themselves, upon reflection, profoundly unsatisfied.... [I]f this earthly life is the whole story, it appears that our deepest longings will remain unfulfilled. But if God is good, He surely will not leave our deepest longings unfulfilled provided He is able to fulfill them—at least to the extent that we are willing to accept His gracious aid. So, since our innermost yearnings are not satisfied in this life, it is likely that they will be satisfied after death.

(2) Human history has been one long story of injustice, of the oppression of the poor and weak by the rich and powerful. The lives of relatively good people are often miserable, while the wicked prosper. Now, if God exists, He is able to correct such injustices, though He does not correct all of them in the present life. But if God is also good, He will not leave such injustices forever unrectified. It thus appears that He will rectify matters at some point after death. This will involve benefits for some in the afterlife—it may involve penalties for others. (However, the... possibility of post-mortem punishment does not necessarily imply the possibility of hell *as standardly conceived*.)

We might sum up the main difference between the secular and religious views by saying that the only goods available from a secular perspective are *earthly* goods. Earthly goods include such things as physical health, friendship, pleasure, self-esteem, knowledge, enjoyable activities, an adequate standard of living, etc. The religious or theistic perspective recognizes these earthly goods *as good*, but it insists that there are non-earthly or *transcendent* goods. These are goods available only if God exists and there is life after death for humans. Transcendent goods include harmonious relations with God prior to death as well as the joys of the afterlife—right relations with both God and redeemed creatures.

* * *

[One secular] defense of the virtues amounts to showing that society cannot function well unless individuals have moral virtue. If we ask, "Why should we as individuals care about society?", the answer will presumably be along the following lines: "Individuals cannot flourish apart from a well-functioning society, so *morality pays for the individual*."

This defense of morality raises two questions we must now consider. First, is it misguided to defend morality by an appeal to self-interest? Many people feel that morality and self-interest are fundamentally at odds: "If you perform an act because you see that it is in your interest to do so, then you aren't doing the right thing *just because it's right*. A successful defense of morality must be a defense of duty for duty's sake. Thus, the appeal to self-interest is completely misguided." Second, *does* morality really pay for the individual? More particularly, does morality always pay in terms of earthly goods? Let us take these questions up in turn.

(1) Do we desert the moral point of view if we defend morality on the grounds that it pays? Consider an analogy with etiquette. Why should one bother with etiquette? Should one do the well-mannered thing simply for its own sake? Do we keep our elbows off the table or refrain from belching just because these things are "proper"?

To answer this question we must distinguish between the *justification of an institution* and *the justification of a particular act within that institution*. (By 'institution' I refer to any system of activities specified by rules.) This distinction can be illustrated in the case of the game (institution) of baseball. If we ask a player why he performs a particular act during a game, he will probably give an answer such as, "To put my opponent out" or "To get a home run." These answers obviously would not be relevant if the question were, "Why play baseball at all?" Relevant answers to this second question would name some advantage for the individual player, e.g., "Baseball is fun" or "It's good exercise." Thus, a justification of the institution of baseball (e.g., "It's good exercise") is quite different from a justification of a particular act within the institution (e.g., "To get a home run").

Now let's apply this distinction to our question about etiquette. If our question concerns the justification of a particular act within the institution of etiquette, then the answer may reasonably be, in effect, "This is what's proper. this is what the rules of etiquette prescribe." ...

But plainly there are deeper questions we can ask about etiquette. Who hasn't wondered, at times, what the point of the institution of etiquette is? Why do we have these quirky rules, some of which seem to make little sense? When these more fundamental questions concerning the entire institution of etiquette are being asked, it makes no sense to urge etiquette for etiquette's sake. What is needed is a description of the human *ends* the institution fulfills—ends which play a justificatory role similar to fun or good exercise in the case of baseball. And it is not difficult to identify some of these ends. For example, the rules of etiquette seem designed, in part, to facilitate social interaction; things just go more smoothly if there are agreed upon ways of greeting, eating, conversing, etc.

If anyone asks, "Why should I as an individual bother about etiquette?", an initial reply might be: "Because if you frequently violate the rules of etiquette, people will shun you." If anyone wonders why he should care about being shunned, we will presumably reply that good social relations are essential to human flourishing, and hence that a person is jeopardizing his own best interests if he places no value at all on etiquette. Thus, in the end, a defense of the institution of etiquette seems to involve the claim that the institution of etiquette *pays* for those who participate in it; it would not be illuminating to answer the question, "Why bother about etiquette?" by saying that etiquette is to be valued for its own sake.

Now, just as we distinguish between justifying the institution of etiquette (or baseball) and justifying a particular act within the institution, so we must distinguish between justifying the institution of morality and justifying a particular act within the institution. When choosing a particular course of action we may simply want to know what's right. But a more ultimate question also cries out for an answer: "What is the point of the institution of morality, anyway? Why should one bother with it?" It is natural to respond by saying that society cannot function well without morality, and individuals cannot flourish apart from a well-functioning society. In short, defending the institution of morality involves claiming that morality pays for the individual in the long run. It seems obscurantist to preach duty for duty's sake, once the more fundamental question about the point of the institution of morality has been raised.

But if morality is defended on the grounds that it pays, doesn't this distort moral motivation? Won't it mean that we no longer do things because they are right, but rather because they are in our self-interest? No. We must bear in mind our distinction between the reasons that justify a particular act within an institution and the reasons that justify the institution itself. A baseball player performs a given act in order to get on base or put an opponent out; he does not calculate whether this particular swing of the bat (or throw of the ball) is fun or good exercise. A well-mannered person is not constantly calculating whether a given act will improve her relations with others, she simply does "the proper thing." Similarly, even if we defend morality on the grounds that it pays, it does not follow that the motive for each moral act becomes, "It will pay." for we are not constantly thinking of the philosophical issues concerning the justification of the entire system of morality; for the most part we simply do things because they are right, honest, fair, loving, etc. Nevertheless, our willingness to plunge wholeheartedly into "the moral game" is apt to be vitiated should it become clear to us that the game does not pay.

At this point it appears that the institution of morality is justified only if it pays for the individuals who participate in it. For if being moral does not pay for individuals, it is difficult to see why they should bother with it. The appeal to duty for duty's sake is irrelevant when we are asking for a justification of the institution of morality itself.

(2) But we must now ask, "Does morality in fact pay?" There are at least four reasons for supposing that morality does not pay from a *secular* perspective. (a) One problem for the secular view arises from the fact that the moral point of view involves a concern for *all* human beings—or at least for all humans affected by one's actions. Thus, within christian theology, the parable of the good Samaritan is well known for its expansion of the category of "my neighbor." But human societies seem able to get along well without extending full moral concern to all outsiders; this is the essence of tribal morality. Thus, explorers in the 1700s found that the Sioux Indians followed a strict code in dealing with each other, but regarded themselves as free to steal horses from the Crow. Later on, American whites repeatedly broke treaties with the American Indians in a way that would not have been possible had the Indians been regarded as equals. It is no exaggeration to say that throughout much of human history tribal morality has been the morality humans lived by.

And so, while one must agree... that the virtues are necessary for the existence of society, it is not clear that this amounts to anything more than a defense of tribal morality.... From a purely secular point of view, it is unclear why the scope of moral concern must extend beyond one's society—or, more precisely, why one's concern must extend to groups of people outside of one's society *who are powerless and stand in the way of things one's society wants*. Why should the members of a modern industrial state extend full moral consideration to a tiny Amazonian tribe? ...

(b) A second problem for secular views concerns the possibility of secret violations of moral rules. What becomes of conscientiousness when one can break the rules in secret, without anyone knowing? After all, if I can break the rules in secret, I will not cause any social disharmony. Of course, there can be no breaking of the rules in secret if there is a God of the Christian type, who knows every human thought as well as every human act. But there are cases in which it is extraordinarily unlikely that any *humans* will discover one's rule breaking. Hence, from a secular perspective, there are cases in which secret violations of morality are possible.

Consider the following case. Suppose *A* has borrowed some money from *B*, but *A* discovers that *B* has made a mistake in his records. Because of the mistake, *B* believes that *A* has already paid the money back. *B* even goes out of his way to thank *A* for prompt payment on the loan. Let us further suppose that *B* is quite wealthy, and hence not in need of the money. Is it in *A*'s interest to pay the money back? Not paying the money back would be morally wrong; but would it be irrational, from a secular point of view? Not necessarily. Granted, it might be irrational in some cases, e.g., if *A* would have intense guilt feelings should he fail to repay the loan. But suppose *A* will not feel guilty because he really needs the money (and knows that *B* does not need it), and because he understands that secret violations belong to a special and rare category of action. Then, from a secular point of view, it is doubtful that paying the loan would be in *A*'s interest.

The point is not that theists never cheat or lie. Unfortunately they do. The point is rather that secret violations of morality arguably pay off from a secular point of view. And so, once again, it seems that there is a "game" that pays off better (in terms of earthly goods) than the relatively idealistic morality endorsed by the great ethicists, viz., one allowing secret "violations."

(c) Even supposing that morality pays for some people, does it pay for *everyone* on the secular view? Can't there be well-functioning societies in which some of the members are "moral freeloaders"? In fact, don't all actual societies have members who maintain an appearance of decency, but are in fact highly manipulative of others? How would one show, on secular grounds, that it is in the interest of these persons to be moral? Furthermore, according to psychiatrists, some people are highly amoral, virtually without feelings of guilt or shame. Yet in numerous cases these amoral types appear to be happy. These "successful egoists" are often intelligent, charming, and able to evade legal penalties for their unconventional behavior.[5] How could one show, on secular grounds, that it is in the interests of such successful egoists to be moral? They seem to find their amoral lives amply rewarding.

(d) Another problem from the secular perspective stems from the fact that in some cases morality demands that one risk death. Since death cuts one off from all earthly goods, what sense does it make to be moral (in a given case) if the risk of death is high?

This point must be stated with care. In many cases it makes sense, from a secular point of view, to risk one's life. For example, it makes sense if the risk is small and the earthly good to be gained is great; after all, one risks one's life driving to work. Or again, risking one's life makes sense from a secular point of view if failing to do so will probably lead to profound and enduring earthly unhappiness. Thus, a woman might take an enormous risk to save her child from an attacker. She might believe that she would be "unable to live with herself" afterward if she stood by and let the attacker kill or maim her child. Similarly, a man might be willing to die for his country, because he could not bear the dishonor resulting from a failure to act courageously.

But failing to risk one's life does not always lead to profound and enduring earthly unhappiness. Many soldiers play it safe in battle when risk taking is essential for victory; they may judge that victory is not worth the personal risks. And many subjects of ruthless tyrants entirely avoid the risks involved in resistance and reform. Though it may be unpleasant for such persons to find themselves regarded as cowards, this unpleasantness does not necessarily lead to profound and enduring earthly unhappiness. It seems strained to claim that what is commonly regarded as moral courage always pays in terms of earthly goods.

At this point it appears that the institution of morality cannot be justified from a secular point of view. For, as we have seen, the institution of morality is justified only if it pays (in the long run) for the individuals who participate in it. But if by "morality" we mean the relatively idealistic code urged on us by the great moralists, it appears that the institution of morality does not pay, according to the secular point of view. This is not to say that no moral code could pay off in terms of earthly goods; a tribal morality of some sort might pay for most people, especially if it were to include conventions which

skirt the problems inherent in my "secret violation" and "risk of death" cases. But such a morality would be a far cry from the morality most of us actually endorse.

Defenders of secular morality may claim that these difficulties evaporate if we look at morality from an evolutionary point of view. The survival of the species depends on the sacrifice of individuals in some cases, and the end of morality is the survival of the species. Hence, it is not surprising that being highly moral will not always pay off for individuals.

This answer is confused for two reasons. First, even if morality does have survival value for the species, we have seen that this does not by itself justify the individual's involvement in the institution of morality. In fact, it does not justify such involvement if what is best for the species is not what is best for the individual member of the species. And I have been arguing that, from a secular point of view, the interests of the species and the individual diverge.

Second, while evolution might explain why humans *feel* obligated to make sacrifices, it is wholly unable to account for genuine moral obligation. If we did not feel obligated to make sacrifices for others, it might be that the species would have died out long ago. So, moral *feelings* may have survival value. However, *feeling obligated* is not the same thing as *being obligated*.... Thus, to show that moral feelings have survival value is not to show that there are any actual moral obligations at all.... The point is, the evolutionary picture does not require the existence of real obligations; it demands only the existence of moral feelings or beliefs. Moral feelings or beliefs would motivate action even if there were in actuality no moral obligations. For example, the belief that human life is sacred may very well have survival value even if human life is not sacred. Moral obligation, as opposed to moral feeling, is thus an unnecessary postulate from the standpoint of evolution.

At this point defenders of the secular view typically make one of two moves: (i) They claim that even if morality does not pay, there remain moral truths which we must live up to; or (ii) they may claim that morality pays in subtle ways which we have so far overlooked. Let us take these claims up in turn.

(i) It may be claimed that moral obligation is just a fact of life, woven into the structure of reality. Morality may not always pay, but certain moral standards remain true, e.g., "Lying is wrong" or "Human life is sacred." These are not made true by evolution or God, but are necessary truths, independent of concrete existence, like "1 + 1 = 2" or "There are no triangular circles."

There are at least three difficulties with this suggestion. First, assuming that there are such necessary truths about morality, why should we care about them or pay them any attention? We may grant that an act is correct from the moral point of view and yet wonder whether we have good reason to participate in the institution of morality. So, even if we grant that various statements of the form "One ought to do X" are necessarily true, this does not show that the institution of morality pays off. It just says that morality is a "game" whose rules are necessary truths.... To defend the institution of morality simply on the grounds that certain moral statements are necessarily true is to urge duty for duty's sake. And ... this is not an acceptable defense of the institution of morality.

Second, the idea that some moral truths are necessary comports poorly with the usual secular account. As Mavrodes points out, necessary moral truths seem to be what Plato had in mind when he spoke about the Form of the Good. And Plato's view, though not contradicted by modern science, receives no support from it either. Plato's Form of the Good is not an emergent phenomenon, but is rather woven into the very structure of reality, independently of physical processes such as evolution. So, Plato's view is incompatible with the typically modern secular view that moral value is an emergent phenomenon, coming into existence with the arrival of the human nervous system. For this reason, Plato's views have "often been taken to be congenial ... to a religious understanding of the world."[6]

Third, it is very doubtful that there are any necessary truths of the form "One ought to do X." We have seen that the institution of morality stands unjustified if participation in it does not pay (in the long run) for individuals. And why should we suppose that there are *any* necessary moral truths if the institution of morality is unjustified? ... [S]tatements of the form "One ought to do X" are not *necessary* truths, though they may be true *if* certain conditions are met.... Hence, if there are any necessary moral truths, they appear to be conditional (if-then) in form: If certain conditions exist, one ought to do X. Among the conditions, as we have seen, is the condition that doing X pays for the individual in the long run. So, it is very doubtful that there are any necessary moral truths of the form "One ought to do X."[7] The upshot is that morality is partly grounded in those features of reality which guarantee that morality pays; and the secular view lacks the metaphysical resources for making such a guarantee....

(ii) But some have claimed that, if we look closely at human psychology, we can see that morality does pay *in terms of earthly goods*. For example, Plato suggested that only a highly moral person could have harmony between the various elements of his soul (such as reason and desire). Others have claimed that being highly moral is the only means to inner satisfaction. We humans are just so constituted that violations of morality never leave us with a net gain. Sure, we may gain earthly goods of one sort or another by lying, stealing, etc., but these are always outweighed by inner discord or a sense of dissatisfaction with ourselves.

There are several problems with this. First, some may doubt that moral virtue is the best route to inner peace. After all, one may experience profound inner discord when one has done what is right. It can be especially upsetting to stand up for what is right when doing so is unpopular; indeed, many people avoid "making waves" precisely because it upsets their inner peace....

Second, how good is the evidence that inner peace *always* outweighs the benefits achievable through unethical action? Perhaps guilt feelings and inner discord are a reasonable price to pay for certain earthly goods. If a cowardly act enables me to stay alive, or a dishonest act makes me wealthy, I may judge that my gains are worth the accompanying guilt feelings. A quiet conscience is not everything.

Third, if inner discord or a sense of dissatisfaction stems from a feeling of having done wrong, why not reassess my standards? Therapists are familiar with the phenomenon of false guilt. For example, a married woman may feel guilty for having sex with her spouse. The cure will involve enabling the patient to view sex as a legitimate means of expressing affection. The point is that just because I feel a certain type of act is wrong, it does not follow that the only route to inner peace is to avoid the action. I also have the option of revising my standards, which may enable me to pursue self-interested goals in a less inhibited fashion. Why drag along any unnecessary moral baggage? How could it be shown, on secular grounds, that it is in my interest to maintain the more idealistic standards endorsed by the great moralists? Certainly, some people have much less idealistic standards than others, and yet seem no less happy.

By way of contrast with the secular view, it is not difficult to see how morality might pay if there is a God of the Christian type. First, God loves all humans and wants all included in his kingdom. So, a tribal morality would violate his demands, and to violate his demands is to strain one's most important personal relationship. Second, there are no secret violations of morality if God exists. Since God is omniscient, willful wrongdoing of any sort will estrange the wrongdoer from God. Third, while earthly society may be able to function pretty well even though there exists a small number of "moral freeloaders," the freeloaders themselves are certainly not attaining harmonious relations with God. Accordingly, their ultimate fulfillment is in jeopardy. Fourth, death is the end of earthly life, but it is not the end of conscious existence, according to Christianity. Therefore, death does not end one's opportunity for personal fulfillment; indeed, if God is perfectly good and omnipotent, we can only assume that the afterlife will result in the fulfillment of our deepest needs—unless we willfully reject God's efforts to supply those needs.

So, it seems to me that the moral life makes more sense from a theistic perspective than from a secular perspective. Of course, I do not claim that I have proved the existence of God, and a full discussion of this metaphysical issue would take us too far from matters at hand.[8] But if I have shown that the moral life makes more sense from a theistic perspective than from a secular one, then I have provided an important piece of evidence in favor of the rationality of belief in God. Moreover, I believe that I have turned back one objection to the Christian teleological view, namely, the allegation that theism is unnecessary metaphysical baggage.

NOTES

1. It can be argued that, even from a secular perspective, some benefits and harms are available after death. For example, vindicating the reputation of a deceased person may be seen as benefiting that person. See, for example, Thomas Nagel, *Mortal Questions* (London: Cambridge University Press, 1979), pp. 1–10. But even if we grant that these are goods for the deceased, it is obvious that, from the secular point of view, such post-mortem goods cannot be consciously enjoyed by the deceased. They are not available in the sense that he will never take pleasure in them.

2. George Mavrodes, "Religion and the Queerness of Morality," in *Rationality, Religious Belief, and Moral Commitment*, ed. Robert Audi and William J. Wainwright (Ithaca, N.Y.: Cornell University Press, 1986), p. 223.

3. Peter Singer, *Practical Ethics*, (London: Cambridge University Press, 1970), p. 209.

4. For an excellent discussion of arguments for immortality, see William J. Wainwright, *Philosophy of Religion* (Belmont, Calif.: Wadsworth, 1988), pp. 99–111.

5. My source for these claims about "happy psychopaths" is Singer, *Practical Ethics*, pp. 214–216. Singer in turn is drawing from Hervey Cleckley, *The Mask of Sanity, (An Attempt to Clarify Some Issues About the So-Called Psychopathic Personality)*, 5th ed. (St. Louis, Mo.: E. S. Cleckley, 1988).

6. Mavrodes, "Religion and the Queerness of Morality," p. 224. I am borrowing from Mavrodes throughout this paragraph.

7. Those acquainted with modal logic may have a question here. By a principle of modal logic, if p is a necessary truth and p necessarily implies q, then q is a necessary truth. So, if it is necessarily true that "certain conditions are met" and necessarily true that "If they are met, one ought to X," then, "One ought to do X" is a necessary truth. But I assume it is not *necessarily true* that "certain conditions are met." In my judgment it would be most implausible to suppose, e.g., that "Morality pays for humans" is a necessary truth.

8. Two fine discussions of moral arguments for theism are Robert Merrihew Adams, "Moral Arguments for Theistic Belief," in *Rationality and Religious Belief*, ed. C. F. Delaney (Notre Dame, Ind.: University of Notre Dame Press, 1979), pp. 116–140, and J. L. Mackie, *The Miracle of Theism* (Oxford: Oxford University Press, 1982), pp. 102–118.

NO
John Arthur

RELIGION, MORALITY, AND CONSCIENCE

My first and prime concern in this paper is to explore the connections, if any, between morality and religion. I will argue that in fact religion is not necessary for morality. Yet despite the lack of any logical or other necessary connection, I will claim, there remain important respects in which the two are related. In the concluding section I will discuss the notion of moral conscience, and then look briefly at the various respects in which morality is "social" and the implications of that idea for moral education. First, however, I want to say something about the subjects: just what are we referring to when we speak of morality and of religion?

MORALITY AND RELIGION

A useful way to approach the first question—the nature of morality—is to ask what it would mean for a society to exist without a social moral code. How would such people think and behave? What would that society look like? First, it seems clear that such people would never feel guilt or resentment. For example, the notions that I ought to remember my parent's anniversary, that he has a moral responsibility to help care for his children after the divorce, that she has a right to equal pay for equal work, and that discrimination on the basis of race is unfair would be absent in such a society. Notions of duty, rights, and obligations would not be present, except perhaps in the legal sense; concepts of justice and fairness would also be foreign to these people. In short, people would have no tendency to evaluate or criticize the behavior of others, nor to feel remorse about their own behavior. Children would not be taught to be ashamed when they steal or hurt others, nor would they be allowed to complain when others treat them badly. (People might, however, feel regret at a decision that didn't turn out as they had hoped; but that would only be because their expectations were frustrated, not because they feel guilty.)

Such a society lacks a moral code. What, then, of religion? Is it possible that a people lacking a morality would nonetheless have religious beliefs? It

From John Arthur, "Religion, Morality, and Conscience," in John Arthur, ed., *Morality and Moral Controversies*, 4th ed. (Prentice Hall, 1996). Copyright © 1996 by John Arthur. Reprinted by permission.

seems clear that it is possible. Suppose every day these same people file into their place of worship to pay homage to God (they may believe in many gods or in one all-powerful creator of heaven and earth). Often they can be heard praying to God for help in dealing with their problems and thanking Him for their good fortune. Frequently they give sacrifices to God, sometimes in the form of money spent to build beautiful temples and churches, other times by performing actions they believe God would approve such as helping those in need. These practices might also be institutionalized, in the sense that certain people are assigned important leadership roles. Specific texts might also be taken as authoritative, indicating the ways God has acted in history and His role in their lives or the lives of their ancestors.

To have a moral code, then, is to tend to evaluate (perhaps without even expressing it) the behavior of others and to feel guilt at certain actions when we perform them. Religion, on the other hand, involves beliefs in supernatural power(s) that created and perhaps also control nature, the tendency to worship and pray to those supernatural forces or beings, and the presence of organizational structures and authoritative texts. The practices of morality and religion are thus importantly different. One involves our attitudes toward various forms of behavior (lying and killing, for example), typically expressed using the notions of rules, rights, and obligations. The other, religion, typically involves prayer, worship, beliefs about the supernatural, institutional forms and authoritative texts.

We come, then, to the central question: What is the connection, if any, between a society's moral code and its religious practices and beliefs? Many people have felt that morality is in some way dependent on religion or religious truths. But what sort of "dependence" might there be? In what follows I distinguish various ways in which one might claim that religion is necessary for morality, arguing against those who claim morality depends in some way on religion. I will also suggest, however, some other important ways in which the two are related, concluding with a brief discussion of conscience and moral education.

RELIGIOUS MOTIVATION AND GUIDANCE

One possible role that religion might play in morality relates to motives people have. Religion, it is often said, is necessary so that people will DO right. Typically, the argument begins with the important point that doing what is right often has costs: refusing to shoplift or cheat can mean people go without some good or fail a test; returning a billfold means they don't get the contents. Religion is therefore said to be necessary in that it provides motivation to do the right thing. God rewards those who follow His commands by providing for them a place in heaven or by insuring that they prosper and are happy on earth. He also punishes those who violate the moral law. Others emphasize less self-interested ways in which religious motives may encourage people to act rightly. Since God is the creator of the universe and has ordained that His plan should be followed, they point out, it is important to live one's life in accord with this divinely ordained plan. Only by living a moral life, it is said, can people live in harmony with the larger, divinely created order.

The first claim, then, is that religion is necessary to provide moral motivation. The problem with that argument, however, is that religious motives are far from the only ones people have. For most of us, a decision to do the right thing (if that is our decision) is made for a variety of reasons: "What if I get caught? What if somebody sees me—what will he or she think? How will I feel afterwards? Will I regret it?" Or maybe the thought of cheating just doesn't arise. We were raised to be a decent person, and that's what we are—period. Behaving fairly and treating others well is more important than whatever we might gain from stealing or cheating, let alone seriously harming another person. So it seems clear that many motives for doing the right thing have nothing whatsoever to do with religion. Most of us, in fact, do worry about getting caught, being blamed, and being looked down on by others. We also may do what is right just because it's right, or because we don't want to hurt others or embarrass family and friends. To say that we need religion to act morally is mistaken; indeed it seems to me that many of us, when it really gets down to it, don't give much of a thought to religion when making moral decisions. All those other reasons are the ones which we tend to consider, or else we just don't consider cheating and stealing at all. So far, then, there seems to be no reason to suppose that people can't be moral yet irreligious at the same time.

A second argument that is available for those who think religion is necessary to morality, however, focuses on moral guidance and knowledge rather than on people's motives. However much people may want to do the right thing, according to this view, we cannot ever know for certain what is right without the guidance of religious teaching. Human understanding is simply inadequate to this difficult and controversial task; morality involves immensely complex problems, and so we must consult religious revelation for help.

Again, however, this argument fails. First, consider how much we would need to know about religion and revelation in order for religion to provide moral guidance. Besides being sure that there is a God, we'd also have to think about which of the many religions is true. How can anybody be sure his or her religion is the right one? But even if we assume the Judeo-Christian God is the real one, we still need to find out just what it is He wants us to do, which means we must think about revelation.

Revelation comes in at least two forms, and not even all Christians agree on which is the best way to understand revelation. Some hold that revelation occurs when God tells us what he wants by providing us with His words: The Ten Commandments are an example. Many even believe, as evangelist Billy Graham once said, that the entire *Bible* was written by God using 39 secretaries. Others, however, doubt that the "word of God" refers literally to the words God has spoken, but believe instead that the *Bible* is an historical document, written by human beings, of the events or occasions in which God revealed Himself. It is an especially important document, of course, but nothing more than that. So on this second view revelation is not understood as *statements* made by God but rather as His *acts* such as leading His people from Egypt, testing Job, and sending His son as an example of the ideal life. The *Bible* is not itself revelation, it's the historical account of revelatory actions.

If we are to use revelation as a moral guide, then, we must first know what is to count as revelation—words given us by God, historical events, or both? But even supposing that we could somehow answer those questions, the problems of relying on revelation are still not over since we still must interpret that revelation. Some feel, for example, that the *Bible* justifies various forms of killing, including war and capital punishment, on the basis of such statements as "An eye for an eye." Others, emphasizing such saying as "Judge not lest ye be judged" and "Thou shalt not kill," believe the *Bible* demands absolute pacifism. How are we to know which interpretation is correct? It is likely, of course, that the answer people give to such religious questions will be influenced in part at least by their own moral beliefs: if capital punishment is thought to be unjust, for example, then an interpreter will seek to read the *Bible* in a way that is consistent with that moral truth. That is not, however, a happy conclusion for those wishing to rest morality on revelation, for it means that their understanding of what God has revealed is itself dependent on their prior moral views. Rather than revelation serving as a guide for morality, morality is serving as a guide for how we interpret revelation.

So my general conclusion is that far from providing a short-cut to moral understanding, looking to revelation for guidance often creates more questions and problems. It seems wiser under the circumstances to address complex moral problems like abortion, capital punishment, and affirmative action directly, considering the pros and cons of each side, rather than to seek answers through the much more controversial and difficult route of revelation.

THE DIVINE COMMAND THEORY

It may seem, however, that we have still not really gotten to the heart of the matter. Even if religion is not necessary for moral motivation or guidance, it is often claimed, religion is necessary in another more fundamental sense. According to this view, religion is necessary for morality because without God there could BE no right or wrong. God, in other words, provides the foundation or bedrock on which morality is grounded. This idea was expressed by Bishop R. C. Mortimer:

> "God made us and all the world. Because of that He has an absolute claim on our obedience.... From [this] it follows that a thing is not right simply because we think it is. It is right because God commands it."[1]

What Bishop Mortimer has in mind can be seen by comparing moral rules with legal ones. Legal statutes, we know, are created by legislatures; if the state assembly of New York had not passed a law limiting speed people can travel, then there would be no such legal obligation. Without the statutory enactments, such a law simply would not exist. Mortimer's view, the *divine command theory*, would mean that God has the same sort of relation to moral law as legislature has to statutes it enacts: without God's commands there would be no moral rules, just as without a legislature there would be no statutes.

Defenders of the divine command theory often add to this a further claim, that only by assuming God sits at the foundation of morality can we explain the objective difference between right and wrong. This point was forcefully argued by F. C. Copleston in a 1948 British

Broadcasting Corporation radio debate with Bertrand Russell.

COPLESTON: ... The validity of such an interpretation of man's conduct depends on the recognition of God's existence, obviously.... Let's take a look at the Commandant of the [Nazi] concentration camp at Belsen. That appears to you as undesirable and evil and to me too. To Adolf Hitler we suppose it appeared as something good and desirable. I suppose you'd have to admit that for Hitler it was good and for you it is evil.

RUSSELL: No, I shouldn't go so far as that. I mean, I think people can make mistakes in that as they can in other things. If you have jaundice you see things yellow that are not yellow. You're making a mistake.

COPLESTON: Yes, one can make mistakes, but can you make a mistake if it's simply a question of reference to a feeling or emotion? Surely Hitler would be the only possible judge of what appealed to his emotions.

RUSSELL: ... You can say various things about that; among others, that if that sort of thing makes that sort of appeal to Hitler's emotions, then Hitler makes quite a different appeal to my emotions.

COPLESTON: Granted. But there's no objective criterion outside feeling then for condemning the conduct of the Commandant of Belsen, in your view.... The human being's idea of the content of the moral law depends certainly to a large extent on education and environment, and a man has to use his reason in assessing the validity of the actual moral ideas of his social group. But the possibility of criticizing the accepted moral code presupposes that there is an objective standard, that there is an ideal moral order, which imposes itself.... It implies the existence of a real foundation of God.[2]

Against those who, like Bertrand Russell, seek to ground morality in feelings and attitudes, Copleston argues that there must be a more solid foundation if we are to be able to claim truly that the Nazis were evil. God, according to Copleston, is able to provide the objective basis for the distinction, which we all know to exist, between right and wrong. Without divine commands at the root of human obligations, we would have no real reason for condemning the behavior of anybody, even Nazis. Morality, Copleston thinks, would then be nothing more than an expression of personal feeling.

To begin assessing the divine command theory, let's first consider this last point. Is it really true that only the commands of God can provide an objective basis for moral judgments? Certainly many philosophers have felt that morality rests on its own perfectly sound footing, be it reason, human nature, or natural sentiments. It seems wrong to conclude, automatically, that morality cannot rest on anything but religion. And it is also possible that morality doesn't have any foundation or basis at all, so that its claims should be ignored in favor of whatever serves our own self-interest.

In addition to these problems with Copleston's argument, the divine command theory faces other problems as well. First, we would need to say much more about the relationship between morality and divine commands. Certainly the expressions "is commanded by God" and "is morally required" do not *mean* the same thing. People and even whole societies can use moral concepts without understanding them to make any reference to God. And while it is true that God (or any other moral being for that matter) would tend to want others to do the right thing, this hardly shows that being right and being commanded by God are the same thing. Parents want their children to do the right thing, too, but that doesn't mean parents, or anybody else, can make a thing right just by commanding it!

I think that, in fact, theists should reject the divine command theory. One reason is what it implies. Suppose we were to grant (just for the sake of argument) that the divine command theory is correct, so that actions are right just because they are commanded by God. The same, of course, can be said about those deeds that we believe are wrong. If God hadn't commanded us not to do them, they would not be wrong.

But now notice this consequence of the divine command theory. Since God is all-powerful, and since right is determined solely by His commands, is it not possible that He might change the rules and make what we now think of as wrong into right? It would seem that according to the divine command theory the answer is "yes": it is theoretically possible that tomorrow God would decree that virtues such as kindness and courage have become vices while actions that show cruelty and cowardice will henceforth be the right actions. (Recall the analogy with a legislature and the power it has to change law.) So now rather than it being right for people to help each other out and prevent innocent people from suffering unnecessarily, it would be right (God having changed His mind) to create as much pain among innocent children as we possibly can! To adopt the divine command theory therefore commits its advocate to the seemingly absurd position that even the greatest atrocities might be not only acceptable but morally required if God were to command them.

Plato made a similar point in the dialogue *Euthyphro*. Socrates is asking Euthyphro what it is that makes the virtue of holiness a virtue, just as we have been asking what makes kindness and courage virtues. Euthyphro has suggested that holiness is just whatever all the gods love.

SOCRATES: Well, then, Euthyphro, what do we say about holiness? Is it not loved by all the gods, according to your definition?
EUTHYPHRO: Yes.
SOCRATES: Because it is holy, or for some other reason?
EUTHYPHRO: No, because it is holy.
SOCRATES: Then it is loved by the gods because it is holy: it is not holy because it is loved by them?
EUTHYPHRO: It seems so.
SOCRATES: ... Then holiness is not what is pleasing to the gods, and what is pleasing to the gods is not holy as you say, Euthyphro. They are different things.
EUTHYPHRO: And why, Socrates?
SOCRATES: Because we are agreed that the gods love holiness because it is holy: and that it is not holy because they love it.[3]

This raises an interesting question: Why, having claimed at first that virtues are merely what is loved (or commanded) by the gods, would Euthyphro so quickly contradict this and agree that the gods love holiness *because* it's holy, rather than the reverse? One likely possibility is that Euthyphro believes that whenever the gods love something they do so with good reason, not without justification and arbitrarily. To deny this, and say that it is merely the gods' love that makes holiness a virtue, would mean that the gods have no basis for their attitudes, that they are arbitrary in what they love. Yet—and this is the crucial point—it's far from clear that a religious person would want to say that God is arbitrary in that way. If we say that it is simply God's loving something that makes it right, then what sense would it make to say God wants us to do right? All that could mean, it seems, is that God wants us to do what He wants us to do; He would have no reason for wanting it. Similarly "God is good" would mean little more than "God does what He pleases." The divine command theory therefore leads us to the results that God is morally arbitrary, and that His wishing us to do good or even God's being just mean nothing more than that God does what He does and wants whatever He wants. Religious people who reject that consequence would also, I am suggesting, have reason to reject the divine command theory itself, seeking a different understanding of morality.

This now raises another problem, however. If God approves kindness because it is a virtue and hates the Nazis because they were evil, then it seems that God discovers morality rather than inventing it. So haven't we then identified a limitation on God's power, since He now, being a good God, must love kindness and command us not to be cruel? Without the divine command theory, in other words, what is left of God's omnipotence?

But why, we may ask, is such a limitation on God unacceptable? It is not at all clear that God really can do anything at all. Can God, for example, destroy Himself? Or make a rock so heavy that He cannot lift it? Or create a universe which was never created by Him? Many have thought that God cannot do these things, but also that His inability to do them does not constitute a serious limitation on His power since these are things that cannot be done at all: to do them would violate the laws of logic. Christianity's most influential theologian, Thomas Aquinas, wrote in this regard that "whatever implies contradiction does not come within the scope of divine omnipotence, because it cannot have the aspect of possibility. Hence it is more appropriate to say that such things cannot be done than that God cannot do them."[4]

How, then, ought we to understand God's relationship to morality if we reject the divine command theory? Can religious people consistently maintain their faith in God the Creator and yet deny that what is right is right because He commands it? I think the answer to this is "yes." Making cruelty good is not like making a universe that wasn't made, of course. It's a moral limit on God rather than a logical one. But why suppose that God's limits are only logical?

One final point about this. Even if we agree that God loves justice or kindness because of their nature, not arbitrarily, there still remains a sense in which God could change morality even having rejected the divine command theory. That's because if we assume, plausibly I think, that morality depends in part on how we reason, what we desire and need, and the circumstances in which we find ourselves, then morality will still be under God's control since God could have constructed us or our environment very differently. Suppose, for instance, that he created us so that we couldn't be hurt by others or didn't care about freedom. Or perhaps our natural environment were created differently, so that all we have to do is ask and anything we want is given to us. If God had created either nature or us that way, then it seems likely our morality might also be different in important ways from the one we now think correct. In that sense, then, morality depends on God whether or not one supports the divine command theory.

"MORALITY IS SOCIAL"

I have argued here that religion is not necessary in providing moral motivation or guidance, and against the divine command theory's claim that God is necessary for there to be morality at all. In this last section, I want first to look briefly at how religion and morality sometimes *do* influence each other. Then I will consider the development of moral conscience and the important ways in which morality might correctly be thought to be "social."

Nothing I have said so far means that morality and religion are independent of each other. But in what ways are they related, assuming I am correct in claiming morality does not *depend* on religion? First, of course, we should note the historical influence religions have had on the development of morality as well as on politics and law. Many of the important leaders of the abolitionist and civil rights movements were religious leaders, as are many current members of the pro-life movement. The relationship is not, however, one sided: morality has also influenced religion, as the current debate within the Catholic church over the role of women, abortion, and other social issues shows. In reality, then, it seems clear that the practices of morality and religion have historically each exerted an influence on the other.

But just as the two have shaped each other historically, so, too, do they interact at the personal level. I have already suggested how people's understanding of revelation, for instance, is often shaped by morality as they seek the best interpretations of revealed texts. Whether trying to understand a work of art, a legal statute, or a religious text, interpreters regularly seek to understand them in the best light—to make them as good as they can be, which requires that they bring moral judgment to the task of religious interpretation and understanding.

The relationship can go the other direction as well, however, as people's moral views are shaped by their religious training and beliefs. These relationships between morality and religion are often complex, hidden even from ourselves, but it does seem clear that our views on important moral issues, from sexual morality and war to welfare and capital punishment, are often influenced by our religious outlook. So not only are religious and moral practices and understandings historically linked, but for many religious people the relationship extends to the personal level—to their understanding of moral obligations as well as their sense of who they are and their vision of who they wish to be.

Morality, then, is influenced by religion (as is religion by morality), but morality's social character extends deeper even than that, I want to argue. First, of course, we possess a socially acquired language within which we think about our various choices and the alternatives we ought to follow, including whether a possible course of action is the right thing to do. Second, morality is social in that it governs relationships among people, defining our responsibilities to others and theirs to us. Morality provides the standards we rely on in gauging our interactions with family, lovers, friends, fellow citizens, and even strangers. Third, morality is social in the sense that we are, in fact, subject to criticism by others for our actions. We discuss with others what we should do, and often hear from them concerning whether our decisions were acceptable. Blame and praise are a central feature of morality.

While not disputing any of this, John Dewey has stressed another, less obvious aspect of morality's social character. Consider then the following comments regarding the origins of morality and conscience in an article he titled "Morality Is Social":

> In language and imagination we rehearse the responses of others just as we dramatically enact other consequences. We foreknow how others will act, and the foreknowledge is the beginning of judgment passed on action. We know *with* them; there is conscience. An assembly is formed within our breast which discusses and appraises proposed and performed acts. The community without becomes an forum and tribunal within, a judgment-seat of charges, assessments and exculpations. Our thoughts of our own actions are saturated with the ideas that others entertain about them.... Explicit recognition of this fact is a prerequisite of improvement in moral education.... Reflection is morally indispensable.[5]

To appreciate fully the role of society in shaping morality and influencing people's sense of responsibility, Dewey is arguing, requires appreciating the fact that to think from the moral point of view, as opposed to the selfish one, for instance, means rejecting our private, subjective perspective in favor of the view of others, envisioning how they might respond to various choices we might make. Far from being private and unrelated to others, moral conscience is in that sense "public." To consider a decision from the moral perspective, says Dewey, requires that we envision an "assembly of others" that is "formed within our breast." In that way, our moral conscience cannot be sharply distinguished from our nature as social beings since conscience invariably brings with it, or constitutes, the perspective of the other. "Is this right?" and "What would this look like were I to have to defend it to others?" are not entirely separable questions.[6]

It is important not to confuse Dewey's point here, however. He is *not* saying that what is right is finally to be determined by the reactions of actually existing other people, or even by the reaction of society as a whole. What is right or fair can never be finally decided by a vote, but instead might not meet the approval of any specific others. But what then might Dewey mean in speaking of such an "assembly of others" as the basis of morality? The answer is that rather than actual people or groups, the assembly Dewey envisions is hypothetical or "ideal." The "community without" is thus transformed into a "forum and tribunal within, a judgment seat of charges, assessments and exculpations." So it is through the powers of our imagination that we can meet our moral responsibilities and exercise moral judgment, using these powers to determine what morality requires by imagining the reaction of Dewey's "assembly of others."

Morality is therefore *inherently* social, in a variety of ways. It depends on socially learned language, is learned from interactions with others, and governs our interactions with others in society. But it also demands, as Dewey put it, that we know "with" others, envisioning for ourselves what their points of view would require along with our own. Conscience demands we occupy the positions of others.

Viewed in this light, God would play a role in a religious person's moral reflection and conscience since it is unlikely a religious person would wish to exclude God from the "forum and tribunal" that constitutes conscience. Rather, for the religious person conscience would almost certainly include the imagined reaction God along with the reactions of others who might be affected by the action. Other people are also important, however, since it is often an open question just what God's reaction would be; revelation's meaning, as I have argued, is subject to interpretation. So it seems that for a religious person morality and God's will cannot be separated, though the connection between them is not the one envisioned by defenders of the divine command theory.

Which leads to my final point, about moral education. If Dewey is correct, then it seems clear there is an important sense in which morality not only can be taught but must be. Besides early moral training, moral thinking depends on our ability to imagine others' reactions and to imaginatively put ourselves into their shoes. "What would somebody (including, perhaps, God) think if this got out?" expresses more than a concern with being embarrassed or punished; it is also the voice of conscience and indeed of morality itself. But that would mean, thinking of education, that listening to others, reading about what others think and do, and reflecting within ourselves about our actions and whether we could defend them to others are part of the practice of morality itself. Morality cannot exist without the broader, social perspective introduced by others, and this social nature ties it, in that way, with education and with public discussion, both actual and imagined. "Private" moral reflection taking place independent of the social world would be no moral reflection at all; and moral education is not only possible, but essential.

NOTES

1. R. C. Mortimer, *Christian Ethics* (London: Hutchinson's University Library, 1950), pp. 7–8.

2. This debate was broadcast on the "Third Program" of the British Broadcasting Corporation in 1948.

3. Plato, *Euthyphro*, tr. H. N. Fowler (Cambridge MA: Harvard University Press, 1947).

4. Thomas Aquinas, *Summa Theologica*, Part I, Q. 25, Art. 3.

5. John Dewey, "Morality Is Social" in *The Moral Writings of John Dewey*, revised edition, ed. James Gouinlock (Amherst, NY: Prometheus Books, 1994), pp. 182–4.

6. Obligations to animals raise an interesting problem for this conception of morality. Is it wrong to torture animals only because other *people* could be expected to disapprove? Or is it that the animal itself would disapprove? Or, perhaps, duties to animals rest on sympathy and compassion while human moral relations are more like Dewey describes, resting on morality's inherently social nature and on the dictates of conscience viewed as an assembly of others?

POSTSCRIPT

Does Morality Need Religion?

As Arthur notes, some of the earliest—and indeed some of the best—arguments on this issue can be found in Plato's dialogue *Euthyphro*, which was written in the fourth century B.C. His arguments were in terms of Greek religious practices and Greek gods, but we can reformulate the points and elaborate on the arguments in monotheistic terms.

One key dilemma in the original Greek version asks us to consider whether holy things (i) are holy because they please the gods or (ii) please the gods because they are holy. In monotheistic terms, the dilemma would be whether holy things (i) are holy because they please God or (ii) please God because they are holy. The question can then be broadened and the dilemma posed in terms of goods things in general. We then ask whether good things are (i) good because God wills them or (ii) willed by God because they are good.

Plato believed that the gods love what is holy because it is holy (i.e., he believed the second option above), just as Christians have traditionally believed that God wills good things because they are good. Traditionally, a contrast is drawn between God, an infinite and all-good being who always wills the good, and humans, finite beings who are not all-good and do not always will the good.

We might also consider a parallel dilemma concerning truths. Are things true because God knows them, or does God know them because they are true? The traditional view is that God is all knowing. God knows all truths because they are truths (and no truths lie outside divine knowledge), whereas people do not know all truths (and many truths lie outside human knowledge).

Nevertheless, there has also been in Christianity a tradition that the almighty power of God is not to be constrained by anything—even if we imagine that what constrains God are good things. This view holds that God creates not only good things but the very fact that a good thing (such as honesty) is good while another thing (such as false witness against your neighbor) is not. Thus, in this view, God in his power determines what is good and what is bad.

These topics are further discussed in Paul Helm, ed., *Divine Commands and Morality* (Oxford University Press, 1981); Robert M. Adams, ed., *The Virtue of Faith and Other Essays in Philosophical Theology* (Oxford University Press, 1987); Richard J. Mouw, *The God Who Commands: A Study in Divine Command Ethics* (University of Notre Dame Press, 1990); E. M. Adams, *Religion and Cultural Freedom* (Temple University Press, 1993); and D. Z. Phillips, ed., *Religion and Morality* (St. Martin's Press, 1996).

On the Internet . . .

Animal Research Data Base
The Animal Research Data Base has been created as a one-stop shopping source for all those informational tidbits that you may need when discussing the issues surrounding the use of animals in research.
http://www.fcs.uga.edu/%7Emhulsey/GDB.html

Rutgers University School of Law Animal Rights Law Center
The Animal Rights Law Center's home page contains links to cases, materials, and descriptions of statutes and regulations devoted to the defense of animals.
http://www.animal-law.org/

Internet Resources on Hate Speech
Sponsored by the University of Iowa Libraries, this is a primary site for anyone interested in controversy over hate speech on the Internet, on college campuses, and internationally.
*http://www.lib.uiowa.edu/gw/journalism/
medialaw/hatespeech.html*

Literature on Poverty and Welfare
This site, sponsored by *Ethics Updates,* contains discussion questions, Internet resources, court decisions, and articles on poverty, homelessness, and welfare.
http://ethics.acusd.edu/poverty.html

PART 2

Morality and Contemporary Social Thought

The issues considered in this section are characteristic of modern society. They are also characteristic of a people who are looking for their moral bearings and trying to decide what kind of society they will live in. Basic issues about the structure and limits of society arise here—issues about men and women, the information revolution, people and animals, rich and poor, and the toleration of "hate speech." The issues considered in this section test the nature and the limits of contemporary society.

■ Does Feminism Provide a Positive Direction for Society?

■ Will the Information Revolution Benefit Society?

■ Should Animals Be Liberated?

■ Should Welfare Benefits Be Unconditional?

■ Should "Hate Speech" Be Tolerated?

ISSUE 4

Does Feminism Provide a Positive Direction for Society?

YES: Ruth Sidel, from *On Her Own: Growing Up in the Shadow of the American Dream* (Viking Penguin, 1990)

NO: Elizabeth Powers, from "A Farewell to Feminism," *Commentary* (January 1997)

ISSUE SUMMARY

YES: Author and social scientist Ruth Sidel argues that although feminism has made some progress, it holds the promise of even greater progress in the future toward a more caring society.

NO: Author and educator Elizabeth Powers argues that feminism naturally leads to strong governmental enforcement; a devaluing of housework, childrearing, and the family; and a struggle against the biology that links women with childbirth.

Feminism seems to be a thoroughly modern view, and, for the most part, it is. In Western societies, men have dominated over women throughout history, and the situation is even more pronounced in many Eastern societies.

From the time of the ancient Greeks (when men went to the market because respectable women stayed at home) to this century (when women in America gained the right to vote in national elections in 1920), there was a nearly unbroken social tradition according to which men were regarded as superior to women in power and status. This social tradition was reflected in the intellectual tradition, so much so that the exceptions to this tradition stand out.

Two exceptional male thinkers were Plato, who held that in an ideal state the rulers would be both men and women (since there are both male and female individuals who are able to achieve wisdom and thus become good political leaders), and John Stuart Mill, who said in *The Subjection of Women* (1869), "The principle which regulates the existing social relation between the two sexes ... is wrong in itself, and [is] now one of the chief hindrances to human improvement.... It ought to be replaced by a principle of perfect equality." Much more common was the view that girls should be obedient to their fathers and women should be obedient to their husbands. Sometimes there were even stronger misogynistic (antiwoman) views. What did the women of the past think about all this? For the most part, women did not have the education or social encouragement and standing to make their voices heard, so in many cases we simply do not know.

There has been a traditional sexual double standard for men and women, and the law has generally prescribed second-class citizenship for women. Nowadays we call that tradition sexist, and we tell ourselves that the situation is different. But can we rightfully say that men and women have an equitable relationship in society?

Consider, for example, the fact that most secretaries are women and most executives are men, that most doctors are men and most nurses are women, and that most kindergarten teachers are women and most university professors are men. If we are asked to picture in our minds a nurse (or a professor, or a secretary), we usually picture one of the "correct" sex. Notice that in every case it is the "male" job that has the greater social prestige and the higher pay. This raises many questions. Is it that women freely prefer to be secretaries, nurses, and kindergarten teachers, and men freely prefer to be executives, doctors, and professors? Or are there some social dynamics at work here? Do women generally seek out jobs that have lower prestige, or is lower prestige attached to the jobs because women have traditionally done them? Are people socialized differently according to their sex? Are social expectations different? Social factors aside, what differences exist between males and females anyway?

In recent history, feminists have rallied against patriarchy and male power structures. The origin of some of these power structures may have been "to keep women in their place"—their place being in the home. It is one thing to challenge this power structure by placing more women in power and prestigious positions—there are, for example, a growing number of women executives, doctors, and professors—but it is an even greater challenge to the system to aim for the destruction of the entire power structure.

In the following selections, Ruth Sidel argues that although many women choose to follow paths once closed to them, the future task of feminism is to make positive changes in the structure of society. The "more caring society" that Sidel envisions would be beneficial not just for women but for men, children, families, and society in general. Elizabeth Powers argues that feminism contains within itself some very negative tendencies. She contends that if the government is to enforce feminist demands, strong governmental power is necessary. Also, if women are to pursue careers traditionally open to men, there is a danger that children and the family will suffer. Powers maintains that it is simply false to assert that women are no different from men and can simply ignore childbirth and all that it entails.

YES   Ruth Sidel

TOWARD A MORE CARING SOCIETY

[T]wenty-five years after the publication of *The Feminine Mystique*, much has changed and much has remained the same. Women are attending college and graduate school in greater numbers than ever before. In the area of work, women have made great strides: the vast increase in the number of women in the labor force; the once unimaginable increase in the number of women in high-status, high-income professions; the growing acceptance, both on the part of women and on the part of many men, that women are competent, committed workers who can get the job done and achieve a considerable amount of their identity through their work roles. In keeping with their greatly increased presence in the world of work, women are often pictured by the media, by the fashion industry, even by politicians as serious, significant members of the labor force.

In recent years women have also gained greater control over their bodies. Largely because of the feminist movement, women have far greater understanding of how their bodies work, more control over their own fertility, and far greater participation in the process of childbirth. As this is being written, some of that control is under siege, particularly the right to abortion; but there have been significant strides nonetheless.

And, perhaps most important, many women recognize that they must make their own way in the world, that they must develop their own identity rather than acquire that identity through a relationship with a man....

But in other areas over this quarter-century there has been very little change, and some aspects of women's lives have deteriorated dramatically. Women are still all too often depicted in advertising, in films, on television, and by the fashion industry as sex objects. Women are still encouraged to focus on their looks—their bodies, their clothes, their makeup, their image. How women are supposed to look may have changed; but the tyranny of physical attractiveness, compounded by the need to appear "fit" and youthful, is omnipresent. Even in an event such as the women's final of the 1988 U.S. Open tennis tournament, in which Steffi Graf was trying to win her fourth major tournament of the year, thereby winning the "Grand Slam"— a feat accomplished by only four other players in the history of tennis—the good looks of her opponent, Gabriela Sabatini, were mentioned numerous times by the male television announcers, who were otherwise scrupulously nonsexist. It is noteworthy that in the record-breaking four-hour-and-fifty-four-minute men's final, which pitted Mats Wilander against Ivan Lendl, there was no mention of Wilander's rugged good looks. It is not, after all, simply how well women play the game but how they look while playing that counts as well.

The area of sex is still extraordinarily problematic for young women today. Of all the mine fields women must navigate, sex is one of the most complex and treacherous.·... [T]he pressures to have sex are enormous and the pressures not to plan for sex nearly as great. Many young women are caught in this incredible bind: some are caught by ignorance, others by the desire to be part of the group; some by fear, others by the need to be held or "loved." And many are caught by the notion that having sex is cool, sophisticated, a rite of passage somehow required in today's culture. But it is still widely seen as something you do inadvertently, almost as an afterthought, for as we have found, if a fifteen-, sixteen-, or seventeen-year-old plans for sex, goes to the local family-planning clinic for contraception, acknowledges her intention, takes responsibility for her actions, truly takes control, she is often seen by her peers, her family, even her community as deviant, as a "bad girl." To acquiesce is permissible; to choose clearly and consciously to embark on a sexual relationship is somehow reprehensible. One is reminded of many magazine advertisements that picture women being "carried away" by feeling or literally carried away by men, vignettes that are clearly metaphors for sex. Are we really saying that being carried away is appropriately feminine while being in control of one's actions is not?

But it is not only the objectification of women that remains a fact of life but the marginalization of women as well, particularly in the workplace and in positions of power.... [F]emale workers still occupy the lowest rungs of most occupations, including the prestigious professions they have recently entered in such large numbers. Women may have entered the labor market in record numbers in recent years, but they are still working predominantly in the lowest-paying jobs within the lowest-paying occupations.

In addition, it has become clear over the past decade that poverty dominates and determines the lives of millions of women in the United States....

Within this context, within the reality of women's true economic situation, what is surprising in talking with young women from various parts of the country ... is the narrowness of their image of success, the uniformity of their dreams. The affluent life as symbolized by the fancy car, the "house on a hill," ... was described yearningly time and time again. ... Success was seen, overwhelmingly, in terms of what they would be able to purchase, what kind of "life-style" they would have. The ability to consume in an upper-middle-class manner was often the ultimate goal....

Given the reality of the job market for women, what will become of their dreams of affluence? Given the reality of the structure of work and the availability of child care, what will become of their image of mothering? Have these young women, in fact, been sold a false dream? Have young women become encouraged to raise their expectations, only to see those expectations unfulfilled because there has not been comparable change within society? Have the major institutions that influence public opinion —the media, advertising, the fashion industry, as well as the industries that produce consumer goods and parts of the educational establishment—fostered these rising expectations because it suits their purposes and, in some cases, their profits? Has the dream of equal opportunity for women and men, of at least partial redistribution of power both within the family and in the society at large, been coopted and commodified, turned into a sprint for consumer goods rather than a long march toward a more humane life for all of us?

Have we indeed over the last quarter-century persuaded women that they, too, are entitled to their fair share of the American Dream, in their own right, not merely as appendages to the primary players, without changing the rules of the game in ways that would permit them truly to compete and succeed? Have women, in short, been hoodwinked into believing that they can "have it all, do it all, be it all" while society itself changes minimally? And have we somehow communicated to them that they must make it on their own, recreating the myth of the rugged individualist seeking the American Dream—alone? The sheriff (or cowboy) alone but for his faithful wife (or horse); the prospector for gold, solitary and in competition with scores of others like him, obsessively searching for an often elusive fortune....

Much has been written about the difficult choices women currently have: how to balance marriage and career; how to balance motherhood and career; the timing of conception; the problems of a demanding job versus the demands and joys of motherhood. But these

books, articles, television programs, and occasionally films put forth a largely false message: that the majority of women in late-twentieth-century America indeed have these choices to make. The illusion is abroad in the land that a young woman can simply "choose" to postpone pregnancy and marriage, acquire the education of her choice (which should, of course, be in a field in which jobs are available and well paying), and then step into the job of her choice. At that point, if she wishes, the man of her dreams will miraculously appear (and will be single and interested in "commitment"!), and, despite years of contraception and possibly even an abortion or two, she will promptly conceive, have a healthy baby or two, and live happily ever after. But of course we know life is not like that—at least not for the vast majority of women.

Most women do not have these magnificent choices....

This illusion of choice is a major impediment to the establishment of conditions that would enable women —and indeed all people—to have real choices. Young women recognize that they are likely to participate actively in both work and home, in "doing" and "caring," but they fail to recognize what they must have in order to do so: meaningful options and supports in their work lives; in childbearing, child rearing, and the structure of their families; in housing, health care, and child care; and, above all, in the values by which they live their lives. Does emphasis on fashion, consumerism, and the lives of the rich and famous create the illusion of choice while diverting attention from serious discussion of policies that would give women genuine options?...

For women to have real choices, we must develop a society in which women and children and indeed families of all shapes and sizes are respected and valued. Despite the mythology of American individualism, it is clear that most women cannot truly go it alone. The young women I interviewed know that they must be prepared to be part of the labor force and still be available to care for others—for children, for older family members, for friends, for lovers —but these often mutually exclusive tasks will be possible only when we develop a society that supports doing and caring. Men must take on caring functions; the society must take some of the responsibility for caring and above all must be restructured to permit, even to encourage, doing and caring. Women simply cannot do it all and cannot do it alone....

[F]undamental change must be made in the workplace. Traditionally male-dominated professions cannot continue to expect their workers to function as if there were a fulltime wife and mother at home. Most male workers no longer live in that never-never land; female workers surely do not. Alternative paths to partnerships, professorships, and promotion must be developed that will neither leave women once again at the bottom of the career ladder without real power and equal rewards nor force them to choose between a demanding work life and a demanding personal life.

Nor should women have to choose a middle ground between work and mothering....

We must reevaluate our system of economic rewards. Do we really want our entertainers, our stockbrokers, our corporate executives, and our divorce lawyers making millions while our nurses and day-care workers barely scrape by? Do we really want the rich to get richer while the poor get poorer and the middle class loses ground? Do we really want to tell our young women that they must play traditional male roles in order to earn a decent living and that caregiving no longer counts, is no longer worth doing?...

Market forces cannot be permitted to rule in all spheres of American life. If our society is to be a caring, humane place to live, to rear our children, and to grow old, we must recognize that some aspects of life—the education of our young people, health care, child care, the texture of community life, the quality of the environment—are more important than profit. We as a nation must determine our priorities and act accordingly. If teaching, the care of young children, providing nursing care, and other human services are essential to the quality of life in the United States, then we must recruit our young people into these fields and pay them what the job is really worth. Only then will we be giving them, particularly our young women, real choices. If we want nurses to care for our sick, we must indicate by decent wages and working conditions that the job is valued by society. We must give nurses and other health workers real authority, a meaningful voice in the health-care system, and then, and only then, will some of our best and brightest and most caring women and men choose to enter nursing. Whatever happened to careers in community organizing, urban planning, Legal Aid, and public-health nursing? Young women and men will be able to consider these options only if they are decently paid, have a future and some degree of security and respect.

In this fin de siècle period of U.S. history characterized (in the words of John Kenneth Galbraith) by "private affluence" and "public squalor," it may be difficult to see our way clear to putting significantly larger amounts of money into health care, community organizing, education, or even a meaningful effort to deter young people from drug abuse, but we must recognize that these issues are central to the well-being of families and thus central to the very fabric and structure of American society....

[P]arents must have some time at home with their children. Why can't parents of young children work a shorter day or week and not risk losing their jobs?...

It must be acceptable in the United States for fathers to take leave to care for a new baby, to stay home with sick children, to leave work in time to pick up a child from day care or after-school care; for sons to attend to the needs of aging parents. It must even become acceptable for fathers to attend a school play or a Halloween party during the work day. Changing male roles may take years of resocialization and structural change within the society, but we must attempt it nonetheless. Mothers can no longer play the solitary domestic role—not while participating in the work force as well. If women are to do and to care, men must also do and care.

Perhaps a vignette from the life of one family and one work site illustrates the need to humanize the workplace. On November 21, 1985, the U.S. Senate agreed not to cast any votes between seven and nine p.m. The following letter was the reason for this unusual action:

Dear Senator Dole:

I am having my second-grade play tonight. Please make sure there aren't any votes between 7 and 9 so my daddy can watch me. Please come with him if you can.

Love,
Corinne Quayle

What is particularly remarkable about this incident is that when the final version of the Parental and Medical Leave Act was being written by the Senate Labor and Human Resources Committee,... J. Danforth Quayle, then a senator, vehemently opposed it and, according to one observer, "offered an amendment in committee that would assure that an employer enjoys the right to fire an employee who takes as much as one day off to be with a seriously ill child."[1] As Judy Mann, the *Washington Post* columnist who brought this incident to light, wrote: "Quayle lives by a set of special rules for the privileged and well-connected and doesn't hesitate to impose another set of rules and obligations, harsher and devoid of compassion, on those who were not to the manner born. Either he doesn't know anything about the reality of most workers' lives, or he doesn't care."[2]...

By demeaning the role of caregiver, society demeans all women and indeed, to one extent or another, exploits all caregivers. It also sets up the exploitation of one group of women by another. The ripples are endless: from the middle- or upper-middle-class career mother who is "stressed out" by trying to do it all to the single mother who really *is* doing it all to the day-care worker who is working in inadequate conditions earning inadequate pay to the child-care worker/domestic who is often shamefully exploited in the home, society's fundamental disregard for caregivers and for raising children diminishes us all. Ultimately, of course, it is the children who suffer, but women at all levels suffer as well. And the poor, the nonwhite, those with least choice suffer the most.

Any society that really wants to enable women to be in control of their lives must provide a comprehensive program of sex education and contraception.... [M]any young women are buffeted about by conflicting attitudes toward sexuality and indeed find it exceedingly difficult to determine what they themselves think and want. By the time they figure it out, it is often too late. They are pregnant and faced with a real Hobson's choice [an apparently free choice in a situation that actually provides no alternatives]: to abort, or to have a baby at a time in their life when they are ill-prepared —economically, physically, socially, or psychologically—to care for a child. We know what it can do to both the mother and the child when the pregnancy is unplanned and the mother is unable to care for the infant properly. We must do everything possible to make every child a planned child, to make every child a wanted child.

We must learn from the experience of other industrialized countries, whose rate of unintended and teenage pregnancy is so much lower than our own. We must institute sex education in our schools at all levels. The ignorance on the part of young women is astonishing and serves no useful purpose. Moreover, in this era of AIDS and other sexually transmitted diseases, such ignorance can literally be life-threatening. We must increase the accessibility of contraceptives, whether through school-based clinics or community-based health centers....

Continued access to abortion must be guaranteed. Efforts to overturn or limit women's right to abortion must be vigorously resisted. For many young women, abortion is the only barrier between them and a life of poverty and despair. Until we stop giving our young women mixed messages—that it is desirable and sometimes even de rigueur to have sex but not legitimate to protect against pregnancy—abortion remains the only resource....

In addition to giving women greater choice over sex and childbearing, we must stop exploiting women as sex objects. As long as the message of jean manufacturers, cereal companies, automobile conglomerates, and perfume distributors is that women are for sale along with the product, that women are, in a very real sense, just another commodity to be bought, used, and traded in when the model wears out, both men and women will perceive women in this way. And until we enable young women to responsibly say either yes or no to sex, to understand their options and the risks involved, we are not permitting them to be in charge of their own destiny. But we cannot expect young women to take control of their own destiny unless they can see alternatives, pathways that will lead to a rewarding life.

It is ironic that young women, a group outside the cultural mainstream in at least two fundamental ways, age and gender, have internalized that most mainstream of ideologies, the American Dream. After examining the realities of women's lives today, it is clear that the American Dream, at least as conventionally conceived, cannot be the blueprint for the majority of women....

We must recognize that even for most men the American Dream, with its belief in the power of the individual to shape his or her own destiny, was a myth. Men usually did not "make it" alone;

they did not, as the image goes, tame the West, develop industrial America, and climb the economic ladder alone—and they certainly did not do it while being the primary caregiver for a couple of preschoolers. Most of those men who "made it" in America, whom we think of when we reaffirm our belief in the American Dream, had women beside them every step of the way—women to iron their shirts, press their pants, mend their socks, cook their meals, bring up their children, and soothe them at the end of a hard day. They did not do it alone. They *still* don't do it alone. How can women do it alone? Who is there to mend and press their clothes, cook their meals, bring up their children, and soothe them at the end of a hard day? How can women possibly make it alone when they earn 65 percent of what men earn, when housing is virtually unaffordable for millions of families, when child care is scarce and all too often second-rate or worse? And where did they get the notion that they *should* be able to make it alone? It may be progress that many young women now realize that they cannot depend on marriage and a man for their identity, their protection, their daily bread; but is it progress or is it illusion for them to believe that they can do the caring and the doing and do it all on their own in a society that has done very little to make women truly independent? ...

We must have the courage and the wisdom as a society to recognize that we need a new vision of America for the twenty-first century, perhaps even a new American Dream. We need a vision that recognizes that we cannot survive without one another, that families must have supports in order to thrive, that women cannot make it alone any more than men ever have.

We must provide many more paths toward a gratifying, economically secure life. Traditional male occupations cannot be the only routes to the good life; traditional female work must be restructured so that it too can lead to power, prestige, and a life of plenty. And the traditional male work style must give way, for both women and men, to the recognition that work is merely one aspect of life and that private concerns, family life, leisure activities, and participation in community life help to define who we are and must be seen as important both to the individual and to the society....

[W]e must develop a vision that recognizes that caring is as important as doing, that caring indeed *is* doing, and that caregivers, both paid and unpaid, are the foundation of a humane society and must be treasured and honored. We need a vision of America that recognizes that we must reorganize our social institutions—our family life, our schools, our places of work, and our communities—to enable all people to care for one another, to enable all people to work and to participate in the public life of the nation. Our courageous, insightful, persevering, and often wise young women deserve no less. Our young men deserve no less. Future generations deserve no less.

NOTES

1. Judy Mann, "Some More Equal Than Others," *The Washington Post*, September 21, 1988.

2. Ibid.

NO   Elizabeth Powers

A FAREWELL TO FEMINISM

She was intelligent and generous; it was a fine free nature; but what was she going to do with herself? This question was irregular, for with most women one had no occasion to ask it.... Isabel's originality was that she gave one an impression of having intentions of her own.

—Henry James, *Portrait of a Lady*

My coming of age in the early 1970's was inextricably linked with what is variously known as feminism, the women's movement, women's liberation. It is a link by which I am much puzzled and troubled. The passing years have brought me a closer look at, so to speak, the fine print, and I shiver now when I observe the evolution that some of my closest friends from that era have undergone, spouting phrases about comparable worth and voicing the most fantastic bureaucratic visions of the future.

But in truth, if I go back to the sources—say, to a *Time* essay by Gloria Steinem in August 1970—I can see that the writing was already on the wall. Steinem, for one, had fully evolved as of that date:

> The [feminist] revolution would not take away the option of being a housewife. A woman who prefers to be her husband's housekeeper and/or hostess would receive a percentage of his pay determined by the domestic-relations courts.

Did I talk like that, advocating state control of private life, with (as Steinem went on) "free nurseries, school lunches, family cafeterias built into every housing complex"? Did I ever stand up in front of people, like the cadres of Red Guards in China, and parroting the words of Kate Millett in *Sexual Politics* (1970), demand "a permissive single standard of sexual freedom... uncorrupted by the crass and exploitative economic bases of traditional sexual alliances"?

As a matter of fact, I do not believe I ever said such things or even contemplated them; nor, I suspect, did most of the women who considered themselves followers of the movement. A dissertation is probably being written which will offer a demographic breakdown of leaders and followers, but my own suspicion is that the leaders were girls whose mothers had been college-educated but became full-time housewives, and so were putatively victimized by what Betty Friedan had defined as the "feminine mystique." The followers, those with backgrounds similar to mine, were not so solidly middle-class or goal-oriented, and had not yet grasped they might be leaders of anything.

We daughters of the working class or the slippery lower reaches of the middle class aspired, by and large, to a greater degree of participation in life outside the home. The shape that participation would take was uncertain. Though a number of highly motivated girls of my generation took advantage of opportunities to enter professional schools, the general affluence of the period allowed those of us who were less motivated or who came from less privileged backgrounds to engage in a lot of shopping around. In my own case, participation did not mean anything practical or even lucrative but rather "fulfillment," a realization of myself in literary and intellectual realms. It was my fortune, as Henry James wrote of Isabel Archer, to care for knowledge that was unfamiliar.

Throughout high school—I grew up in a rather cloistered environment in Kentucky—my aspirations seemed to run in thoroughly conventional directions: I wanted to be a cheerleader and prom queen and, of course, I wanted a boyfriend. But the same thing that kept me from becoming a cheerleader or prom queen also meant I was essentially dateless. I simply did not possess that combination of attributes which, for a brief time, confers unexpected grace on otherwise undeserving teenage girls. When I went to college, in 1965, still desiring to be exceptional in some way,

I quickly perceived other possibilities of achievement.

This was a moment when university standards were still sacrosanct and an Ivy League institution was not the only place at which to receive a first-rate education. Though a fair number of women prominent today in public life probably graduated from women's colleges, I suspect the majority went, as I did, to schools like Indiana University (Jane Pauley, my classmate!). It was hard going for me—I was terribly uneducated when I got to college—but for the first time in my life I began to train my mind and came close to perfecting myself in something, namely, a foreign language.

Yet this youthful accomplishment, immeasurably assisted by two years of work and study in Europe, was attended by new challenges, chiefly of a social and sexual nature. Europe produced in me the same feeling that assailed Christopher Newman, the central character of Henry James's novel *The American*, in the presence of Old Master paintings: a vague self-mistrust. Possessing a fair share of Newman's innate American confidence and naturalness, but not his steady moral compass, I found myself entranced by the relaxed cultural habits that had evolved in Europe by the late 1960's. These I could not help contrasting with mid-century America's moral certitudes, centering on sex and the cold war, which now seemed to me to be a caricature of inflexibility.

Not three years before, where I came from, sex had been a matter cloaked in a great deal of mystery. I had been much fascinated by a girl I knew only by sight who became pregnant at fifteen and was married, probably shotgun-style, to her boyfriend of seventeen. Without being able to articulate it, I felt she must have been marked by her experience in a way that ordinary mortals, hewing to the straight and narrow, were not. Transgression may have resulted in shame and social denigration, but through her risk she had become an object of interest. Still, to stand outside the moral order was a fearsome prospect.

My Catholic attitudes were shot through with the fire and brimstone of other American cultural remnants —the sermons of Jonathan Edwards, Hawthorne's *The Scarlet Letter.* In an educated European of the late 1960's, such attitudes provoked only condescending smiles. Europeans, it seemed, got to have the experience minus the soul-scorching. I was ignorant in those days of the social arrangements, mainly an intensive welfare bureaucracy, that cushioned these permissive sentiments and perhaps had even helped bring them into being. Instead, in the presence of mores so different from my own, and influenced as well by superior church architecture and other evidence of cultural tradition, I came to conclude that European attitudes in the matter of sex were wiser than those of Americans. I wanted to be wise like Europeans.

* * *

"I told you just now I'm very fond of knowledge," Isabel answered.

"Yes, of happy knowledge—of pleasant knowledge. But you haven't suffered, and you're not made to suffer. I hope you'll never see the ghost!" ...

"I don't think that's a fault," she answered. *"It's not absolutely necessary to suffer; we were not made for that."*

The birth-control pill, available in Europe in the 1950's, was first approved by the FDA in 1960; the last state ban on contraception was struck down by the Supreme Court in 1965. The pill would seem to have solved the problem for which, historically, the movement for women's emancipation had struggled: freedom from constant reproduction.

Yet the pill was one of those technical achievements, like gunpowder and printing, like the desk-top computer, the effects of which flowed all over the social and political landscape. One of its effects was to alter a perilously achieved historical understanding regarding the responsibility of men to their offspring. With the pill, this responsibility was taken from them overnight. It was at this point, in 1969, returning from Europe, that I entered graduate school at the University of Texas. One of the first things I did after getting an apartment, registering for classes, and picking up my paycheck as a teaching assistant was to go to a doctor and get a prescription—even though I was still a virgin. That knowledge of which Isabel Archer spoke, which could be obtained without difficulty, had suddenly offered itself: all one had to do was take a pill 21 days in a row.

To get at some of the larger confusions engendered by this new dispensation it may be helpful to turn to a prominent book of the early women's movement, Ingrid Bengis's *Combat in the Erogenous Zone* (1972). I wonder if anyone has actually gotten to the end of this exercise in rage and self-pity; despite Bengis's avowed admiration for artists, it seems never to have occurred to *her* to shape her material or give form to her experiences. The book is instead hardly more than an accumulation of horrors, an inventory of the infallible tendency of the nicest-seeming males to take advantage of Ingrid Bengis. The gallery of villains ranges from construction workers whistling at her on the street to the boy she shared a room with who fondled her as she lay blissfully zonked out in her sleeping bag, to the Mexican restaurant owner who gave her a free meal and then demanded sex, to the truck driver who picked her up while hitchhiking and then got upset when she refused to put out.

These were experiences many of us had in the 1970's. In hindsight, the source of Bengis's rage, a rage felt by so many women of our generation, can be discerned as early as the second page of her book, where she speaks of the men (plural) she has loved. The long and the short of it is that, thanks to the pill, young American females of the 1970's were suddenly behaving with the license, but without the sensibility, of jaded aristocrats. We women instinctively knew that what we were conferring was important and had something to do with love, and, like Ingrid Bengis, we used that word when we spoke of sex. Yet the terms of the bargain between men and women had radically changed. The old bargain —sex in exchange for commitment— had issued out of conditions of what might crassly be called a balance of supply and demand. These conditions were undermined in the 1970's by the flooding of the market with casual sex.

Feminists tend to blame men for their cavalier treatment of women, but, in the realm which Goethe spoke of as *Sittlichkeit* (roughly, morals), men follow the lead of women. Young males, it turns out, will only be protective and caring of females if something is at stake. When women sleep with men they barely know, assuming on their own the responsibility for regulating reproduction, men will be equally casual. A reward not having been fought for or truly earned is not a reward for which any individual will feel more than momentary indebtedness.

No wonder the whistle of construction workers, once a sign of appreciation for rewards not yet earned, and perhaps unattainable, came to sound to us like a hiss of contempt at our availability. The resulting sense of bafflement can be gleaned from where, in her prose, Bengis stamps her foot in emphasis, and where her inimitable ellipses fall:

> *Of course* I was proud to be a woman... proud as well of a subtle kind of sexuality. But I was not proud of the way in which that sexuality was systematically abused in the service of something that ultimately cheapened both me and it.

By such displacements outward did rage at men become the fate of an entire generation.

* * *

The role of the women's movement was to turn this rage into something powerful—sisterhood. As unexpected as it may sound, the experience of becoming a feminist was, for many, akin to a sudden spiritual conversion, a radical turnaround of the kind Tolstoy described in *Confession*, in which "everything that was on the right hand of the journey is now on the left." An essay by Jane O'Reilly, "Click! The Housewife's Moment of Truth" (from the whimsically entitled *The Girl I Left Behind*, 1980), perfectly captures the quality of transformation promised by the movement, and just as perfectly exposes its hollowness.

The essay inhabits a genre the publishing market has long catered to: morality tales in which adolescents learn the deceptiveness of appearance through painful lessons that lead them to maturity and true values. Just so, Jane O' Reilly finally grew up when she encountered women's liberation. Her book is a tale of setting aside the unimportant things, the very things she had once (in the 1950's) perceived that being a woman meant: debutante balls, identification bracelets, popularity, 75 people singing carols on Christmas Eve, drinking cocoa out of Dresden cups, real pearls. The illumination she underwent was to recognize that all these were a snare and a delusion, a cover and a preparation for deferring and submitting to men. Instead, what women needed was to become "equal members of the human society."

O'Reilly's essay contains Erma Bombeck-like hints for negotiating the transition from Cinderella-*cum*-domestic-drone to liberated human being: "(1) Decide what housework needs to be done. Then cut the list in half." In the realm of love, her language is up-to-date, *circa* 1980: "I practiced and practiced taking the sexual initiative"; "I need to get laid." But the subtext is still the same old thing: romance. It turns out Jane O'Reilly truly wanted the flowers, the passionate declarations, and all the rest. For her, too, though perhaps less grimly than for Ingrid Bengis, women's sexual liberation was a bust. The new social arrangements —here is an entry for February 29 from the *Liberated Woman's Appointment Calendar:* "Leap Year Day. Propose to the person of Your Choice"—failed.

At the end, Jane O'Reilly gives up, though she puts a brave face on it: "I now think love is somehow beside the point." Having sloughed off the demands of boyfriends, husbands, children, parents, in-laws, she is left to craft her own "lifestyle" out of the limp slogans of sisterhood:

> Nontradition has become tradition. My friends are my family, and we will provide for each other. Gathered about the [Christmas] tree will be the intact family from upstairs, the broken family from across the park, an extended family from out of town, my own reconstituted family, and the various inexplicable attachments we have all acquired along the way.

Thus, by 1980, had Kate Millett's turgid and off-putting rhetoric of revolution been refashioned into O'Reilly-style sentimentality. Moreover, this sentimentality had become a staple, peddled in magazines and books, in TV programs and movies. Seldom was it asked whether or how it could actually carry you through long-term illness, financial jeopardy, or personal crises of a truly acute nature. Instead, as many women went through affair after affair, as they failed with one Mr. Right after another, as they approached forty and saw the possibilities of a family of their own diminishing, as they found themselves living alone, scrambling for an invitation for Christmas dinner, O'Reilly's defeated alternative became more and more a necessary article of faith....

* * *

The women's movement is usually seen as having grown from the movement for civil rights for blacks, and, to many people, it had to do primarily with equality of economic opportunity. From the late 1960's on, mainstream journalists dutifully trotted out the statistics concerning women's economic and professional disadvantages. Yet feminists agitating about the pay scales of lawyers or accountants were in fact after something else: a change in the very meaning of equality.

For women to be "equal," as Jane O'Reilly dimly perceived ("The point of feminism is not that the world should be the same, but that it should be different"), something more drastic than admission to medical school was required. Female biology itself would have to be interpreted as a humanly limiting condition, established not by nature but by a cabal otherwise known as the patriarchy. There was much at stake, and a 1969 article in the *Nation* spelled it out: the women's movement, intoned the writer, was dedicated "to a total restructuring of society, ... and is not content simply to integrate women into male-defined goals and values."

This thoroughgoing radicalism, a (relatively) new aspect of the century-old movement for female emancipation, elicited criticism even on the Left. Among the opponents was the socialist and literary critic Irving Howe. In December 1970 Howe published in *Harper's* a long review-essay of Kate Millett's *Sexual Politics*, which a few months earlier had been baptized by *Time* magazine as the *Communist Manifesto* of the women's movement. Howe took the book sharply to task not only for its intellectual and literary failings but also for what he perceived as Millett's dangerous political agenda, which he considered "a parody of the Marxist vision of class struggle." In one of the nastiest literary put-downs of all time, he declared that "the emotions of women toward children don't exactly form an overwhelming preoccupation in *Sexual Politics:* there are times when one feels the book was written by a female impersonator." This was a comment, I recall, that particularly exercised me and my sisters in the movement at the time. That I

had not read Millett was beside the point; it was enough that Howe attacked the woman who articulated our rage for us.

Were sexual differences amenable to the kind of social reconfiguration Millett was advocating? Howe, for one, certainly did not think so. To the contrary, he thought they should not be jettisoned on the trash heap of history in the pursuit of some bloodless ideal. In speaking of the struggles of his own parents, toiling as garment workers while raising children in wretched poverty, Howe sounded almost like a conservative. Besides suggesting that the differences between the sexes might in fact contribute to the melioration of our fallen human condition, he also defended the family as being not necessarily oppressive to women:

> That the family ... has been coextensive with human culture itself and may therefore be supposed to have certain powers of endurance and to yield certain profound satisfactions to human beings other than merely satisfying the dominating impulses of the "master group," hardly causes Miss Millett to skip a phrase. Nor does the thought that in at least some of its aspects the family has protected the interests of women as against those of men.

In retrospect, this may have been the moment when the Left gave way definitively to the New Left. That Howe was fighting a rear-guard action is clear from the fact that he soon withdrew from this polemical field—as did Norman Mailer, another leftist stalwart whose lone contribution to the anti-feminist canon was his 1971 *The Prisoner of Sex*. By now, moreover, both the women's movement and the New Left had begun to find a new source of legitimation in a philosophy that had sunk roots in the universities. Call it deconstruction, call it post-structuralism, its intent was to demolish the notion that there could be anything like cultural standards, or agreed-upon truths, or, it went without saying, objective sexual differences.

Today, of course, this relativism-in-the-service-of-a-new-absolutism has contaminated far more than the upper reaches of academia and the fringes of the Modern Language Association. All introductory college courses, be they in literature, sociology, anthropology, religion, etc., have become shot through with the insights of deconstruction, and an afternoon of watching Oprah is enough to demonstrate how they have filtered down into the general culture. The goal of this new orientation is, ostensibly, radical human freedom and equality, without ties to oppressive institutions of any kind, especially not to the patriarchy, that shibboleth of social reconstructionists. But what deconstruction has really done is to banish, as nothing more than a set of arbitrary conventions, the moral promptings that lead people to notice oppression in the first place, and along with them the ability to distinguish true oppression from false.

* * *

He had told her, the first evening she ever spent at Gardencourt, that if she should live to suffer enough she might some day see the ghost with which the old house was duly provided. She apparently had fulfilled the necessary condition; for the next morning, in the cold, faint dawn, she knew that a spirit was standing by her bed.

There is a cart-before-the-horse quality about feminism. An explosion of economic forces, starting after World War II, sent women into the workplace in large numbers. It was only after this process was in high gear, and when women began directly competing with men in the upper echelons, that feminism came into being. An ideology then arose to justify the unprecedented autonomy on the part of women (and perhaps to assuage some of their felt guilt over the abandonment of hearth and home) and to allocate spoils. A panoply of institutions formed in its turn, to buttress the ideology: women's-studies departments in universities, tax-exempt institutions setting themselves up as lobbyists for "women's issues," a larger and larger government bureaucracy. By now, many women have come to believe that their opportunities stem wholly from the struggles of their feminist forebears and not at all from the steady expansion of the market.

But ideology, as Karl Marx noted long ago, is replete with tensions. These tensions are in abundant evidence in an essay by Diane Johnson in a recent issue of the *New York Review of Books.* Johnson is aware of the distress signals being sent out by contemporary feminism, and she demonstrates that even a liberal like herself can recognize the ridiculousness of academic feminist highjinks:

> ... endless testimonials, diatribes, and spurious science from people who imagine that their personal experience, the dynamics of their particular family, sexual taste, childhood trauma, and personal inclination constitute universals.

Johnson even circles back to the incommensurables of human existence, going so far as to refer to God and original sin. Since she is a novelist, such incommensurables may be on her mind.

Yet on the subject of women and women's issues, she inevitably begins from premises that are at odds with the way individuals struggle to craft their individual solutions to life's demands, a task that, ironically enough, the novel has traditionally taken it as its prerogative to illuminate. Johnson's constant use of the word "class" in connection with women alerts the reader to the non-novelistic sources of her thinking. Her enumeration of the minimal rights that feminists should urge on everyone is unalloyed bureaucratic boilerplate: personal safety, autonomy in sexual and health matters, equal pay for equal work.

Among my friends who are working women of middle age, there are very few who do not consider themselves feminists. Their attitudes, like Johnson's, are permeated by a belief in the inevitable progress of humanity—from which, they hold, women, prior to the 1960's, were excluded. They remain upbeat concerning the bureaucratic arrangements that will bring about the inevitable progress. Such has been the infiltration of feminist-think that women who 30 years ago would have recoiled from the social engineering extolled by Gloria Steinem now accept the rationale for suspending a six-year-old boy from school for sexual harassment because he has kissed a six-year-old girl.

Johnson herself adduces several sociological studies which purportedly demonstrate that all the parameters are finally lining up and settling into place. She quotes Dr. Daniel J. ("mid-life crisis") Levinson: "Humanity is now in the early phases of a transformation in the meanings of gender and the place of women and men in every society." The same doctor also holds, from the loftiest Archimedean perspective, that such gender transformation (here I am quoting Johnson) "is an irreversible historical trend which will take another century to

achieve." And people think Newt Gingrich is a crackpot for spouting Alvin Toffler.

Johnson declines to question whether the "transformation in the meanings of gender" projected by Levinson is a desirable state, whether it is a state any of us would wish to morph into. An irreversible trend, after all, is an irreversible trend. But she compliments France and Scandinavia, "whose governments have committed themselves to large-scale child-care arrangements." These arrangements, like the model farms the Soviets used to allow foreign visitors to see, seem to offer evidence that rational social planning will work and that the awful dislocations and disruptions occurring all around us are only temporary and in any case justified by the march of History.

* * *

But maybe Dr. Levinson is on to something. It strikes me that one of the peculiar results of the reign of feminism is that women have actually become unimportant, indeed nonessential. This has come about by feminism's making radically suspect the influence that women, *qua* women, have traditionally exercised on the souls of those with whom they come into contact. The first effective thrust was to deny that any of the endless tasks performed by women within the marriage union contributed in any way to its spiritual wholeness. Housekeeping and child-raising were transformed into a purely material operation, consisting of the kind of mindless, mechanical steps that characterize the assembly of an automobile or a computer. It is no surprise that the most ambitious women of my generation fled this scenario of drudgery, and, by extension, also avoided traditional women's occupations as they would the plague. A generation of women who would have been excellent teachers instead became attorneys, in what they were told and seemed to believe would be a net gain for humanity.

This abandonment of the female realm has also led to the production of a class that appears to be in the vanguard of the nanny state: women who "have it all," whose marriage are not so much unions as partnerships of two career paths, and whose children, once assembled and produced, are willingly turned over by them to caretakers. Most of these women have probably not dwelt on the consequences of the Faustian bargain they have struck, but their example says loudly and clearly that children are interchangeable units and that the values they learn can be equally well acquired from a Norwegian au pair and after-school public television as from parents.

Whether such women really do have it all is for them, perhaps, to say. Even so, there remains a lack of synchronicity between the highest levels of feminist achievers and ordinary women. Housework and the raising of children, denigrated by the movement and by so many elite women, is looked upon very differently by my unmarried friends, even those who call themselves feminist. They sense that the struggle to form one's life in conjunction with another—including all those horrible minutiae of daily existence that Jane O'Reilly described as the murder of a woman's soul—is a spiritual enterprise of the highest sort, involving the "discovery," as Midge Decter put it with her habitual precision in *The New Chastity* (1972), "that to be in charge of oneself also requires the courage to recognize the extent of one's frailty and dependence on others." And they sense acutely

that, in declining or refusing to make those compromises of daily living-with-another, they have missed out on the greatest of human challenges and have indeed failed in point of courage. They still yearn to meet someone with whom, as the current parlance goes, they can share their life.

The tragic part is the egocentrism of their current existence, the days and years devoted to self-maintenance, with minimal effect on the lives of others. Women now get to fulfill themselves—O'Reilly's passionate wish—but they do so in the most resolute solitude. If there is any validity to what Aristotle said long ago—that one's existence has a goal toward which the soul strives—then the care of one's physical and mental self can only be a subordinate part of a larger existential plan. The women I am talking about do not have such a plan, be it marriage or children or a high-powered career. Instead of caring for the direction of their souls, they tend to their "personal space."

The greatest loss for my friends who have not married is of course the children they never had. Exhortations to self-fulfillment aside, by the time they reached forty many women of my generation were in a desperate race with their bodies. Magazines in the late 1980's began featuring articles on "Mommie Oldest," as women underwent Herculean efforts to get their aging uteruses into shape. *In vitro* fertilization, artificial insemination, hormone shots—if only they could go back and undo all those abortions!

* * *

Here, indeed, is the great unnameable, the subject that many of us have refused to face squarely in its terrible personal dimension but that, like the purloined letter, has always been there, before our eyes. Childbirth, contraception, abortion: these dividers of women also illuminate the terrible contradictions of feminist ideology, and particularly the contention that women are no different from men.

The divide between the goals of radical, society-transforming feminism and ordinary women is inadvertently captured by Diane Johnson in her criticism of the social thinker Elizabeth Fox-Genovese, whose latest book, *Feminism Is Not the Story of My Life*, dwells precisely on this divide. Fox-Genovese, she writes, "stops just short of saying that feminists will murder infants in their cradles." Even setting partial-birth abortions aside, Johnson's refusal to see what feminism has, in fact, done in this realm is breathtaking. And because she will not acknowledge it, she must also censure Fox-Genovese for speaking of women's sexual decisions as being somehow fraught with special danger. To speak in this way, says Johnson, suggests that women are not up to "independent moral choice." But Fox-Genovese

does not deny women moral choice; she merely underscores what most women have always known: that sex, for them, *is* fraught with special danger. Ingrid Bengis knew that, though it made her very angry.

I have made my way back to my starting point. Is sex merely a material manifestation, a physical fact and act, a discharge of physical tension? Does it make any difference that the man who caresses a woman's body is a man she met only a few hours before? Or is a woman's experience of sex part of a larger moral, indeed spiritual, equation? Does she require that the man with whom she shares her bed be one whose love has settled unwaveringly and discriminatingly on her? Does she expect him to take responsibility for the child she may conceive? These are the hard questions, ones that many of us have not confronted. But whenever a woman does confront them, and arrives at the latter point of view, you will probably find that she has severed her ties with feminism.

POSTSCRIPT

Does Feminism Provide a Positive Direction for Society?

Sidel argues that feminism has not been effective enough on a societal level. It has been relatively effective on an individual basis, and young women today have thoughts and hopes and dreams that women could never have entertained before the feminist movement. But Sidel complains that society itself threatens to dash these hopes if it does not reform itself into what she calls a "more caring society."

Sidel and Powers seem to have different ideas about feminism's impact on men. Sidel believes that the "caring" that has traditionally been associated with females will have to be shared by males. Powers does not explicitly speak of changes that feminism would require of men. However, she seems to think that what feminists expect from women is that either they will be unmarried and independent or married and independent (with no children to take care of, whether because a woman has no children or because she has hired a nanny to take care of them).

Powers believes that it is futile to pretend—as she thinks feminists do—that all the same freedoms and possibilities that have traditionally existed for men can also exist for women. She does not see the effort to grant women freedom comparable to that traditionally enjoyed by men—through the encouragement of nannies, professional child care, etc.—as a positive development. Rather, Powers claims, it threatens to alienate women from family life.

A good historical overview of feminism can be found in Rosemarie Tong, *Feminist Thought: A Comprehensive Introduction* (Westview Press, 1989). Other relevant readings are Susan Faludi, *Backlash: The Undeclared War Against American Women* (Crown Publishers, 1991); Christina Hoff Sommers, *Who Stole Feminism? How Women Betrayed Women* (Simon & Schuster, 1994); Barbara Findlen, ed., *Listen Up: Voices from the Next Feminist Generation* (Seal Press, 1995); Cornelius F. Murphy, Jr., *Beyond Feminism: Toward a Dialogue on Difference* (Catholic University of America, 1995); Virginia Held, ed., *Justice and Care: Essential Readings in Feminist Ethics* (Westview Press, 1995); Sondra Farganis, *The Social Construction of the Feminine Character*, 2d ed. (Rowman & Littlefield, 1996); Pamela Grande Jensen, ed., *Finding a New Feminism: Rethinking the Woman Question for Liberal Democracy* (Rowman & Littlefield, 1996); Elizabeth Fox-Genovese, *Feminism Is Not the Story of My Life: How Today's Feminist Elite Has Lost Touch With the Real Concerns of Women* (Doubleday, 1996); Ellen R. Klein, *Feminism Under Fire* (Prometheus, 1996); and Sheila Tobias, *Faces of Feminism* (Westview Press, 1997).

ISSUE 5

Will the Information Revolution Benefit Society?

YES: John S. Mayo, from "Information Technology for Development: The National and Global Information Superhighway," *Vital Speeches of the Day* (February 1, 1995)

NO: James H. Snider, from "The Information Superhighway as Environmental Menace," *The Futurist* (March/April 1995)

ISSUE SUMMARY

YES: John S. Mayo, president emeritus of Lucent Technologies Bell Laboratories, formerly AT&T Bell Laboratories, argues that many benefits will follow from the information superhighway. One primary benefit will be that, since there will be less need to be in an urban location, people will be able to choose to live and work in rural or small-town environments and still have access to many of the resources that were previously available only in large cities.

NO: Political scientist James H. Snider argues that the very benefits brought by the information revolution also have tremendous environmental impacts, as the population is concentrated less in metropolises, spreads out more evenly across the country, and is drawn to currently rural areas.

There is no doubt that the development and proliferation of modern information technology has brought many benefits to people. And further growth of the industry promises even more benefits.

However, critics have pointed to costs as well as benefits: Modern information technology could bring increased threats to security, both on national and individual levels, as computer hackers and others gain access to the nation's sensitive information and to people's personal information. Critics have also drawn attention to the opportunity for computer crime (e.g., someone makes a bank withdrawal from your account or uses your credit card number for purchases). The possibility of sending secret (or encrypted) e-mail messages could also aid criminals and terrorists.

Nevertheless, one of the great claims for benefits to individuals is that people will be able to do so much from their home computers. For example, it will be possible to work and shop; obtain financial, medical, and legal advice; and even enjoy virtual trips to museums and art galleries. Many individuals, no longer having to commute to (or even live near) large metropolises, could spend more time with their children. Children could be brought up in safer, more crime-free areas. Individuals—without having to travel or even leave their homes—could virtually view artistic masterpieces located in the museums of New York, Paris, and Rome. Since there will be far less need to commute to large cities, traffic problems associated with rush hour will be greatly alleviated or will disappear entirely, as will the need for more highway construction, the increase in pollution caused by road travel, and so on.

But if all this comes to pass—and some of it is indeed already coming to pass—the very success of the information superhighway could bring with it a vast change in the population distribution, and this, in turn, may have a serious impact on the environment. Proponents of information technology point to its ability to bring to nonurban areas jobs that had hitherto required one's physical presence in an urban area. This is a benefit to those who already live in nonurban areas in that they have a larger selection of jobs available to them that do not require their having to relocate far away from family and friends. And it is also a benefit to individuals who might wish to retain the positions that they currently occupy in a large city—but without many of the problems associated with living in a congested area, such as crime, pollution, and a high cost of living.

Ironically, however, if a great many people seek peace and quiet in the country, there may be a countryside full of people—and very little peace and quiet. Moreover, if the population is spread out more evenly—rather than the way it is now, with high population densities in a few small areas, and large areas with very low population densities—the environmental damage could be devastating.

In the following selections, John S. Mayo describes what he feels will be the beneficial results of new information technology, while James H. Snider warns that the information superhighway is an environmental threat whose vast scope has hardly been recognized by many leading environmentalists.

YES

John S. Mayo

INFORMATION TECHNOLOGY FOR DEVELOPMENT: THE NATIONAL AND GLOBAL INFORMATION SUPERHIGHWAY

Delivered at the National Research Council/World Bank Symposium, Marshalling Technology For Development, Technology Trends And Applications Session, Irvine, California (by video), November 28, 1994

[In late 1995 and early 1996, AT&T underwent restructuring that resulted in three separate companies. The new systems and technology company is called Lucent Technologies. All references to AT&T in this selection should be considered synonymous with Lucent Technologies.—Ed.]

I plan to discuss major trends in information technology by first examining the driving forces propelling the emerging multimedia communications revolution and the evolution of the so-called information superhighways—to use the popular term. Then I will glance at this multimedia revolution and at AT&T's vision of information superhighways. And I will conclude by touching on the impact of all this information technology on developing countries.

Now, it's clear that the key underlying information technologies are the prime drivers and the key enablers behind the emerging multimedia communications revolution and the evolution of information superhighways—as well as a host of other advances that together are changing the way we live, work, play, travel and communicate. Because these key information technologies are changing the work and home environments, these same technologies are helping to address customer needs. The more they can do, the more new products and services the customer wants. It has been an upward spiral that has lasted over three decades, and will surely last at least one or two decades more.

What are these key underlying information technologies? They are silicon chips, computing, photonics or lightwaves, and software. And we've seen technology capabilities doubling every year in a number of such domains—

From John S. Mayo, "Information Technology for Development: The National and Global Information Superhighway," *Vital Speeches of the Day* (February 1, 1995). Copyright © 1995 by *Vital Speeches of the Day*. Originally delivered at the National Research Council/World Bank Symposium, Marshalling Technology for Development, Technology Trends and Applications Session, Irvine, California (by video), November 28, 1994. Reprinted by permission.

for example, in computing and photonics —and doubling every 18 months in silicon chips. Even software—once a "bottleneck" technology because of quality and programmer-productivity problems—is beginning to advance rapidly in major areas like telecommunications, thanks to advanced programming languages and reuse of previously developed software modules.

To cite perhaps the most widely known example, we've witnessed explosive growth in the power of silicon chips —one measure of which is the number of transistors we can cram onto a chip the size of a fingernail. And this number, now in the millions, is moving steadily toward known physical limits. In the early part of the next century, today's familiar solid state devices may mature with transistors measuring about 400 atoms by 400 atoms each—the smallest such transistors likely to operate reliably at room temperature. The new frontier then will not be in making the devices smaller, but in creatively and economically using the vast increase in complexity and power made possible by this remarkable technology.

The amazing progress of silicon chips forms a microcosm of the broad thrust of information technology and all the associated forces that are leading to the multimedia communications revolution and the evolution of information superhighways. Let's look at the progress and impacts of these related driving forces.

After the invention of the integrated circuit, every time the number of transistors on a silicon chip increased by a factor of a thousand, something had to be reengineered—that is, something had to be radically changed or improved, because it was a new ball game. So the first reengineering that we did—as we headed toward that first thousand-fold increase

—was to change all of our design processes, which had been based on discrete components.

When we reached a thousand transistors per chip, we used the new digital circuitry to reengineer our products from analog to digital, as did many other industries. Let me stress that this early progress toward digital products, enabled by silicon chips and software, brought about the digitalization of most systems and services—domestically and, more and more, globally. This digitalization created a powerful force that is driving us toward multimedia communications and information superhighways.

Then, about a decade ago, we reached toward a million transistors per chip— and powerful microcomputers became possible, along with all the periphery related to microcomputers and the needed software systems. All this led to an explosion of advanced communications services that forced the judicial process that led to the reengineering of our company: from a company that provided largely voice and data-on-voice telecommunications services to a company focused on universal information services. The theme of universal information services is voice, data and images anywhere, anytime with convenience and economy. Providing advanced services on an increasingly intelligent global network was the beginning of multimedia communications, now emerging as the revolution of the 1990s and beyond.

We are currently in the era of yet another thousand-fold increase in transistors per chip. And reengineering has now extended beyond our company and is leading to the merging of communications, computers, consumer electronics and entertainment. The bringing together of these four industries has started out in obvious ways—that is, through joint projects, joint ventures, mergers, acquisitions and some new start-up companies. This reengineering of our industry appears to be the next-to-the-last step of the information revolution brought on by the invention of the transistor.

The last step, and one that may go on forever, is the reengineering of society—of how we live, work, play, travel and communicate. It will create a whole new way of life. For example, it will change education through distance learning and school at home; it will change work life through virtual offices and work at home; and it will diminish the need to transport our bodies for work or routine tasks such as visiting and shopping. Let me quickly add, however, that it will take social change as well as technology to make many of these changes happen.

Another driving force toward multimedia communications and information superhighway evolution is the worldwide push toward common standards and open, user-friendly interfaces that will encourage global networking, and maximum interoperability and connectivity.... [S]ervice providers and customers will be able to use equipment from many different vendors without worry about compatibility. This will facilitate the upgrading of existing networks and the construction of new networks on a worldwide basis.... Similar standards in domestic networks will enable digital communications to the workplace and home, and will make possible high data-rate services.

But let me be clear on this point: although we have a lot of good work on standards, universal connectivity and interoperability will remain a big challenge as the communications and computing industries merge....

Now, the pacing force behind the multimedia and information superhighway revolution is not so much the technology as it is marketplace demands. For the greater part of this century, the user willingly accepted whatever technological capabilities we were able to achieve. Thus, the telecommunications industry was supplier-driven, and the suppliers managed the evolution of the industry and the information highways. But, as you may know, the technology became so rich that it made many more capabilities possible than the user could accept. To put it differently, we could design a lot more products and services than the customer was willing to pay for. That marked the transition from a supplier-driven industry to today's customer-driven industry—from supplier push to marketplace pull.

And, importantly, the global transfer and assimilation of information technology are combining with political and regulatory forces such as the move to privatization of telecommunications around the world—in both developed and developing countries. The result is the growth of ever-stronger global competition in the provision of communications products and services. Such emerging competition is another force driving the evolution of both multimedia communications and information superhighways. And there is an on-going challenge to public policy—not just in the U.S., but globally—to provide a framework for that evolution to occur, a framework that ensures full and fair competition for all players.

These, then, are some of the important forces driving us into the multimedia communications revolution and the associated evolution of information superhighways.

Let's look a bit further into these subjects and start with the multimedia revolution. After all, the pursuit of multimedia is creating social pressures on the evolution of information superhighways—both here and around the world. So what is "multimedia?" A reasonable working definition is that the term "multimedia" refers to information that combines more than one medium, where the media can include speech, music, text, data, graphics, fax, image, video and animation. And we at AT&T tend to focus on multimedia products and services that are networked; that is, connected over a communications and information network.

Examples of such networked multimedia communications range from videotelephony and videoconferencing; to real-time video on demand, interactive video and multimedia messaging; to remote collaborative work, interactive information services such as electronic shopping, and multimedia education and training. Eventually, we will have advanced virtual reality services, which will enable people to indirectly and remotely experience a place or an event in all dimensions.

Now, we are excited about multimedia because public switched networks—or information highways, if you will—can presently accommodate a wide array of networked multimedia communications, and the evolutionary directions of those networks will enable them to handle an increasingly vast range of such communications. Moreover, there is also a potentially vast market for multimedia hardware and supporting software. Although actual projections differ widely, the most commonly quoted projection for the total worldwide market for multimedia products and services is roughly $100 billion by the year 2000.

We at AT&T are playing a major role in facilitating the emerging multimedia revolution—as a service provider, as a provider of network products to local service providers, and as a provider of products to end users. These are familiar roles for AT&T, so let me briefly describe another, perhaps less familiar, major role we are studying in relation to the multimedia revolution. That is the role of what we call "the missing industry"— and that role is a "host" for a wide variety of digital content and multimedia applications developed by others. Hosting is a function that connects end users to the content they seek. Customers will gain easy, timely and convenient access to personal communications, transactions, information services and entertainment via wired and wireless connections to telephones, handheld devices, computers and eventually television sets. Independent sources for this digital content eventually will range from publishers to large movie studios to small cottage-industry software houses.

This role is also of interest here because of the key information superhighway challenge it illustrates—specifically, because openness of critical interfaces and global standards are vital to this complex hosting function. The entertainment industry, for example, must have software systems that are compatible with those of the hosting industry, and these software systems must, in turn, be compatible with those of the communications and information-networking industry, which then must be compatible with the customer-premises equipment industry.

In addition, the tremendous growth in available information and databases will stimulate the need for personal intelligent agents. These "smart agents" are software programs that are activated by electronic messages in the network, and that find, access, process and deliver desired information to the customer. They can perform many of the time-consuming tasks that have discouraged a number of users from taking advantage of on-line services and the emerging electronic marketplace. "Smart agents" are one feature of AT&T's recently announced enhanced network service called AT&T PersonaLink^{SM} Services.

Let me say I'm looking forward to these "smart agents"—software that can take the hassle out of life. Shopping for the best mortgage, or finding the best new car deal, or finding out which store has the item I want is a hassle, and has people at the interface who add negative value. Just last week I needed a replacement part. I called the store twice and got no satisfactory response to my calls. So I went to the store, waited in line, and then the salesperson queried the database and said, "We don't have it in stock." My "smart agent" could have queried their database and saved them and me a big investment in a zero-revenue operation. There was never a problem with the database; the problem was that people were inadvertently in the way of my ability to access it—adding negative value, but diligently trying to do their jobs. A "smart agent" could simply have done it better.

Now, it's important to note that in the age of multimedia communications, people who are geographically separated from each other will not, for example, just play games together over networks —they will visit and find what is emotionally nourishing, and build their relationships. According to AT&T's vision, in this evolving age, consumers and business associates will seek new relationships based on telepresence, a new type of community, and a social experience independent of geography. This potential for interactive networks is quite unlike that found in the proposed availability in the U.S. of 500 pre-programmed TV channels on the CATV cable. The beauty is that people will have the freedom to choose any subject or service from the intelligent terminals in their homes and offices. A key point is that they will be able to network clusters of friends or associates to enjoy such services as a group.

I must stress that networked multimedia communications will dramatically change the nature of work, and will therefore have a broad impact on business—first in developed nations and eventually in developing nations. Video-conferencing, for example, is first coming into businesses to enhance productivity, save time, and reduce travel. And current developments in multimedia telephony are making the possibility of remote collaborative work more and more realistic. In a few years, for example, a person could be working with colleagues or suppliers in branch offices in New York, Irvine, Hong Kong, Paris, and Sydney. Working in real time, they could accomplish the combined task of producing printed materials, presentation slides, and a videotape introducing a new product line.

As I noted, the pursuit of multimedia communications is driving social issues relating to the evolution of the information superhighway. Now, what is AT&T's vision of the information superhighway?

Our vision is to bring people together, giving them easy access to each other and to the information and services they want and need—anytime, anywhere. In our view, the information superhighway is a seamless web of communications and information networks —together with other elements of our national information infrastructure, such as computers, databases, and consumer electronics—which will put vast amounts of information at the fingertips of a variety of users. And we see the information superhighway, quite simply, as a vast interoperable network of networks —embracing local, long distance and global networks, wireless, broadcast and cable, and satellites. In addition, the information superhighway also embraces the Internet.... Importantly, the information superhighway is *not* a uniform end-to-end network developed and operated by government or any one company. It is the totality of networks in our nation, interconnected domestically and globally. And it is an important part of evolving global information superhighways.

Now, let's turn to the impacts of these technology trends on developing nations. These advanced information technology trends, multimedia communications and information superhighways will have a variety of broad, beneficial social impacts on developing nations, including the following:

Item 1. Advanced communications, growing in ubiquity, could slow the migration of rural people to urban areas— a traditional problem in countries such as The People's Republic of China.

Item 2. Access to jobs and services. People living in rural areas would be less inclined to move to the cities if advanced communications systems gave them access to jobs and sophisticated social services where they already live. (In the U.S., for example, our pervasive communications infrastructure has enabled information-intensive businesses to flourish anywhere in the country.)

Item 3. Information superhighways could alleviate congestion and commuter-traffic pollution in cities by making telecommuting possible—by bringing good jobs to people, wherever they are. (In the U.S., as you know, the work-at-home movement is gaining momentum, and trials with certain types of jobs show that employees can be even more highly productive without leaving their homes. One side benefit here is reduced costs for urban office space.)

Item 4. Information superhighways could also revolutionize education and eliminate differences in quality between rural and urban education systems—by enabling a limited number of the very best teachers and professors to reach huge numbers of students. Both students and teachers could be located practically anywhere, in "virtual" classrooms—and they could enhance learning by accessing multimedia network databases on a great variety of content areas.

Item 5. Information superhighways could also revolutionize medical care by helping to deliver high-quality medical care far from large population centers. Advanced communications would permit frequent meetings between rural health workers and physicians located in more populated areas. The same capability would also permit direct doctor-to-patient consultation and follow-up.

Item 6. Advances in information technology are stitching together a truly global society and a global economy —which developing nations would be able to participate in fully.

Item 7. Peoples and countries would be able to retain their ethnic and cultural identities, but at the same time they would be able to communicate, transact and interact seamlessly across geographic and political boundaries.

Item 8. In addition to these capabilities, a modern information infrastructure would help strengthen the ties that hold a nation's people together. In a large country such as China, for example, the huge distances between cities and regions, and the enormous complexity of regional dialects, have made communication among the Chinese people exceptionally difficult. So an information superhighway would have the potential to help lessen both the obstacle of distance and the barrier of language. And information technology will also eventually make possible real-time translation of languages.

These, then, are some of the social impacts of information technology on developing nations. In addition to social impacts, the key information technology trends, multimedia communications and information superhighways will have some broad public-policy impacts on developing nations, including the following:

Item 1. In general, investment in communications infrastructure would contribute greatly to a nation's overall economic development. Moreover, the new technologies that developing countries would be investing in are becoming more and more cost-effective. So there is a strong need to ensure sufficient investment in construction and management of a country's communications infrastructure.

Item 2. There is an opportunity to choose a technology path that would move a developing nation into the information age most directly. The opportunity is to "leapfrog" many of the older technologies that preceded today's advanced network systems—for example, to install glass fiber in local distribution networks. A country thus has the opportunity to economize on scarce capital resources by investing in a national information superhighway in the initial stages.

Item 3. There is technology to "jumpstart" a developing nation. For example, cellular radio can provide telephony almost overnight and serve large markets while the fiberoptic infrastructure is put in place.

Item 4. In addition, there is a need for heavy investment in the development of the *human* infrastructure, not just the *physical* infrastructure. The global leaders of the 21st century will be those countries that have not only invested in the right technologies, but also in the intellectual growth of their people.

Item 5. Information technology is vital to economic reform and development —to improving the economic and social life of a nation's people, and to attracting and meeting the needs of foreign investors.

Item 6. Information technology would also enhance financial management— for example, by enabling a country to move away from a cash economy to one in which electronic transactions are not only faster, but also provide for much greater visibility into economic activity.

Item 7. Information technology would both *facilitate and complicate* the job of governing; *facilitate* by making available to decision-makers vastly expanded resources of timely information; *complicate* by vastly expanding the numbers of people who would be informed about important issues and who would inevitably want to play a role in deciding them.

These are some of the broad public-policy impacts of information technology on developing nations. Although the government of the U.S. clearly does not have all the answers, some of our steps, as well as missteps, might be helpful for such nations to consider.

As you know, the U.S. government has played a crucial role in nurturing rapid technological progress, as well as rapid application of new technologies in the marketplace. In the communications sector, for example, the government has established a clear set of national objectives—such as universal service, technological leadership, and broadband capability into all population centers. The government has also created a strong, independent regulatory structure designed to ensure that private companies serve the public interest in a fair and competitive marketplace—although we still have a long way to go toward genuine and effective competition in the local exchange. Many, if not most, developing nations are still evolving their policies, laws and regulations governing the communications industry. And I cannot overemphasize the importance of this task.

In summary, rich information technology, the worldwide push toward global standards, ever-increasing customer demands, and growing global competition are key driving forces behind the emerging multimedia communications revolution and the evolution of national information superhighways. The growth of multimedia communications and the further competitive evolution of these information superhighways, as well as of global information superhighways promise a broad range of Information Age benefits to virtually every citizen of our nation. And they also promise to extend these Information Age benefits to virtually every citizen of the world, including the developing nations.

NO

James H. Snider

THE INFORMATION SUPERHIGHWAY AS ENVIRONMENTAL MENACE

Over the years environmentalists have cautioned us against threats to the environment—the population explosion, nuclear radiation, pesticides, aerosols, nonrecyclable garbage, and automobile exhaust, to name just a few. But what they haven't noticed yet is the environmental menace posed by the information superhighway.

If you look at the literature of some of the organizations concerned with preserving the land, such as the Wilderness Society or the Sierra Club, you don't see the information superhighway listed as a threat. On the contrary, the information superhighway is supposed to help the environment by reducing the need for automobile and airplane travel and all the pollution they bring. In fact, some of the most-ardent environmentalists also happen to be ardent advocates of the information superhighway.

U.S. Vice President Al Gore is a prime example. In his book *Earth in the Balance* (Houghton Mifflin, 1992), Gore attempts to recount the present dangers to the environment. In the chapter, "A Global Marshall Plan," he advocates building an information superhighway to facilitate telecommuting as a partial solution to our problems. This, he believes, will reduce the demand for cars and the pollution that cars inevitably bring. He notes that, for "a dozen years, I have been the principal author and advocate of a proposal to build a national network of information superhighways."

More recently, the Clinton administration has directed the U.S. Environmental Protection Agency and the Department of Transportation to promote telecommuting, largely to improve air quality, reduce future environmental risks, and conserve energy resources. High-population centers such as New York City, Los Angeles, and Chicago are among the areas targeted. Among the many policy proposals are tax incentives for employers and individuals to change to home-based telecommuting arrangements, as well as "flexiplace" incentives similar to current "flexitime" ones.

Yet, unbeknownst to the advocates of telecommuting, the coming information superhighway portends an environmental disaster of the first magnitude. In the United States, where population growth is relatively subdued, it may

From James H. Snider, "The Information Superhighway as Environmental Menace," *The Futurist*, vol. 29, no. 2 (March/April 1995). Copyright © 1995 by The World Future Society. Reprinted by permission of *The Futurist*, World Future Society, Bethesda, Maryland, *wfsinfo@wfs.org*.

lead to the massive destruction of the remaining forests, open land, and wild flora and fauna over the next few decades.

RURAL VS. METROPOLITAN

Despite the huge increase over the last few hundred years, the world's population has been highly concentrated on a limited landmass. Only about 2% of the earth's land surface is covered by cities and towns. Though human beings affect much landmass through farming, tree growing, pollution, or other means, the mass of humanity has tended to congregate in metropolitan (urban or suburban) areas. Even now, the ratio of people living in metropolitan vs. rural areas continues to increase, substantially reducing the pressure on open spaces that would otherwise ensue from population increases.

In the United States, the population is also highly concentrated. About 80% of Americans live in metropolitan areas, which cover just 16% of the contiguous states. The number of Americans living in rural areas has decreased not just because of population increases in other areas, but because of changing job opportunities. In 1800, more than 90% of U.S. jobs were agricultural. Today, that figure is under 2%, and the vast majority of the remaining jobs can only be done in metropolitan areas.

Thanks to the information superhighway, this hundred-year-old trend toward metropolitan areas is about to reverse. In fact, a recent *Wall Street Journal* article argues that, "Like the coming of the railroad a century ago and the arrival of the interstate highway system in the 1950s, telecommunications is dramatically rearranging rural life.... Almost unnoticed are recent census figures showing an abrupt turnabout in the rural diaspora.... In all, during the first two years of the 1990s, rural counties gained nearly 900,000 new residents."

TRANSPORTATION AND POPULATION DISPERSION

Throughout history, transportation technology has largely determined where people live. Before the Industrial Age, when boats dominated the movement of people and goods, major population centers were located next to major bodies of water. During the nineteenth century, railroads opened up the hinterlands and led to a vast dispersion of towns and cities clustered around railroad stops and junctions.

As transportation historian Stephen Goddard says in *Getting There: The Epic Struggle Between Road and Rail in the American Century* (Basic Books, 1994), the West was worthless until the railroads "opened up the West to settlement. Pioneers rode the rails into the wilderness and seemingly overnight built new towns with supplies manufactured in the East. Towns called Omaha, Tulsa, and Wichita grew from tiny settlements to cities overnight."

In the twentieth century, the automobile led to the massive growth of suburbs surrounding traditional urban areas, as well as the growth of new cities along the interstate highway system. The interstates, says Goddard, altered "beyond recognition where and how Americans lived. They allowed a breadwinner to commute double the distance in the same time. Sleepy farming villages at the outskirts of cities doubled their population within a decade as their cornfields gave way to row upon row of tract houses."

The information superhighway could potentially spread people out much farther than the train or automobile ever could. People may have created new urban areas or moved to suburban areas, but the difficulty of driving to "civilization" has kept them within relatively narrow distances. By eliminating the remaining transportation barriers, the information superhighway threatens a massive migration out of metropolitan areas to the relatively unspoiled hinterlands.

THE DEATH OF RURAL AMERICA

Public officials representing rural areas throughout the United States (including Alaska, Idaho, Iowa, Maine, Montana, Nebraska, North Carolina, and Vermont) are advocating the information superhighway in order to stimulate business in their states. For example, U.S. Senator Conrad Burns of Montana explains in the *Congressional Record* his rationale for accelerating its building:

> Workers will travel to work on the information highways instead of our traditional highways. The cars on these information highways will be bits of information which can travel anywhere in the world instantly....
>
> Think of it, a stockbroker could live in Circle, Montana, with a population of 931, and be in instant contact with anyone, anywhere, anyway. That person wouldn't have to burn thousands of gallons of fossil fuel each year to drive to and from work.... And, best of all, that person will be able to live and work in rural America.

Burns also expects the information superhighway to stem the historical outflow of population from rural Montana to metropolitan areas in other states:

> In Montana, many of our graduating seniors want to stay in our beautiful state where the skies are blue, the water is crisp, the air is healthy, and the quality of life is good. But they are forced to leave the state to find jobs. We need to keep our best and brightest at home.

Until now, a large number of jobs have only been available in metropolitan areas. Occupations such as accounting, law, advertising, management consulting, and architecture tend not to thrive in more-rural areas. In occupations such as movie production, book publishing, and international finance, only a few metropolitan areas hold the vast majority of jobs.

Similarly, most cultural activities have only been available in metropolitan areas. Movies, theaters, playhouses, video stores, sports events, concerts, high-quality schools, and pools of potential friends are still heavily concentrated geographically. In the future, the information superhighway will make high-quality entertainment and education increasingly available in the home or anywhere else on the planet. And as "virtual" communities sprout, the need to be physically close to friends and relatives will continue to diminish.

At the same time, the allure of open spaces is unlikely to diminish. In *A Fierce Green Fire* (Hill and Wang, 1993), a history of the environmental movement, author Philip Shabecoff says, "The migration to the suburbs was, for many if not most of the families who moved, an environmental choice for open space, greenery, cleaner air, less noise, and a generally healthier place to live." More than ever, environmental quality is seen as an integral part of a search for a higher standard of living. With economic and cultural restrictions removed from the quest to live in open spaces, such a quest is likely to reach a new and environmentally destructive phase.

"Every survey shows that more people want to live in small towns than can find jobs there," says Calvin Beale, a senior demographer for the U.S. Department of Agriculture. "If you wire them, they will come."

"THE NEW YORKERS ARE COMING! THE NEW YORKERS ARE COMING!"

So what will happen if the information superhighway is built and the population can disperse evenly throughout the land? Let's take Vermont, the self-described "Green Mountain State." The *Wall Street Journal* recently rated metropolitan Burlington, Vermont, as the best place in the United States to raise a family. What would happen if the relatively nearby inhabitants of New York City could find good work in Vermont (whose current population is 560,000)? Would this attract millions of people to not just visit but live in Vermont?

No definitive answer can be found. I did ask this question to half a dozen of my friends in Manhattan. All of those with families told me that they'd readily move to Vermont if only they could find good work and a solid career. Whether justified or not, it certainly can be said that Vermonters live in constant fear of an onslaught of "flatlanders" from the south. Vermont is widely perceived as a highly desirable place to live. Much of its 50% increase in population since 1950 has resulted from out-of-staters seeking the quality of life that Vermont's environment makes possible. By 1994, a majority and ever-increasing proportion

of Vermont's voting-age population were out-of-staters. Vermont's governor and U.S. representative are both transplanted New Yorkers.

If we allow the information superhighway to be built, it does seem reasonable to believe that it could absolutely blight this little gem of a state. Already the few suburban areas in Vermont are chock full of expatriates from nearby metropolitan areas such as New York City and Boston. But that is merely a trickle compared with the millions who are likely to come if the information superhighway flourishes. The best and brightest will leave the urban blights and turn Vermont into one huge and spread-out suburb. They will spoil Vermont, but it will still be far better than where they came from. They will telework from their home or nearby office. Maybe Vermont will become one of the premium telelifestyle locations, but the destruction visited upon its land will not be unique.

If all Americans succeed in getting their dream homes with several acres of land, the forests and open lands across the entire continental United States will be destroyed. Even if the U.S. population were to quadruple to 1 billion, the havoc wrought on the land would not be as great as from a more even dispersal of its present 250 million. Today's one-acre apartment building with 200 families will turn into 200 five-acre homesteads spread out over 1,000 acres. Even if the average home lot only increases from a quarter of an acre to an acre, the environmental destruction would be huge.

In the past, environmentalists have not been oblivious to the environmental impact of new communications technologies. Many, for example, have bemoaned the tendency of the car to destroy open spaces and ecosystems. Shabecoff recounts Lewis Mumford's warning that "the swelling size and power of the cities was overwhelming the countryside." For Mumford, "the automobile filled in the last open spaces and was the true Frankenstein's monster of the twentieth century, surpassed only in its destructive potential by the hydrogen bomb, but more dangerous because more complacently indulged." More recently in *Healing the Planet* (Touchstone, 1990), Paul Ehrlich calls for "a near absolute ban on the building of new freeways and roads." But environmentalists have yet to discover that the information superhighway might not only be destructive, but far more so than the physical highways of the past.

PRESERVING OPEN SPACES

The emerging information superhighway offers the potential to dramatically improve education, consumer information, democracy, entertainment, and economic growth. But it also has the potential to be the most environmentally destructive technology of the early twenty-first century.

Is there any way to gain the benefits of the information superhighway while preserving the earth's open spaces? The ideal solution would be to strengthen land-conservation incentives and laws. The government could buy or protect more land. Zoning laws could be tightened and more strictly enforced. Many such efforts are currently under way in the United States, but the pace will have to be dramatically accelerated to ward off the new onslaught on the land.

The paradox is that the very reason the land is threatened is because having open space around one's home is equated with a high standard of living. People's environmental values lead them to want to leave crowded cities and suburbs. But in doing so, they destroy the environment that attracts them there in the first place. The tendency to want a homestead with at least an acre is deeply rooted, and efforts to preserve open spaces will come into conflict with this powerful drive and the economic forces that cater to it.

This leads to pessimism that traditional land-conservation measures will be enough to hold back the flood of spreading humanity. The only way to stop the flood might be to dam it at its source—to prevent information superhighways, just like interstate highways, from being built in environmentally important areas. This is the path I urge upon land conservationists—at least until traditional land-conservation measures are significantly strengthened.

POSTSCRIPT

Will the Information Revolution Benefit Society?

The problems that Snider sees as resulting from the information superhighway are to a large extent what Mayo views as successes. If Mayo is correct, and the resources that he anticipates being brought to areas of low population density actually are brought to those areas, then there very well may be a growth in the human population in those areas. Environmentalists, however, have often claimed that human population growth is one of the primary roots of environmental degradation. Snider would agree that this would be a serious problem.

On the other hand, it is often very difficult to predict social responses to new technology. Are there reasons that people would prefer to live in cities anyway, even if jobs and many resources could be brought to nonmetropolitan areas? Perhaps some people who live in cities could not imagine life without an array of ethnic restaurants or city nightlife; and some people simply prefer the crowds and excitement of a city over the peace and quiet of rural life. Snider reports asking some people in Manhattan whether or not they would prefer to live in Vermont (if they could maintain their careers) and receiving an affirmative answer. Snider muses that perhaps they say this now but would never really move; or perhaps they would move but would find themselves missing things that could only be supplied in a city—and would move back.

Books relevant to this topic are Constance Penley and Andrew Ross, *Technoculture* (University of Minnesota Press, 1991); Chuck Huff and Thomas Finholt, eds., *Social Issues in Computing: Putting Computing in Its Place* (McGraw-Hill, 1994); Daniel Burstein and David Kline, *Road Warriors: Dreams and Nightmares Along the Information Highway* (E. P. Dutton, 1995); Kirkpatrick Sale, *Rebels Against the Future: The Luddites and Their War on Industrial Revolution: Lessons for the Computer Age* (Addison-Wesley, 1995); Clifford Stoll, *Silicon Snake Oil: Second Thoughts on the Information Highway* (Doubleday, 1995); James Brook and Iain A. Boal, eds., *Resisting the Virtual Life: The Culture and Politics of Information* (San Francisco City Lights, 1995); Nicholas Negroponte, *Being Digital* (Random House, 1995); Mark Dery, *Flame Wars: The Discourse of Cyberculture* (Duke University Press, 1995); Donald Altschiller, ed., *The Information Revolution* (H. W. Wilson, 1995); Dinty W. Moore, *The Emperor's Virtual Clothes: The Naked Truth About Internet Culture* (Algonquin, 1995); William J. Mitchell, *City of Bits: Place, Space, and Infobahn* (MIT Press, 1995); Peter Ludlow, ed., *High Noon on the Electronic Frontier: Conceptual Issues in Cyberspace* (MIT Press, 1996); and M. David Ermann, *Computers, Ethics, and Society*, 2d ed. (Oxford University Press, 1997).

ISSUE 6

Should Animals Be Liberated?

YES: Peter Singer, from *Practical Ethics*, 2d ed. (Cambridge University Press, 1993)

NO: Michael P. T. Leahy, from *Against Liberation: Putting Animals in Perspective* (Routledge, 1991)

ISSUE SUMMARY

YES: Australian philosopher Peter Singer argues that since animals can suffer pain, and since pain is a bad experience for whatever being has that experience, human beings need to take the suffering of animals into consideration. He denounces speciesism because, like racism and sexism, it takes the view that the suffering of one group does not count as much as the suffering of another.

NO: British philosopher Michael P. T. Leahy argues that although it may be necessary to be more humane to animals, drastic changes in human behavior toward animals are not called for. He maintains that abolishing meat-eating, a practice that is indulged in by millions of people, would be severely disruptive to people's lives and cannot be justified by concerns for animals.

People's relationship to (other) animals is ambivalent—as the parentheses in this sentence suggest. On one hand, we say that human beings are animals; on the other hand, we say that people are not animals.

Most of Western culture stresses the differences between humans and animals, not our interrelationships with them. According to the Bible, for example, God created both the animal kingdom and human beings, but he specified that human beings are to be the masters of all the animals.

Other cultural and religious traditions, however, stress the continuity of all living things. Some cultures hold that a soul that inhabits a human being's body will be reborn attached to the body of an animal and vice versa. Other cultures abstain from eating meat altogether out of respect for animals. Still others recognize an intimate connection between hunters and the hunted, and they require hunters to perform rituals and ceremonies in order to maintain the correct spiritual relationships between them.

In the West, various revolutions have displaced human beings from the center of our own moral universe. And recent public environmental awareness has highlighted the idea that human beings and animals are tied together in ways never before realized. Some people have begun to rethink the moral place of animals. An important point advanced by those who favor animal liberation is that human beings and animals can suffer and feel pain. Moreover, they claim, any beings that suffer the same amount should be given equal moral consideration. To regard ourselves as superior to and, thus, as deserving of more consideration than animals is to fall into the same self-serving way of thinking that racists, sexists, and chauvinists of all kinds have fallen into.

Many animal liberationists agree that the liberation of animals—which they think of as analogous to liberation movements for various socially and politically oppressed groups—will be resisted by those who benefit from the current status of animals (such as meat eaters) and who are therefore naturally reluctant to change. The responses of these liberationists to what they see as cruel treatment of animals range from the clandestine practices of those who break into the laboratories of scientists who use animals for research (and literally liberate the animals) to the purely educational practices of those who write books and articles in order to inform the public about current conditions that are harmful to animals.

Not only are the clandestine and sometimes violent activities condemned by most people against animal liberation, but even much of the so-called educational material is criticized as overly projective (it projects human attitudes, feelings, etc., onto animals) and one-sided (it concentrates on cases in which animals are abused rather than on more typical cases).

Those who are against liberation maintain that there is nothing essentially wrong with human beings using animals (as food for example), although there may be abuses, as there are in any system. But there is a strong sense that animals are not part of the human circle at all (they cannot be parties to a social contract, for example). Therefore, although individual animals can be harmed by human actions, no general liberation is called for.

In the essays that follow, Peter Singer, an animal liberation leader in the intellectual and the political spheres, makes a case for animal liberation, while Michael P. T. Leahy argues against animal liberation.

YES

Peter Singer

EQUALITY FOR ANIMALS?

RACISM AND SPECIESISM

I gave reasons for believing that the fundamental principle of equality, on which the equality of all human beings rests, is the principle of equal consideration of interests. Only a basic moral principle of this kind can allow us to defend a form of equality that embraces all human beings, with all the differences that exist between them. I shall now contend that while this principle does provide an adequate basis for human equality, it provides a basis that cannot be limited to humans. In other words I shall suggest that, having accepted the principle of equality as a sound moral basis for relations with others of our own species, we are also committed to accepting it as a sound moral basis for relations with those outside our own species—the non-human animals.

This suggestion may at first seem bizarre. We are used to regarding discrimination against members of racial minorities, or against women, as among the most important moral and political issues facing the world today. These are serious matters, worthy of the time and energy of any concerned person. But animals? Isn't the welfare of animals in a different category altogether, a matter for people who are dotty about dogs and cats? How can anyone waste their time on equality for animals when so many humans are denied real equality?

This attitude reflects a popular prejudice against taking the interests of animals seriously—a prejudice no better founded than the prejudice of white slaveowners against taking the interests of their African slaves seriously. It is easy for us to criticise the prejudices of our grandfather, from which our fathers freed themselves. It is more difficult to distance ourselves from our own views, so that we can dispassionately search for prejudices among the beliefs and values we hold. What is needed now is a willingness to follow the arguments where they lead, without a prior assumption that the issue is not worth our attention.

The argument for extending the principle of equality beyond our own species is simple, so simple that it amounts to no more than a clear understanding of the nature of the principle of equal consideration of interests. We have seen that this principle implies that our concern for others ought not to depend on what they are like, or what abilities they possess (although precisely what this concern requires us to do may vary according to the characteristics of those affected by what we do). It is on this basis that we are able to say that the fact that some people are not members of our race does not entitle us to exploit them, and similarly the fact that some people are less intelligent than others does not mean that their interests may be disregarded. But the principle also implies that the fact that beings are not members of our species does not entitle us to exploit them, and similarly the fact that other animals are less intelligent than we are does not mean that their interests may be disregarded.

... [M]any philosophers have advocated equal consideration of interests, in some form or other, as a basic moral principle. Only a few have recognised that the principle has applications beyond our own species, one of the few being Jeremy Bentham, the founding father of modern utilitarianism. In a forward-looking passage, written at a time when African slaves in the British dominions were still being treated much as we now treat non-human animals, Bentham wrote:

> The day may come when the rest of the animal creation may acquire those rights which never could have been withholden from them but by the hand of tyranny. The French have already discovered that the blackness of the skin is no reason why a human being should be abandoned without redress to the caprice of a tormentor. It may one day come to be recognised that the number of the legs, the villosity of the skin, or the termination of the *os*
> *sacrum*, [the presence or absence of a tail] are reasons equally insufficient for abandoning a sensitive being to the same fate. What else is it that should trace the insuperable line? Is it the faculty of reason, or perhaps the faculty of discourse? But a fullgrown horse or dog is beyond comparison a more rational, as well as a more conversable animal, than an infant of a day, or a week, or even a month, old. But suppose they were otherwise, what would it avail? The question is not, Can they *reason*? nor Can they *talk*? but, *Can they suffer?*

In this passage Bentham points to the capacity for suffering as the vital characteristic that entitles a being to equal consideration. The capacity for suffering —or more strictly, for suffering and/or enjoyment or happiness—is not just another characteristic like the capacity for language, or for higher mathematics. Bentham is not saying that those who try to mark 'the insuperable line' that determines whether the interests of a being should be considered happen to have selected the wrong characteristic. The capacity for suffering and enjoying things is a prerequisite for having interests at all, a condition that must be satisfied before we can speak of interests in any meaningful way. It would be nonsense to say that it was not in the interests of a stone to be kicked along the road by a schoolboy. A stone does not have interests because it cannot suffer. Nothing that we can do to it could possibly make any difference to its welfare. A mouse, on the other hand, does have an interest in not being tormented, because mice will suffer if they are treated in this way.

If a being suffers, there can be no moral justification for refusing to take that suffering into consideration. No matter what the nature of the being, the principle of equality requires that the suffering be counted equally with the like suffering —in so far as rough comparisons can be made—of any other being. If a being is not capable of suffering, or of experiencing enjoyment or happiness, there is nothing to be taken into account. This is why the limit of sentience (using the term as a convenient, if not strictly accurate, shorthand for the capacity to suffer or experience enjoyment or happiness) is the only defensible boundary of concern for the interests of others. To mark this boundary by some characteristic like intelligence or rationality would be to mark it in an arbitrary way. Why not choose some other characteristic, like skin colour?

Racists violate the principle of equality by giving greater weight to the interests of members of their own race when there is a clash between their interests and the interests of those of another race. Racists of European descent typically have not accepted that pain matters as much when it is felt by Africans, for example, as when it is felt by Europeans. Similarly those I would call 'speciesists' give greater weight to the interests of members of their own species when there is a clash between their interests and the interests of those of other species. Human speciesists do not accept that pain is as bad when it is felt by pigs or mice as when it is felt by humans.

That, then, is really the whole of the argument for extending the principle of equality to nonhuman animals; but there may be some doubts about what this equality amounts to in practice. In particular, the last sentence of the previous paragraph may prompt some people to reply: 'Surely pain felt by a mouse just is not as bad as pain felt by a human. Humans have much greater awareness of what is happening to them, and this makes their suffering worse. You can't equate the suffering of, say, a person dying slowly from cancer, and a laboratory mouse undergoing the same fate.'

I fully accept that in the case described the human cancer victim normally suffers more than the nonhuman cancer victim. This in no way undermines the extension of equal consideration of interests to nonhumans. It means, rather, that we must take care when we compare the interests of different species. In some situations a member of one species will suffer more than a member of another species. In this case we should still apply the principle of equal consideration of interests but the result of so doing is, of course, to give priority to relieving the greater suffering. A simpler case may help to make this clear.

If I give a horse a hard slap across its rump with my open hand, the horse may start, but it presumably feels little pain. Its skin is thick enough to protect it against a mere slap. If I slap a baby in the same way, however, the baby will cry and presumably does feel pain, for the baby's skin is more sensitive. So it is worse to slap a baby than a horse, if both slaps are administered with equal force. But there must be some kind of blow—I don't know exactly what it would be, but perhaps a blow with a heavy stick—that would cause the horse as much pain as we cause a baby by a simple slap. That is what I mean by 'the same amount of pain' and if we consider it wrong to inflict that much pain on a baby for no good reason then we must, unless we are speciesists, consider it equally wrong to inflict the same amount of pain on a horse for no good reason.

There are other differences between humans and animals that cause other complications. Normal adult human beings have mental capacities that will, in certain circumstances, lead them to suffer more than animals would in the same circumstances. If, for instance, we decided to perform extremely painful or lethal scientific experiments on normal adult humans, kidnapped at random from public parks for this purpose, adults who entered parks would become fearful that they would be kidnapped. The resultant terror would be a form of suffering additional to the pain of the experiment. The same experiments performed on nonhuman animals would cause less suffering since the animals would not have the anticipatory dread of being kidnapped and experimented upon. This does not mean, of course, that it would be *right* to perform the experiment on animals, but only that there is a reason, and one that is not speciesist, for preferring to use animals rather than normal adult humans, if the experiment is to be done at all. Note, however, that the same argument gives us a reason for preferring to use human infants—orphans perhaps—or severely intellectually disabled humans for experiments, rather than adults, since infants and severely intellectually disabled humans would also have no idea of what was going to happen to them. As far as this argument is concerned, nonhuman animals and infants and severely intellectually disabled humans are in the same category; and if we use this argument to justify experiments on nonhuman animals we have to ask ourselves whether we are also prepared to allow experiments on human infants and severely intellectually disabled adults. If we make a distinction between animals and these humans, how can we do it, other than on the basis of a morally indefensible preference for members of our own species?

There are many areas in which the superior mental powers of normal adult humans make a difference: anticipation, more detailed memory, greater knowledge of what is happening, and so on. These differences explain why a human dying from cancer is likely to suffer more than a mouse. It is the mental anguish that makes the human's position so much harder to bear. Yet these differences do not all point to greater suffering on the part of the normal human being. Sometimes animals may suffer more because of their more limited understanding. If, for instance, we are taking prisoners in wartime we can explain to them that while they must submit to capture, search, and confinement they will not otherwise be harmed and will be set free at the conclusion of hostilities. If we capture wild animals, however, we cannot explain that we are not threatening their lives. A wild animal cannot distinguish an attempt to overpower and confine from an attempt to kill; the one causes as much terror as the other.

It may be objected that comparisons of the sufferings of different species are impossible to make, and that for this reason when the interests of animals and humans clash, the principle of equality gives no guidance. It is true that comparisons of suffering between members of different species cannot be made precisely. Nor, for that matter, can comparisons of suffering between different human beings be made precisely. Precision is not essential.... [E]ven if we were to prevent the infliction of suffering on animals only when the interests of humans will not be affected to anything like the extent that animals are affected, we would be forced to make radical changes in our treatment of animals that would involve our diet, the farming methods we use, experimental procedures in many fields of science, our approach to wildlife and to hunting, trapping and the wearing of furs, and areas of entertainment like circuses, rodeos, and zoos. As a result, the total quantity of suffering caused would be greatly reduced; so greatly that it is hard to imagine any other change of moral attitude that would cause so great a reduction in the total sum of suffering in the universe. . . .

SPECIESISM IN PRACTICE

Animals as Food

For most people in modern, urbanised societies, the principal form of contact with nonhuman animals is at meal times. The use of animals for food is probably the oldest and the most widespread form of animal use. There is also a sense in which it is the most basic form of animal use, the foundation stone on which rests the belief that animals exist for our pleasure and convenience.

If animals count in their own right, our use of animals for food becomes questionable—especially when animal flesh is a luxury rather than a necessity. Eskimos living in an environment where they must kill animals for food or starve might be justified in claiming that their interest in surviving overrides that of the animals they kill. Most of us cannot defend our diet in this way. Citizens of industrialised societies can easily obtain an adequate diet without the use of animal flesh. The overwhelming weight of medical evidence indicates that animal flesh is not necessary for good health or longevity. Nor is animal production in industrialised societies an efficient way of producing food, since most of the animals consumed have been fattened on grains and other foods that we could have eaten directly. When we feed these grains to animals, only about 10 per cent of the nutritional value remains as meat for human consumption. So, with the exception of animals raised entirely on grazing land unsuitable for crops, animals are eaten neither for health, nor to increase our food supply. Their flesh is a luxury, consumed because people like its taste.

In considering the ethics of the use of animal flesh for human food in industrialised societies, we are considering a situation in which a relatively minor human interest must be balanced against the lives and welfare of the animals involved. The principle of equal consideration of interests does not allow major interests to be sacrificed for minor interests.

The case against using animals for food is at its strongest when animals are made to lead miserable lives so that their flesh can be made available to humans at the lowest possible cost. Modern forms of intensive farming apply science and technology to the attitude that animals are objects for us to use. In order to have meat on the table at a price that people can afford, our society tolerates methods of meat production that confine sentient animals in cramped, unsuitable conditions for the entire duration of their lives. Animals are treated like machines that convert fodder into flesh, and any innovation that results in a higher 'conversion ratio' is liable to be adopted. As one authority on the subject has said, 'Cruelty is acknowledged only when profitability ceases.' To avoid speciesism we must stop these practices. Our custom is all the support that factory farmers need. The decision to cease giving them that support may be difficult, but it is less difficult than it would have been for a white Southerner to go against the traditions of his society and free his slaves; if we do not change our dietary habits, how can we censure those slaveholders who would not change their own way of living?

These arguments apply to animals who have been reared in factory farms —which means that we should not eat chicken, pork, or veal, unless we know that the meat we are eating was not produced by factory farm methods. The same is true of beef that has come from cattle kept in crowded feedlots (as most beef does in the United States). Eggs will come from hens kept in small wire cages, too small even to allow them to stretch their wings, unless the eggs are specifically sold as 'free range' (or unless one lives in a relatively enlightened country like Switzerland, which has prohibited the cage system of keeping hens).

... Apart from taking their lives there are ... many other things done to animals in order to bring them cheaply to our dinner table. Castration, the separation of mother and young, the breaking up of herds, branding, transporting, and finally the moments of slaughter—all of these are likely to involve suffering and do not take the animals' interests into account. Perhaps animals could be reared on a small scale without suffering in these ways, but it does not seem economical or practical to do so on the scale required for feeding our large urban populations. In any case, the important question is not whether animal flesh *could* be produced without suffering, but whether the flesh we are considering buying was produced without suffering. Unless we can be confident that it was, the principle of equal consideration of interests implies

that it was wrong to sacrifice important interests of the animal in order to satisfy less important interests of our own; consequently we should boycott the end result of this process.

For those of us living in cities where it is difficult to know how the animals we might eat have lived and died, this conclusion brings us close to a vegetarian way of life....

Experimenting on Animals

Perhaps the area in which speciesism can most clearly be observed is the use of animals in experiments. Here the issue stands out starkly, because experimenters often seek to justify experimenting on animals by claiming that the experiments lead us to discoveries about humans; if this is so, the experimenter must agree that human and nonhuman animals are similar in crucial respects. For instance, if forcing a rat to choose between starving to death and crossing an electrified grid to obtain food tells us anything about the reactions of humans to stress, we must assume that the rat feels stress in this kind of situation.

People sometimes think that all animal experiments serve vital medical purposes, and can be justified on the grounds that they relieve more suffering than they cause. This comfortable belief is mistaken. Drug companies test new shampoos and cosmetics they are intending to market by dripping concentrated solutions of them into the eyes of rabbits, in a test known as the Draize test. (Pressure from the animal liberation movement has led several cosmetic companies to abandon this practice. An alternative test, not using animal, has now been found. Nevertheless, many companies, including some of the largest, still continue to perform the Draize test.) Food additives, including artificial colourings and preservatives, are tested by what is known as the LD50—a test designed to find the 'lethal dose', or level of consumption that will make 50 per cent of a sample of animals die. In the process nearly all of the animals are made very sick before some finally die and others pull through. These tests are not necessary to prevent human suffering: even if there were no alternative to the use of animals to test the safety of the products, we already have enough shampoos and food colourings. There is no need to develop new ones that might be dangerous.

In many countries, the armed forces perform atrocious experiments on animals that rarely comes to light. To give just one example: at the U.S. Armed Forces Radiobiology Institute, in Bethesda, Maryland, rhesus monkeys have been trained to run inside a large wheel. If they slow down too much, the wheel slows down, too, and the monkeys get an electric shock. Once the monkeys are trained to run for long periods, they are given lethal doses of radiation. Then, while sick and vomiting, they are forced to continue to run until they drop. This is supposed to provide information on the capacities of soldiers to continue to fight after a nuclear attack.

Nor can all university experiments be defended on the grounds that they relieve more suffering than they inflict. Three experimenters at Princeton University kept 256 young rats without food or water until they died. They concluded that young rats under conditions of fatal thirst and starvation are much more active than normal adult rats given food and water. In a well-known series of experiments that went on for more than fifteen years, H. F. Harlow of the Primate Research Center, Madison, Wisconsin, reared monkeys under conditions of maternal deprivation and total isolation. He found that in this way he could reduce the monkeys to a state in which, when placed among normal monkeys, they sat huddled in a corner in a condition of persistent depression and fear. Harlow also produced monkey mothers so neurotic that they smashed their infant's face into the floor and rubbed it back and forth. Although Harlow himself is no longer alive, some of his former students at other U.S. universities continue to perform variations on his experiments.

In these cases, and many others like them, the benefits to humans are either nonexistent or uncertain, while the losses to members of other species are certain and real. Hence the experiments indicate a failure to give equal consideration to the interests of all beings, irrespective of species.

In the past, argument about animal experimentation has often missed this point because it has been put in absolutist terms: would the opponent of experimentation be prepared to let thousands die from a terrible disease that could be cured by experimenting on one animal? This is a purely hypothetical question, since experiments do not have such dramatic results, but as long as its hypothetical nature is clear, I think the question should be answered affirmatively—in other words, if one, or even a dozen animals had to suffer experiments in order to save thousands, I would think it right and in accordance with equal consideration of interests that they should do so. This, at any rate, is the answer a utilitarian must give. Those who believe in absolute rights might hold that it is always wrong to sacrifice one being, whether human or animal, for the benefit of another. In that case the experiment should not be carried out, whatever the consequences.

To the hypothetical question about saving thousands of people through a single experiment on an animal, opponents of speciesism can reply with a hypothetical question of their own: would experimenters be prepared to perform their experiments on orphaned humans with severe and irreversible brain damage if that were the only way to save thousands? (I say 'orphaned' in order to avoid the complication of the feelings of the human parents.) If experimenters are not prepared to use orphaned humans with severe and irreversible brain damage, their readiness to use nonhuman animals seems to discriminate on the basis of species alone, since apes, monkeys, dogs, cats, and even mice and rats are more intelligent, more aware of what is happening to them, more sensitive to pain, and so on, than many severely braindamaged humans barely surviving in hospital wards and other institutions. There seems to be no morally relevant characteristic that such humans have that nonhuman animals lack. Experimenters, then, show bias in favour of their own species whenever they carry out experiments on nonhuman animals for purposes that they would not think justified them in using human beings at an equal or lower level of sentience, awareness, sensitivity, and so on. If this bias were eliminated, the number of experiments performed on animals would be greatly reduced.

Other Forms of Speciesism

I have concentrated on the use of animals as food and in research, since these are examples of large-scale, systematic speciesism. They are not, of course, the only areas in which the principle of equal consideration of interests, extended beyond the human species, has practical implications. There are many other areas that raise similar issues, including the fur trade, hunting in all its different forms, circuses, rodeos, zoos, and the pet business. Since the philosophical questions raised by these issues are not very different from those raised by the use of animals as food and in research, I shall leave it to the reader to apply the appropriate ethical principles to them.

NOTES

1. My views on animals first appeared in *The New York Review of Books*, 5 April 1973, under the title 'Animal Liberation'. This article was a review of R. and S. Godlovitch and J. Harris (eds.), *Animals, Men and Morals* (London, 1972). A more complete statement was published as *Animal Liberation*, 2d ed. (New York, 1990). Richard Ryder charts the history of changing attitudes towards speciesism in *Animal Revolution* (Oxford, 1989).

Among other works arguing for a drastic revision in our present attitudes to animals are Stephen Clark, *The Moral Status of Animals* (Oxford, 1977); and Tom Regan *The Case for Animal Rights* (Berkeley, 1983). *Animal Rights and Human Obligations*, 2d ed., edited by T. Regan and P. Singer (Englewood Cliffs, N.J., 1989) is a collection of essays, old and new, both for and against attributing rights to animals or duties to humans in respect of animals. P. Singer (ed.), *In Defence of Animals* (Oxford, 1985), collect essays by both activists and theorists involved with the animal liberation movement. Steve Sapontzis, *Morals, Reason and Animals* (Philadelphia, 1987), is a detailed and sympathetic philosophical analysis of arguments about animal liberation, while R. G. Frey, *Rights, Killing and Suffering* (Oxford, 1983), and Michael Leahy, *Against Liberation* (London, 1991), offer philosophical critiques of the animal liberation position. Mary Midgley, *Animals and Why They Matter* (Harmondsworth, Middlesex, 1983), is a readable and often penetrating account of these issues. James Rachels, *Created from Animals* (Oxford, 1990), draws the moral implications of the Darwinian Revolution in our thinking about our place among the animals. Finally, Lori Gruen's 'Animals' in P. Singer (ed.), *A Companion to Ethics*, explores the predominant recent approaches to the issue.

Bentham's defence of animals, quoted in the section 'Racism and Speciesism' is from his *Introduction to the Principles of Morals and Legislation*, chap. 18, sec. 1, n.

A more detailed description of modern farming conditions can be found in *Animal Liberation*, chap. 3; and in James Mason and Peter Singer, *Animal Factories*, 2d ed. (New York, 1990). Similarly, *Animal Liberation*, chap. 2, contains a fuller discussion of the use of animals in research than is possible in this book, but see also Richard Ryder, *Victims of Science*, 2d ed. (Fontwell, Sussex, 1983). Publication details of the experiment on rhesus monkeys carried out at the U.S. Armed Forces Radiobiology Institute are: Carol Frantz, 'Effects of Mixed Neutron-gamma Total-body Irradiation on Physical Activity Performance of Rhesus Monkeys', *Radiation Research*, vol. 101 (1985): 434–41. The experiments at Princeton University on starving rats, and those by H. F. Harlow on isolating monkeys, referred to in the sub-section 'Experimenting on Animals', were originally published in *Journal of Comparative and Physiological Psychology*, vol. 78 (1972): 202, *Proceedings of the National Academy of Science*, vol. 54 (1965): 90, and *Engineering and Science*, vol. 33, no. 6 (April 1970): 8. On the continuation of Harlow's work, see *Animal Liberation*, 2d ed., pp. 34–5.

NO
Michael P. T. Leahy

AGAINST LIBERATION: PUTTING ANIMALS IN PERSPECTIVE

Bernard Williams touches upon several themes... which will directly affect the practical conclusions of this [discussion]:[1]

> A concern for nonhuman animals is indeed a proper part of human life, but we can acquire it, cultivate it, and teach it only in terms of our understanding of our selves. Human beings both have that understanding and are the objects of it, and this is one of the basic respects in which our ethical relations to each other must always be different from our relations to other animals. Before one gets to the question of how animals should be treated, there is the fundamental point that this is the only question there can be: how they should be treated. The choice can only be whether animals benefit from our practices or are harmed by them. This is why speciesism is falsely modelled on racism and sexism, which really are prejudices. To suppose that there is an ineliminable white or male understanding of the world, and to think that the only choice is whether blacks or women should benefit from 'our' (white, male) practices or be harmed by them: this is already to be prejudiced. But in the case of human relations to animals, the analogues to such thoughts are simply correct. (Williams 1985: 118–19)

The message here is straightforward. If we are required to make a decision which has consequences for other people, and if we wish to treat them properly, then it is vital that we take into account their own views on the matter. Simply to decide upon the basis of what *we* think is best for them can be a form of prejudice. ...

With animals it is different. The *best* that can be hoped for, on their behalf, is that human beings are kindly disposed towards them. ...

Most of the calls for the abolition of our routines involving animals, particularly those appearing in the Press or the propaganda material issued by organisations like Animal Aid or the League Against Cruel Sports, ignore ... [a] basic logical point. So-called 'horror stories' (gory illustrations depicting the de-beaking of turkeys, dogs being hanged, huntsmen exulting over the corpse of a fox, or reports of a senile researcher who failed properly to anaesthetise his animal subjects) may well be effective copy and have an impact upon gullible readers but are of limited argumentative worth. A genuine case for abolition, if it is so based, needs to establish both that the alleged abuses are as stated and that they are endemic to the practice; thus *unavoidable*.

KILLING FOR FOOD

The number of animals killed to satisfy our taste for meat dwarfs those used in the other main areas of controversy, those of experimentation and hunting. Richard Askwith (1988: 22) gives the British Home Office figures for 1986, which are a typical comparison for the UK. Just over 3 million experiments were performed upon animals, mostly rats and mice. Richard Ryder's figures for 1987 are slightly higher at 3.6 million (1989: 242).[2] UK Government statistics for 1988 and 1989 show a steady decline in the use of research animals since 1977 (Highfield 1990). But around 400 *million* animals are eaten annually in the UK. The irony, of course, is that since a considerable proportion of these were bred for the purpose, a large number of animals would not otherwise have lived were they not destined to die prematurely. (Askwith also mentions 'some 100 million birds and small rodents' estimated to have fallen prey to domestic cats, although surely such a statistic could hardly be arrived at with any confidence.)

What these figures will not have taken account of is, for example, the 34,000 kilos of frogs legs imported in 1986 mainly from Bangladesh and Indonesia. Frog-catching gangs ensure that this is a thriving trade in these countries although it is conducted in hideously unhygienic conditions and there are adverse ecological implications due to the increase in malarial and other waterborne pests. Partly for these reasons, and partly due to pressure from western organisations like Compassion in World Farming, the Indian government has recently banned the slaughter of frogs for this purpose.

A related example, which provides a useful introduction to a more detailed look at the complaints levelled at our own practices, frequently surfaces in the national Press. Campaigns are being waged against the Republic of Korea where laws forbidding the eating of cats and dogs, the latter a traditional source of medicinal potency, are openly flouted in the ubiquitous 'boshintang' (dog-meat soup) houses. 'Gae sogu', a dog-meat wine, is also popular. Yet the so-called 'International Alert' issued by the World Society for the Protection of Animals, which highlights the charges, is curiously ill-focussed. Its petition refers to the 'inherent cruelty' of dog eating (the use of 'inherent' seeming to imply that abuse is inevitable) but the supporting literature does little to substantiate this. The dogs are raised mainly on breeding farms and are described as 'generally well kept in outdoor pens with adequate room'. The traditional method of slaughter by slow strangulation might well seem revolting but that is admitted to be a 'waning practice'. Its replacement by 'a sharp blow on the back of the neck or a blow from a mallet to the forehead' is relatively humane if administered skillfully. The transport to market is certainly slipshod but the dogs illustrated look in good condition and, indeed, would not sell if they were dilapidated since the animals are generally sold live. If there *are* abuses then they are clearly avoidable, and this, as we have seen, provides inadequate grounds for abolishing the (in Korea's case admittedly illegal) practice of dog eating....

The liberationists, with the possible exception of Rollin, do seem to regard the use of animals for food as the cardinal vice, although it is run close by the fuss over furs and field sports. Perhaps it is due to the disproportionate numbers killed for food, or possibly that becoming vegetarian is an unmistakable gesture that it is within anyone's competence to make. From it follows a series of hardline implications for the other practical issues. The only other dissenter is Mary Midgley, who, with good sense, questions the pride of place given to an unambiguous vegetarianism (1983: 25–7): 'What the animals need most urgently is probably a campaign for treating them better before they are eaten', and she augments this by advocating a gradual move towards the consumption of less meat (27). She needs to have added the caution that much depends upon the reasons why people are vegetarians. My brother just dislikes the taste of meat and is faintly surprised that other people do not. But he is not critical of meat eaters. (He is, I suspect, in a minority among vegetarians.) But if there were a sea change, and they became the majority that meat eaters are at present, and if this were fueled by the arguments of Regan or Singer, then surely it would be reasonable to expect a knock-on effect in the other contentious areas.

Considerations of Utility: Human Welfare

In *Animal Liberation* and all his subsequent writings on the topic, Singer employs his animal-enhanced equality principle to argue that the consequences for all concerned would on balance be best served by almost total vegetarianism. (The 'almost' allows for exceptional circumstances where, let us say, killing is the only way to obtain food (1979: 55,

105).) What are the interests put in the scales? Firstly, there are considerations of *human* well-being. The evidence that it is inefficient to use meat for food is well documented. If the grains, soy beans and fishmeal, which are used in the feeding of food animals in the developed world, were consumed directly by human beings then there would be something like a ninefold gain in the nutritional spinoff. In other words, 90 per cent of the nutrients are lost in the transformation of the grains into meat. It is worth noting that the beneficiaries would not be the members of the developed world: 'If we stopped feeding animals on grains, soybeans and fishmeal the amount of food saved would—if distributed to those who need it—be more than enough to end hunger throughout the world' (1979: 160).

Now the ending of all hunger would undoubtedly benefit many in underdeveloped countries in the short term; although the demographic and political implications might be slightly chilling if one ponders upon international stability in the next century. But what of the claimed benefits for the health of developed nations? The only fact upon which dieticians seem agreed is that in general we eat too much meat and too few vegetables, which distorts the balance of fat in our bodies. Research suggests that the incidence of cancer, cardiovascular complaints and other degenerative diseases, quite apart from the general ill-health resulting from obesity and lack of exercise, diminishes if our intake of meat, and other sources of fat, is lowered. For instance, in Japan the diet, still mainly fish and rice, contains considerably less fat than that of Europe, North America and Australia. The Japanese also enjoy a lower incidence of cancer. But as Carl Simonton, the radiation oncologist prominent in the holistic health movement, and others point out, this does not isolate diet as the sole or even the main cause and it is likely that cultural factors, for which Japan is unique among industrialised nations, may be more significant (Simonton *et al.* 1986: 38–40)....

Utility and Western Society

But let us, for argument's sake, concede the nutritional point. Whatever weight this would add to the utilitarian scales would need to be colossal to offset the social and economic ills which might well follow. Frey in *Rights, Killing and Suffering* (1983) paints a detailed picture of the possible downfall of whole economies the minutiae of which, although hinting strongly at overkill, are nonetheless plausible enough to be disturbing (197–203). I will mention only three areas of potential catastrophe. In the first place, a huge number of industries would be undermined, bringing the misery of unemployment to employees and their families where alternative jobs were not available. Many localities in Europe are dominated by livestock and poultry farming and vaster areas such as the states of Iowa, South Dakota and Texas are deeply involved. Argentina, Australia and New Zealand would have a considerable proportion of their national economies wiped out. Secondly, our social lives would need readjustment. If it is difficult to change habits like smoking or drinking, despite the best of intentions, then the switch to nut steaks and vegetable lasagne might be just as painful, and for those forced to it because of the unavailability of meat it would also be deeply resented. Most traditional French, Italian, British, American and even Oriental restaurants would cease to exist in their present forms. Thirdly, the idea of the European countryside, valuable to many as a source of beauty, history, and national pride would also be transformed. Sheep would not safely graze nor would spring lambs nor calves; the average farmer could hardly be expected to stock them for old times' sake. Clark is beady-eyed in his dismissal of what he seems to regard as sentimentality:

> We are entitled to ask why it matters, if it is true, that there should be no such poor slaves to be seen. Because we get aesthetic pleasure from the scene, and are therefore entitled to instigate whatever distress be necessary to achieve our satisfaction? (Clark 1977: 65)

His alternatives are predictably bleak: 'Much of what is now sheep country could profitably be reforested with nut-trees' (1977: 60). Rural Britain would more and more resemble parts of the American mid-west. Life would be strange indeed.

Singer's attempt to duck these difficulties by arguing that social changes of this magnitude would need to be phased in slowly will not survive scrutiny. The problems would re-emerge in other forms. What, for example, would be the time-scale envisaged? Thirty years? Would impatient abolitionists like Regan be prepared to wait that long? If Frey is an exponent of gloom and doom, then Regan is a master of myopia on this issue and shows an unbecoming lack of sensitivity which suggests that his answer would be No. In the first place, he argues, farming is a risky business (he compares it to 'road racing') and if the demand for his products dries up then it is just bad luck on the farmer and his dependants. In the wider context Regan contends that, 'though the (economic) heavens fall' there is no case for protecting society 'if the protection in question involves violating the rights of others [viz. farm animals]' (1983: 346–7).

The Dark Side of Farming

Most vegetarians are so, I suspect, primarily because they object to the death and what they see as the suffering to which animals are consigned by meat eating. The suffering involved which receives most publicity takes place in intensive or factory farms, although it is not confined to them. These are a practical necessity[3] and it would be quite impossible to meet the present demand for meat and dairy products, except in certain rural areas, from the products of traditional farms that were the order of the day in Europe and North America up until the Second World War:

> Now, virtually all of our poultry products and about half of our milk and red meat come from animals mass-produced in huge factory-like systems. In some of the more intensively managed 'confinement' operations, animals are crowded in pens and cages stacked up like so many shipping crates.... There are no pastures, no streams, no seasons, not even day and night. Health and productivity come not from frolics ... but from syringes and additive laced feed.... The typical cage in today's egg factory holds four or five hens on a 12- by 18-inch floor area. (Mason 1985: 89, 91)

Jim Mason is writing of Britain in the early 1980s. The percentages for the rest of modernised Europe, with the exception of Switzerland, are slightly higher and for North America they are higher still. Patrick Sutherland estimates that of 170 million farm animals in Britain 'about two thirds never walk on or eat grass' (1989: 62).

Horror stories abound, originally fuelled by the publication of Ruth Harrison's *Animal Machines* (1964), a book which in Britain directly influenced the setting up of the first parliamentary inquiry into the new methods of animal husbandry under the chairmanship of F. W. R. Brambell. (It reported in 1965; nothing was acted upon for about six years and even then very little was implemented.) Close confinement encourages aggression and distorts instinctive behaviour patterns. The result is often cannibalism, especially in chickens and turkeys, which are debeaked and often have their toes cut by the same hot-knife machine as a preventative. Pigs also are prone to the habit. With these it is often initiated by acute tail-biting which gets out of hand 'and then the attacking pig or pigs continue to eat further into the back. If the situation is not attended to, the pig will die and be eaten' (quoted by Mason 1985: 95). The factories are rife with diseases needing attention and routine dosing of the animals with vitamins and drugs takes place, often to the point of dependency.

Singer, like Ruth Harrison, gives prominence to the methods employed in the production of veal that were pioneered in Holland. By now, due in part to media coverage, these are fairly well known. The calves, when only a few days old, are tethered by the neck in a stall about 60 cms wide and 150 cms long, until they are too large to turn. It has a slatted wooden floor and is often without bedding lest it be eaten. The calves remain 'crated' until taken out for slaughter between three and four months later during which time they are fed a milk-derivative liquid diet 'enhanced' in the usual ways with vitamins, medication, and sometimes growth-promoters. The feed needs to be as iron-free as possible in order that the eventual meat will be the light colour preferred by consumers. Because the animal is denied the natural iron in what would be its natural food it develops anaemia. As Singer puts it 'pale pink flesh is in fact anaemic flesh' (Regan and Singer 1976: 32). This is not the end of its troubles. The instincts to suck and later to eat roughage are often vented on the wood of its stall. Stomach ulcers and other digestive disorders are rife and there is a high mortality rate amongst veal calves despite their brief lifetime.

Defects of Utilitarian Abolition

Now Singer thinks it is undeniable that what we have here is a catalogue of inequality. Unless we are confident that the meat we eat was produced without suffering, the equality principle 'implies that it was wrong to sacrifice important interests of the animal in order to satisfy less important interests of our own' (1979: 57). However, this conclusion is not without its difficulties.

1. Even if *all* meat and dairy products were produced by intensive husbandry and the alleged abuses were rife it would nonetheless be perfectly fair to argue that the possible catastrophic consequences of widespread vegetarianism for human beings, which have been pointed out, would more than outweigh the continued suffering of the animals. Clark not only dissents but is hopeful enough to scorn utilitarian considerations about humane husbandry and so forth:

> This at least cannot be true, that it is proper to be the cause of avoidable ill... this at least is dogma. And if this minimal principle be accepted, there is no other honest course than the immediate rejection of all flesh-foods

and most bio-medical research. (Clark 1977: Preface)

2. Not all meat and dairy products are produced intensively and Singer seems to allow that if we are confident that ours came from animals humanely bred and slaughtered then we are doing nothing wrong in eating it. Admittedly he has some reservations even about free-range farming such as the need for castration, transportation and slaughtering techniques but, as Francis and Norman point out (1978: 516), since Singer himself thinks that much of this suffering could be eliminated, it is simply a matter of working to bring these improvements about. Someone concerned at the suffering might well think it more appropriate to work for reformation rather than abolition.

3. Although it is undoubtedly the case that farm animals *do* suffer from many of the horrors of intensive husbandry (it cannot be pleasant for a pig to be eaten alive) there are serious questions to be asked about the extent and nature of the alleged suffering.... Injuries in war and disasters provide numerous anecdotes of the anaesthetic effects of shock; a doctor in the aftermath of London's Clapham rail crash of 1988 reported having treated several victims lying or sitting by the track in a state of bewilderment and oblivious of serious wounds; in one case an ankle was completely severed other than for a few shreds of flesh. In most of the accounts of animal abuse, be they in factory farm or primate laboratory, even the more sensitive monkeys are portrayed in similar ways: comatose, agitated, even neurotic, often with serious injuries, but not necessarily *in pain*. This is so even of accounts by activists anxious

to maximise the horror (Pacheco and Francione 1985:136–7, Barnes 1985: 160). We owe it to clarity to disentangle the varieties of suffering possible in a given situation.

Here is another example of the need for vigilance when assessing usually well-intentioned accounts of distress. Singer, in his depiction of the hapless veal calf, protests that, 'Obviously the calves sorely miss their mothers. They also miss something to suck on' (Regan and Singer 1976: 31). The previously-mentioned use of the wood of their stalls as a substitute is adequate grounds for the second complaint. But to describe their state as one of *missing their mothers* sounds suspiciously like hyperbole designed to wring illicit sympathy from the reader.... Are we meant to take it seriously? Premature babies are routinely taken from their mothers on the maternity ward into intensive care, or sterile areas, often for long periods and although their mothers might miss them, it would be thought sentimental to claim the opposite. What *is* true is that the absence of, say, its mother's milk may affect the baby's medical condition and, to this extent, it misses the milk (although unable to be aware of the fact) but not its mother. The baby can certainly suffer complications if deprived of mother's milk and it might well be claimed that talk of its missing its mother is a special language-game pointing only to the source of the deprivation, but Singer is certainly not using the phrase with this in mind. His use is anthropomorphic. The calf is supposed to miss its mother as it might be said of a 4-year-old child. But this requires the *self*-awareness of a developing language-user: a grasp of the significance of its mother, her absence and hoped-for return, and so on. This is something that not even a Washoe or Lucy,* far less a baby calf, begins to approach....

Conclusion

It is certainly possible to defend vegetarianism. Apart from merely disliking the taste of meat, like that of anything else, one might also decide that the cruelty involved in some intensive farming, although not endemic to it, is unacceptable even in the short term. Others might be persuaded by the current furore over the possible spread of spongiform encephalopathy (BSE) to nonruminants such as poultry and pigs, and decide to give up all meat (contrary to the majority of expert opinion). But it is equally justifiable to eat meat whilst being concerned about current abuses in its production and preparation, none of which, given time and energy, are thought by bodies like the RSPCA, [Royal Society for the Prevention of Cruelty to Animals] to be irremovable. Intensive farming is, after all, in its infancy and the campaigns against it, both in Britain and the USA, have resulted already in remedial legislation on such issues as debeaking, overcrowding, cage sizes, and the use of steroids and other growth promoters.

But attempts to convince us that the eating of meat and fish is an evil invasion of the inalienable rights of animals and that it should cease forthwith are a sham. They can only succeed with the help either of opportunistic flights of fancy ... or by otherwise obscuring the differences between creatures like ourselves, who use language, and those that do not. The result of so doing is the sad and mischievous error of seeing little or no

*[Washoe and Lucy are apes that have been taught to use American Sign Language.—Ed.]

moral difference between the painless killing of chickens and that of unwanted children.

NOTES

1. I have benefited greatly from reading Williams but I intend no implication that he would support my conclusions. But it is fair to quote his comment on Clark (1977): 'I cannot see why, on any realistic view of our and other animals' "natural" relations to one another, it should be thought to exclude our eating them' (1985: 216 fn.).

2. Readers who would like to follow up the more intricate details of the political campaigns of the 1970s and 1980s to further reforms of alleged animal abuse on every front, can find them in Ryder's *Animal Revolution* (1989: 261–71). The book also provides a useful general history of the issues. Ryder writes as a vehement critic of contemporary practices. He is a political activist and a supporter of both Singer and Regan.

3. Aided and abetted in Europe by EEC regulations which financially encourage farmers to take surplus land out of use rather than to employ it in using less intensive methods.

REFERENCES

Askwith, R. (1988) 'Experiments on animals: time to open our eyes', *Sunday Telegraph Magazine*, 10 July.

Barnes, D. J. (1985) 'A matter of change', in P. Singer (ed.) *In Defence of Animals*, Oxford: Basil Blackwell.

Clark, S. R. L. (1977). *The Moral Status of Animals*, Oxford: Clarendon Press.

Francis, L. P. and Norman, R. (1978) 'Some animals are more equal than others', *Philosophy*, 53.

Frey, R. G. (1980) *Interests and Rights: The Case Against Animals*, Oxford: Clarendon Press.

—— (1983) *Rights, Killing and Suffering*, Oxford: Basil Blackwell.

Harrison, R. (1964). *Animal Machines*, London: Vincent Stuart.

Highfield, R. (1990) 'Animal tests lowest for 30 years', *Daily Telegraph*, 23 July.

Mason, J. (1985) 'Brave new farm?' in P. Singer (ed.) *In Defence of Animals*, Oxford: Basil Blackwell.

Midgley, M. (1983) *Animals and Why They Matter*, Harmondsworth: Penguin Books.

Pacheco, A. and Francione, A. (1985) "The Silver Spring monkeys', in P. Singer (ed.) *In Defence of Animals*, Oxford: Basil Blackwell.

Regan T. (1983) *The Case for Animal Rights*, Berkeley: University of California Press.

Regan, T. and Singer, P. (eds.) (1976) *Animal Rights and Human Obligations*, Englewood Cliffs, NJ: Prentice-Hall.

Rollin B. E. (1981) *Animal Rights and Human Morality*, Buffalo, NY: Prometheus Books.

Ryder, R. (1989) *Animal revolution: Changing Attitudes towards Speciesism*, Oxford: Basil Blackwell.

Simonton, O. C., Mathews-Simonton, S., and Creighton, J. L. (1986) *Getting Well Again*, London: Bantam Books.

Singer, P. (1979) *Practical Ethics*, Cambridge: Cambridge University Press.

—— (1983) *Animal Liberation*, Wellingborough: Thorsons. (First pub. 1975.)

—— (ed.) (1985) *In Defence of Animals*, Oxford: Basil Blackwell.

Sutherland, P. (1989) 'Farm Blight', *Independent Magazine*, 7 October.

Williams, B. (1985) *Ethics and the Limits of Philosophy*, London: Fontana Press.

POSTSCRIPT

Should Animals Be Liberated?

Sometimes animal liberationists make provocative-sounding claims that "all animals are equal." Singer makes an effort here to explain such ideas more carefully. His principle of equality does not mean that a mouse or a horse has moral standing equal to that of a human being but that pain (or pleasure) experienced by any being should be given equal consideration, whether that being is a mouse, a horse, or a human being. So important to Singer is the idea of pain or pleasure, and so irrelevant is the question of which species experiences the pain or pleasure, that Singer seems more than willing to blur the line between human beings and animals.

Leahy agrees that there are individual cases of animal abuse, but he does not believe that any radical change in the relation between human beings and animals is necessary. Leahy criticizes the anthropomorphic consideration of animals that is evident in the writings of animal liberationists. That is, he feels that they attribute to animals feelings or thoughts that only a human being could have. Leahy's charge of anthropomorphism is not just simply that liberationists are overly sentimental or emotional about animals. It goes to the heart of Singer's claim about animal suffering. He states that Singer's claim that calves raised for food "miss their mothers" is a good example of how liberationists attribute human emotions to animals to elicit sympathy. This is not to deny the suffering of such animals but only to deny that it can be described in human terms—terms that are unavailable to the animals. We know what it is for human beings to miss their mothers, but it would be a mistake to attribute this to animals.

A good historical account of Western attitudes toward animals is Richard D. Ryder, *Animal Revolution: Changing Attitudes Towards Speciesism* (Basil Blackwell, 1989). Other relevant sources are Jeremy Rifkin, *Beyond Beef: The Rise and Fall of the Cattle Culture* (E. P. Dutton, 1992); Greta Gaard, ed., *Ecofeminism: Women, Animals, Nature* (Temple University Press, 1993); F. Barbara Orlans, *In the Name of Science: Issues in Responsible Animal Experimentation* (Oxford University Press, 1993); Evelyn B. Pluhar, *Beyond Prejudice: The Moral Significance of Human and Nonhuman Animals* (Duke University Press, 1995); Bernard Rollin, *Farm Animal Welfare: Social, Biological, and Research Issues* (Iowa State University Press, 1995); David DeGrazia, *Taking Animals Seriously: Mental Life and Moral Status* (Cambridge University Press, 1996); Andrew Harnack, ed., *Animal Rights: Opposing Viewpoints* (Greenhaven Press, 1996); John Lawrence Hill, *The Case for Vegetarianism: Philosophy for a Small Planet* (Rowman & Littlefield, 1996); and Stephen R. L. Clark, *Animals and Their Moral Standing* (Routledge, 1997).

ISSUE 7

Should Welfare Benefits Be Unconditional?

YES: Trudy Govier, from "The Right to Eat and the Duty to Work," *Philosophy of the Social Sciences* (vol. 5, 1975)

NO: Tom Bethell, from "They Had a Dream," *National Review* (August 23, 1993)

ISSUE SUMMARY

YES: Canadian philosopher Trudy Govier argues that society does have an obligation to care for the less well off and that welfare benefits should be provided without being made contingent upon something (a willingness to work, for example).

NO: Tom Bethell, a contributing editor to the *National Review,* argues that a liberal social welfare policy encourages laziness and nonproductivity. He believes that the incentives of a generous welfare program encourage welfare dependency and discourage work and family life.

The first question that might be asked about the less well off is, How desperate are they? If it is the case that income and wealth simply vary, so that some people have more and some have less, then, unless we favor some strict form of egalitarianism, this economic discrepancy alone should not present a problem. But how should we respond if those who are less well off are unable to provide for themselves even basic needs, such as food, shelter, and medicine? Some social critics argue that a rich society that does not provide all members with the basic necessities is failing at a most fundamental level.

Clearly, some people in the United States (and in other similarly wealthy industrial nations) do not have even their basic needs met. In any large city, we can see people sleeping on sidewalks, next to subway grates, or under bridges. Moreover, the ranks of the homeless now include not only single men but also women, children, and families. If you live in a town where the homeless are not visible, the plight of the homeless may not be familiar to you firsthand, but it should be familiar from newspaper stories, magazine articles, and television reports. There is even a danger that the homeless have been overexposed in the media and that we have consequently become callous to them and insensitive to their problems.

Government statistics show that poverty and unemployment rates are particularly high among young urban minorities and for families headed by single women. Poor people in the United States are more likely to be victims of violent crimes, have higher infant mortality rates, and are less healthy than the general population.

In American society, which is predominantly capitalistic, people fulfill needs, including basic needs, through the mechanism of the marketplace —people purchase the goods and services they require. But the market does not provide for the needs of those who simply do not have the money to purchase basic goods.

How should we respond? One might argue that society has an obligation to meet the basic needs of its less fortunate citizens, whether those people can afford goods or not, and whether those people are willing to contribute to a free enterprise system or not. Another approach is to argue that the generous provision of welfare does a disservice to the very people welfare is supposed to help. Instead of being a temporary boost, it can trap people and hold them back from doing productive work.

In the following selections, Trudy Govier argues that society has a direct obligation to meet the fundamental needs of its members and to do so unconditionally (and not, for example, only on the condition that people are willing to work). Tom Bethell takes the position that unconditional welfare encourages welfare dependency and discourages productive work. Moreover, so-called workfare leads to the proliferation of government programs and more work for social workers.

YES

Trudy Govier

THE RIGHT TO EAT
AND THE DUTY TO WORK

Although the topic of welfare is not one with which philosophers have often concerned themselves, it is a topic which gives rise to many complex and fascinating questions—some in the area of political philosophy, some in the area of ethics, and some of a more practical kind. The variety of issues related to the subject of welfare makes it particularly necessary to be clear just which issue one is examining in a discussion of welfare. In a recent book on the subject, Nicholas Rescher asks:

> In what respects and to what extent is society, working through the instrumentality of the state, responsible for the welfare of its members? What demands for the promotion of his welfare can an individual reasonably make upon his society? These are questions to which no answer can be given in terms of some *a priori* approach with reference to universal ultimates. Whatever answer can appropriately be given will depend, in the final analysis, on what the society decides it should be.[1]

Rescher raises this question only to avoid it. His response to his own question is that a society has all and only those responsibilities for its members that it thinks it has. Although this claim is trivially true as regards legal responsibilities, it is inadequate from a moral perspective. If one imagines the case of an affluent society which leaves the blind, the disabled, and the needy to die of starvation, the incompleteness of Rescher's account becomes obvious. In this imagined case one is naturally led to raise the question as to whether those in power ought to supply those in need with the necessities of life. Though the needy have no legal right to welfare benefits of any kind, one might very well say that they ought to have such a right. It is this claim which I propose to discuss here.

I shall approach this issue by examining three positions which may be adopted in response to it. These are:

1. *The Individualist Position:* Even in an affluent society, one ought not to have any legal right to state-supplied welfare benefits.

2. *The Permissive Position:* In a society with sufficient resources, one ought to have an unconditional legal right to receive state-supplied welfare benefits. (That is, one's right to receive such benefits ought not to depend on one's behaviour; it should be guaranteed.)

3. *The Puritan Position:* In a society with sufficient resources one ought to have a legal right to state-supplied welfare benefits; this right ought to be conditional, however, on one's willingness to work....

1. The Individualist View

It might be maintained that a person in need has no legitimate moral claim on those around him and that the hypothetical inattentive society which left its blind citizens to beg or starve cannot rightly be censured for doing so. This view is vividly portrayed in the writings of Ayn Rand and her followers.[2] The Individualist sets a high value on uncoerced personal choice. He sees each person as a responsible agent who is able to make his own decisions and to plan his own life. He insists that with the freedom to make decisions goes responsibility for the consequences of those decisions. A person has every right, for example, to spend ten years of his life studying Sanskrit—but if, as a result of this choice, he is unemployable, he ought not to expect others to labour on his behalf. No one has a proper claim on the labour of another, or on the income ensuing from that labour, unless he can repay the labourer in a way acceptable to that labourer himself. Government welfare schemes provide benefits from funds gained largely by taxing earned income. One cannot "opt out" of such schemes. To the Individualist, this means

that a person is forced to work part of his time for others.

Suppose that a man works forty hours and earns two hundred dollars. Under modern-day taxation, it may well be that he can spend only two-thirds of that money as he chooses. The rest is taken by government and goes to support programmes which the working individual may not himself endorse. The beneficiaries of such programmes —those beneficiaries who do not work themselves—are as though they have slaves working for them. Backed by the force which government authorities can command, they are able to exist on the earnings of others. Those who support them do not do so voluntarily, out of charity; they do so on government command.

> Someone across the street is unemployed. Should you be taxed extra to pay for his expenses? Not at all. You have not injured him, you are not responsible for the fact that he is unemployed (unless you are a senator or bureaucrat who agitated for further curtailing of business which legislation passed, with the result that your neighbour was laid off by the curtailed business). You may voluntarily wish to help him out, or better still, try to get him a job to put him on his feet again; but since you have initiated no aggressive act against him, and neither purposefully nor accidentally injured him in any way, you should not be legally penalized for the fact of his unemployment.[3]

The Individualist need not lack concern for those in need. He may give generously to charity; he might give more generously still, if his whole income were his to use, as he would like it to be. He may also believe that, as a matter of empirical fact, existing government programmes do not actually help the poor. They support a cumbersome bureaucracy and they use financial resources which, if untaxed, might be used by those with initiative to pursue job-creating endeavours. The thrust of the Individualist's position is that each person owns his own body and his own labour; thus each person is taken to have a virtually unconditional right to the income which that labour can earn him in a free market place. For anyone to preempt part of a worker's earnings without that worker's voluntary consent is tantamount to robbery. And the fact that the government is the intermediary through which this deed is committed does not change its moral status one iota.

On an Individualist's view, those in need should be cared for by charities or through other schemes to which contributions are voluntary. Many people may wish to insure themselves against unforeseen calamities and they should be free to do so. But there is no justification for non-optional government schemes financed by taxpayers money....

2. The Permissive View
Directly contrary to the Individualist view of welfare is what I have termed the Permissive view. According to this view, in a society which has sufficient resources so that everyone could be supplied with the necessities of life, every individual ought to be given the legal right to social security, and this right ought not to be conditional in any way upon an individual's behaviour. *Ex hypothesi* the society which we are discussing has sufficient goods to provide everyone with food, clothing, shelter and other necessities. Someone who does without these basic goods is scarcely living at all, and a society which takes no steps to change this state of affairs implies by its inaction that the life of such a person is

without value. It does not execute him; but it may allow him to die. It does not put him in prison; but it may leave him with a life of lower quality than that of some prison inmates. A society which can rectify these circumstances and does not can justly be accused of imposing upon the needy either death or lifelong deprivation. And those characteristics which make a person needy—whether they be illness, old age, insanity, feeblemindedness, inability to find paid work, or even poor moral character—are insufficient to make him deserve the fate to which an inactive society would in effect condemn him. One would not be executed for inability or failure to find paid work; neither should one be allowed to die for this misfortune or failing....

The adoption of a Permissive view of welfare would have significant practical implications. If there were a legal right, unconditional upon behaviour, to a specified level of state-supplied benefits, then state investigation of the prospective welfare recipient could be kept to a minimum. Why he is in need, whether he can work, whether he is willing to work, and what he does while receiving welfare benefits are on this view quite irrelevant to his right to receive those benefits.... If the Permissive view of welfare were widely believed, then there would be no social stigma attached to being on welfare. There is such a stigma, and many long-term welfare recipients are considerably demoralized by their dependent status.[4] These facts suggest that the Permissive view of welfare is not widely held in our society.

3. The Puritan View
This view of welfare rather naturally emerges when we consider that no

one can have a right to something without someone else's, or some group of other persons', having responsibilities correlative to this right. In the case in which the right in question is a legal right to social security, the correlative responsibilities may be rather extensive. They have been deemed responsibilities of "the state." The state will require resources and funds to meet these responsibilities, and these do not emerge from the sky miraculously, or zip into existence as a consequence of virtually effortless acts of will. They are taken by the state from its citizens, often in the form of taxation on earned income. The funds given to the welfare recipient and many of the goods which he purchases with these funds are produced by other members of society, many of whom give a considerable portion of their time and their energy to this end. If a state has the moral responsibility to ensure the social security of its citizens then all the citizens of that state have the responsibility to provide state agencies with the means to carry out their duties. This responsibility, in our present contingent circumstances, seems to generate an obligation to *work*.

A person who works helps to produce the goods which all use in daily living and, when paid, contributes through taxation to government endeavours. The person who does not work, even though able to work, does not make his contribution to social efforts towards obtaining the means of life. He is not entitled to a share of the goods produced by others if he chooses not to take part in their labours. Unless he can show that there is a moral justification for his not making the sacrifice of time and energy which others make, he has no legitimate claim to welfare benefits. If he is disabled or unable to obtain work, he cannot work;

hence he has no need to justify his failure to work. But if he does choose not to work, he would have to justify his choice by saying "others should sacrifice their time and energy for me; I have no need to sacrifice time and energy for them." This principle, a version of what Rawls refers to as a free-rider's principle, simply will not stand up to criticism.[5] To deliberately avoid working and benefit from the labours of others is morally indefensible.

Within a welfare system erected on these principles, the right to welfare is conditional upon one's satisfactorily accounting for his failure to obtain the necessities of life by his own efforts. Someone who is severely disabled mentally or physically, or who for some other reason cannot work, is morally entitled to receive welfare benefits. Someone who chooses not to work is not. The Puritan view of welfare is a kind of compromise between the Individualist view and the Permissive view....

The Puritan view of welfare, based as it is on the interrelation between welfare and work, provides a rationale for two connected principles which those establishing welfare schemes in Canada and in the United States seem to endorse. First of all, those on welfare should never receive a higher income than the working poor. Secondly, a welfare scheme should, in some way or other, incorporate incentives to work. These principles, which presuppose that it is better to work than not to work, emerge rather naturally from the contingency which is at the basis of the Puritan view: the goods essential for social security are products of the labour of some members of society. If we wish to have a continued supply of such goods, we must encourage those who work to produce them....

APPRAISAL OF POLICIES: SOCIAL CONSEQUENCES AND SOCIAL JUSTICE...

1. Consequences of Welfare Schemes

First, let us consider the consequences of the non-scheme advocated by the Individualist. He would have us abolish all non-optional government programmes which have as their goal the improvement of anyone's personal welfare. This rejection extends to health schemes, pension plans and education, as well as to welfare and unemployment insurance. So following the Individualist would lead to very sweeping changes.

The Individualist will claim (as do Hospers and Ayn Rand) that on the whole his non-scheme will bring beneficial consequences. He will admit, as he must, that there are people who would suffer tremendously if welfare and other social security programmes were simply terminated. Some would even die as a result. We cannot assume that spontaneously developing charities would cover every case of dire need. Nevertheless the Individualist wants to point to benefits which would accrue to businessmen and to working people and their families if taxation were drastically cut. It is his claim that consumption would rise, hence production would rise, job opportunities would be extended, and there would be an economic boom, if people could only spend all their earned income as they wished. This boom would benefit both rich and poor.

There are significant omissions which are necessary in order to render the Individualist's optimism plausible. Either workers and businessmen would have insurance of various kinds, or they would be insecure in their prosperity. If they did have insurance to cover health problems, old age and possible job loss, then they would pay for it; hence they would not be spending their whole earned income on consumer goods. Those who run the insurance schemes could, of course, put this money back into the economy—but government schemes already do this. The economic boom under Individualism would not be as loud as originally expected. Furthermore the goal of increased consumption-increased productivity must be questioned from an ecological viewpoint: many necessary materials are available only in limited quantities.

Finally, a word about charity. It is not to be expected that those who are at the mercy of charities will benefit from this state, either materially or psychologically. Those who prosper will be able to choose between giving a great deal to charity and suffering from the very real insecurity and guilt which would accompany the existence of starvation and grim poverty outside their padlocked doors. It is to be hoped that they would opt for the first alternative. But, if they did, this might be every bit as expensive for them as government-supported benefit schemes are now. If they did not give generously to charity, violence might result. However one looks at it, the consequences of individualism are unlikely to be good.

Welfare schemes operating in Canada today (1976) are almost without exception based upon the principles of the Puritan view....

Both the Special Senate Committee Report on Poverty and the Real Poverty Report criticize our present system of welfare for its demoralization of recipients, who often must deal with several levels of government and are vulnerable to arbitrary interference on the part of administering officials. Welfare officials have the power to check on welfare recipients and cut off or limit their benefits under a large number of circumstances. The dangers to welfare recipients in terms of anxiety, threats to privacy and loss of dignity are obvious. According to the Senate Report, the single aspect shared by all Canada's welfare systems is "a record of failure and insufficiency, of bureaucratic rigidities that often result in the degradation, humiliation and alienation of recipients."[6] The writers of this report cite many instances of humiliation, leaving the impression that these are too easily found to be "incidental aberrations."[7] Concern that a welfare recipient either be unable to work or be willing to work (if unemployed) can easily turn into concern about how he spends the income supplied him, what his plans for the future are, where he lives, how many children he has....

In fairness, it must be noted here that bureaucratic checks and controls are not a feature only of Puritan welfare systems. To a limited extent, Permissive systems would have to incorporate them too. Within those systems, welfare benefits would be given only to those whose income was inadequate to meet basic needs. However, there would be no checks on "willingness to work," and there would be no need for welfare workers to evaluate the merits of the daily activities of recipients. If a Permissive guaranteed income system were administered through income tax returns, everyone receiving the basic income and those not needing it paying it back in taxes, then the special status of welfare recipients would fade. They would no longer be singled out as a special group within the population. It is to be expected that living solely on government-supplied benefits would

be psychologically easier in that type of situation.

Thus it can be argued that for the recipients of welfare, a Permissive scheme has more advantages than a Puritan one. This is not a very surprising conclusion.... The concern which most people have regarding the Permissive scheme relates to its costs and its dangers to the "work ethic." It is commonly thought that people work only because they have to work to survive in a tolerable style. If a guaranteed income scheme were adopted by the government, this incentive to work would disappear. No one would be faced with the choice between a nasty and boring job and starvation. Who would do the nasty and boring jobs then? Many of them are not eliminable and they have to be done somehow, by someone. Puritans fear that a great many people— even some with relatively pleasant jobs —might simply cease to work if they could receive non-stigmatized government money to live on. If this were to happen, the permissive society would simply grind to a halt.

In addressing these anxieties about the consequences of Permissive welfare schemes, we must recall that welfare benefits are set to ensure only that those who do not work have a bearable existence, with an income sufficient for basic needs, and that they have this income regardless of why they fail to work. Welfare benefits will not finance luxury living for a family of five! If jobs are adequately paid so that workers receive more than the minimum welfare income in an earned salary, then there will still be a financial incentive to take jobs. What guaranteed income schemes will do is to raise the salary floor....

Furthermore it is unlikely that people work solely due to (i) the desire for money and the things it can buy and (ii) belief in the Puritan work ethic. There are many other reasons for working, some of which would persist in a society which had adopted a Permissive welfare system. Most people are happier when their time is structured in some way, when they are active outside their own homes, when they feel themselves part of an endeavour whose purposes transcend their particular egoistic ones. Women often choose to work outside the home for these reasons as much as for financial ones. With these and other factors operating I cannot see that the adoption of a Permissive welfare scheme would be followed by a level of slothfulness which would jeopardize human well-being.

Another worry about the Permissive scheme concerns cost. It is difficult to comment on this in a general way, since it would vary so much from case to case. Of Canada at the present it has been said that a guaranteed income scheme administered through income tax would cost less than social security payments administered through the present bureaucracies. It is thought that this saving would result from a drastic cut in administrative costs....

In summary, we can appraise Individualism, Puritanism and Permissivism with respect to their anticipated consequences, as follows: Individualism is unacceptable; Puritanism is tolerable, but has some undesirable consequences for welfare recipients; Permissivism appears to be the winner. Worries about bad effects which Permissive welfare schemes might have due to high costs and (alleged) reduced work-incentives appear to be without solid basis.

2. Social Justice Under Proposed Welfare Schemes

We must now try to consider the merits of Individualism, Puritanism and Permissivism with regard to their impact on the distribution of the goods necessary for well-being. Nozick has argued against the whole conception of a distributive justice on the grounds that it presupposes that goods are like manna from heaven: we simply get them and then have a problem—to whom to give them. According to Nozick we know where things come from and we do not have the problem of to whom to give them. There is not really a problem of distributive justice, for there is no central distributor giving out manna from heaven! It is necessary to counter Nozick on this point since his reaction to the (purported) problems of distributive justice would undercut much of what follows.[8]

There is a level at which Nozick's point is obviously valid. If A discovers a cure for cancer, then it is A and not B or C who is responsible for this discovery. On Nozick's view this is taken to imply that A should reap any monetary profits which are forthcoming; other people will benefit from the cure itself. Now although it cannot be doubted that A is a bright and hardworking person, neither can it be denied that A and his circumstances are the product of many co-operative endeavours: schools and laboratories, for instance. Because this is so, I find Nozick's claim that "we know where things come from" unconvincing at a deeper level. Since achievements like A's presuppose extensive social cooperation, it is morally permissible to regard even the monetary profits accruing from them as shareable by the "owner" and society at large.

Laws support existing income levels in many ways. Governments specify taxation so as to further determine net income. Property ownership is a legal matter. In all these ways people's incomes and possibilities for obtaining income are affected by deliberate state action. It is always possible to raise questions about the moral desirability of actual conventional arrangements. Should university professors earn less than lawyers? More than waitresses? Why? Why not? Anyone who gives an account of distributive justice is trying to specify principles which will make it possible to answer questions such as these, and nothing in Nozick's argument suffices to show that the questions are meaningless or unimportant.

Any human distribution of anything is unjust insofar as differences exist for no good reason. If goods did come like manna from heaven and the Central Distributor gave A ten times more than B, we should want to know why. The skewed distribution might be deemed a just one if A's needs were objectively ten times greater than B's, or if B refused to accept more than his small portion of goods. But if no reason at all could be given for it, or if only an irrelevant reason could be given (e.g., A is blue-eyed and B is not), then it is an unjust distribution. All the views we have expounded concerning welfare permit differences in income level.... But we ... deal here solely with the question of whether everyone should receive a floor level of income; decisions on this matter are independent of decisions on overall equality or principles of variation among incomes above the floor. The Permissivist contends that all should receive at least the floor income; the Individualist and the Puritan deny this. All would claim justice for their side.

The Individualist attempts to justify extreme variations in income, with some people below the level where they can fulfill their basic needs, with reference to the fact of people's actual accomplishments. This approach to the question is open to the same objections as those which have already been raised against Nozick's non-manna-from-heaven argument, and I shall not repeat them here. Let us move on to the Puritan account. It is because goods emerge from human efforts that the Puritan advances his view of welfare. He stresses the unfairness of a system which would permit some people to take advantage of others. A Permissive welfare system would do this, as it makes no attempt to distinguish between those who choose not to work and those who cannot work. No one should be able to take advantage of another under the auspices of a government institution. The Puritan scheme seeks to eliminate this possibility, and for that reason, Puritans would allege, it is a more just scheme than the Permissive one.

Permissivists can best reply to this contention by acknowledging that any instance of free-riding would be an instance where those working were done an injustice, but by showing that any justice which the Puritan preserves by eliminating free-riding is outweighted by *injustice* perpetrated elsewhere. Consider the children of the Puritan's free-riders. They will suffer greatly for the "sins" of their parents. Within the institution of the family, the Puritan cannot suitably hurt the guilty without cruelly depriving the innocent. There is a sense, too, in which Puritanism does injustice to the many people on welfare who are not free-riders. It perpetuates the opinion that they are non-contributors to society and this doctrine, which is over-simplified if not downright false, has a harmful effect upon welfare recipients.

Social justice is not simply a matter of the distribution of goods, or the income with which goods are to be purchased. It is also a matter of the protection of rights. Western societies claim to give their citizens equal rights in political and legal contexts; they also claim to endorse the larger conception of a right to life. Now it is possible to interpret these rights in a limited and formalistic way, so that the duties correlative to them are minimal. On the limited, or negative, interpretation, to say that A has a right to life is simply to say that others have a duty not to interfere with A's attempts to keep himself alive. This interpretation of the right to life is compatible with Individualism as well as with Puritanism. But it is an inadequate interpretation of the right to life and of other rights. A right to vote is meaningless if one is starving and unable to get to the polls; a right to equality before the law is meaningless if one cannot afford to hire a lawyer. And so on.

Even a Permissive welfare scheme will go only a very small way towards protecting people's rights. It will amount to a meaningful acknowledgement of a right to life, by ensuring income adequate to purchase food, clothing and shelter —at the very least. These minimum necessities are presupposed by all other rights a society may endorse in that their possession is a precondition of being able to exercise these other rights. Because it protects the rights of all within a society better than do Puritanism and Individualism, the Permissive view can rightly claim superiority over the others with regard to justice.

NOTES

1. Nicholas Rescher, *Welfare: Social Issues in Philosophical Perspective*, p. 114.
2. See, for example, Ayn Rand's *Atlas Shrugged*, *The Virtue of Selfishness*, and *Capitalism: The Unknown Ideal*.
3. John Hospers, *Libertarianism: A Political Philosophy for Tomorrow*, p. 67.
4. Ian Adams, William Cameron, Brian Hill, and Peter Penz, *The Real Poverty Report*, pp. 167–187.
5. See *A Theory of Justice*, p. 124, 136. Rawls defines the free-rider as one who relies on the principle "everyone is to act justly except for myself, if I choose not to," and says that his position is a version of egoism which is eliminated as a morally acceptable principle by formal constraints. This conclusion regarding the tenability of egoism is one which I accept and which is taken for granted in the present context.
6. *Senate Report on Poverty*, p. 73.
7. The Hamilton Public Welfare Department takes automobile license plates from recipients, making them available again only to those whose needs meet with the Department's approval. (*Real Poverty Report*, p. 186.) The *Globe and Mail* for 12 January 1974 reported that welfare recipients in the city of Toronto are to be subjected to computerized budgeting. In the summer of 1973, the two young daughters of an Alabama man on welfare were sterilized against their own wishes and without their parents' informed consent. (See *Time*, 23 July 1973.)
8. Robert Nozick, "Distributive Justice," *Philosophy and Public Affairs*, Fall 1973.

NO

Tom Bethell

THEY HAD A DREAM

On May 10, [1993,] ABC television correspondent Brit Hume pointed out on the evening news that President Clinton, in trouble with the voters, was on the road again, in Ohio. The President was shown in an auditorium talking about welfare reform, saying what he has already said many times: welfare as we know it should be ended. The audience duly applauded, as it always does on these occasions. In case we hadn't been following the script, Hume jogged our memories. Talk of welfare reform is calculated to lift Clinton in the polls, he said. Since then, the politically opportune nature of Clinton's interest in welfare has been widely noted.

... [But] the care and maintenance of welfare programs is perhaps the first order of business for liberal activists. The redistribution of income is the cause to which their lives are dedicated (and upon which, in many cases, their jobs depend). Many of them believe that welfare programs should become more generous, not more onerous. Richard P. Nathan, the director of the Nelson A. Rockefeller Institute of Government, wrote at the end of 1991 that welfare policy was turning "mean and harsh," imbued with "David Duke's racist spirit." Even as he wrote, welfare rolls were rapidly expanding.

CHARLES MURRAY'S HERESY

Welfare reform is important because welfare is the central cause of the mounting chaos in the war-zones that used to be our city centers. This is the thesis of Charles Murray's *Losing Ground* (1984): the rapid expansion of welfare in the 1960s changed the incentives of the poor, making welfare more attractive than entry-level jobs, making unwed motherhood tolerable, making husbands dispensable. This in turn gave rise to the underclass that is progressively ruining urban life. Poverty is not the "root cause" of this underclass. Nor is joblessness. Nor is racism. Sixty years ago, when poverty and unemployment and racism were far more severe than they are today, the cities remained in good shape. The trouble began at a time of unprecedented prosperity, when eligibility for welfare was exploding.

The defenders of welfare rushed to their typewriters when Murray's heresy was promulgated. How dare he say such things about their Model Cities and their Demonstration Projects, their Pilot Projects and their Housing Projects! The real cause of the continuing distress was the niggardliness of the middle class. Robert Greenstein, director of the Center on Budget and Policy Priorities, came tearing into print in *The New Republic*. The facts didn't bear Murray out! During the 1970s, benefit levels for Aid to Families with Dependent Children, the basic welfare program, had actually dropped because they weren't adjusted for inflation. On Murray's theory, the welfare rolls should have declined, too. Instead, they remained flat.

But, Murray says today, the erosion of AFDC was pretty much offset by increases in other components of the welfare package—housing, Food Stamps: benefits that for some reason are still not counted in determining the poverty rate. It should also be pointed out that, in 1970, the bad incentives of welfare still had not fully overpowered the good work habits inculcated in earlier generations. Dependency is not something that is acquired overnight. It took a few years for the eligible to realize the government was giving them these benefits with no strings attached—except for the crucial string that, to remain eligible, they would have to continue leading unproductive lives.

Another objection to Murray's thesis was raised by David T. Ellwood, a Harvard professor and the author of *Poor Support*. He is now assistant secretary of HHS with responsibility for welfare reform. Clinton's rhetoric about a time limit for welfare came from Ellwood, who has since made it clear that he thinks single mothers can be taken off welfare only if an extensive package of benefits remains available to them (child support, Medicaid, day care, and so on). In other words, they can be taken off welfare only if they remain on it.

Ellwood objected to Murray as follows: The level of AFDC varies from state to state, and if it's true that young women have children in order to qualify for benefits, one would expect more illegitimacy in high-benefit states, such as California, than in low-benefit states, such as Mississippi. In reality there is very little difference. Murray replied that welfare should be thought of not as something that bribes women to have babies but as something that enables them to do so. When you look at the total package of cash and in-kind benefits, and take into consideration the cost of living (as the General Accounting Office did in a 1978 study), then "poor young women in a stingy AFDC location (New Orleans) and in a generous AFDC location (San Francisco) were looking at nearly identical choices relative to the local economy."

THE SYSTEM IS THE PROBLEM

The problem is not one of "fraud and abuse." It is not that "welfare queens" receive multiple benefits using fake IDs. The real problem lies in the lawful operation of the system, not in the circumvention of it. Another misconception is that welfare outlays are busting the budget. Liberals are eager to refute this. "AFDC is less than 1 per cent of the federal budget," says Mario Cuomo. "Throw in Food Stamps and you're up to 3 per cent." Mickey Kaus of *The New Republic*, a liberal but also a welfare revisionist, retorted in his recent book, *The End of Equal-*

ity, that these comparatively low percentages only prove "that through a relatively small expenditure, Money Liberals have managed to poison voters against government spending in general."

Other calculations suggest that the cost of welfare may not be so low after all. Robert Rector of the Heritage Foundation estimates that since the onset of Lyndon Johnson's war on poverty, total welfare spending expressed in 1990 dollars has amounted to $3.5 trillion, "more than the full cost of World War II after adjusting for inflation." The war metaphor has turned out to be more appropriate than LBJ imagined, of course, in view of the state of the inner cities.

The welfare problem, nonetheless, should be thought of in terms of individual incentives rather than collective costs. The problem is that the total value of benefits available to the welfare client approaches or exceeds the dollar amount that can be earned in entry-level jobs. This is the welfare trap. Try to escape by taking a job, and you may have to accept a pay cut, you may lose your health insurance, you will certainly have to go to work every day. Don't forget, welfare recipients are rewarded with leisure in addition to cash, Food Stamps, housing, Medicaid, energy assistance, legal assistance (in case they feel like suing someone), school breakfast and lunch benefits, day-care, and so on. Picking up a check from the mailbox, and visiting the local welfare office occasionally, is much less demanding than showing up at the factory gate at 8 A.M. Hence welfare dependency. According to Rector, "the average mother in the average state can get benefits worth about $12,000 or $13,000 a year.

If the woman on welfare decides to marry a man earning, say, $14,000 a year, his earnings will count toward determining her eligibility, and at that level will disqualify her. But if they live apart, or live together without admitting it, she can stay on welfare. Notice that this is not just the folly of the law, as Amitai Etzioni implies in his ... book *The Spirit of Community*. "At present, in nearly every jurisdiction," he writes, "welfare payments are cut off if a recipient marries a working person, thus discouraging marriage." In fact it is not marriage that is penalized (non-working married couples can receive welfare), but work.

The law cannot very easily be changed because millions of couples manage to work, stay married, and stay off welfare. If the law were changed so that one spouse's earnings no longer disqualified the other from receiving welfare, the welfare rolls could expand by 10 to 15 million families overnight. The cost of *that* really would be staggering. Couples might have to get divorced briefly, enabling the woman to go on welfare. Then they could remarry and keep the benefits (according to Etzioni's prescription). In fact, New Jersey recently did change its law to allow a recipient to retain benefits after marrying someone with a job. But to circumvent precisely this problem, the law specified that the woman would have to marry someone other than the father of her children. One way or another, generous welfare benefits have perverse consequences.

In New York City, over one million people now receive welfare—more people than attend the public-school system. (In 1943, according to Senator Moynihan, 73,000 New Yorkers were on relief.) David Shaffer of the Public Policy Institute recently compared work and welfare for a mother with two children (as reported by *New York Times* Metro columnist Sam Roberts): On welfare, the mother "receives a $2,856 basic grant, $636 in home energy payments, a $3,432 housing allowance, $2,784 in Food Stamps for a total of $9,708 annually, or 80 per cent of the poverty level. If the mother had a minimum-wage job, she would make $8,829 in salary, $2,880 in Food Stamps, $3,360 in public assistance, a $1,200 earned-income credit, and would pay $4,200 ($175 a month per child) for day care, $2,500 ($50 a week) in work-related expenses, and $678 in Social Security taxes for a net income of $8,891. Working for $8.50 an hour—twice the minimum wage—would disqualify the mother for public assistance and for Medicaid after one year, which would reduce her net income to under $9,000." All of which explains why it is difficult to get off welfare. We are told by welfare apologists, including David Ellwood, that half of all new recipients are off the rolls in two years. But this is a statistical deception caused by high turnover among short-term recipients. "At any one time, about 82 per cent of all recipients are in the midst of spells that will last five years or more," Douglas Besharov and Amy Fowler recently wrote in *The Public Interest*. "And about 65 per cent are caught up in spells of eight years or more."

THE CUCKOLDING STATE

The number of people who receive welfare in the U.S. is usually equated with the number of people enrolled in the AFDC program. In 1992 this was 13.5 million people, in 4.7 million families —up from 3.7 million families in 1988. This June [1993], HHS reported that the number of families on AFDC had risen to 5 million, a record. These figures show how much welfare has grown since it was last reformed—in 1988. Between 1989 and 1992, caseloads rose by 27 per cent. Nearly all recipients are single parents, and the great majority are women.

"Single men are eligible for very little in the way of federally sponsored welfare benefits," Ellwood has written, rebutting the claim that welfare undermines the "work ethic of young black men." In *Wealth and Poverty*, George Gilder refuted this argument with perhaps his most valuable contribution to the welfare debate: "The welfare culture tells the man he is not a necessary part of the family: he feels dispensable, his wife knows he is dispensable, his children sense it." Men are "cuckolded by the compassionate state." But women aren't too perturbed if it's the state that looks after them rather than husbands.

The argument has annoyed liberals, who imagine men and women to be basically the same. In *The Undeserving Poor*, Michael Katz disapprovingly notes that Gilder is not a social scientist but "primarily a moralist." (Gilder's bold insight would not have been possible, of course, if he had been a social scientist because he would never have been able to quantify it.)

Here is Gilder on the L.A.-style inner-city today:

It appears to be almost a matriarchy. The women receive all the income, dominate the social-worker classes, and most of the schools. But a matriarchy is contrary to nature, so what happens is that gangs of young men rule the society. And they utterly rule it, with their violence and recklessness. The women cower in their apartments and the mothers cower before their sons. If men don't dominate as husbands and providers, then they form violent gangs and dominate as thugs and muggers and drug lords.

The Agriculture Department most recently reported that 27.4 million people, or one in nine Americans, are now enrolled in the Food Stamp program. Cost: $24 billion.... The Department of Housing and Urban Development provides housing aid to about 4.5 million families, and estimates that a further 13 million families are qualified to receive assistance. Translation: HUD would like a big budget increase, and if taxpayers can be persuaded to send more of their money to Washington, HUD has lots of potential clients....

In addition, please note, the Congress has now passed legislation that will require states to allow welfare recipients to register to vote at welfare offices. Senate Republicans at first wisely stalled with a filibuster, but Senator Dave Durenberger of Minnesota relented, and was cravenly joined by Pete Domenici of New Mexico and Arlen Specter of Pennsylvania. John Stuart Mill, the Victorian liberal who was ahead of his time in supporting the enfranchisement of women, thought it axiomatic that those who received welfare ("parish relief") should not be allowed to vote. Legislators today want to encourage them to do so. "We have made it easier for the American people to be a part of their government," said a gullible Senator Wendell Ford (D., Ky.), who managed the bill....

HOW TO BREAK THE CYCLE

How, then, might welfare be reformed? What about time limits? Clinton's proposal "will put a time limit on welfare." ... After that, people who've been through the education and training programs will have to work." Conservatives should rid themselves of any illusions about time limits. As Kate O'Beirne of the Heritage Foundation has said, any such measure will certainly come with a federal jobs program and a child-care program attached. "They've figured me out," Representative Tom Downey of New York told a *Wall Street Journal* reporter... when this objection to time limits was raised. "If you want to time-limit welfare make sure there's a job at the end of that rainbow."

This brings us to work requirements for those on welfare. In recent years they have acquired growing support. But the results of the Reagan Administration's attempt to enact them should make everyone leery. The liberal strategy is first to complain bitterly about "slavefare." The putative requirements are then riddled with loopholes; for example, women with small children are exempted (as happened in 1988), which takes care of half the recipients right off. Then come the countervailing demands. Work requirements are catnip for social workers; they see counseling galore in the educational programs and training seminars that Congress will construe as meeting the requirements. Result: a new sandbox for the welfare bureaucracies to romp in. Social workers sometimes grumble about work requirements, for the sake of appearances; secretly they love them.

"Making welfare mothers work is one of the silliest ideas I've ever heard of," says George Gilder. "Government will not only have to provide the jobs, it will also have to provide day care. It has to do two things that it can't do at all: create jobs and raise children. It takes on still more responsibility for the lives of welfare recipients, with no perceptible benefits to society. In return for valueless work, recipients get to abandon their kids." The only useful reform, he says, is to "reduce the level of benefits, and that's the one thing that nobody wants to do."

Martin Anderson of the Hoover Institution points out that there is something odd about requiring people to work for welfare. "The reason for welfare is that people can't take care of themselves," he says. "If they can work, they shouldn't be on welfare." (AFDC started up, incidentally, as small grants to widows, in the 1930s. The idea was to keep the mothers at home and the children out of orphanages; not put the women in "jobs" and the children in programs.) "Take a young mother with two small kids," says Anderson, the author of *Welfare*. "You're going to kick her out of the house?" It is hardly a conservative notion.

The goal of workfare is to make welfare less appealing but if this means losing welfare clients, the social workers won't stand for it. Mickey Kaus points out in *The End of Equality* that "workfare" always gets watered down into something mushy. "Welfare mothers are offered elaborate menus of activities, including vocational instruction, 'job search,' and remedial education," he writes. "Taking such courses, one after another, can easily become a way to avoid going into the labor market." When California enacted a reform in 1986 with "workfare" provisions, he points out, "exactly 1,235 recipients" out of 650,000 were working for their checks five years later.

Nonetheless, Kaus himself proposes an ambitious new work program for welfare recipients—a new kind of WPA with welfare mothers being herded about with Marine Corps discipline on the job site. No paycheck until the end of the week, lady! "The danger is that the men would try to live off the women, relying as before on a compassion-padded system," Kaus admits. His solution: "You have to make mothers work at least enough so that they are faced with the unpleasant consequences of having an out-of-wedlock child. If you don't, you perpetuate the underclass."

To get the Kausian picture, imagine a construction site with pregnant mums under the supervision of a Lou Gossett–type drill sergeant. The very unthinkableness of it brings the irresponsible males rushing over from their gang-warfare activities and street-corner lookout posts. Kaus's admirable goal is to shame them into coming to the rescue, picking up the shovels, going to work, marrying the women. Ergo, with a strict regime, two-parent working families will replace one-parent non-working families.

Hmmmm, it might work, Charles Murray allows, but he can't see Congress enacting it, somehow. "Napoleonic," says Myron Magnet, the mutton-chopped author of *The Dream and the Nightmare: The Sixties Legacy to the Underclass*.

It's instructive to take a look at the 1988 welfare reform, labeled the Family Support Act, to see what happened when work requirements were introduced into legislative deliberations then. The result was a disguised liberal triumph, not acknowledged at the time. The *New York Times* strategically praised the emerging legislation in a succession of editorials as "A Break with the Past," "Welfare without Dependency," and "a rare social policy step forward in the Reagan era." When the bill reached the crucial conference committee it was hailed as "the first major revision of welfare since the creation of AFDC." Its central principle: "Able-bodied recipients must accept or train for [work] in return for benefits."

After Labor Day, Reagan sternly promised to veto the bill if it lacked a work requirement. On cue, the liberals grumbled about slavefare, then demanded concessions. Senator Moynihan warned that if the bill didn't pass, "we will have spoiled the next century." Finally Congressman Henry Waxman (D., Calif.) insisted that if workfare provisions were to be tolerated, there would have to be an expansion of Medicaid and day care, with these benefits made available for one year to those who left welfare to take jobs. Those who read the fine print might have noticed that the so-called work provisions would not take effect for another five years, and so could be quietly repealed by a future Congress.... Even then, the requirement would apply to only 5 per cent of recipients, and "work" could be construed as job-training, secondary education, and the like. All of which put the social-worker classes in a very good mood. It's not clear what Reagan thought he was getting out of it; perhaps simply something called "welfare reform with work requirements."

The *New York Times* was ecstatic: "Real Welfare Reform at Last." The paper asked Robert Rector to contribute an op-ed article about the legislation, but he highlighted the defects that are now apparent, and the piece was not published. Today, Rector says, "Less than 1 per cent of all AFDC parents are actually required to work in exchange for benefits."

Charles Murray did get into print, in the *Wall Street Journal*. He pointed out that giving Medicaid and day care to women who got jobs would put them side by side with others who lacked those benefits. Unavoidably confronted with the unfairness of their position, some of these workers would be enticed into the welfare system themselves, even if

only for a few months. Then, when they went back to work, they too would enjoy Medicaid and day-care coverage. Murray "ventured the prediction" that welfare would expand as a result, and it has. Welfare defenders blame the recession, but the increase preceded it, and is now continuing beyond it.

"1988 Welfare Act Is Falling Short, Researchers Say," was the headline of a March 1992 *New York Times* article by Jason DeParle. While the law "has succeeded in expanding services," DeParle reported, "it is failing to convert welfare from a system that permits long-term dependency to one that stresses skills, jobs, and financial independence." Oh. It *succeeded* in expanding services? Now they tell us.

The central feature of the reform was something called JOBS (Job Opportunities and Basic Skills), telling the states to run training and work programs for parents on welfare. The Feds would put up $1 billion a year and the states were to find matching funds and design their own programs. These were duly set up, each blazoned with its hopeful acronym. Ohio's LEAP stood for Learning, Earning, and Parenting. Then there was GAIN in California, REACH in New Jersey, WORK in Arkansas, SWIM in San Diego, etc. Newspaper accounts of these experiments have been suffused with, well, HOPE, and usually they include an upbeat quote from Judith Gueron, president of the Ford Foundation–funded Manpower Demonstration Research Corporation in New York.

LOVELY NEW EXPERIMENTS

Here were lots of lovely new social experiments for liberals to play with. Pilot projects, day-care programs, control groups, experimental subjects! Small, monitored groups often behave themselves while under observation, and sure enough, when our welfare moms (the experimental group) were ushered into classrooms, given child support, day care, counseling services, individual attention, job-placement advice, lectures on AIDS, and no doubt free condoms, they seemed to demonstrate measurable "earnings gains" (compared to the control group). But somehow, after the data had been collected and the social workers had moved on to another pilot project, little proved to have changed.

Douglas Besharov of the American Enterprise Institute points out that between 1987 and 1991 HHS carried out the Teenage Parent Demonstration in Chicago, Newark, and Camden, requiring all teen mothers to participate. No exceptions were allowed. Those who didn't show up were subject to a sizable reduction in their AFDC grant, losing about $160 a month. The great majority (88 per cent) did appear for registration, but the actual program entailed going to public-school classes and other time-consuming chores. At that point "participation fell off sharply, dropping to about half," Besharov says. In other words, a lot of the teen mothers were willing to lose one-third (or more) of their AFDC rather than sit in classrooms. Almost certainly, attendance entailed loss of (unreported) outside income for some. The result suggests that welfare is now so generous that many of those who get it prefer a "pay cut" to jumping through the bureaucracy's hoops.

Still, experimentation at the state level is probably the only hope of change right now. As Kaus says, if the requirements are strict enough they will make welfare less appealing, and officials in a number of states do seem willing to make things a good deal tougher. Wisconsin Governor Tommy Thompson has a proposal under which cash benefits really would stop after two years....

Some liberals, of course, are still talking about fully funding the inner cities. Maybe we should let them have the money and see what happens. Charles Murray predicted a few years ago that the cities would continue to deteriorate and that those who could afford it would withdraw to gated suburbs and beyond. That too will come to pass—is already doing so.

LIBERAL ANXIETY

Meanwhile we should note with some satisfaction the growing anxiety in liberal circles. It is unthinkable for them to give up on their egalitarian ideology. Yet they don't know what to do about the underclass. Mickey Kaus's attack on "money liberals"—on the belief that social problems can be solved by transferring money from rich to poor—tells us that all is not well. The truth is, their favorite class of experimental subjects inner-city blacks, are not behaving themselves properly. The black leadership is fine. They have been bought off with affirmative action, racial set-asides, gerrymandered districts, local power, and ample patronage. Liberal schemes have benefited them personally, and so they remain obedient-Nouveaux Toms. But the rank and file frankly, have been disorderly: the women having too many children and just plain enjoying life on the dole, not even trying to join the middle class; the young men of course beyond the pale—downright uncooperative and dangerous.

The liberals hadn't bargained for this. They used to scoff confidently at conservatives who said that welfare would undermine work habits. Hadn't we heard? In America, there is a work ethic. Now the liberals are wondering what to do next. . . .

"Most of the people we persist in calling poor are really a sort of lower leisure class, subsidized in idleness, never forced by circumstance to acquire the old middle-class habits," Joe Sobran wrote in a recent column. "Why should these young women 'better themselves,' as the Victorians would have put it? They might gain materially, but they would lose the security they have. Only a few of them are willing to take the risk and give up what they already possess in order to compete with a completely different class of people who have inherited those middle-class habits."

The point is that the liberals themselves often despise these "middle class" virtues and have actively sought to undermine them. "I don't think they even believe in them for themselves, let alone feel they can impose them on others," said Gertrude Himmelfarb, who has written extensively on poverty in Victorian England. She said that historians usually write about these values—thrift, prudence, temperance, providence, and so on—as though they were specific to the middle class. "But that is not the way the Victorian reformers thought of them. These were eternal verities, true for all classes. They truly believed that the working classes were as capable of realizing those values in their lives as they themselves were in theirs. So in a sense they were far more democratic than our present-day reformers."

The key difference between the English ruling class in the nineteenth century and ours today is that the Victorians tried to instill the virtues needed to lift the poor out of poverty. American liberals have tried to stamp them out. Both succeeded, the Victorians admirably, American liberals shamefully. In *The Dream and the Nightmare*, Myron Magnet points to the meretricious and degraded values of American elites, transmitting to the underclass the endlessly repeated message that "you can't succeed without special treatment; the values that allow us haves to succeed have no application to you have-nots; your own self-destructive behavior is a legitimate expression of your history and your oppression," and so on.

I spoke to Marvin Olasky, the author of *The Tragedy of American Compassion* and a professor at the University of Texas. His book contrasts American compassion of a hundred years ago with the bureaucratic version today. He sees the future of the inner cities as "bleak." We have two cultures very much in conflict today, he says. "As long as we cannot say that one is better than the other, then we are not going to be able to reform the welfare system. You have to be able to say, 'This is better, this is the proper way to live, we're going to help you live this way.'" . . .

A comment that senator Jacob Javits made in 1966 [is relevant]. He asked the chairman of New York City's Human Rights Commission, then appearing before the Judiciary Committee: "Commissioner Booth, as New York *has* an antidiscrimination-in-housing law, an excellent law, why do we still have riots? How is it that our situation has not been perfected?" Oh, Senator, would that you were with us today, $3.6 trillion later. Our situation still has not been perfected. And will not be any time soon.

POSTSCRIPT

Should Welfare Benefits Be Unconditional?

One point at issue between Govier and Bethell is whether or not unconditional welfare benefits are really helpful to the poor. Govier is concerned with delivering the benefits without subjecting the recipients to potentially demeaning and prying questions (about why the person does not have a job, about how a welfare check will be spent, and so on) that could be humiliating. Moreover, she is concerned about a social stigma that might be associated with receiving welfare benefits. In Govier's view, if these disagreeable elements are eliminated, then welfare benefits really will be helpful to the poor. Bethell, on the other hand, sees welfare as a trap that can encourage what he calls welfare dependency. Moreover, from his perspective, if Govier's ideas were put into practice, welfare would be even more of a trap. Bethell claims that free and unconditional welfare benefits do not really help poor people to escape from their poverty and to better themselves. On the contrary, such a program encourages the poor to stay where they are. Even liberal-inspired ideas about "workfare"—according to which the poor are supposed to be led from welfare to jobs—often generate a host of further government programs, an inflated bureaucracy, and even more costs to the taxpayers.

Ironically, Govier, who takes a liberal position on welfare, and Bethell, who approaches welfare from a conservative position, seem to switch positions when it comes to the matter of the power of the government over individuals and their private lives. Govier plays the conservative here and argues for a limited governmental role, as well as the utmost personal freedom and discretion for the individual. Bethell, insofar as he supports the idea of conditions being placed on welfare benefits, seems willing to allow the government to play an active role in determining whether or not those conditions are met, even if probing questions and inquiries have to be made into individuals' lives. Moreover, Govier, with her "no questions asked" approach, refuses to confront welfare recipients with any judgments about how the welfare monies are being spent or how well their lives are proceeding, while Bethell seems much more interested in getting judgmental messages from the government to the individual.

Relevant readings are Charles Murray, *Losing Ground: American Social Policy 1950–1980* (Basic Books, 1984); Robert E. Goodin, *Reasons for Welfare: The Political Theory of the Welfare State* (Princeton University Press, 1988); David R. Riemer, *The Prisoners of Welfare: Liberating America's Poor from Unemployment and Low Wages* (Praeger, 1988); Richard E. Wagner, *To Promote the General Welfare: Market Processes vs. Political Transfers* (Pacific Research Institute for

Public Policy, 1989); Peter H. Rossi, *Down and Out in America: The Origins of Homelessness* (University of Chicago Press, 1989); Theodore R. Marmor, Jerry L. Mashaw, and Philip L. Harvey, *America's Misunderstood Welfare State: Persistent Myths, Enduring Realities* (Basic Books, 1990); George Gilder, *Wealth and Poverty*, 2d ed. (ICS Press, 1993); Victor George, *Welfare and Ideology* (Prentice Hall, 1995); Neil Lunt and Douglas Coyle, eds., *Welfare and Policy: Agendas and Issues* (Taylor & Francis, 1996); Thomas R. Barton and Vijayan K. Pillai, *Welfare As We Know It: A Family-Level Analysis of AFDC Receipt* (Edwin Mellen Press, 1997); and Paul Winters and Charles Cozic, eds., *Welfare* (Greenhaven Press, 1997).

ISSUE 8

Should "Hate Speech" Be Tolerated?

YES: Jonathan Rauch, from "In Defense of Prejudice: Why Incendiary Speech Must Be Protected," *Harper's Magazine* (May 1995)

NO: Thomas W. Peard, from "Hate Speech on Campus: Exploring the Limits of Free Speech," *From the Center: A Newsletter* (Spring 1997)

ISSUE SUMMARY

YES: Writer and social commentator Jonathan Rauch argues that since it is impossible to eliminate bigotry from society completely, intellectual pluralism, which permits the verbal expression of various forms of bigotry, should be promoted.

NO: Philosopher Thomas W. Peard argues that some forms of hate speech—especially racist hate speech in the form of "fighting words"—are rightfully regulated. He maintains that such language causes serious harm and that this harm outweighs any interest on the part of the speaker.

First, it should be made clear that the question of whether or not "hate speech"—generally defined as speech that is racist, sexist, homophobic, or otherwise denigrating and offensive to someone or some group—should be tolerated is about authorities, such as university administrators, councils, and law-making bodies. The question is whether such authorities should allow hate speech or ban it, not whether a specific individual should or should not tolerate such speech.

One question we might ask concerning hate speech is whether or not it is more an expression of hate than of opinion. One defense of speech codes that limit or prohibit hate speech is that the grounds for limiting some forms of speech have nothing to do with whether or not we believe that such speech makes false assertions. Rather, the grounds are simply that such speech expresses hate and other extremely negative attitudes.

For example, those who would like to silence individuals who argue that the Holocaust never happened rely on this argument. From this standpoint, the problem with Holocaust deniers is not that they make false assertions but that they use their freedom of speech rights and the language of open-mindedness to package their own vision of the world—one that includes a strong anti-Semitism.

In line with this type of argument, it might be said that the fundamental problem with hate speech is not so much that it contains false claims but that it is grounded in, exemplifies, and encourages a harmful vision of the world. According to this argument, hate speech is really a form of harassment and its occurrence as speech is incidental to its real purposes. Thus, for example, taunting language aimed at minorities or racial slurs are not perceived simply as speech—and therefore sheltered under a principle of freedom of expression —but are interpreted as a manifestation of racism itself and therefore given no shelter.

A strong defender of freedom of expression could admit much of this. We do not have to approve of or like everything that is permitted under the idea of freedom of speech, whether it is obscene matter, hate speech, right-wing political propaganda, left-wing political propaganda, and so on. In fact, it is guaranteed that we will not like all free speech, because some of it will express the very things that we find abhorrent. But, it might be said, a true supporter of freedom will not draw a line separating what is to be allowed (tolerated) from what is not to be allowed (not tolerated). From this viewpoint, if you are truly committed to ideas of toleration, freedom, and liberty, then you will accept the expression of any speech, even if you think such speech is wrong, disagreeable, or misguided.

One area in which hate speech has become especially controversial concerns the imposition of speech codes on college campuses. These codes, which have been adopted at a number of colleges and universities, punish people for making derogatory remarks based on race, gender, religion, or sexual orientation. Now, assuming that a college is a community of learning that provides a civilizing influence on students, which is the enlightened and civilized approach: to ban hate speech as incompatible with the mission and goals of higher education, or to allow that the toleration of all speech (even hate speech) is an even higher value?

In the selections that follow, Jonathan Rauch argues in favor of what he calls intellectual pluralism. Rauch says that it is impossible to eradicate prejudice completely and that we should learn to live with it rather than try to eliminate its expression. Thomas W. Peard argues in favor of regulating racist hate speech, such as on college campuses. Although such regulation will not bring prejudice and bigotry to an end, it is nevertheless valuable, he argues, because it addresses a matter of serious harm.

YES
Jonathan Rauch

IN DEFENSE OF PREJUDICE: WHY INCENDIARY SPEECH MUST BE PROTECTED

The war on prejudice is now, in all likelihood, the most uncontroversial social movement in America. Opposition to "hate speech," formerly identified with the liberal left, has become a bipartisan piety. In the past year, groups and factions that agree on nothing else have agreed that the public expression of any and all prejudices must be forbidden. On the left, protesters and editorialists have insisted that Francis L. Lawrence resign as president of Rutgers University for describing blacks as "a disadvantaged population that doesn't have that genetic, hereditary background to have a higher average." On the other side of the ideological divide, Ralph Reed, the executive director of the Christian Coalition, responded to criticism of the religious right by calling a press conference to denounce a supposed outbreak of "namecalling, scapegoating, and religious bigotry." Craig Rogers, an evangelical Christian student at California State University, recently filed a $2.5 million sexual-harassment suit against a lesbian professor of psychology, claiming that anti-male bias in one of her lectures violated campus rules and left him feeling "raped and trapped."

In universities and on Capitol Hill, in workplaces and newsrooms, authorities are declaring that there is no place for racism, sexism, homophobia, Christian-bashing, and other forms of prejudice in public debate or even in private thought. "Only when racism and other forms of prejudice are expunged," say the crusaders for sweetness and light, "can minorities be safe and society be fair." So sweet, this dream of a world without prejudice. But the very last thing society should do is seek to utterly eradicate racism and other forms of prejudice.

I suppose I should say, in the customary I-hope-I-don't-sound-too-defensive tone, that I am not a racist and that this is not an article favoring racism or any other particular prejudice. It is an article favoring intellectual pluralism, which permits the expression of various forms of bigotry and always will. Although we like to hope that a time will come when no one will believe

From Jonathan Rauch, "In Defense of Prejudice: Why Incendiary Speech Must Be Protected," *Harper's Magazine*, vol. 290, no. 1740 (May 1995). Copyright © 1995 by *Harper's Magazine*. All rights reserved. Reproduced from the May issue by special permission.

that people come in types and that each type belongs with its own kind, I doubt such a day will ever arrive. By all indications, *Homo sapiens* is a tribal species for whom "us versus them" comes naturally and must be continually pushed back. Where there is genuine freedom of expression, there will be racist expression. There will also be people who believe that homosexuals are sick or threaten children or—especially among teenagers—are rightful targets of manly savagery. Homosexuality will always be incomprehensible to most people, and what is incomprehensible is feared. As for anti-Semitism, it appears to be a hardier virus than influenza. If you want pluralism, then you get racism and sexism and homophobia, and communism and fascism and xenophobia and tribalism, and that is just for a start. If you want to believe in intellectual freedom and the progress of knowledge and the advancement of science and all those other good things, then you must swallow hard and accept this: for as thickheaded and wayward an animal as us, the realistic question is how to make the best of prejudice, not how to eradicate it.

Indeed, "eradicating prejudice" is so vague a proposition as to be meaningless. Distinguishing prejudice reliably and nonpolitically from non-prejudice, or even defining it crisply, is quite hopeless. We all feel we know prejudice when we see it. But do we? At the University of Michigan, a student said in a classroom discussion that he considered homosexuality a disease treatable with therapy. He was summoned to a formal disciplinary hearing for violating the school's policy against speech that "victimizes" people based on "sexual orientation." Now, the evidence is abundant that this particular hypothesis is wrong, and any American homosexual can attest to the harm that the student's hypothesis has inflicted on many real people. But was it a statement of prejudice or of misguided belief? Hate speech or hypothesis? Many Americans who do not regard themselves as bigots or haters believe that homosexuality is a treatable disease. They may be wrong, but are they all bigots? I am unwilling to say so, and if you are willing, beware. The line between a prejudiced belief and a merely controversial one is elusive, and the harder you look the more elusive it becomes. "God hates homosexuals" is a statement of fact, not of bias, to those who believe it; "American criminals are disproportionately black" is a statement of bias, not of fact, to those who disbelieve it.

Who is right? You may decide, and so may others, and there is no need to agree. That is the great innovation of intellectual pluralism (which is to say, of post-Enlightenment science, broadly defined). We cannot know in advance or for sure which belief is prejudice and which is truth, but to advance knowledge we don't need to know. The genius of intellectual pluralism lies not in doing away with prejudices and dogmas but in channeling them—making them socially productive by pitting prejudice against prejudice and dogma against dogma, exposing all to withering public criticism. What survives at the end of the day is our base of knowledge.

* * *

What they told us in high school about this process is very largely a lie. The Enlightenment tradition taught us that science is orderly, antiseptic, rational, the province of detached experimenters and high-minded logicians. In the popular view, science stands for reason against prejudice, open-mindedness against dogma, calm consideration against passionate attachment —all personified by pop-science icons like the magisterially deductive Sherlock Holmes, the coolly analytic Mr. Spock, the genially authoritative Mr. Science (from our junior-high science films). Yet one of science's dirty secrets is that although science as a whole is as unbiased as anything human can be, scientists are just as biased as anyone else, sometimes more so. "One of the strengths of science," writes the philosopher of science David L. Hull, "is that it does not require that scientists be unbiased, only that different scientists have different biases." Another dirty secret is that, no less than the rest of us, scientists can be dogmatic and pigheaded. "Although his pigheadedness often damages the careers of individual scientists," says Hull, "it is beneficial for the manifest goal of science," which relies on people to invest years in their ideas and defend them passionately. And the dirtiest secret of all, if you believe in the antiseptic popular view of science, is that this most ostensibly rational of enterprises depends on the most irrational of motives—ambition, narcissism, animus, even revenge. "Scientists acknowledge that among their motivations are natural curiosity, the love of trust, and the desire to help humanity, but other inducements exist as well, and one of them is to 'get that son of a bitch,'" says Hull. "Time and again, scientists whom I interviewed described the powerful spur that 'showing that son of a bitch' supplied to their own research."

Many people, I think, are bewildered by this unvarnished and all too human view of science. They believe that for a system to be unprejudiced, the people in it must also be unprejudiced. In fact, the opposite is true. Far from eradicat-

ing ugly or stupid ideas and coarse or unpleasant motives, intellectual pluralism relies upon them to excite intellectual passion and redouble scientific effort. I know of no modern idea more ugly and stupid than that the Holocaust never happened, nor any idea more viciously motivated. Yet the deniers' claims that the Auschwitz gas chambers could not have worked led to closer study and in 1993, research showing, at last, how they actually did work. Thanks to prejudice and stupidity, another opening for doubt has been shut.

An enlightened and efficient intellectual regime lets a million prejudices bloom, including many that you or I may regard as hateful or grotesque. It avoids any attempt to stamp out prejudice, because stamping out prejudice really means forcing everyone to share the same prejudice, namely that of whatever is in authority. The great American philosopher Charles Sanders Peirce wrote in 1877: "When complete agreement could not otherwise be reached, a general massacre of all who have not thought in a certain way has proved a very effective means of settling opinion in a country." In speaking of "settling opinion," Peirce was writing about one of the two or three most fundamental problems that any human society must confront and solve. For most societies down through the centuries, this problem was dealt with in the manner he described: errors were identified by the authorities—priests, politburos, dictators —or by mass opinion, and then the error-makers were eliminated along with their putative mistakes. "Let all men who reject the established belief be terrified into silence," wrote Peirce, describing this system. "This method has, from the earliest times, been one of the chief means of upholding correct theological and political doctrines."

Intellectual pluralism substitutes a radically different doctrine: we kill our mistakes rather than each other. Here I draw on another great philosopher, the late Karl Popper, who pointed out that the critical method of science "consists in letting our hypotheses die in our stead." Those who are in error are not (or are not supposed to be) banished or excommunicated or forced to sign a renunciation or required to submit to "rehabilitation" or sent for psychological counseling. It is the error we punish, not the errant. By letting people make errors—even mischievous, spiteful errors (as, for instance, Galileo's insistence on Copernicanism was taken to be in 1633) —pluralism creates room to challenge orthodoxy, think imaginatively, experiment boldly. Brilliance and bigotry are empowered in the same stroke.

Pluralism is the principle that protects and makes a place in human company for that loneliest and most vulnerable of all minorities, the minority who is hounded and despised among blacks and whites, gays and straights, who is suspect or criminal among every tribe and in every nation of the world, and yet on whom progress depends: the dissident. I am not saying that dissent is always or even usually enlightened. Most of the time it is foolish and self-serving. No dissident has the right to be taken seriously, and the fact that Aryan Nation racists or Nation of Islam anti-Semites are unorthodox does not entitle them to respect. But what goes around comes around. As a supporter of gay marriage, for example, I reject the majority's view of family, and as a Jew I reject its view of God. I try to be civil, but the fact is that most Americans regard my views on marriage as a reckless assault on the most fundamental of all institutions, and many people are more than a little discomfited by the statement "Jesus Christ was no more divine than anybody else" (which is why so few people ever say it). Trap the racists and anti-Semites, and you lay a trap for me too. Hunt for them with eradication in your mind, and you have brought dissent itself within your sights.

The new crusade against prejudice waves aside such warnings. Like earlier crusades against antisocial ideas, the mission is fueled by good (if cocksure) intentions and a genuine sense of urgency. Some kinds of error are held to be intolerable, like pollutants that even in small traces poison the water for a whole town. Some errors are so pernicious as to damage real people's lives, so wrongheaded that no person of right mind or goodwill could support them. Like their forebears of other stripe—the Church in its campaigns against heretics, the McCarthyites in their campaigns against Communists —the modern anti-racist and anti-sexist and anti-homophobic campaigners are totalists, demanding not that misguided ideas and ugly expressions be corrected or criticized but that they be eradicated. They make war not on errors but on error, and like other totalists they act in the name of public safety—the safety, especially, of minorities.

*   *   *

The sweeping implications of this challenge to pluralism are not, I think, well enough understood by the public at large. Indeed, the new brand of totalism has yet even to be properly named. "Multiculturalism," for instance, is much too broad. "Political correctness" comes closer but is too trendy and snide. For lack of anything else, I will call the new anti-pluralism "purism," since its major tenet is that society cannot be just until the last traces of invidious prejudice have been scrubbed away. Whatever you call it, the purists' way of seeing things has spread through American intellectual life with remarkable speed, so much so that many people will blink at you uncomprehendingly or even call you a racist (or sexist or homophobe, etc.) if you suggest that expressions of racism should be tolerated or that prejudice has its part to play.

The new purism sets out, to begin with, on a campaign against words, for words are the currency of prejudice, and if prejudice is hurtful then so must be prejudiced words. "We are not safe when these violent words are among us," wrote Mari Matsuda, then a UCLA law professor. Here one imagines gangs of racist words swinging chains and smashing heads in back alleys. To suppress bigoted language seems, at first blush, reasonable, but it quickly leads to a curious result. A peculiar kind of verbal shamanism takes root, as though certain expressions, like curses or magical incantations, carry in themselves the power to hurt or heal—as though words were bigoted rather than people. "Context is everything," people have always said. The use of the word "nigger" in *Huckleberry Finn* does not make the book an "act" of hate speech—or does it? In the new view, this is no longer so clear. The very utterance of the word "nigger" (at least by a non-black) is a racist act. When a *Sacramento Bee* cartoonist put the "nigger" mockingly in the mouth of a white supremacist, there were howls of protest and 1,400 canceled subscriptions and an editorial apology, even though the word was plainly being invoked against racists, not against blacks.

Faced with escalating demands of verbal absolutism, newspapers issue lists of forbidden words. The expression "gyp" (derived from "Gypsy") and "Dutch treat" were among the dozens of terms stricken as "offensive" in a much-ridiculed (and later withdrawn) *Los Angeles Times* speech code. The University of Missouri journalism school issued a *Dictionary of Cautionary Words and Phrases*, which included *"Buxom:* Offensive reference to a woman's chest. Do not use. See 'Woman.' *Codger:* Offensive reference to a senior citizen."

As was bound to happen, purists soon discovered that chasing around after words like "gyp" or "buxom" hardly goes to the roots of the problem. As long as they remain bigoted, bigots will simply find other words. If they can't call you a kike then they will say Jewboy, Judas, or Hebe, and when all those are banned they will press words like "oven" and "lampshade" into their service. The vocabulary of hate is potentially as rich as your dictionary, and all you do by banning language used by cretins is to let them decide what the rest of us may say. The problem, some purists have concluded, must therefore go much deeper than laws: it must go to the deeper level of ideas. Racism, sexism, homophobia, and the rest must be built into the very structure of American society and American patterns of thought, so pervasive yet so insidious that, like water to a fish, they are both omnipresent and unseen. The mere existence of prejudice constructs a society whose very nature is prejudiced.

... [W]hat is now under way is a growing drive to eliminate prejudice from every corner of society. I doubt that many people have noticed how far-reaching this anti-pluralist movement is becoming.

In universities: Dozens of universities have adopted codes proscribing speech and other expression that (this is from Stanford's policy, which is more or less representative) "is intended to insult or stigmatize an individual or a small number of individuals on the basis of their sex, race, color, handicap, religion, sexual orientation or national and ethnic origin." Some codes punish only persistent harassment of a targeted individual, but many, following the purist doctrine that even one racist is too many, go much further. At Penn, an administrator declared: "We at the University of Pennsylvania have guaranteed students and the community that they can live in a community free of sexism, racism, and homophobia." Here is the purism that gives "political correctness" its distinctive combination of puffy high-mindedness and authoritarian zeal....

In criminal law: Consider two crimes. In each, I am beaten brutally; in each, my jaw is smashed and my skull is split in just the same way. However, in the first crime my assailant calls me an "asshole"; in the second he calls me a "queer." In most states, in many localities, and, as of September 1994, in federal cases, these two crimes are treated differently: the crime motivated by bias—or deemed to be so motivated by prosecutors and juries—gets a stiffer punishment. "Longer prison terms for bigots," shrilled Brooklyn Democratic Congressman Charles Schumer, who introduced the federal hate-crimes legislation, and those are what the law now provides. Evidence that the assailant holds prejudiced beliefs, even if he doesn't actually express them while committing an offense, can serve to elevate the crime. Defendants in hate-crimes cases may be grilled on how many black friends they have and whether they have told racist jokes. To increase a prison sentence only because of the defendant's "prejudice" (as gauged by prosecutor and jury) is, of course, to try minds and punish beliefs. Purists say, Well, they are dangerous minds and poisonous beliefs.

In the workplace: Though government cannot constitutionally suppress bigotry directly, it is now busy doing so indirectly by requiring employers to eliminate prejudice. Since the early 1980s, courts and the Equal Employment Opportunity Commission have moved to bar workplace speech deemed to create a hostile or abusive working environment for minorities. The law, held a federal court in 1988, "does require that an employer take prompt action to prevent ... bigots from expressing their opinions in a way that abuses or offends their co-workers," so as to achieve "the goal of eliminating prejudices and biases from our society." So it was, as UCLA law professor Eugene Volokh notes, that the EEOC charged that a manufacturer's ads using admittedly accurate depictions of samurai, kabuki, and sumo were "racist" and "offensive to people of Japanese origin"; that a Pennsylvania court found that an employer's printing Bible verses on paychecks was religious harassment of Jewish employees; that an employer had to desist using gender-based job titles like "foreman" and "draftsman" after a female employee sued.

On and on the campaign goes, darting from one outbreak of prejudice to another like a cat chasing flies. In the American Bar Association, activists demand that lawyers who express "bias or prejudice" be penalized. In the Education Department, the civil-rights office presses for a ban on computer bulletin board comments that "show hostility toward a person or group based on sex, race or color, including slurs, negative stereotypes, jokes or pranks." In its security checks for government jobs, the FBI takes to asking whether applicants are "free of biases against any class of citizens," whether, for instance, they have told racist jokes or indicated other "prejudices." Joke police! George Orwell, grasping the close relationship of jokes to dissent, said that every joke is a tiny revolution. The purists will have no such rebellions.

The purist campaign reaches, in the end, into the mind itself. In a lecture at the University of New Hampshire, a professor compared writing to sex ("You and the subject become one"); he was suspended and required to apologize, but what was most insidious was the order to undergo university-approved counseling to have his mind straightened out. At the University of Pennsylvania, a law lecturer said, "We have ex-slaves here who should know about the Thirteenth Amendment"; he was banished from campus for a year and required to make a public apology, and he, too, was compelled to attend a "sensitivity and racial awareness" session. Mandatory reeducation of alleged bigots is the natural consequence of intellectual purism. Prejudice must be eliminated! ...

* * *

What is especially dismaying is that the purists pursue prejudice in the name of protecting minorities. In order to protect people like me (homosexual), they must pursue people like me (dissident). In order to bolster minority self-esteem, they

suppress minority opinion. There are, of course, all kinds of practical and legal problems with the purists' campaign: the incursions against the first Amendment; the inevitable abuses by prosecutors and activists who define as "hateful" or "violent" whatever speech they dislike or can score points off of; the lack of any evidence that repressing prejudice eliminates rather than inflames it. But minorities, of all people, ought to remember that by definition we cannot prevail by numbers, and we generally cannot prevail by force. Against the power of ignorant mass opinion and group prejudice and superstition, we have only our voices. If you doubt that minorities' voices are powerful weapons, think of the lengths to which Southern officials went to silence the Reverend Martin Luther King Jr. (recall that the city commissioner of Montgomery, Alabama, won a $500,000 libel suit, later overturned in *New York Times v. Sullivan* [1964], regarding an advertisement in the *Times* placed by civil-rights leaders who denounced the Montgomery police). Think of how much gay people have improved their lot over twenty-five years simply by refusing to remain silent. Recall the Michigan student who was prosecuted for saying that homosexuality is a treatable disease, and notice that he was black. Under that Michigan speech code, more than twenty blacks were charged with racist speech, while no instance of racist speech by whites was punished. In Florida, the hate-speech law was invoked against a black man who called a policeman a "white cracker"; not so surprisingly, in the first hate-crimes case to reach the Supreme Court, the victim was white and the defendant black.

In the escalating war against "prejudice," the right is already learning to play by the rules that were pioneered by the purist activists of the left. [In 1994] leading Democrats, including the President, criticized the Republican Party for being increasingly in the thrall of the Christian right. Some of the rhetoric was harsh ("fire-breathing Christian radical right"), but it wasn't vicious or even clearly wrong. Never mind: when Democratic Representative Vic Fazio said Republicans were "being forced to the fringes by the aggressive political tactics of the religious right," the chairman of the Republican National Committee, Haley Barbour, said, "Christian-bashing" was "the left's preferred form of religious bigotry." Bigotry! Prejudice! "Christians active in politics are now on the receiving end of an extraordinary campaign of bias and prejudice," said the conservative leader William J. Bennett. One discerns, here, where the new purism leads. Eventually, any criticism of any group will be "prejudice."

Here is the ultimate irony of the new purism: words, which pluralists hope can be substituted for violence, are redefined by purists *as* violence.

"The experience of being called 'nigger,' 'spic,' 'Jap,' or 'kike' is like receiving a slap in the face," Charles Lawrence wrote in 1990. "Psychic injury is no less an injury than being struck in the face, and it often is far more severe." This kind of talk is commonplace today. Epithets, insults, often even polite expressions of what's taken to be prejudice are called by purists "assaultive speech," "words that wound," "verbal violence." "To me, racial epithets are not speech," one University of Michigan law professor said. "They are bullets." In her speech accepting the 1993 Nobel Prize for Literature in Stockholm, Sweden, the author Toni Morrison said this: "Oppressive language does more than represent violence; it is violence."

It is not violence. I am thinking back to a moment on the subway in Washington, a little thing. I was riding home late one night and a squad of noisy kids, maybe seventeen or eighteen years old, noisily piled into the car. They yelled across the car and a girl said, "Where do we get off?"

A boy said, "Farragut North."

The girl: *"Faggot* North!"

The boy: "Yeah! Faggot North!"

General hilarity.

First, before the intellect resumes control, there is a moment of fear, an animal moment. Who are they? How many of them? How dangerous? Where is the way out? All of these things are noted preverbally and assessed by the gut. Then the brain begins an assessment: they are sober, this is probably too public a place for them to do it, there are more girls than boys, they were just talking, it is probably nothing.

They didn't notice me and there was no incident. The teenage babble flowed on, leaving me to think. I became interested in my own reaction: the jump of fear out of nowhere like an alert animal, the sense for a brief time that one is naked and alone and should hide or run away. For a time, one ceases to be a human being and becomes instead a faggot.

* * *

The fear engendered by these words is real. The remedy is as clear and as imperfect as ever: protect citizens against violence. This, I grant, is something that American society has never done very well and now does quite poorly. It is no solution to define words as violence or prejudice as oppression, and then by cracking down on words or thoughts pretend that we are doing something about violence and oppression. No doubt it is easier to pass a speech code or hate-crimes law and proclaim the streets safer than actually to make the streets safer, but the one must never be confused with the other. Every cop or prosecutor chasing words is one fewer chasing criminals. In the world rife with real violence and oppression, full of Rwandas and Bosnias and eleven-year-olds spraying bullets at children in Chicago and in turn being executed by gang lords, it is odious of Toni Morrison to say that words are violence.

Indeed, equating "verbal violence" with physical violence is a treacherous, mischievous business. Not long ago a writer was charged with viciously and gratuitously wounding the feelings and dignity of millions of people. He was charged, in effect, with exhibiting flagrant prejudice against Muslims and out-rageously slandering their beliefs. "What is freedom of expression?" mused Salman Rushdie a year after the ayatollahs sentenced him to death and put a price on his head. "Without the freedom to offend, it ceases to exist." I can think of nothing sadder than that minority activists, in their haste to make the world better, should be the ones to forget the lesson of Rushdie's plight: for minorities, pluralism, not purism, is the answer. The campaigns to eradicate prejudice—all of them, the speech codes and workplace restrictions and mandatory therapy for accused bigots and all the rest—should stop, now. The whole objective of eradicating prejudice, as opposed to correcting and criticizing it, should be repudiated as a fool's errand. Salman Rushdie is right, Toni Morrison wrong, and minorities belong at his side, not hers.

NO

Thomas W. Peard

HATE SPEECH ON CAMPUS: EXPLORING THE LIMITS OF FREE SPEECH

White students on the campus of the University of Wisconsin followed a female African-American student shouting "We've never tried a nigger."[1] Appalling examples such as these which abound in the literature represent the type of seriously abusive racist speech that I wish to address.

In this paper I outline and apply an analytical framework for determining when it is morally permissible to regulate such speech. I also delineate several policy considerations to be consulted in addressing the form such regulation should take.

I focus here on "first-strike" racist fighting words hate speech (hereafter "racist hate speech"). These are fighting words that (i) are directed to minority members who are strangers to the speaker, (ii) are intended to insult or stigmatize such individuals on the basis of their race[2] and (iii) are unprovoked and unanticipated. Fighting words are words addressed directly to the hearer[3] which "by their very utterance inflict injury or tend to incite an immediate breach of the peace."[4]

I

Difficult moral questions, including the moral permissibility of restricting hate speech, often require one to balance the interests of the relevant parties. The balancing test I adopt is intended to weigh the interests of the speaker who engages in hate speech against the interests of the hearer. On one scale of the balance is the seriousness of the harm or offense caused by the speech. This is weighed against the reasonableness of the speaker's conduct.

The seriousness of the offense or harm is determined by (1) the *magnitude* of the risk of harm, if any (compounded out of *gravity* and *probability* of harm); (2) the *intensity, durability,* and *degree of directedness* of the offense, if any; (3) the ease with which the victim can avoid the offensive/harmful conduct; (4) whether the victim assumed the risk of harm/offense; and (5) whether and to what extent the harm/offense can be mitigated.

From Thomas W. Peard, "Hate Speech on Campus: Exploring the Limits of Free Speech," *From the Center: A Newsletter,* vol. 16, no. 1 (Spring 1997). Copyright © 1997 by Thomas W. Peard. Reprinted by permission.

Factors determining reasonableness of the conduct are (6) its personal importance to the actor and its social value generally; and (7) the extent to which the conduct is motivated by spite, malice or the intent to harm/offend the victim.[5]

Following Feinberg, we will understand harms to be wrongful setbacks to significant interests, such as interests in mental and physical health, intellectual acuity, etc.[6] The term "offense" encompasses various disliked mental states caused by wrongful conduct.[7] The principal offended states of mind relevant here are shame, embarrassment, anxiety, fear, resentment, humiliation and anger.[8]

II

In this section I apply the proposed test to racist hate speech. A complete analysis is not possible due to space limitations. But we can cover salient points.

Harms and Offenses

Principal harms that may be caused by racist hate speech include harms resulting from (i) racial subordination; (ii) group and individual defamation; and (iii) breach of the peace.

Racial subordination. Racist speech is a pervasive means for conveying discriminatory attitudes. It is a severe dignitary affront which may cause immediate emotional and physical distress and impair an individual's self-worth. In some cases it is an integral part of assaultive conduct. A single incident of racist hate speech typically causes incremental harm that builds on past discrimination and increases the victim's susceptibility to future harm. Racist speech on campus may also result in educational inequalities. Intimidated minority members are less likely to participate fully in academic and extracurricular activities. Effects of repeated discriminatory treatment include psychological, sociological, physical and economic harm, and even harm to the victim's children through the effects of racism on parenting practices.[9]

Defamation. Full consideration of harms caused by defamatory hate speech requires a theory of defamation which is beyond the scope of this paper. I note, however, that under standard defamation law it is unlikely that racist hate speech typically constitutes provable individual or group defamation.[10]

Breach of the peace. Racist hate speech both *provokes* the victim and *challenges* the hearer to fisticuffs or even more severe forms of physical violence.[11] Accordingly, such conduct may pose a significant risk of harm from breach of the peace.

Offense. As several writers have observed,[12] the offense caused by racist fighting words is generally intense, durable and sharply directed. It is varied as well and may include shame, embarrassment, anxiety, fear, resentment, humiliation and anger.

Total disvalue of harm and offense. The disvalue of harms and offenses may be added. The total disvalue (risk of harm + offense) of an act of racist hate speech generally exceeds the disvalue of the harm or offense alone. For example, where the incident causes a setback to educational equality *and* immediate offense, the total disvalue of the act is greater than that of either addendum.

Factors (3)–(5). Typically, a victim of racist hate speech does not assume the risk of the conduct, cannot avoid it and cannot mitigate the harm or offense, e.g., by "more speech" or by steeling oneself against the conduct.[13]

Reasonableness of Conduct

As the Supreme Court has recognized, fighting words are no essential part of any exposition of ideas.[14] Racist hate speech has little to do with discovery of the truth; rather it impedes robust discussion and debate through intimidation of minority members. Such speech primarily consists in emotive utterances intended to express and vent hostility, animosity and the like and to personally vilify the speaker's audience. Undoubtedly, the speech may have propositional content—often indeterminate—but the essential cognitive content of the propositions can be communicated without the use of racist hate speech.

It may be thought that racist hate speech has value to the extent it plays a role in *emotive* advocacy—persuasion through the *venting* or *expression* of emotions and attitudes. However, the purpose of such advocacy is usually to weaken the opposition through intimidation, harassment and similar means and perhaps to issue a rallying cry to others perversely motivated by the personal vilification of minority members. Emotive advocacy also may be used defensively to counter advocacy of opponents, but this is largely irrelevant to first-strike utterances.

The social value, if any, of emotive advocacy through intimidation and similar conduct is low owing to the risks of multiple societal harms such as racial inequality, divisiveness and incivility. Moreover, emotive advocacy of this type is usually malicious conduct intended solely to harm and offend others. The reasonable-

ness of such conduct must then be *further* discounted under factor (7) of our test. Additionally, empirical studies dispute any social benefit from allowing speakers to vent emotions that might otherwise be expressed in violence.[15]

The personal value of racist hate speech is also low. The conduct hardly promotes the speaker's interests in acquiring information or making considerate judgments —interests sometimes associated with the value of free speech.[16] Certainly, the speaker's interests in communication are implicated. But base impulses to deprecate others typically play no significant role in the speaker's network of interests and may be self-defeating, as where the conduct results in debilitating guilt. There are extremists for whom such conduct plays a more integral role, but even this may be relatively minor. In any case, *whatever* its personal value the reasonableness of such conduct must be drastically reduced under factor (7). Further, any interference with speaker interests such as liberty and autonomy, due to speech regulation, is wholly offset by the speaker's interference with correlative victim interests.

One final consideration. There is unfairness in requiring an innocent party harmed or offended by the actor's conduct to pay the costs of promoting the actor's interests, especially where the harm/offense is intentional. In such cases greater weight should be given to the innocent party's interests. Call this the *fairness principle*. Its applicability to racist hate speech requires us to give additional weight to the victim's interests.

Assessing the Balance

As we noted, the offense caused by racist hate speech may be extreme, and there is typically a substantial risk of incremental harm. There is also risk of serious harm, as where the victim is especially vulnerable to discriminatory treatment. On the other balance, the personal and social value of racist hate speech is low and must be further reduced under factor (7). Also, the fairness principle applies, requiring more favorable treatment of the victim's interests.

There is another point. It is sometimes claimed that mere offensiveness is an insufficient reason for regulating speech because too much speech would be subject to restriction. However, the exceedingly high risk of serious offense posed by racist hate speech may distinguish it from less offensive speech. This distinction would then permit principled regulation of racist hate speech even absent a showing of significant harm, provided that the offensiveness is not due merely to the opinions expressed. The risk of breach of the peace further distinguishes racist hate speech from some less offensive forms of expression.

Two objections to our analysis should be considered. The first is that racist hate speech has *propositional* content that cannot be effectively conveyed through other forms of expression. Regulation of racist hate speech may then threaten impermissible content censorship. The second objection is that racist *opinions* —not their forms of expression—are the principal cause of the harm/offense described above. Thus regulation of racist hate speech may have minimal value because it can be circumvented through more civil expression of racist opinion.

The first objection assumes, without argument, that the propositional content in question is individuated by its form of expression.[17] Even if that is true, the *essential* propositional *and* emotive content necessary for robust discussion may be expressible without using racist hate speech. Additionally, propositional content may be restricted where it threatens sufficient harm/offense. Spitting in another's face is proscribable even if the conduct conveys an otherwise inexpressible proposition.

The second objection rests on questionable empirical assumptions about the harm/offense caused by civil expression of racist opinions. Testimony of minority members[18] and other evidence[19] corroborate the view that racist hate speech causes greater harm and offense than more civil language and that such speech is sufficiently prevalent to require redress. There are racial insults less harmful and offensive than racist hate speech. But even if these should not be enjoined, there may be significant social value in restricting the worst forms of hate speech, due in part to the symbolic function of the regulation.[20]

The foregoing analysis suggests that the university may regulate racist hate speech. However, additional empirical evidence of the magnitude of harm/offense would be helpful in drawing more definite conclusions.

III

If hate speech may be restricted, what type of regulation should be imposed? The decision ought to be based in part on policy considerations such as whether the regulation: (a) is facially invalid because it prohibits protected speech; (b) can be fairly and efficiently administered; (c) constitutes content discrimination; (d) has an undue chilling effect on protected speech; (e) impermissibly inhibits equal access to expressive opportunities;[21] (f) unduly encourages the filing of fraudulent, vexatious or frivolous claims or charges; (g) provides for a reasonable assignment and apportionment of fault and a reasonable assessment and apportionment of damages; and (h) duplicates other regulations or claims.

Space does not permit elaboration. But I will briefly consider (c), a topic of recent interest. Consider the Stanford regulation which regulates insulting or fighting words

> ... intended to insult or stigmatize an individual or a small group of individuals on the basis of their sex, race, color, handicap, religion, sexual orientation, or national and ethnic origin.[22]

This regulation apparently constitutes subject matter discrimination because it regulates fighting words only on matters stated in the regulation.[23] It does not regulate, for instance, hate speech directed against bigotry. The regulation may also constitute viewpoint discrimination since egalitarians are permitted to use the most virulent language available to them while their opponents may not.[24]

There are two brief replies that, at least, shift the burden of proof. First, the content discrimination at issue does not significantly threaten to exclude ideas from the marketplace of ideas because they can be expressed by means other than fighting words hate speech.[25] Fighting words hate speech may pose a more significant threat in this regard by excluding minority speech through intimidation.

Second, the objection assumes that the regulation is unfair and will skew political debate by taking weapons from the communicative arsenal of racists (and others) without effecting a proportionate taking from the communicative arsenal of their opponents. But there is no showing that proponents of equality have like weapons in their arsenal (those that cause substantially the same offense and harm). If they have no like weapons, then it is the use of fighting words hate speech that unfairly skews debate. Furthermore, some inequality in hate speech regulation may be tolerated to promote compelling social interests such as the alleviation of significant injustices.

I conclude that the foregoing objections to the Stanford regulation are not decisive.

NOTES

1. Thomas C. Grey, "Civil Rights Versus Civil Liberties," reprinted in *Philosophy of Law*, 5th ed., ed. Joel Feinberg and Hyman Gross (Belmont: Wadsworth Publishing Co., 1995), 294–310 at 296.

2. See the Stanford regulation below.

3. See *Cohen v. California*, 408 U.S. 15 (1971).

4. *Chaplinsky v. New Hampshire*, 315 U.S. 568, 572 (1942).

5. This test is derived from Joel Feinberg's mediating maxims for application of the harm and offense principles. See Joel Feinberg, *The Moral Limits of the Criminal Law: Offense to Others*, vol. 2 (New York: Oxford University Press, 1985; Oxford University Press Paperback, 1987), 26; *The Moral Limits of the Criminal Law: Harm to Others*, vol. 1 (New York: Oxford University Press Paperback, 1987), 216.

6. See Feinberg, *Harm to Others*, Chapter I, 31–64.

7. Feinberg, *Offense to Others*, 1–5.

8. See Ibid.

9. This paragraph is an exceedingly brief summary of Richard Delgado's comprehensive discussion of harms caused by racial insults in "Words That Wound: A Tort Action for Racial Insults, Epithets and Name-Calling," *Harvard Civil Rights-Civil Liberties Law Review* 17 (1982), 133–81 at 135–49.

10. See e.g., Delgado, "Words That Wound," 157–159; John Arthur, *The Unfinished Constitution: Philosophy and Constitutional Practice* (Belmont: Wadsworth Publishing Company, 1989), 90–91.

11. See Feinberg, *Offense to Others*, 226–36.

12. See, e.g., Charles R. Lawrence III, "If He Hollers Let Him Go: Regulating Racist Speech on Campus," reprinted in *Social and Personal Ethics*, 2d ed., ed. William H. Shaw (Belmont: Wadsworth Publishing Company, 1996), 272–80.

13. See Delgado, "Words That Wound," 146.

14. *Chaplinsky v. New Hampshire*, 315 U.S. 568, 571–72 (1942).

15. See Delgado, "Words That Wound," 140.

16. See, e.g., Joshua Cohen, "Freedom of Expression," *Philosophy and Public Affairs* (1994), 207-63 at 224, 228–29; Kent Greenawalt, *Speech, Crime and the Use of Language* (New York: Oxford University Press, 1989), 26–27.

17. This raises rich philosophical issues concerning proposition individuation which I cannot address here.

18. See, e.g., Lawrence, "If He Hollers Let Him Go."

19. See generally Delgado, "Words That Wound."

20. See Grey, "Civil Rights Versus Civil Liberties," 305–306.

21. See Cohen, "Freedom of Expression," 245–50.

22. The Stanford Discriminatory Harassment Provision was adopted as a disciplinary rule at Stanford University. Thomas Grey was one of the original drafters. For the full text of the provision, see Grey, "Civil Rights Versus Civil Liberties," 306–307.

23. See Grey, "Civil Rights Versus Civil Liberties," 302.

24. See Ibid.

25. See Cohen, "Freedom of Expression," 255.

POSTSCRIPT

Should "Hate Speech" Be Tolerated?

Rauch claims that an intellectual pluralism that deserves support must tolerate hate speech. Rauch feels that it is not possible to rid a society of prejudice and racism. One reason is that the human species is a "tribal species" that is naturally drawn to the "us versus them" attitudes that lie behind various forms of bigotry. Rauch provides another reason for tolerating hate speech, stemming from the Enlightenment. According to this idea, people do not judge prior to investigation whether a given statement is an expression of truth or of prejudice. Enlightenment thinking does not impose an orthodoxy or set of dogmas that must be followed. It does not reject out of hand any claim. Enlightment permits Galileo to claim that the Earth moves, the Michigan student to state that homosexuality is a treatable disease, and the Holocaust deniers to spread their own ideas. Rauch is confident that post-Enlightenment science is in a position to show that the Earth does move, that homosexuality is no disease, and that the Holocaust did happen.

Rauch seems to think of people as claim makers who should not be prohibited from making what might sound to others like outrageous claims, because sometimes these claims turn out to be true. Galileo sounded outrageous to many people in the early 1600s, but he was right. Holocaust deniers sound outrageous, and they are wrong. So let people say outrageous things—some of them might turn out to be right. However, Peard argues, not all language is of the claim-making kind: Words can be used as weapons against people. If they are used as weapons, they can injure people. And if they can injure people, people need to be protected from them.

Further readings on this issue include Nat Hentoff, *Free Speech for Me—But Not for Thee: How the American Left and Right Relentlessly Censor Each Other* (HarperCollins, 1992); Cass R. Sunstein, *Democracy and the Problem of Free Speech* (Free Press, 1993); Andrew Altman, "Speech Acts and Hate Speech," in M. N. Sellers, ed., *An Ethical Education: Community and Morality in the Multicultural University* (Berg, 1994); Samuel Walker, *Hate Speech: The History of an American Controversy* (University of Nebraska Press, 1994); Bruno Leone, ed., *Free Speech* (Greenhaven Press, 1994); Kent Greenawalt, *Fighting Words: Individuals, Communities, and Liberties of Speech* (Princeton University Press, 1995); Steven J. Heyman, ed., *Hate Speech and the Constitution*, 2 vols. (Garland, 1996); and Paul A. Winters, ed., *Hate Crimes* (Greenhaven Press, 1996). Of particular relevance to the campus situation are Richard Miniter, "Campus Speech Wars: Waving the Tacky Shirt," *Insight on the News* (January 24, 1994) and Robert M. O'Neil, *Free Speech in the College Community* (Indiana University Press, 1997).

On the Internet . . .

http://www.dushkin.com

Literature on Sexual Orientation
This site, sponsored by *Ethics Updates,* contains discussion questions, Internet resources, legislative initiatives, and court cases on issues related to sexual orientation. *http://ethics.acusd.edu/sexual_orientation.html*

NARAL Online
This is the home page of the National Abortion and Reproductive Rights Action League (NARAL), an organization that works to promote reproductive freedom and dignity for women and their families. *http://www.naral.org/*

The Ultimate Pro-Life Resource List
The Ultimate Pro-Life Resource List is one of the most comprehensive listings of right-to-life resources on the Internet. *http://www.prolife.org/ultimate/*

PART 3

Morality, Sex, and Reproduction

The issues in this section specifically address matters of sexuality and reproduction. Since we are sexual and reproductive beings, and since human beings are social and naturally interact with each other, it is imperative to have some idea of what is allowable and what is not with respect to sexual and reproductive matters.

The issues in this section do not presuppose that there is anything morally questionable about sex itself, but they do raise questions about how, in today's world, we should regard certain matters of sex and reproduction.

■ Should Society Be More Accepting of Homosexuality?

■ Is Pornography Degrading to Women?

■ Is Abortion Immoral?

ISSUE 9

Should Society Be More Accepting of Homosexuality?

YES: Michael Nava and Robert Dawidoff, from *Created Equal: Why Gay Rights Matter to America* (St. Martin's Press, 1994)

NO: Carl F. Horowitz, from "Homosexuality's Legal Revolution," *The Freeman* (May 1991)

ISSUE SUMMARY

YES: Attorney Michael Nava and history teacher Robert Dawidoff argue that basic constitutional freedoms and liberties require the social acceptance of homosexuality.

NO: Carl F. Horowitz, a policy analyst at the Heritage Foundation, argues that legal acceptance of homosexuality has gone too far. He maintains that open displays of homosexual affection, the homosexualization of entire neighborhoods, and gay mannerisms are deeply offensive to heterosexuals.

One question that frequently lies behind questions of homosexual acceptance is whether or not homosexuality is immoral. If it is, then it is hard to see why society should be more accepting of it. Many arguments do aim to show that homosexuality is indeed immoral. Some claim in this context that homosexuality is unnatural, that its acceptance is a threat to heterosexual people, and that it is condemned by the Roman Catholic Church, among other arguments. But arguments that homosexuality is immoral are much more difficult to state clearly than many people suppose. Part of the problem is that heterosexuals often know very little about homosexuality and often rely upon stereotypical thinking or their feelings rather than logic.

A particular problem associated with the question of whether or not homosexuality should be accepted is that individuals who are not attracted to members of the same sex at all may conclude that, in a personal sense, they do not "accept homosexuality" at all. Yet the question here does not concern any particular individual—it concerns society.

Clearly, there can be degrees of social acceptance of homosexuality. At the lowest levels of acceptance, same-sex relationships (if they existed at all) would be publicly unacknowledged, and homosexuals would have to keep their sexual preferences hidden ("in the closet"). It is questionable whether the existence of homosexuality would even be acknowledged; whether the sexual orientation of celebrities and historical figures would be made known;

whether the homosexuality of foreigners would be acknowledged; and whether homosexual practices in other cultures would be recognized. At the highest levels of social acceptance, homosexuality might be considered so unremarkable that it would not have a name. Or at least nothing socially significant would be affected by someone's sexual orientation.

Our society seems to stand somewhere in the large middle area, although it is probably much closer to the low end of acceptance of homosexuality. Homosexuality is condemned by most people speaking from a religious point of view, and the U.S. Supreme Court has ruled that the Constitution does not guarantee the rights of consenting adults to engage in homosexual acts, even in the privacy of their homes (*Bowers v. Hardwick*, 1986). On the other hand, there are some ways in which society does accept homosexuality. Some insurance companies recognize homosexual relationships and will cover homosexual partners as well as heterosexual spouses. Sometimes rent-control legislation treats a surviving partner of a homosexual union like a surviving spouse. And some legal jurisdictions guarantee homosexuals rights of nondiscrimination.

In the following selections, Michael Nava and Robert Dawidoff argue that basic freedoms and liberties (as enshrined, for example, in the U.S. Constitution) guarantee the rights of gay men and lesbians, although social prejudice often leads to the violation of these rights. Carl F. Horowitz argues that society's legal acceptance of homosexuality is already excessive, to the extent that the rights of homosexuals are impinging on those of heterosexuals.

YES   Michael Nava and Robert Dawidoff

THE ICK FACTOR: HOMOSEXUALITY, CITIZENSHIP, AND THE CONSTITUTION

A QUESTION OF TASTE

Homosexuality disqualifies an American for citizenship. Whatever rights someone may enjoy on account of other identities, attributes, accomplishments, and positions cannot ensure either the free exercise of individual liberty or equal protection of the laws if that person is known to be lesbian or gay. American society still automatically accepts homosexuality as a sufficient cause for deprivation of normal civil rights, and American culture promotes the prejudice that sustains this second-class citizenship. For instance, in September of 1993 a Virginia judge took a child away from his mother solely because she was a lesbian. Routinely exposed to official persecution, common violence, prejudicial treatment, and denied legal recourse, gay and lesbian Americans are only whimsically protected in life, liberty, and property, let alone the myriad understandings of happiness.

Consider what amounts to a national epidemic of gay-bashing. A 1987 Justice Department study reported that gays are the "most frequent victims" of hate crimes. More telling is the fact that 73 percent of these attacks were not reported to police because, as another study concludes, 14 percent of the victims feared more harm from the police. In 1991, anti-gay harassment and violence increased 31 percent in five major cities, including New York, San Francisco, Chicago, Boston, and Minneapolis–St. Paul. A 1993 study found that 28 percent of lesbians and gay men surveyed were subject to anti-gay harassment or gay-bashed within a one-year period, the vast majority not reporting the incidents to authorities. Yet, despite such evidence of the sometimes lethal effects of hatred of lesbians and gay men, the anti-gay right continues to object even to classifying attacks on homosexuals as hate crimes.[1] ...

At times, the controversy surrounding the recognition of sexual orientation as a category of individual liberty makes it seem that what homosexual Americans are claiming differs in some fundamental way from what other groups of individuals have claimed in their movements for the recognition of their civil rights. Frequently, for instance, when gays talk about gay rights, heterosexuals hear talk about sex, not personal freedom. The claim that gays want "special rights" reflects the degree to which lesbians and gay men are seen as so out of the ordinary that their claims to ordinary rights seem special.

But in fact, gays want an end to their special status, their status as pariahs under the Constitution. In twenty-three states sodomy statutes criminalize certain sexual practices—specifically, oral and anal sex—that both homosexuals and heterosexuals engage in. In the 1986 decision *Bowers v. Hardwick,* the Supreme Court held, in effect, that these laws are valid when applied to homosexuals but not when applied to heterosexuals. It doesn't take a legal scholar to ask how these laws, which govern the most intimate behavior, can be an affront to the protected liberty interests of heterosexual people, and not also be an affront to the protected liberty of homosexual people? It was a question the Court declined, with startling animosity, to answer. Yet this refusal was itself an answer: The sexual behavior of homosexuals, the Court implied, is not constitutionally protected *because they are not heterosexuals,* even though the practices are identical....

A patriotic American who happens to be lesbian or gay can only serve in the military by hiding the existence of a private life. The recent and thwarted attempt to lift the ban against gays and lesbians in the armed forces has not changed the message that has greeted returning homosexual soldiers in every American war: You can give your life for your country, but you can't live your life in your country. The line between private and public life overlaps for everybody, not just heterosexuals. The effort to compel gays to lie about their lives and deny their own human experience is itself a deprivation of liberty.

The constitutional status of homosexuals is inextricably bound up with the intense prejudice against them. The straight majority acquiesces in the constitutional disenfranchisement of the gay minority because lesbians and gays have sex with partners of the same sex and because that goes against the majority's grain. That, rather than any truth about homosexuals, has resulted in the common belief that gay rights are about sex. This struggle is not about sex. It is about privacy, individuality, and civil equality and the right of all Americans, not just gay and lesbian Americans, to be free. And, yes, that freedom must include the freedom to express one's own desire for sexual intimacy, homosexual or heterosexual.

The routine denial of civil rights to gays and lesbians reflects a powerful prejudice, one so pervasive and so connected to everything else in society that it is treacherously hard to isolate. Even when not activated into energetic hostility, this prejudice is deeply rooted in and continually reaffirmed by the rituals of family formation, child-rearing, and gender in our culture. One of the tragic ironies in the lives of lesbians and gay men is the degree to which they inevitably assimilate much of this prejudice against them. Another is how the prejudice against homosexuals thrives, even among the family and friends of gay people. (But it is also true that people who know someone who is lesbian or gay are less likely to oppose gay rights than people who claim not to know someone gay; indeed, a recent survey of American voters showed that 53 percent of respondents who know someone gay are inclined to be more favorable to gay rights than the 47 percent who think they do not know someone gay.[2]...

The decision to regard homosexuality as a species of alien behavior, and to punish it, makes a law of the majority's personal taste and habits. For most people, the "sin" of homosexuality is a question of taste. The question embarrasses people not because they can't imagine it, but because they can and do. The revulsion many men and women feel at the thought of sexual activity between people of their own sex remains a formidable obstacle on the path of gay rights. This revulsion, which we call the Ick Factor, equates distaste with immorality. It is a child's vision of life, in which the things one wants to do are natural, and the things one doesn't want to do are matters of morality: "I don't like it; it's bad." The undertone of the debate and the refusal to entertain a discussion about gay rights echoes the schoolyard din of "Ick," "Yuck," and "Gross." Teenagers apparently react this way to scenes of gay affection in movies. Of course, teenagers react that way to all but a few things. Adults are supposed to leave this stage when they assume the responsibilities and privileges of citizenship.

We believe that adults can think about issues of sexual orientation without being threatened as if they were adolescents imprisoned in the metabolism of puberty. We think that adults can learn to treat lesbians and gay men with the calm and neighborly regard democracy requires to survive. The prejudice against homosexuality is not so much religious as visceral, but neither religious nor visceral feelings justify the denial of constitutional rights in our system of government. Discrimination against gays reflects an awkward and inevitably failed attempt to isolate some people on account of whom they love, a matter that is supremely and constitutionally their own business.

Prejudice requires an elaborate social support to thrive, and the formidably articulated system of reinforcing prejudice toward homosexuality remains the bulwark of legal discrimination against gays and lesbians. What it all boils down to, however, is neither elaborate nor particularly complicated. At the core of the alleged "unnaturalness" of homosexuality is how unnatural it would feel to someone for whom it would indeed be unnatural. This distaste—understandable, though not constitutionally privileged—lurks among even those who wish gays and lesbians well and indeed would sympathize with, if not champion, their claiming of their rights. What blocks gay equality is prejudice. What fuels the movement for gay equality is the conviction that this prejudice is not constitutionally protected, but that the individual rights of homosexual Americans are....

WHAT'S AT STAKE

At stake in the movement for lesbian and gay equality are established constitutional protections of a species of individual liberty, called by the courts the right of privacy, and the more familiar guarantee of equal protection of the laws. The agitation for gay civil rights confronts the nation with the question of whether these rights will be subordinated to the religious and ideological views of a minority that blames gays and lesbians for what it dislikes and fears in society. Unquestionably, their attack on gays and lesbians amounts to an attack on individual freedom itself.

At its core, gay rights are an issue of individual liberty, the very individual liberty protected by the Constitution....

[T]he price you must pay for the enjoyment of your own liberty is the recognition that other people, especially people with whom you may not like to identify, have an equal claim to the same liberty. America requires an allegiance to a stern principle of individual liberty. This is the reason gay rights matter to Americans generally and not just to lesbians and gay men.

... [T]he opponents of gay rights, like the opponents of every other historical struggle for civil rights, have to encroach on the liberty of the majority to prevent liberty from being extended to the minority....

THE AMERICAN ROOTS
OF GAY RIGHTS

Gay rights restates, as all great civil rights and liberties movements do, the essential grounds of American constitutional nationhood....

In our system it is the individual who makes moral choices as well as material, sexual, and political ones. While the individual's choices in these matters are not unmediated by the community, they are not to be dictated by it. The moral history of this nation might well be seen as the assumption by more and more individuals of their fundamental rights and their insistence on their part of the social contract. That we are used to thinking of these rights as belonging to classes comes from convenience and legal habit. But the equal protection of the law extends through classes to the individual, and the rights belong to the individual, not the class.

... [T]he movement for gay rights relies on two broad principles, the first is the individual right of homosexuals to enjoy the privacy that is the precondition for the enjoyment of civil liberty. The second is the enjoyment by homosexuals as a class or group of equal protection of the laws, which means essentially that one's individual right to equal treatment under the law may not be violated because one belongs to the class of people whose sexual orientation is toward members of the same sex. The individual right to privacy is a supreme constitutional value; equal protection of the laws is an inescapable constitutional guarantee. Without privacy and without equal protection of the laws, one simply does not enjoy American citizenship. The deprivation of privacy and equal protection constitutes the central ground for the gay civil rights movement.

When we talk about the right of privacy, we are talking, as the Supreme Court did in a recent abortion case, about a right that exists "at the heart of liberty," the right "to define one's own concept of existence, of meaning, of the universe and the mystery of human life. Beliefs about these matters could not define the attributes of personhood were they formed under the compulsion of the state."[3] Gays and lesbians do not constitute an identifiable minority along the lines of ethnic, racial, or class minorities. Being gay cuts across all human lines; gays and lesbians exist in all strata of society and in each group within those strata. For this reason, their struggle for equal rights particularly calls on the underlying constitutional principle of individual liberty.

In addition, not only the status of being gay but also the process of self-discovery is particularly individual. The lesbian and gay population consists of women and men who have arrived, by very different paths, at the same self-knowledge. The feelings that prompt ordinary people to love members of their own gender against the grain of convention, and the decision to honor those feelings, are different for every person. The decision to accept one's homosexuality occurs in that interior space where a person's deepest truths reside: the core of personal liberty. It is exactly that part of the self to which neither government nor other people's religion has legitimate access. This argument is not about sexual practices or particular lifestyles. It hinges on whether gay and lesbian Americans are entitled to the same enjoyment as their fellow citizens of the freedom to make choices about how to live their lives without suffering discrimination in consequence....

SEX, RACE, AND GAY RIGHTS

The gay and lesbian Americans' movement for civil equality raises constitutional principles as well as legal arguments, and it makes sense to consider the general problem of individual freedom in light of that movement. When we speak of equality under the law and of personal freedom, we are not—as even a majority of the Supreme Court appears to believe—talking about the right to have sex. People have always engaged in homosexual practices, with or without the sanction of family, church, and state. But sexual orientation goes beyond sex, because it involves not only the body but also the heart, mind, and soul. Sexual orientation involves the intimate associations—happily, including the sexual—that individuals form and that help give

meaning and richness to life. The continuing categorical denial of basic civil rights to lesbian and gay Americans sends the message that their lives are less valuable than the lives of heterosexuals.

Sexual desire is natural. Sexual formation is social. To criminalize a kind of sexual desire, a society must articulate a common good that is rationally served by elevating some desires over others. It is possible, for instance, that a theocratic Christian fundamentalist state might criminalize homosexuality—along with adultery, nonmarital sexual relations of any sort, and all sexual practices but the missionary position—for reasons that make sense to its purpose as a regime dedicated to furthering its adherents' notions of divine revelation. The United States, however, is explicitly not such a regime, and it may not impose restrictions on individual freedom in order to serve the purposes of religious sects. The First Amendment protects religious freedom in the same way it protects individual freedom; such protection does not license the invasion of individual freedom even on God's business or permit the substitution of particular moralities for the individual, rational choices the Bill of Rights enshrines.

Criminalizing behavior is not sufficient to establish that a kind of behavior is in fact criminal. For example, intermarriage between whites and blacks was once criminalized in this country. Criminalizing such behavior served the recognized social purpose of racial hegemony, but it did not transform that behavior itself into something criminal, let alone unnatural. In a similar fashion, decriminalization of rape and violence directed by whites against blacks did not remove the criminal quality from such acts. The criminalization of the subject race in a racially defined society is an example of the kind of criminalization that homosexuals experience. To criminalize some people because their sexual orientation is in the minority is a crude tool of social policy —and, as it happens, that social policy serves no function in our society other than the preservation of a heterosexual privilege that does not appear to have had a beneficial effect on the social or moral common life.

Legal preference for heterosexual over homosexual orientation must be based on arguments about the human good in this society, not just on moralistic pronouncements. What reasons can be advanced for restricting individual sexual desire that apply to homosexual and not to heterosexual people? Stereotypical libels notwithstanding, gays do not commit sexual abuse more often than straights; the opposite is true, judging by rape statistics.[4] Family formation is not at risk because of gay and lesbian equality. In fact, if the goal of social policy is healthy family life, the equal recognition of families in which homosexual children and adults play a part will advance the purposes of those for whom strong families are the foundation of a good society. Lesbians and gay men do not prevent heterosexuals from forming families; and, as parents and children, lesbians and gays are equally capable of carrying on the social functions of families....

Although there are many grounds for identity and community among homosexuals—even across the important divide between lesbians and gay men —the deepest ground of sharing arises from a common oppression that has created a common culture and a shared form of desire that no doubt contributes to some common values. There is no reason to believe that the millions of lesbians and gay men in fact share connections analogous to the obvious and compelling ones of race, religion, gender, and nationality, or that even the groups that do share such connections founded in homosexuality are in the majority. The common experience of being gay is deeply individual. You discover your sexual identity yourself, your closet is your own, your coming out is individual.

It may be that the key contribution of the gay and lesbian movement to the history of civil rights and civil liberties is its re-emphasis on the individual. Being gay is an individuality that cuts across all the other identities around which civil rights movements have formed. It presents a challenge by individuality to group identity and group allegiance. The only culture we can say for certain that American homosexuals share is the common American culture. Central to this culture is a professed belief in individual freedom, yours as well as mine. The drama of the gay civil rights movement is less its statement of group aims than its necessary return to the ground of the individual asserting personal rights to personal freedom for personal choice about the personal life....

HOW GAY RIGHTS RESTATES INDIVIDUAL RIGHTS

Lesbians and gay men who have come out and begun to insist that their lives and their choices about how to live deserve parity with the lives and choices of heterosexuals symbolize the fears of many Americans that freedom is going too far. For some, homosexuality is a marker of moral and social decay; the emergence of the lesbian and gay rights movement suggests to them not freedom but license. Moreover, among the religious right and self-styled cultural conservatives, lesbians and gays occupy the place once held by Jews and Communists in the practice of paranoid politics. Right-wing and restrictionist activists speak as darkly of the "homosexual agenda" as anti-Semites used to talk of *The Protocols of the Elders of Zion*, pretending knowledge of what they fear to know. Reactionary religionists warn of gays converting unsuspecting heterosexuals in the same way anticommunists used to warn of femmes fatales dispatched from Moscow to seduce innocent American boys. The scapegoating of gays and lesbians has less to do with homosexuality than with powerful cultural anxieties about family and sexuality, which express themselves in a wave of anti-individualist rhetoric. . . .

The labeling of gays as sexually degenerate and unnatural is the same kind of labeling that has always been used to justify the denial of rights to individuals belonging to "minority" communities. It was less than forty years ago that a Virginia Supreme Court judge wrote in defense of the Old Dominion's miscegenation law: "[The] law which forbids their intermarriage and the social amalgamation which leads to the corruption of the races is as clearly divine as that which imparted to them their different natures."[5] Similarly, assertions of "natural law," warnings of corruption, and the invocation of the divine repeatedly find their way into arguments justifying discrimination against gays and lesbians. Such appeals are arguments against individual freedom because they deny the validity of personal experience when it is at odds with convention. Much of the fierce opposition to gay rights consists of this kind of denial. In effect, gay men and women are taught that their experience of themselves as decent, productive, loving humans is false, because homosexuality is unnatural and sinful. In this case, however, their own self-knowledge has helped gays and lesbians overcome the labels attached to their sexual natures. The process of coming out is harrowing, but it can leave in its wake an unshakable core of certainty of self.

Coming out is more than an acknowledgment, acceptance, or even announcement of one's sexual identity. It represents a continuing process founded on an act of compassion toward oneself—a compassion, alas, seldom shown by one's own family or friends, let alone society. That act is the acceptance of one's fundamental worth, including, and not despite, one's homosexuality, in the face of social condemnation and likely persecution. Coming out is the process through which one arrives at one's values the hard way, testing them against what one knows to be true about oneself. Gay men and lesbians must think about family, morality, nature, choice, freedom, and responsibility in ways most people never have to. Truly to come out, a gay person must become one of those human beings who, as psychiatrist Alice Miller writes, "want to be true to themselves. Rejection, ostracism, loss of love, and name calling will not fail to affect them; they will suffer as a result and they will dread them, but once they have their authentic self they will not want to lose it. And when they sense something is being demanded of them to which their whole being says no, they cannot do it. They simply cannot."[6]

It bears repeating that what is sought by gays and lesbians is not new or special rights, but, rather, the extension of existing rights guaranteed to all American citizens by the Constitution and identified by the Declaration of Independence as the purpose, not the gift, of government. Nor would the removal of legal disabilities suffered by gays and lesbians "promote" homosexuality, as is sometimes argued. Ending discrimination does no more than dismantle the props by which one group of citizens unfairly enjoys a superior status over another group of citizens.

We must also again emphasize that gays and lesbians do not seek the right to *be* homosexual. This "right" is not one within the authority of government to give. They are fighting for the right to secure the conditions under which they may lead ordinary, civilized lives....

The movement for gay rights would have surprised the Founders, many of whom, after all, were slaveholders, and who limited the franchise to male property owners. But they wrote a binding set of laws that were meant to surprise them. Their own habits and prejudices were among the conventions that the Constitution was meant to trump. They believed in the progress of liberty, which they based on their conception of human beings as rational creatures. The issue of gay rights is often lost in a morass of prejudice, religious and secular, but prejudice can be overcome by reason and reflection. We believe that when bias is put to one side, reason reveals that the cause of gay rights is a matter of simple justice.

NOTES

1. Hate crime statistics: *USA Today*, March 30, 1992; news release of the Anti-Violence Project of the Los Angeles Gay and Lesbian Community Services Center, March 11, 1993. For an example of how antigay extremists try to exclude gay-bashing from the category of hate crimes, see Marian Wallace, "Junior Scholastic Pushes Gay Agenda," in *Family Voice*, May 1993 (vol. 15, no. 5), p. 29.

2. *U.S. News and World Report*, July 5, 1993, p. 42.

3. *Casey v. Planned Parenthood of Southeastern Pennsylvania* (1992), 120 L.Ed.2d 674, 698.

4. Bureau of Justice Statistics, *Sourcebook of Criminal Justice Statistics*, (Washington, D.C.: Department of Justice, 1992), p. 266.

5. *Loving v. Virginia* (1966), 388 US 1, 3.

6. Alice Miller, *For Your Own Good: Hidden Cruelty in Child Rearing and the Roots of Violence* (New York: Farrar, Straus, Giroux, 1989), p. 85.

NO

Carl F. Horowitz

HOMOSEXUALITY'S LEGAL REVOLUTION

Last April, a brief series of events occurred in a Madison, Wisconsin, restaurant that spoke volumes about the current character of the homosexual rights movement. An employee of the Espresso Royal Cafe asked two women—presumably lesbians—to refrain from passionately kissing as they sat at a window table. Madison's gay community was not amused. The very next day, about 125 homosexual demonstrators showed up on the premises, and conducted a "kiss-in" for several minutes. A spokeswoman for the protesters, Malvene Collins, demanded, "You say gays and lesbians cannot show affection here? Why not here but in every other restaurant in Madison?" The establishment's chastised owner, Donald Hanigan, assured the crowd, "I regret that this incident ever happened. I want all of you to come in here every day."[1]

In October, several dozen homosexual males, many of them dressed in women's clothing, openly hugged and kissed in a terminal of Seattle-Tacoma Airport, and handed out condoms and leaflets to travelers. Matt Nagel spokesman for the Seattle chapter of . . . [the] homosexual organization, Queer Nation, seemed to sum up the feeling among militants in the local homosexual community. "We're going to homophobic bars, we're going to pack them, we're going to be openly affectionate, we're going to dance together and make it uncomfortable for all the straight people there."[2]

At the same time in Chicago, six homosexual couples staged a "kiss-in" at the cosmetics counter of a Bloomingdale's department store until they were escorted out by security guards. Far from being deterred, the couples shortly went down to the cafeteria of a nearby office building, where they resumed their public display of affection.[3]

A BID FOR LEGITIMACY

After some two decades of confrontation, the homosexual rights movement is consolidating its bid for legitimacy. The phrase, "Out of the closet, and into the streets," sounds quaint. That battle has already been won. Openly

From Carl F. Horowitz, "Homosexuality's Legal Revolution," *The Freeman* (May 1991). Copyright © 1991 by The Foundation for Economic Education, Irvington-on-Hudson, NY. Reprinted by permission. Some notes omitted.

homosexual adults are certainly in the streets—and in stores, airports, and "homophobic" bars. Openly gay television characters, each with handsome, well-scrubbed looks, populate daytime and evening drama. Gay-oriented news programming is available on radio and television. Homosexual activists have all but completed their campaign to persuade the nation's educational establishment that homosexuality is normal "alternative" behavior, and thus any adverse reaction to it is akin to a phobia, such as fear of heights, or an ethnic prejudice, such as anti-Semitism.[4]

The movement now stands on the verge of fully realizing its use of law to create a separate homosexual society paralleling that of the larger society in every way, and to intimidate heterosexuals uncomfortable about coming into contact with it. Through aggressive lobbying by such gay organizations as the Human Rights Campaign Fund, the Lambda Legal Defense and Education Fund, and the National Gay and Lesbian Task Force, the first part of that mission has enjoyed enormous success. About 90 counties and municipalities now have ordinances banning discrimination on the basis of gender orientation. There are roughly 50 openly gay public officials, up from less than a half-dozen in 1980.[5]

Gay couples are increasingly receiving the full benefits marriage, if not through state recognition of homosexual marriage ceremonies, then through enactment of domestic partnership laws.[6] The State of California recently took a big step toward legalization of such marriages: this December [1990] it announced that "non-traditional" families, including homosexual couples, could formally register their unions as "unincorporated non-profit associations."[7] Divorced gay parents are receiving with increasing frequency the right to custody of natural children. Gay adults without children are increasingly receiving the right to adopt them. Aspiring homosexual clergy are demanding—and receiving—the right to be ordained. Openly gay teachers are teaching in public schools. Homosexual soldiers, aware that their sexual orientation is grounds for expulsion from the military, openly declare their proclivities.

A Federal gay rights bill is the ultimate prize, and homosexual activists are blunt and resolute in pursuing such legislation. For example, Jeff Levi, spokesman for the National Gay and Lesbian Task Force, remarked at a press conference coinciding with the national gay march on Washington in October 1987:

> ... we are no longer seeking just a right to privacy and a protection from wrong. We also have a right—as heterosexual Americans already have—to see government and society affirm our lives.... until our relationships are recognized in the law —through domestic partner legislation or the definition of beneficiaries, for example—until we are provided with the same financial incentives in tax law and government programs to affirm our family relationships, then we will not have achieved equality in American society.[8]

Yet, homosexual activists know that this legal revolution will never succeed without the unpleasant task of coercing heterosexuals into masking their displeasure with homosexuality. It is thus not enough merely to break down all existing barriers to homosexual affection being expressed through marriage, child-rearing, or employment. The law must additionally be rewritten to make it as difficult as possible for heterosexuals to avoid contact with such displays, or to show discomfort toward them.

This two-edged approach would create a world in which stringent laws at all levels, aggressively enforced and strictly interpreted, force business owners to refuse to discriminate against the openly homosexual in patronage, leasing, and hiring. Removing overtly homosexual patrons from a bar, an airport, or any other public space would result in heavy fines and even jail sentences against property owners or their employees (or in lieu of these sanctions, mandatory purgation). Derogatory remarks directed at homosexuals, even with sexuality only incidental, would likewise result in criminal penalties.

1990: A PIVOTAL YEAR

The year 1990 was pivotal for the homosexual legal revolution. The states of Massachusetts and Wisconsin in the late 1980s had enacted laws forbidding discrimination against homosexuals. The victories would come quickly now, especially at the local level. In March, the City of Pittsburgh voted to include sexual orientation as a right protected under the City Code. In October, Stanford University allowed homosexual couples to qualify for university student housing. In November, voters in San Francisco, buoyed by a heavy turnout of that city's large gay population, produced a "lavender sweep," not only passing Proposition K, a city initiative to allow homosexuals to register as domestic partners at City Hall (a similar measure was defeated in 1989), but electing two openly lesbian candidates to the City Board of Supervisors, and an openly homosexual male candidate to the Board of Education.

Voters in Seattle refused to repeal an existing gender orientation ordinance. Congress did its part early in the year by overwhelmingly passing the Hate Crimes Statistics Act (or Hate Crimes Act), which requires the Justice Department to publish hate crime statistics according to classifications that include sexual orientation.[9] ...

"GAY CIVIL RIGHTS"

The homosexual lobby speaks of itself as struggling for "civil rights." "The gay community's goal is integration—just as it was with Martin Luther King," argues homosexual activist and San Francisco Board of Supervisors President Harry Britt.[10] Yet, underneath the surface, gay civil rights seems analogous to black "civil rights" *after* Reverend King's death. Far from seeking integration with the heterosexual world, it vehemently avoids it. More important, the movement seeks to win sinecures through the state, and over any objections by "homophobic" opposition. With a cloud of a heavy fine or even a jail sentence hanging over a mortgage lender, a rental agent, or a job interviewer who might be discomforted by them, homosexuals under these laws can win employment, credit, housing, and other economic entitlements. Heterosexuals would have no right to discriminate against homosexuals, but apparently, not vice versa. Libertarians as well as traditionalists ought to be troubled by this.

Consider a recent controversy in Madison, Wisconsin, as noted earlier a national bastion of "enlightened" attitudes. Three single women had recently moved into the same apartment, and one announced that she was a lesbian. The other two, not unreasonably, asked her to move. The lesbian filed a grievance with the local Human Rights Board, and, predictably, won. The shock came in the punishment. The two heterosexual women had to pay

$1,500 in "damages" to the lesbian, send her a public letter of apology, attend a two-hour "briefing" on homosexuality (conducted, needless to say, by homosexuals), and submit to having their living arrangements monitored for two years.[11]

With such laws in effect, this outcome would not be so much played out as simply avoided. Let one hypothetical example suffice, one that no doubt *has* been played out regularly, and that goes a long way in explaining why in any metropolitan area gays tend to cluster in a few neighborhoods.

A man enters an apartment rental office, inquiring about a vacancy. He openly indicates he is a homosexual, or at least implies as much through certain mannerisms. For good measure, he brings along his lover. The rental manager fudges, clears his throat, and says, "Well, er, several people are looking at the apartment. Call me later." An hour later, a second man, alone, walks in. He does not announce his sexuality. Who gets the apartment?

In the absence of gay protectionism, and assuming equal incomes, the manager (sighing with relief) would probably award the apartment to the second applicant. Gay militants would cry, "Discrimination!"—and miss the point. Discrimination based on sexual orientation is fundamentally different from that based on race. Homosexuality constitutes a behavioral, not a genetic trait. It is within the moral right of a landlord, job interviewer, banker, or anyone else performing a "gatekeeper" function to discourage economically risky behavior, sexual or otherwise. Libertarian columnist Doug Bandow articulates this:

> The point is, homosexuals have no right to force others to accept or support their lifestyle. Certainly government has no business discriminating against them: Anti-sodomy laws, for instance, are a vicious intrusion in the most intimate form of human conduct. And gays who pay taxes have as much right to government services and employment as anyone else.
>
> But someone who decides to live openly as a homosexual should accept the disapproval of those around him. For many Americans still believe that there is a fundamental, unchangeable moral code by which men are to live....
>
> Using government to bludgeon homophobics into submission is even more intolerant than the original discrimination.[12]

Under normal circumstances, the rental manager would not want to lease to gays who, once moved in, might tell their friends that the neighborhood could have possibilities as a "gay" one. Word-of-mouth travels fast within their world. Beyond a certain "tipping-point," many heterosexual residents near and within the complex, rather than risk feeling stigmatized, would choose to move. Their places largely would be taken by overt homosexuals.

In fact this is exactly how neighborhoods such as Castro (San Francisco), West Hollywood (formerly part of Los Angeles, now separately incorporated largely due to gay pressure), the West Village (New York City), and Dupont Circle (Washington, D.C.) all rapidly developed reputations as "gay neighborhoods," and how large sections of Martha's Vineyard, Fire Island, and Rehoboth Beach became "gay resorts."[13] The tipping-point principle also applies to public facilities such as restaurants. At the Grapevine Cafe in Columbus, Ohio, for example, heterosexual customers stopped coming when the clientele became heavily gay.[14]

What would happen with a sexual orientation law in place? The rental manager knows that if he turns down an openly homosexual applicant, he risks prosecution. Any rejection can serve as proof of discriminatory intent, even with factors such as length of employment, income, and previous tenant record taken into account.[15] In response to such a fear, the manager, though reluctantly, is likely to award the apartment to the homosexual.

For gay activists, therein lies the payoff. By codifying into law "protection" of homosexual mannerisms, they can intimidate gatekeepers into providing job security and housing for the openly homosexual. Thus, without necessarily mentioning anything about quotas or, for that matter, homosexuality, law in the U.S. is increasingly mandating *homosexual affirmative action.* ...

SEXUAL SCHISM

If the homosexual rights movement is in large measure an affirmative action strategy, certain consequences should be evident. ...

First, wherever such laws exist, they will attract homosexuals to the jurisdictions enacting them. Common sense dictates that any community laying out the welcome mat for homosexuality lays it for homosexuals, implicitly telling others to kindly step aside. Aside from legal protection, there is political strength in concentrated numbers. Most aspiring elected officials in San Francisco, for example, must now pay homage to the achievement of local gays, and show up at gay events. As Proposition K coordinator Jean Harris remarked following the

November elections, "We've shocked the world and made history with this lavender sweep.... It's clear that if you don't get the support of the gay-lesbian community you're going to be in trouble."[16] While the homosexual voting bloc will never be a majority in any city, even San Francisco, it can wield enormous veto power over the objections of all other blocs.

Second, having learned the power of the gatekeeper role, many homosexuals will seek to become gatekeepers themselves. It takes no great stretch of imagination, for example, to understand that the growing number of college administrations severely punishing anti-gay harassment (even if such "harassment" takes no more sinister a form than a satirical campus newspaper editorial or cartoon) has much to do with the growing number of college administrators and faculty who are themselves homosexual (and possibly were hired on that very basis). Nor does it take much imagination to understand that gay employers have more reason than ever to favor homosexuals in their hiring and promotion practices.

Third, these laws will create market bottlenecks. Heterosexuals and even "closeted" homosexuals will be at a competitive disadvantage for jobs and housing. For them, prices will be higher and wages lower than in the absence of such "safeguards." This is especially significant since gay culture is visible in high-cost cities such as New York and San Francisco.

Gays view economic victories to be won here, and few have been as resounding as the *Braschi* decision.[17] In July 1989, the New York State Court of Appeals ruled that a gay lover had the right to stay in his deceased partner's rent-controlled apartment because he qualified as a member of the partner's family, a decision recently upheld by the Appellate Division of the State Supreme Court. "We conclude that the term 'family,'" the lower court argued, "should not be rigidly restricted to those people who have formalized their relationship by obtaining, for instance, a marriage certificate or an adoption order.... a more realistic, and certainly equally valid, view of a family includes two adult lifetime partners whose relationship is long term and characterized by an emotional and financial commitment and interdependence."[18]

Gay activists understandably were elated at this imprimatur for homosexual marriage; they know household economics. Homosexual couples defined as "married" could reduce not only their housing costs, but also their income taxes (by filing jointly), pensions, and insurance premiums. They also would qualify for paid medical leave, spousal bereavement leave, and other employee benefits. At this writing, the San Francisco chapter of the American Civil Liberties Union is considering suing several locally based corporations that deny benefits to their homosexual employees' partners.[19]

Fourth, the new legalism will increase heterosexual anger—and even violence—toward homosexuals. Reports of "gay bashing" (the real kind) simultaneous with increased homosexual visibility cannot be a coincidence. What economist Thomas Sowell[20] and psychologist Stephen Johnson[21] have each revealed about racial affirmative action can apply to sexual affirmative action as well; unprotected groups, lacking recourse through rule of law, may resort to violence against innocent members of protected groups. Those who make it their bailiwick to monitor every incident of petty harassment of gays are impervious to any possibility that when laws force heterosexuals to bottle up dialogue, their feelings may erupt in more destructive ways. *Gay bashing, then, is in some measure a product of the very laws designed to punish it.*

THE LANGUAGE OF VICTIMHOOD

The radical homosexual movement seeks centralization of state power in the name of "civil rights." What began as a demand for the state not to interfere against private homosexual behavior has evolved into a demand for the state to intercede on behalf of public homosexual behavior. In so doing, the movement has advanced further into the same totalitarian netherworld that various black and feminist movements also have come to occupy. In each case, activists proclaim "victim" status, malign the intentions of critics, and demand government entitlements that necessarily discriminate against others. "Once upon a time," syndicated columnist Paul Greenberg writes in *The Washington Times*, "civil rights were unifying and universal—a way to open society to the claims of individual merit. Now 'civil rights' becomes a code word for dividing society into competing, resentful groups."[22]

Gay militants know the cue-card language of victimhood. For example, Gara LaMarche and William B. Rubenstein write in *The Nation*, "The targets of the 1950s witch hunts were both Communists and other leftists, labeled 'subversives,' and homosexuals, labeled 'sexual perverts.' Today, as the cold war mentality collapses, enemies are again being found at home, but this time lesbians and gay men are leading the list."[23] With former President Ronald Reagan and Cardinal John O'Connor leading the list of personages in the "McCarthy" role, the authors can make believe this really is the 1950s.

Just as opposing current racial and ethnic civil rights orthodoxies inevitably invites being labelled "racist" and "ethnocentric," opposing the current homosexual orthodoxy almost guarantees being denounced as "homophobic." One is simply not free to not pay tribute to them.... When early in 1990, Martin Luther King III remarked in a speech in Poughkeepsie, New York, that "something must be wrong" with homosexuals, enraged gay leaders demanded (and got) an apology.

Heterosexuals need not even fire the first shot to invoke gay wrath. When a pair of Queer Nation activists disrupted the airing of the December 14, 1990, segment of *The Arsenio Hall Show,* they insisted that the host explain why so few of his guests were gay. Unappeased by Hall's assurance that many are, the activists continued their on-camera ranting for about 10 minutes. Hall, of course, must now bear the onus as a "homophobe."[24]

Gay activists may incessantly speak of their "rights," yet oddly care little for those of others. Articles in *Outweek,* a year-old tabloid dedicated to exposing homosexual liaisons (real or imagined) of public figures believed otherwise to be heterosexual, routinely call for removing freedom of speech from anyone alleged to be "homophobic."[25] A placard at a recent gay rights march in Washington read, "BAN HOMOPHOBIA, NOT HOMOSEXUALITY."[26] Radical homosexuals apparently do not reciprocate when it comes to the First Amendment....

Homosexual militants also have little use for the right to privacy save their own. They view any public figure's possible homosexual behavior as grist for voyeuristic public consumption. The mere existence of a spurious scandal sheet like *Outweek* ought to outrage the sensibilities of all individualists. The hypocrisy of it all begs a comparison. Suppose the *National Enquirer* or some other general circulation gossip magazine exposed as homosexuals the very same celebrities that *Outweek* does. Homosexual activists would properly see this as character assassination. Yet apparently when a homosexual publication engages in the identical practice, it is creating "positive gay role models."[27]

"Now, the idea that one must be either in the closet or out of it is an invention of those who would politicize sex and abolish privacy," Thomas Short writes in *National Review.* "They wrongly make whatever is not publicly proclaimed seem secret, furtive. This dichotomy of being either in the closet or out of it should not exist.... We all have some secrets to keep."[28] Homosexual radicals do not keep sexual secrets. Since a homosexual act is political, even the most casual encounter by an otherwise heterosexual person must be made public, at whatever cost to that person. *Outweek,* and the mentality to which it caters, is more than indiscreet; it is totalitarian.

THE GROWING THREAT OF VIOLENCE

There is something about encountering homosexuality in its militant and pugnacious form that touches a deep, almost reflexive anger, even among most heterosexual liberals. That is why attempts at "mainstreaming" gay culture, even when holding an olive branch, are bound to fail. One of the saddest books to appear in recent years is *After the Ball: How America Will Conquer Its Fear and Hatred of Gays in the 90s*.[29] The authors, Marshall Kirk and Hunter Madsen, both homosexual, advocate a national campaign to cheerfully "sell" gay culture. They suggest, for example, that gay organizations buy up advertising space in "straight" newspapers with pictures of historical figures such as Alexander the Great, asking: "Did you know he was gay?"

Kirk and Madsen, like their surlier compatriots, fail to grasp that public homosexuality strikes at both a heterosexual's fear of loss of sexual identity and sense of belonging to a family. For even in this age of artificial insemination, families are not sustainable without heterosexuality. No matter how much the homosexual activist naively protests, "Gays are people, too," such a plea will receive in return grudging respect, and little else.

In a summary piece for *Newsweek's* March 12, 1990, cover story, "The Future of Gay America," Jonathan Alter revealed a rare understanding of this dynamic.[30] He notes, "'Acting gay' often involves more than sexual behavior itself. Much of the dislike for homosexuals centers not on who they are or what they do in private, but on so-called affectations —'swishiness' in men, the 'butch' look for women—not directly related to the more private sex act." Quite rightly so—one doubts if more than a tiny fraction of heterosexuals have even *inadvertently* witnessed a homosexual act. Alter then gets to the core of the issue. "Heterosexuals," he writes, "tend to argue that gays can downplay these characteristics and 'pass' more easily in the straight world than blacks can in a white world.... This may be true, but

it's also irrelevant. For most gays those traits aren't affectations but part of their identities; attacking their swishiness is the same as attacking *them*."

Yet if gays, through their carefully practiced "gay" mannerisms, know fully well they are antagonizing many heterosexuals, then why do they display them? Is it not in part to make heterosexuals sweat? By aggressively politicizing these traits, and demanding that those objecting must grin and bear it, they are in a sense restricting heterosexual freedom of speech. Male and even female opposition to persons with these traits is slowly taking a nasty turn, moving from violence of language to violence of fists. And yet, given the emerging legal climate, one discovers within oneself a disquieting empathy with the inchoate rage behind such acts.

Most heterosexuals are reasonably libertarian; an October 1989 Gallup Poll indicted that by a 47-to-36 margin (with the remainder undecided), Americans prefer legalization of homosexual relations between consenting adults.[31] This is all to the good. Anti-sodomy laws serve no purpose but to intimidate people out of private, consensual acts. On the other hand, the brazen, *open* display of homosexuality—as if to taunt, to tease, to maliciously sow confusion into sexual identities—is something most heterosexuals do not handle gracefully. With an unofficial government mandate for preferential treatment, it is not difficult to imagine a backlash....

Should a sober discussion of the possibilities for heterosexual violence be forbidden? Nobody in a *rational* state of mind would seek to emulate the exploits of "skinheads" or the late San Francisco Supervisor Dan White. Yet let readers here imagine themselves in that Madison restaurant or Seattle airport, being witness to mass displays of homosexual kissing, and feeling utterly helpless to evince the slightest disapproval. Would not such a scenario provoke an impulse, however fleeting and irrational, to do bodily harm? Does not the knowledge that the law is now stacked against even nonviolent disapproval ("hate crimes") merely add to the likelihood of a conflagration?

The principal motive of the gay movement is coming into focus with each passing month: to bait heterosexuals' less morally sturdy side, goading them into verbal or (better) physical assaults against the openly homosexual. That way, cries of homosexual victimhood would carry even more self-fulfilling prophecy, so much the better to vilify heterosexuals.

Gay militants aren't hesitant about admitting to such motives. Some want nothing less than war in the streets. Homosexual playwright and ACT-UP founder, Larry Kramer, recently called upon a gay audience to take gun practice for use in eventual combat against police and gay-bashers. "They hate us anyway," he rationalized. A cover of a recent issue of *Outweek* displayed a lesbian pointing a gun at the reader, with the headline, "Taking Aim at Bashers," while another cover announced, "We Hate Straights."[32] ...

The crowning legacy of the new gay legalism may yet be widespread violence, a violence brought on by state inhibition of rational dialogue at the behest of gay radicals, and in the name of "sensitivity." That alone is enough reason to oppose it.

NOTES

1. "Gay Rights Protesters Win Right to Kiss," *The Washington Times*, April 18, 1990.

2. Joyce Price, "Queer Nation Decides It's Time to Bash Back," *The Washington Times*, October 15, 1990.

3. Price, "Queer Nation."

4. One of the best arguments that homosexuality is not simply a statistical aberration, but a behavioral abnormality, can be found in Steven Goldberg, "Is Homosexuality Normal?" *Policy Review*, Summer 1982, pp. 119–38.

5. "The Future of Gay America," *Newsweek*, March 12, 1990, pp. 21–22.

6. "Gay Measure Stirs Florida," *The Washington Times*, August 24, 1990.

7. Tupper Hall, "Gay Couples Allowed to File as 'Non-Profit' Associations," *The Washington Times*, December 17, 1990.

8. Jeff Levi, speech to National Press Club, October 10, 1987.

9. The term "hate crime," in the hands of the homosexual lobby, is so vague that even an accidental epithet could qualify as an offense. For example, of the 462 anti-homosexual "hate crimes" committed in Virginia in 1987, 423—over 90 percent—involved mere name-calling. See Patrick Buchanan, "The Real Victims of Hate Crimes," *The Washington Times*, March 7, 1990. The National Gay and Lesbian Task Force (NGLTF), in its own estimate of hate crimes committed nationwide in 1988, admitted that 77 percent were verbal. In fact, the origin of the legislation lay in a 1985 NGLTF presentation before the National Institute of Justice. See Congressman William Dannemeyer, *Shadow in the Land: Homosexuality in America* (San Francisco: Ignatius Press, 1989), pp. 71–75. Congressman Dannemeyer's book is the best currently available on the homosexual lobby.

10. Quoted in *Newsweek*, "The Future of Gay America," p. 21.

11. Phyllis Schlafly, "A Choice, Not an Echo in California," *The Washington Times*, March 2, 1990.

12. Doug Bandow, "Government as God," in *The Politics of Plunder: Misgovernment in Washington* (New Brunswick, NJ: Transaction, 1990), pp. 18–20.

13. Even sympathetic observers of this process admit that the public identification of a neighborhood as "gay" induces non-gays to move out.

14. James N. Baker and Shawn D. Lewis, "Lesbians: Portrait of a Community," *Newsweek*, March 12, 1990, p. 24.

15. For evidence of this, see Dannemeyer, *Shadow in the Land*, p. 70.

16. Valerie Richardson, "Gay Voters Claim Biggest Victory in San Francisco," *The Washington Times*, November 9, 1990.

17. *Braschi v. Stahl Associates Co.*, 74 N.Y.2d 201.

18. Dennis Hevesi, "Court Extends 'Family' Rule to Rent-Stabilized Units," *The New York Times*, December 6, 1990.

19. Richardson, "Gay Voters Claim Biggest Victory,"

20. Thomas Sowell, "Affirmative Action: A Worldwide Disaster," *Commentary,* December 1989, pp. 21–41; see also Sowell, *Preferential Policies: An International Perspective* (New York: William Morrow, 1990).

21. Stephen Johnson, "Reverse Discrimination and Aggressive Behavior," *Journal of Psychology,* January 1980, pp. 11–19; Johnson, "Consequences of Reverse Discrimination," *Psychological Reports,* December 1980, pp. 1035–1038.

22. Paul Greenberg, "Decline and Fall of Civil Rights," *The Washington Times,* November 8, 1990.

23. Gara LaMarche and William B. Rubenstein, "The Love That Dare Not Speak," *The Nation,* November 5, 1990, p. 524.

24. "Gay Protesters Confront Arsenio Hall," *The Washington Times,* December 17, 1990.

25. Quoted in Andrew Sullivan, "Gay Life, Gay Death," *The New Republic,* December 27, 1990, p. 24. That Sullivan, an ally of the homosexual legal revolution, is alarmed over the totalitarianism inherent in such pronouncements should be taken seriously; he supports—on conservative grounds, no less—legalizing homosexual marriage. See Sullivan, "Here Comes the Groom," *The New Republic,* August 28, 1989, pp. 20–22.

26. David Rieff, "The Case Against Sensitivity," *Esquire,* November 1990, p. 124.

27. The evidence suggests that increased social tolerance of homosexuality does not necessarily lead to homosexuals themselves being happier. See Martin S. Weinberg and Colin J. Williams, *Male Homosexuals* (New York: Oxford University Press, 1974); Samuel McCracken, "Are Homosexuals Gay?" *Commentary,* January 1979, pp. 19–29.

28. Thomas Short, "Gay Rights or Closet Virtues?" *National Review,* September 17, 1990, pp. 43–44.

29. Marshall Kirk and Hunter Madsen, *After the Ball: How America Will Conquer Its Fear and Hatred of Gays in the 90s* (Garden City, NY: Doubleday, 1989).

30. Jonathan Alter, "Degrees of Discomfort," *Newsweek,* March 12, 1990, p. 27.

31. The Gallup Report, Report No. 289 (Princeton, NJ: The Gallup Poll, October 1989), p. 13.

32. See Sullivan, "Gay Life, Gay Death," p. 25.

POSTSCRIPT

Should Society Be More Accepting of Homosexuality?

Horowitz writes about some specific instances of homosexual "kiss-ins" and confrontational activism. Are these typical of gay activism? Homosexuals, for the most part, face a difficult catch-22. The existence of gay activism virtually requires gay rights, and the existence of gay rights virtually requires gay activism. But the confrontational tactics that Horowitz describes do not seem politically useful. Yet Horowitz claims that the confrontation is the point. Moreover, according to Horowitz, much of what is claimed to be unfair prejudice against homosexuals stems from the socially confrontational and aggressive behavior of homosexuals themselves. He cites the impulses of some heterosexuals to do bodily harm to homosexuals who "taunt" them through open homosexual affection, or what Horowitz calls "gay mannerisms."

This line of thought raises an interesting question: How much weight should be given to the idea of allowing certain people to do something that puts some other people ill at ease? Should society accept homosexuality even if some people might be strongly motivated to ill-treat homosexuals? In general, should the likes and dislikes of people be taken as a given, to which the behaviors of others must answer? Or should the behaviors of others be taken as a given, to which the likes and dislikes of others must answer?

There is much literature about homosexuality. Relevant sources include John Money, *Gay, Straight, and In-Between: The Sexology of Erotic Orientation* (Oxford University Press, 1988); Richard Mohr, *Between Men—Between Women: Lesbian and Gay Cultures* (Columbia University Press, 1988); William Dannemeyer, *Shadow in the Land: Homosexuality in America* (Ignatius Press, 1989); Wayne Dynes, ed., *The Encyclopedia of Homosexuality* (Garland, 1990); E. L. Pattullo, "Straight Talk About Gays," *Commentary* (December 1992); Michelangelo Signorile, *Queer in America: Sex, the Media, and the Closets of Power* (Random House, 1993); John Finnis and Martha Nussbaum, "Is Homosexual Conduct Wrong? A Philosophical Exchange," *The New Republic* (November 15, 1993); Bruce Bawer, *A Place at the Table: The Gay Individual in American Society* (Poseidon, 1993); Pim Pronk, *Against Nature? Types of Moral Argumentation Regarding Homosexuality* (William B. Eerdmans, 1993); John Finnis, "Law, Morality, and 'Sexual Orientation,'" *Notre Dame Law Review* (vol. 69, 1994); Timothy Murphy, ed., *Gay Ethics: Controversies in Outing, Civil Rights, and Sexual Science* (Harrington Park Press, 1994); Andrew Sullivan, *Virtually Normal: An Argument About Homosexuality* (Alfred A. Knopf, 1995); Robert M. Baird and M. Katherine Baird, eds., *Homosexuality: Debating the Issues* (Prometheus, 1995); Chandler Burr, *A Separate Creation: The Search for the*

Biological Origins of Sexual Orientation (Hyperion, 1996); Norman Podhoretz, "How the Gay Rights Movement Won," *Commentary* (November 1996); Francis M. Mondimore, *A Natural History of Homosexuality* (Johns Hopkins University Press, 1996); Simon LeVay, *Queer Science: The Use and Abuse of Research on Homosexuality* (MIT Press, 1996); Colin Spencer, *Homosexuality in History* (Harcourt Brace, 1996); Tamara L. Roleff, ed., *Gay Rights* (Greenhaven Press, 1997); Amy Gluckman and Betsy Reed, *Homo Economics: Capitalism, Community, and Lesbian and Gay Life* (Routledge, 1997); and John Corvino, *Same Sex: The Ethics, Science and Culture of Homosexuality* (Rowman & Littlefield, 1997).

Joseph Nicolosi argues that homosexuality is something that can be cured in "Let's Be Straight: A Cure Is Possible," *Insight on the News* (December 6, 1993). Nicolosi is answered by Carlton Cornett in "Gay Ain't Broke; No Need to Fix It," *Insight on the News* (December 6, 1993).

Literature on religion and homosexuality includes J. Boswell, *Christianity, Social Tolerance, and Homosexuality: Gay People in Western Europe from the Beginning of the Christian Era to the Fourteenth Century* (University of Chicago Press, 1980); Keith Hartman, *Congregations in Conflict: The Battle Over Homosexuality* (Rutgers University Press, 1996); and Donald J. Wold, *Out of Order: Homosexuality in the Bible and the Ancient Near East* (Baker, 1997).

The topic of gays in the military is discussed in Randy Shilts, *Conduct Unbecoming: Gays and Lesbians in the U.S. Military* (St. Martin's Press, 1993); Lois Shawver, *And the Flag Was Still There: Straight People, Gay People, and Sexuality in the U.S. Military* (Haworth Press, 1995); and Marc Wolinsky and Kenneth Sherrill, *Gays and the Military* (Princeton University Press, 1993).

Books on same-sex marriage include William N. Eskridge, *The Case for Same-Sex Marriage: From Sexual Liberty to Civilized Commitment* (Free Press, 1996); Andrew Sullivan, ed., *Same-Sex Marriage, Pro and Con: A Reader* (Random House, 1997); and Mark Strasser, *Legally Wed: Same-Sex Marriage and the Constitution* (Cornell University Press, 1997).

ISSUE 10

Is Pornography Degrading to Women?

YES: Helen E. Longino, from "Pornography, Oppression, and Freedom: A Closer Look," in Laura Lederer, ed., *Take Back the Night: Women on Pornography* (William Morrow, 1980)

NO: Alan Soble, from "Pornography: Defamation and the Endorsement of Degradation," *Social Theory and Practice* (Spring 1985)

ISSUE SUMMARY

YES: Philosopher Helen E. Longino argues that pornography defames women, endorses the degradation of women, and contributes to a sexist culture that fosters psychological and physical violence against women. Pornography, she maintains, is a proper concern of anyone who supports the social equality of the sexes.

NO: Philosopher Alan Soble argues that pornography is generally a product of male fantasy and does not assert anything about women. He contends that portrayals of degradation do not necessarily endorse it and that pornography is not responsible for violence against women.

Pornography is somewhat difficult to define, and one might well sympathize with the judge who said, "I can't define pornography, but I know it when I see it!" Assuming that we do have some idea about what pornography is, let us hazard the following suggestions: pornography is sexually explicit; it is intended to cause sexual arousal; and pornographic items are generally for sale, or at least are closely related to commercial operations.

One objection that has been raised is that pornography endorses the sexual degradation of women. The sexual nature of pornography is not the offending element in this criticism. What is offensive is the degradation of women and the fact that this degradation is endorsed or presented in a positive manner. The latter is the serious problem. A news report, for example, could describe or show the degradation of individuals, but such a report would likely not *endorse* the degradation and thus would not be considered pornography. Pornography's endorsement of degradation is one that affects all women— not just those in the pornographic material—because it sends the message that this is the proper way to treat women. Thus, it is an offense against all women. In addition, women may be harmed if viewers of pornography act upon the message.

Objectors claim that in a free society, individuals have the right to make, buy, and sell pornography. Pornography may be disagreeable to some people, but any attempt to censor it is in violation of the principle of free expression. The only possible justification for restricting pornography would be on the grounds that it harms some people, but those who participate in pornographic productions do so voluntarily, and there is no proof that pornography actually does harm others.

But, opponents of pornography might respond, women's "voluntary" participation in pornography may be an indication of how limited their life choices really are. And from a larger, societal perspective, there are connections between pornographic representations of women and the social realization of sexual equality. As long as pornographic representations of women are socially acceptable, there will remain obstacles to real social equality between the sexes. The harm is primarily a social one; a sexist society naturally produces pornography.

It is not reasonable to think that the elimination of pornography would eliminate sexism. But it is quite different—and perhaps more reasonable— to think that the elimination of sexism would bring about the elimination of pornography.

In the following selections, Helen E. Longino and Alan Soble discuss the idea that pornography defames women. Longino argues that pornography spreads lies about women, that pornography is a social concern, and that its presence in society endorses the degradation of women. Soble claims that pornography does not make any assertions about women (and hence that it does not make false assertions about women). Rather, he says, pornography is mainly the depiction of male fantasies.

YES

Helen E. Longino

PORNOGRAPHY, OPPRESSION, AND FREEDOM: A CLOSER LOOK

I. INTRODUCTION

The much-touted sexual revolution of the 1960's and 1970's not only freed various modes of sexual behavior from the constraints of social disapproval, but also made possible a flood of pornographic material....

Traditionally, pornography was condemned as immoral because it presented sexually explicit material in a manner designed to appeal to "prurient interests" or a "morbid" interest in nudity and sexuality, material which furthermore lacked any redeeming social value and which exceeded "customary limits of candor." While these phrases, taken from a definition of "obscenity" proposed in the 1954 American Law Institute's *Model Penal Code*,[1] require some criteria of application to eliminate vagueness, it seems that what is objectionable is the explicit description or representation of bodily parts or sexual behavior for the purpose of inducing sexual stimulation or pleasure on the part of the reader or viewer. This kind of objection is part of a sexual ethic that subordinates sex to procreation and condemns all sexual interactions outside of legitimated marriage. It is this code which was the primary target of the sexual revolutionaries in the 1960's, and which had given way in many areas to more open standards of sexual behavior.

One of the beneficial results of the sexual revolution has been a growing acceptance of the distinction between questions of sexual mores and questions of morality. This distinction underlies the old slogan, "Make love, not war," and takes harm to others as the defining characteristic of immorality. What is immoral is behavior which causes injury to or violation of another person or people. Such injury may be physical or it may be psychological. To cause pain to another, to lie to another, to hinder another in the exercise of her or his rights, to exploit another, to degrade another, to misrepresent and slander another are instances of immoral behavior. Masturbation or engaging voluntarily in sexual intercourse with another consenting adult of the same or the other sex, as long as neither injury nor violation of either individual or another is involved, are not immoral. Some sexual behavior is morally objectionable, but not because of its sexual character. Thus, adultery is immoral not because it involves sexual intercourse with someone to whom one is not legally married, but because it involves breaking a promise (of sexual and emotional fidelity to one's spouse). Sadistic, abusive, or forced sex is immoral because it injures and violates another.

The detachment of sexual chastity from moral virtue implies that we cannot condemn forms of sexual behavior merely because they strike us as distasteful or subversive of the Protestant work ethic, or because they depart from standards of behavior we have individually adopted. It has thus seemed to imply that no matter how offensive we might find pornography, we must tolerate it in the name of freedom from illegitimate repression. I wish to argue that this is not so, that pornography is immoral because it is harmful to people.

II. WHAT IS PORNOGRAPHY?

I define pornography as *verbal or pictorial explicit representations of sexual behavior that,* in the words of the Commission on Obscenity and Pornography, *have as a distinguishing characteristic "the degrading and demeaning portrayal of the role and status of the human female . . . as a mere sexual object to be exploited and manipulated sexually."*[2] In pornographic books, magazines, and films, women are represented as passive and as slavishly dependent upon men. The role of female characters is limited to the provision of sexual services to men. To the extent that women's sexual pleasure is represented at all, it is subordinated to that of men and is never an end in itself as is the sexual pleasure of men. What pleases women is the use of their bodies to satisfy male desires. While the sexual objectification of women is common to all pornography, women are the recipients of even worse treatment in violent pornography, in which women characters are killed, tortured, gang-raped, mutilated, bound, and otherwise abused, as a means of providing sexual stimulation or pleasure to the male characters. It is this development which has attracted the attention of feminists and been the stimulus to an analysis of pornography in general.[3]

Not all sexually explicit material is pornography, nor is all material which contains representations of sexual abuse and degradation pornography.

A representation of a sexual encounter between adult persons which is characterized by mutual respect is, once we have disentangled sexuality and morality, not morally objectionable. Such a representation would be one in which the desires and experiences of each participant were regarded by the other participants as having a validity and a subjective importance equal to those of the individual's own desire and experiences. In such an encounter, each participant acknowledges the other participant's basic human dignity and personhood. Similarly, a representation of a nude human body (in whole or in part) in such a manner that the person shown maintains self-respect—e.g., is not portrayed in a degrading position—would not be morally objectionable. The educational films of the National Sex Forum, as well as a certain amount of erotic literature and art, fall into this category. While some erotic materials are beyond the standards of modesty held by some individuals, they are not for this reason immoral.

A representation of a sexual encounter which is not characterized by mutual respect, in which at least one of the parties is treated in a manner beneath her or his dignity as a human being, is no longer simple erotica. That a representation is of degrading behavior does not in itself, however, make it pornographic. Whether or not it is pornographic is a function of contextual features. Books and films may contain descriptions or representations of a rape in order to explore the consequences of such an assault upon its victim. What is being shown is abusive or degrading behavior which attempts to deny the humanity and dignity of the person assaulted, yet the context surrounding the representation, through its exploration of the consequences of the act, acknowledges and reaffirms her dignity. Such books and films, far from being pornographic, are (or can be) highly moral, and fall into the category of moral realism.

What makes a work a work of pornography, then, is not simply its representation of degrading and abusive sexual encounters, but its implicit, if not explicit, approval and recommendation of sexual behavior that is immoral, i.e., that physically or psychologically violates the personhood of one of the participants. Pornography, then, is verbal or pictorial material which represents or describes sexual behavior that is degrading or abusive to one or more of the participants *in such a way as to endorse the degradation.* The participants so treated in virtually all heterosexual pornography are women or children, so heterosexual pornography is, as a matter of fact, material which endorses sexual behavior that is degrading and/or abusive to women and children. As I use the term "sexual behavior," this includes sexual encounters between persons, behavior which produces sexual stimulation or pleasure for one of the participants, and behavior which is prepara-

tory to or invites sexual activity. Behavior that is degrading or abusive includes physical harm or abuse, and physical or pyschological coercion. In addition, behavior which ignores or devalues the real interests, desires, and experiences of one or more participants in any way is degrading. Finally, that a person has chosen or consented to be harmed, abused, or subjected to coercion does not alter the degrading character of such behavior.

Pornography communicates its endorsement of the behavior it represents by various features of the pornographic context: the degradation of the female characters is represented as providing pleasure to the participant males and, even worse, to the participant females, and there is no suggestion that this sort of treatment of others is inappropriate to their status as human beings. These two features are together sufficient to constitute endorsement of the represented behavior. The contextual features which make material pornographic are intrinsic to the material. In addition to these, extrinsic features, such as the purpose for which the material is presented—i.e., the sexual arousal/pleasure/satisfaction of its (mostly) male consumers—or an accompanying text, may reinforce or make explicit the endorsement. Representations which in and of themselves do not show or endorse degrading behavior may be put into a pornographic context by juxtaposition with others that are degrading, or by a text which invites or recommends degrading behavior toward the subject represented. In such a case the whole complex—the series of representations or representations with text—is pornographic....

To summarize: Pornography is not just the explicit representation or description of sexual behavior, nor even the explicit representation or description of sexual behavior which is degrading and/or abusive to women. Rather, it is material that explicitly represents or describes degrading and abusive sexual behavior so as to endorse and/or recommend the behavior as described. The contextual features, moreover, which communicate such endorsement are intrinsic to the material; that is, they are features whose removal or alteration would change the representation or description.

... The female characters of contemporary pornography ... exist to provide pleasure to males, but in the pornographic context no pretense is made to regard them as parties to a contractual arrangement. Rather, the anonymity of these characters makes each one Everywoman, thus suggesting not only that all women are appropriate subjects for the enactment of the most bizarre and demeaning male sexual fantasies, but also that this is their primary purpose. The recent escalation of violence in pornography—the presentation of scenes of bondage, rape, and torture of women for the sexual stimulation of the male characters and male viewers—while shocking in itself, is from this point of view merely a more vicious extension of a genre whose success depends on treating women in a manner beneath their dignity as human beings.

III. PORNOGRAPHY: LIES AND VIOLENCE AGAINST WOMEN

What is wrong with pornography, then, is its degrading and dehumanizing portrayal of women (and *not* its sexual content). Pornography, by its very nature, requires that women be subordinate to men and mere instruments for the fulfillment of male fantasies. To accomplish this, pornography must lie. Pornography lies when it says that our sexual life is or ought to be subordinate to the service of men, that our pleasure consists in pleasing men and not ourselves.... Pornography lies explicitly about women's sexuality, and through such lies fosters more lies about our humanity, our dignity, and our personhood.

Moreover, since nothing is alleged to justify the treatment of the female characters of pornography save their womanhood, pornography depicts all women as fit objects of violence by virtue of their sex alone. Because it is simply being female that, in the pornographic vision, justifies being violated, the lies of pornography are lies about all women. Each work of pornography is on its own libelous and defamatory, yet gains power through being reinforced by every other pornographic work. The sheer number of pornographic productions expands the moral issue to include not only assessing the morality or immorality of individual works, but also the meaning and force of the mass production of pornography....

The entrenchment of pornography in our culture also gives it a significance quite beyond its explicit sexual messages. To suggest, as pornography does, that the primary purpose of women is to provide sexual pleasure to men is to deny that women are independently human or have a status equal to that of men. It is, moreover, to deny our quality at one of the most intimate levels of human experience. This denial is especially powerful in a hierarchical, class society such as ours, in which individuals feel good about themselves by feeling superior to others. Men in our society have a vested interest in maintaining their belief in the inferiority of the female sex, so that no matter how oppressed and exploited by the society in which they live and work, they can feel that they are at least superior to someone and some category of individuals—a woman or women. Pornography, by presenting women as wanton, depraved, and made for the sexual use of men, caters directly to that interest. The ... lack of any explicit social disavowal of the pornographic image of women enables this image to continue fostering sexist attitudes even as the society publicly proclaims its (as yet timid) commitment to sexual equality.

In addition to finding a connection between the pornographic view of women and the denial to us of our full human rights, women are beginning to connect the consumption of pornography with committing rape and other acts of sexual violence against women. Contrary to the findings of the Commission on Obscenity and Pornography a growing body of research is documenting (1) a correlation between exposure to representations of violence and the committing of violent acts generally, and (2) a correlation between exposure to pornographic materials and the committing of sexually abusive or violent acts against women.[4] While more study is needed to establish precisely what the causal relations are, clearly so-called hard-core pornography is not innocent.

From "snuff" films and miserable magazines in pornographic stores to *Hustler*, to ... album covers and advertisements, to *Vogue*, pornography has come to occupy its own niche in the communications and entertainment media and to acquire a quasi-institutional character (signaled by the use of diminutives such as "porn" or "porno" to refer to pornographic material, as though such familiar naming could take the hurt out). Its

acceptance by the mass media, whatever the motivation, means a cultural endorsement of its message. As much as the materials themselves, the social tolerance of these degrading and distorted images of women in such quantities is harmful to us, since it indicates a general willingness to see women in ways incompatible with our fundamental human dignity and thus to justify treating us in those ways. The tolerance of pornographic representations of the rape, bondage, and torture of women helps to create and maintain a climate more tolerant of the actual physical abuse of women....

In sum, pornography is injurious to women in at least three distinct ways:

1. Pornography, especially violent pornography, is implicated in the committing of crimes of violence against women.

2. Pornography is the vehicle for the dissemination of a deep and vicious lie about women. It is defamatory and libelous.

3. The diffusion of such a distorted view of women's nature in our society as it exists today supports sexist (i.e., male-centered) attitudes, and thus reinforces the oppression and exploitation of women.

Society's tolerance of pornography, especially pornography on the contemporary massive scale, reinforces each of these modes of injury: By not disavowing the lie, it supports the male-centered myth that women are inferior and subordinate creatures. Thus, it contributes to the maintenance of a climate tolerant of both psychological and physical violence against women.

IV. PORNOGRAPHY AND THE LAW

Congress shall make no law respecting the establishment of religion, or prohibiting the free exercise thereof; or abridging the freedom of speech, or of the press; or the right of the people peaceably to assemble, and to petition the Government for a redress of grievances.

—First Amendment, Bill of Rights of the United States Constitution

Pornography is clearly a threat to women. each of the modes of injury cited above offers sufficient reason at least to consider proposals for the social and legal control of pornography. The almost universal response from progressives to such proposals is that constitutional guarantees of freedom of speech and privacy preclude recourse to law.[5] While I am concerned about the erosion of constitutional rights and also think for many reasons that great caution must be exercised before undertaking a legal campaign against pornography, I find objections to such a campaign that are based on appeals to the First Amendment or to a right to privacy ultimately unconvincing.

Much of the defense of the pornographer's right to publish seems to assume that, while pornography may be tasteless and vulgar, it is basically an entertainment that harms no one but its consumers, who may at worst suffer from the debasement of their taste; and that therefore those who argue for its control are demanding an unjustifiable abridgment of the rights to freedom of speech of those who make and distribute pornographic materials and of the rights to privacy of their customers. The account of pornography given above shows that the assumptions of this position are false. Nevertheless, even some who acknowl-

edge its harmful character feel that it is granted immunity from social control by the First Amendment, or that the harm that would ensue from its control outweighs the harm prevented by its control.

There are three ways of arguing that control of pornography is incompatible with adherence to constitutional rights. The first argument claims that regulating pornography involves an unjustifiable interference in the private lives of individuals. The second argument takes the first amendment as a basic principle constitutive of our form of government, and claims that the production and distribution of pornographic material, as a form of speech, is an activity protected by that amendment. The third argument claims not that the pornographer's rights are violated, but that others' rights will be if controls against pornography are instituted.

The privacy argument is the easiest to dispose of. Since the open commerce in pornographic materials is an activity carried out in the public sphere, the publication and distribution of such materials, unlike their use by individuals, is not protected by rights to privacy. The distinction between the private consumption of pornographic material and the production and distribution of, or open commerce in, it is sometimes blurred by defenders of pornography. But I may entertain, in the privacy of my mind, defamatory opinions about another person, even though I may not broadcast them. So one might create without restraint—as long as no one were harmed in the course of preparing them—pornographic materials for one's personal use, but be restrained from reproducing and distributing them. In both cases what one is doing—in the privacy of one's mind or basement—

may indeed be deplorable, but immune from legal proscription. Once the activity becomes public, however—i.e., once it involves others—it is no longer protected by the same rights that protect activities in the private sphere.*

In considering the second argument (that control of pornography, private or public, is wrong in principle), it seems important to determine whether we consider the right to freedom of speech to be absolute and unqualified. If it is, then obviously all speech, including pornography, is entitled to protection. But the right is, in the first place, not an unqualified right: There are several kinds of speech not protected by the First Amendment, including the incitement to violence in volatile circumstances, the solicitation of crimes, perjury and misrepresentation, slander, libel, and false advertising. That there are forms of proscribed speech shows that we accept limitations on the right to freedom of speech if such speech, as do the forms listed, impinges on other rights. The manufacture and distribution of material which defames and threatens all members of a class by its recommendation of abusive and degrading behavior toward some members of that class simply in virtue of their membership in it seems a clear candidate for inclusion on the list. The right is therefore not an unqualified one.

Nor is it an absolute or fundamental right, underived from any other right: If it were there would not be exceptions or limitations. The first ten amendments were added to the Constitution as a way of guaranteeing the "blessings of liberty" mentioned in its preamble, to protect citizens against the unreasonable usurpation of power by the state. The specific rights mentioned in the First Amendment—those of religion, speech, assembly, press, petition—reflect the recent experiences of the makers of the Constitution under colonial government as well as a sense of what was and is required generally to secure liberty.

It may be objected that the right to freedom of speech is fundamental in that it is part of what we mean by liberty and not a right that is derivative from a right to liberty. In order to meet this objection, it is useful to consider a distinction explained by Ronald Dworkin in his book *Taking Rights Seriously*.[6] As Dworkin points out, the work "liberty" is used in two distinct, if related, senses: as "license," i.e., the freedom from legal constraints to do as one pleases, in some contexts; and as "independence," i.e., "the status of a person as independent and equal rather than subservient," in others. Failure to distinguish between these senses in discussions of rights and freedoms is fatal to clarity and understanding.

If the right to free speech is understood as a partial explanation of what is meant by liberty, then liberty is perceived as license: The right to do as one pleases includes a right to speak as one pleases. But license is surely not a condition the First Amendment is designed to protect. We not only tolerate but require legal constraints on liberty as license when we enact laws against rape, murder, assault, theft, etc. If everyone did exactly as she or he pleased at any given time, we would have chaos if not lives, as Hobbes put it, that are "nasty, brutish, and short."

---

*Thus, the right to use such materials in the privacy of one's home, which has been upheld by the United States Supreme Court (*Stanley v. Georgia*, 394 U.S. 557), does not include the right to purchase them or to have them available in the commercial market. See also *Paris Adult Theater I v. Slaton*, 431 U.S. 49.

We accept government to escape, not to protect, this condition.

If, on the other hand, by liberty is meant independence, then freedom of speech is not necessarily a part of liberty; rather, it is a means to it. The right to freedom of speech is not a fundamental, absolute right, but one derivative from, possessed in virtue of, the more basic right to independence. Taking this view of liberty requires providing arguments showing that the more specific rights we claim are necessary to guarantee our status as persons "independent and equal rather than subservient." In the context of government, we understand independence to be the freedom of each individual to participate as an equal among equals in the determination of how she or he is to be governed. Freedom of speech in this context means that an individual may not only entertain beliefs concerning government privately, but may express them publicly. We express our opinions about taxes, disarmament, wars, social-welfare programs, the function of the police, civil rights, and so on. Our right to freedom of speech includes the right to criticize the government and to protest against various forms of injustice and the abuse of power. What we wish to protect is the free expression of ideas even when they are unpopular. What we do not always remember is that speech has functions other than the expression of ideas.

Regarding the relationship between a right to freedom of speech and the publication and distribution of pornographic materials, there are two points to be made. In the first place, the latter activity is hardly an exercise of the right to the free expression of ideas as understood above. In the second place, to the degree that the tolerance of material degrading to women supports and reinforces the attitude that women are not fit to participate as equals among equals in the political life of their communities, and that the prevalence of such an attitude effectively prevents women from so participating, the absolute and fundamental right of women to liberty (political independence) is violated.

This second argument against the suppression of pornographic material, then, rests on a premise that must be rejected, namely, that the right to freedom of speech is a right to utter anything one wants. It thus fails to show that the production and distribution of such material is an activity protected by the First Amendment. Furthermore, an examination of the issues involved leads to the conclusion that tolerance of this activity violates the rights of women to political independence.

The third argument (which expresses concern that curbs on pornography are the first step toward political censorship) runs into the same ambiguity that besets the arguments based on principle. These arguments generally have as an underlying assumption that the maximization of freedom is a worthy social goal. Control of pornography diminishes freedom —directly the freedom of pornographers, indirectly that of all of us. But again, what is meant by "freedom"? It cannot be that what is to be maximized is license—as the goal of a social group whose members probably have at least some incompatible interests, such a goal would be internally inconsistent. If, on the other hand, the maximization of political independence is the goal, then that is in no way enhanced by, and may be endangered by, the tolerance of pornography. To argue that the control of pornography would create a precedent for suppressing political speech is thus to confuse license with political independence. In addition, it ignores a crucial basis for the control of pornography, i.e., its character as libelous speech. The prohibition of such speech is justified by the need for protection from the injury (psychological as well as physical or economic) that results from libel. A very different kind of argument would be required to justify curtailing the right to speak our minds about the institutions which govern us. As long as such distinctions are insisted upon, there is little danger of the government's using the control of pornography as precedent for curtailing political speech.

In summary, neither as a matter of principle nor in the interests of maximizing liberty can it be supposed that there is an intrinsic right to manufacture and distribute pornographic material.

The only other conceivable source of protection for pornography would be a general right to do what we please as long as the rights of others are respected. Since the production and distribution of pornography violates the rights of women—to respect and to freedom from defamation, among others—this protection is not available.

V. CONCLUSION

I have defined pornography in such a way as to distinguish it from erotica and from moral realism, and have argued that it is defamatory and libelous toward women, that it condones crimes against women, and that it invites tolerance of the social, economic, and cultural oppression of women. The production and distribution of pornographic material is thus a social and moral wrong. Contrasting both the current volume of pornographic production and its growing infiltration of the communications media with the status of women in this culture makes clear the necessity for its control. Since the goal of controlling pornography does not conflict with constitutional rights, a common obstacle to action is removed.

Appeals for action against pornography are sometimes brushed aside with the claim that such action is a diversion from the primary task of feminists—the elimination of sexism and of sexual inequality. This approach focuses on the enjoyment rather than the manufacture of pornography, and sees it as merely a product of sexism which will disappear when the latter has been overcome and the sexes are socially and economically equal. Pornography cannot be separated from sexism in this way: Sexism is not just a set of attitudes regarding the inferiority of women but the behaviors and social and economic rules that manifest such attitudes. Both the manufacture and distribution of pornography and the enjoyment of it are instances of sexist behavior. The enjoyment of pornography on the part of individuals will presumably decline as such individuals begin to accord women their status as fully human. A cultural climate which tolerates the degrading representation of women is not a climate which facilitates the development of respect for women. Furthermore, the demand for pornography is stimulated not just by the sexism of individuals but by the pornography industry itself. Thus, both as a social phenomenon and in its effect on individuals, pornography, far from being a mere product, nourishes sexism. The campaign against it is an essential component of women's struggle for legal, economic, and social equality, one which requires the support of all feminists.

Many women helped me to develop and crystallize the ideas presented in this paper. I would especially like to thank Michele Farrell, Laura Lederer, Pamela Miller, and Dianne Romain for their comments in conversation and on the first written draft. Portions of this material were presented orally to members of the Society for Women in Philosophy and to participants in the workshops on "What Is Pornography?" at the Conference on Feminist Perspectives on Pornography, San Francisco, November 17, 18, and 19, 1978. Their discussion was invaluable in helping me to see problems and to clarify the ideas presented here.

REFERENCES

1. American Law Institute *Model Penal Code*, sec. 251.4.
2. *Report of the Commission on Obscenity and Pornography* (New York: Bantam Books, 1979), p. 239. The Commission, of course, concluded that the demeaning content of pornography did not adversely affect male attitudes toward women.
3. Among ... feminist discussions are Diana Russell, "Pornography: A Feminist Perspective" and Susan Griffin, "On Pornography," *Chrysalis*, Vol. I, No. 4, 1978; and Ann Garry, "Pornography and Respect for Women," *Social Theory and Practice*, Vol. 4, Spring 1978, pp. 395–421.
4. Urie Bronfenbrenner, *Two Worlds of Childhood* (New York: Russell Sage Foundation, 1970); H. J. Eysenck and D. K. B. Nias, *Sex, Violence and the Media* (New York: St. Martin's Press, 1978); and Michael Goldstein, Harold Kant, and John Hartman, *Pornography and Sexual Deviance* (Berkeley: University of California Press, 1973); and the papers by Diana Russell, Pauline Bart, and Irene Diamond included in [Laura Lederer, ed., *Take Back the Night: Women on Pornography* (New York: Morrow, 1980)]
5. Cf. Marshall Cohen, "The Case Against Censorship," *The Public Interest*, No. 22, Winter 1971, reprinted in John R. Burr and Milton Goldinger, *Philosophy and Contemporary Issues* (New York: Macmillan, 1976), and Justice William Brennan's dissenting opinion in *Paris Adult Theater I v. Slaton*, 431 U.S. 49.
6. Ronald Dworkin, *Taking Rights Seriously* (Cambridge: Harvard University Press, 1977), p. 262.

NO

Alan Soble

PORNOGRAPHY: DEFAMATION AND THE ENDORSEMENT OF DEGRADATION

1. INTRODUCTION

In one of the more significant papers in the feminist anti-pornography collection *Take Back the Night*, Helen Longino advances two arguments for the censorship of pornography.[1] Longino argues that much pornography defames women (it is libelous), and that it endorses the degradation of women. Pornography defames women by telling lies about the nature of women and women's sexuality; in particular, it maliciously asserts that women naturally cater to the sexual needs of men and that women enjoy being sexually degraded. And by endorsing the degradation of women, pornography promotes that degradation and contributes causally to acts harmful to women....

In Section 2 it will be argued that the defamation argument fails because pornography is nonpropositional, and that even though much pornography is in some sense false, it does not promulgate lies about women. In Sections 3 and 4 the accusation that pornographic materials degrade women is discussed, an accusation that is common to the defamation and endorsement arguments. Finally, in Section 5, I argue that the endorsement argument fails because a depiction of degradation is not by itself an endorsement of that degradation.

2. PORNOGRAPHIC FANTASY IS NONPROPOSITIONAL

... Suppose that the main function served by pornography for the consuming male is to induce sexual arousal. We can safely say, on the basis of what feminists and others have described as the content of much pornography, that the fantasies contained in pornographic material depict a world in which sexual activity for its own sake, sex without commitments, prohibited or scorned types of sexual activity, sexually attractive bodies, and sexually adventurous women are more plentiful than they are in the lives of the consumers. If the function of pornography is to provide stimuli that enable men to imagine that women fully accommodate to their sexual desires (either by being passive

From Alan Soble, "Pornography: Defamation and the Endorsement of Degradation," *Social Theory and Practice*, vol. 11, no. 1 (Spring 1985). Copyright © 1985 by *Social Theory and Practice*. Reprinted by permission. Some notes omitted.

attendants, or by being active seekers of their own pleasure, whichever works at the time for the individual), then any thesis about the propositional content of pornography will be irrelevant; it will simply not be grappling with what is central to the phenomenon. If pornography is consumed primarily for the sexual arousal it induces, and if this arousal is generated by fantasies contained in and provoked by pornographic depictions, then the issue of what might be asserted by pornography drops out.[2] Pornography does not arouse by advancing arguments, defending theses, or laying out a metaphysics, and it is not consumed for any arguments, theses or metaphysics it might just happen to contain. It is, in fact, a common complaint about pornography that it is made by men, and that as a result it is nothing but a one-sided man's fantasy of a woman's fantasy, a projection that "says" something only about the men who produce and consume it. This observation has merit. But if we are going to be this sophisticated about pornography, then we are already acknowledging that men's fantasies do not assert anything about women and therefore could not defame them.

Pornographic fantasies go beyond the merely factually false to the grossly unrealistic, and things in this category are not usefully seen as propositional. In *some* sense, all fantasies *are* false, and so it is quite right to claim that pornography does not depict the actual state of the world or the nature of women's sexuality. All fantastic literature fails to correspond with reality. Indeed, the failure of pornographic fantasy to match reality probably contributes to its ability to generate sexual arousal; if women in reality always accommodated to the sexual desires of men, if women

were in fact full sexual slaves, then the depiction of their accommodation in pornography might not arouse. But fantasy material is not false in the same way that nonfantasy material (a disproven scientific theory) is false. Pornography is false in some weak sense, in whatever sense, say, science fiction is false. Fantasy material never purports to be telling the truth about its subject matter; *Star Wars* is false, but as fantasy its falsity is beside the point. Men consume pornography because they find that entering its fantasy world is enjoyable, not because it is sexually arousing to perpetuate discredited theories about the nature of women. Similarly, the massive consumption of romance novels by women is motivated by the enjoyment of contemplating a fantasy world in which everlasting loves are more plentiful than they happen to be; these novels hardly depict men as they are, yet they are not defamatory. The key here is that to engage in pretense is not to disseminate lies. Pornography is understood better by analogy with playing cops and robbers, than by analogy with a piece of journalism.

The suggestion that pornography is a vehicle of fantasy, and therefore perhaps not legally-speaking speech, pleases conservatives who use it to defend the legal prohibition of pornography. Harry Clor, for example, insists that pornography ("obscenity") does not "espouse or discuss opinions," but invites its audience "to experience sensations" and "wallow" in degradation.[3] Clor is right insofar as what is psychologically and socially important about pornography is its sexual function and not its possible propositional content. From this perspective, an item of pornography is more like a bit of technology such as contraceptive foam (both contribute to sexual enjoyment) than it is a religious pamphlet. It is more like a piece of machinery like a vibrator (both are "sexual aids") than it is a scandal sheet....

3. DEGRADATION: THREE APPROACHES

The defamation and endorsement arguments presuppose that pornography degrades women, or at least that specific items of pornography degrade women. The former holds that pornography defames women by telling the lie that women enjoy being sexually degraded; the latter holds that pornographic depictions of the degradation of women endorse and thereby promote that degradation. Let us assume that if there are sexual acts that are degrading to women, and these are depicted by pornography, then pornography is degrading to women.[4] But which sexual acts are degrading to women, and how frequently are these degrading acts depicted by pornography? Consider two descriptions of pornography, the first by Griffin, the second by Kathleen Barry:

> If all the literature of pornography were to be represented by one performance, and if that performance were to move into its most dramatic moments, the scenes... which would embody the entire action and meaning of the play... would have to be the moments (which are inevitable in the pornographic *oeuvre*) in which most usually a woman, sometimes a man, often a child, is abducted by force, verbally abused, beaten, bound hand and foot and gagged, often tortured, often hung, his or her body suspended, wounded, and then murdered.[5]
>
> The most prevalent theme in pornography is one of utter contempt for women. In movie after movie women are raped, ejaculated on, urinated on, anally penetrated, beaten, and, with the advent of snuff films, murdered in an orgy of sexual pleasure.[6]

These claims are factually false. That both summaries mention murder suggests that these writers got carried away.... One can agree that pornographic depictions of rape and abuse are degrading, because these acts are degrading, without being committed to the view that most pornography is degrading or that other sexual acts are degrading to women. In particular, anal penetration and the smearing of the ejaculate (or their depictions) are not clearly degrading.

It is useful to distinguish three ways of understanding the claim that pornography degrades women. First, the *definitional* approach: pornography degrades women because pornography *is* sexually explicit material that degrades women. Although a number of feminists, among others, define pornography in these terms, it is not an ideal definition. It works persuasively to make a defender of pornography look like a cad, and it closes the door immediately on serious investigation into the extent of degradation in the content of pornography.

Second, there is the *descriptive* approach. Pornography is defined, say, as sexually explicit material designed to induce sexual arousal, and then some of it can be described, in virtue of its content, as degrading to women. If there are criteria for the presence of degradation in pornography, the descriptive approach can provide important information. However, one standard view, common among liberals, is that descriptions of the degrading content of pornography are subjective or presuppose essentially contestable values. This view, I think, is empty when applied to depictions of brutal sexual assault; Barry's claim that rape is degrading does not involve a malignant sort of subjectivism. The reason is that this judgment—brutal assault is degrading—is based on a nearly universal consensus. At the same time, because there is not such consensus about anal penetration or the smearing of the ejaculate, Barry's claim that these acts are degrading to women does succumb to the liberal critique. Consider, too, Rosemarie Tong's claim that sexual activity without love is quite acceptable and that only degrading pornography should be censored. The Pope agrees that degradation is immoral, depicted and in practice, but also claims that it is degrading for any woman to engage in sexual activity outside of the proper context. If the defamation and endorsement arguments are to avoid probably unresolvable debates about what counts as degradation, they must be severely qualified, claiming at most that universally condemned brutality is degrading and that only pornographic depictions of brutality are to be censored.

Third, there is the *metaphysical* approach. When examining pornography we could focus on the "deeper" messages that can be teased out of it. To investigate degradation in pornography we would examine it intellectually, somewhat like doing dream analysis or literary interpretation. Claims like Griffin's (see her expression, the "meaning of the play") and Barry's do not have to be taken as true by definition, as largely false descriptions, or as essentially contestable evaluations. They could be understood as attempts to probe beneath the surface of pornography in order to reveal its latent meaning....

Arguments... that one interpretation is superior to another will be delicate at best and speculative at worst. But even if it can be demonstrated that the deep meaning of an item of pornography is the degradation of women, that demonstration will not help the defamation and endorsement arguments. For those arguments refer only to degradation that is immediately and easily witnessed by viewers of pornography. Those who consume pornography are not concerned with the deep interpretations of the material they are using to achieve sexual arousal. If the degrading content of pornography is located only in the metaphysical level, it will not be successful in defaming women for these people, or in endorsing the degradation of women for them.

4. DEGRADATION AND INEQUALITY

Some feminists argue that there is another source of the degrading character of pornography; it is not that women are portrayed performing degrading acts, but rather that there is a type of inequality in pornography that constitutes degradation....

Ann Garry has... argued that pornography, to be acceptable must be egalitarian. She finds unobjectionable a kind of nonsexist pornography in which

> men and woman [are] equal sex partners. The man would not control... the choice of positions or acts; the woman's preference would be counted equally.[7]

Garry does not say whether equality in this sense should occur in each scene of every film and novel. But I am not convinced that nonsexist pornography would be egalitarian in this sense. Think about a man and a woman (or two women,) engaging in sexual activity and disagreeing about the position or the act. In this situation the preference of one person carries the day, and for that particular time the preference of the other person counts for nothing. For any single sexual act there is no way to avoid this; compromising by employing some third position, or calling the whole thing off, means that neither preference is satisfied.... [T]here is no way that both preferences can count equally. Thus, nonsexist pornography might contain some scenes in which the man controls the position, and other scenes in which the woman controls, their preferences counting equally not in any given scene but only sequentially or alternatively. I wonder: should the scenes be distributed equally in each item of pornography, or only in the genre as a whole (in which case there might be films depicting men, or women, as full sexual slaves)? Even this account of the equality achievable in pornography is misleading. Because pornography attempts to create a fantasy of an ideal world, men and women quibble very little if at all about what positions to use; in fantasy the parties agree spontaneously to do the same thing at the same time. It is therefore beside the point to insist that in nonsexist pornography the depicted preferences of women will count equally.

Rather than insist that the depicted preferences of the woman in a film count equally with the man's preferences, we could insist that her depicted preferences match the preferences of women in the audience, or that her depicted preferences are those that the women in the audience want to see depicted. Nonsexist pornography, then, could be defined not in terms of the content of the material, but

in terms of its being designed equally for the pleasure of the women and men who consume it. There is still the problem of whether this sort of equality should occur in each scene, in each item of pornography, or only in general in the bulk of the genre. This is just a minor tangle; after all, most pornography produced today is made for and consumed by men, and at the very least nonsexist pornography should be designed to appeal to women. This talk of *designing* pornography, however, suggests a third sense of nonsexist pornography: that which is produced by men and women equally. In this case, should every film be produced by men and women together, or should some films be produced by men and others by women?

5. HOW CAN A DEPICTION ENDORSE?

The endorsement argument can be understood[8] as admitting that pornography contains and elicits fantasies of what the male consumers think of as a better sexual world. As fantasy, pornography is a vision of the way things ought to be or could be, regardless of the way things actually happen to be. Pornography cannot be charged with falsely and maliciously describing women and, therefore, avoids the defamation argument. The endorsement argument picks up the slack: as a depiction of the way things ought to be, pornography endorses that things be the way they are depicted, and by endorsing these values, pornography causally helps to bring these states of affairs into existence. "Pornography, especially violent pornography, is implicated in the committing of crimes of violence against women" and it "supports sexist... attitudes, and thus reinforces the oppression and exploitation of women."[9]...

Why has the endorsement argument been popular...? What is the motivation behind the insistence that pornography endorses what it depicts...? Part of the answer is that feminists have been hard pressed to find convincing arguments against pornography. But if in virtue of endorsing the abusive treatment of women, pornographic depictions promote that degradation, contribute to the oppression of women, or undermine their civil rights, then a good case can be made for the legal control of pornography. There is, however, more to the story.

Longino is one of the... writers on pornography who credit it with reliable harmful causal effects; her argument against pornography turns on a causal connection between pornographic endorsements of acts harmful to women and the occurrence of acts harmful to women....

The assumption... is that endorsing an act is an especially effective way to increase the frequency of that act. However, the assumption is probably false. Quite often, whether my endorsing X gets others to do X depends on factors out of my control: they already believe X should not be done, or they already do X and my endorsement is superfluous, etcetera. (Football players endorse after-shave; newspapers endorse candidates; the *Nihil Obstat* endorses. Are these effective?)... [A]n argument against pornography that turns on a connection between endorsements and harmful consequences is as weak as any other causal-consequences argument against pornography.

But this does not mean that Longino must abandon ship. The endorsement argument can be maintained even when there is no evidence of pornography's harmful effects. If attempting but failing to perform a criminal act is itself criminal, and if encouraging others to commit crimes is itself a crime even when the encouragement fails, then there is some reason to say that the endorsement of acts harmful to women is criminal, even if those endorsements are known to be unsuccessful in causing the actions endorsed or cannot be proved to be successful. This argument against pornography, that is, might be subsumed under the law of attempts, encouragement, and conspiracy. This is the hidden beauty of the endorsement argument, apparently overlooked by its sponsors: it does not necessarily depend on contentious claims about the causal effects of pornography.

The issue, then, is whether depictions of degradation can endorse what they depict, and if so, what conditions must be satisfied for a depiction to be an endorsement....

In explaining how pornography endorses degradation, Longino begins with:

> ... the degradation of the female characters is represented as providing pleasure to the participant males and... to the participant females, and there is no suggestion that this sort of treatment of others is inappropriate.... These two features are together sufficient to constitute endorsement of the represented behavior.[10]

... It is not obvious, however, that depicting degradation as pleasurable or depicting a happy adulterer is to endorse degradation or adultery. A corollary of the suggested principle would seem to be that depicting degradation as unpleasurable and adulterers as unhappy is to disapprove of these behaviors. But consider John Barth's *The End of the Road*; does linking extramarital sex and abortion with a tragic death amount to disapproving of extramarital sex and abortion? Or consider Judith Rossner's *Looking for Mr. Goodbar;* does linking barhopping with calamity amount to a condemnation of barhopping? No. From Barth one could just as easily extract the advice that if one is going to engage in extramarital sex, one should use efficient birth control, or that if one is going to have an abortion, one should avoid quacks. And from Rossner one could just as easily extract the idea that barhopping is safe fun, as long as one is adequately attuned to the psychological complexities of potential sex partners. I use the word "extract" quite intentionally, for it focuses attention not on the mysterious ability of a depiction to implicitly endorse, but on the ability of the viewer of the depiction to construct a commentary from it.

The centrality of the characteristics of the audience is easy to illustrate. Consider the old documentary film, "Reefer Madness," which was intended to disapprove of marijuana by linking the smoking of marijuana with immoral sexual behavior, crime, and insanity. Audiences today howl with laughter at this film, which shows that depicting a behavior as a disaster of unhappiness is not sufficient for endorsing its avoidance. Similarly, for audiences today of scenes of a happy nuclear family (as in "Ozzie and Harriet"), the happiness linked to that structure hardly serves to endorse the nuclear family. In both cases, even if the depictions are meant as endorsements, they are not taken as endorsements....

The fact that whether an item of pornography implicitly endorses degradation is partially a function of the nature of the audience creates an unanticipated complication for the endorsement argument. The pornography that Longino wishes to have censored is that which *endorses* degradation. The pornography to be censored, then, is that which *accomplishes* the endorsement of degradation, or that which is *successful* as an endorsement. I do not mean that the pornography to be censored must be causally successful in bringing about an increase in the frequency of the acts depicted and endorsed; that is a different sense of "successful endorsement" and a sense not necessarily presupposed by the endorsement argument (as I argued earlier). Rather, the pornography must at least succeed in *being* an endorsement, even if it doesn't have any causal effects. But whether an item of pornography succeeds in being an endorsement depends on whether it is taken as an endorsement (rather than, say, ignored or even laughed at) by its audience. If the censorship of pornography turns on being able to show that it succeeds in being an implicit endorsement for an audience, there will be too many counterexamples to satisfy the goal of the argument. That a depiction is intended or meant to implicitly endorse degradation is not sufficient for it to succeed in being an implicit endorsement, in which case proving success in being an implicit endorsement will be difficult.

NOTES

1. Helen Longino, "Pornography, Oppression, and Freedom: A Closer Look," in L. Lederer, ed., *Take Back the Night* (New York: William Morrow, 1980), pp. 40–54. Rosemarie Tong, in "Feminism, Pornography, and Censorship," *Social Theory and Practice,* 8 (1982): 1–17, elaborates Longino's defamation argument.

2. It is unconvincing for Susan Lurie to claim *both* that pornography asserts an "insidious lie" about women and that it "articulates the fantasy" that women accommodate to male sexual desires ("Pornography and the Dread of Women," in *Take*

Back the Night, pp. 159–73, at pp. 160 and 171, respectively).

3. Harry M. Clor, *Obscenity and Public Morality* (Chicago: University of Chicago Press, 1970), pp. 52 and 234, respectively.

4. This assumption requires argument. . . .

5. Susan Griffin, *Pornography and Silence* (New York: Harper and Row, 1979), p. 46.

6. Kathleen Barry, *Female Sexual Slavery* (Englewood Cliffs, NJ: Prentice-Hall, 1979), p. 175.

7. Ann Garry, "Pornography and Respect for Women," *Social Theory and Practice*, 4 (1978): 138.

8. I say "can be," and I also mean "should be," because this is not the way the argument is expressed by Longino. She conflates the defamation and endorsement arguments when she says that pornography lies because it recommends that women should be subservient to the sexual needs of men. To recommend a state of affairs, even an obnoxious one, is not to tell a lie.

9. Longino, "Pornography, Oppression, and Freedom," p. 48.

10. Longino, "Pornography, Oppression, and Freedom," pp. 43–44.

POSTSCRIPT

Is Pornography Degrading to Women?

It seems paradoxical that progressive people would argue on the side of a cause that has in the past been championed by very conservative elements in society. But conservative groups and iconoclastic feminist groups—who disagree on many subjects—nowadays often find agreement in opposition to pornography. One point that still separates the feminist opposition from the conservative kind, however, is that the former (but not the latter) still allows a place for erotica. Erotica can be considered different from pornography in that it lacks the element of degradation that antipornography activists find offensive.

Soble and those who support his side of the debate say that Longino and others are simply mistaken about the content of popular pornography. Mainly, Soble suggests, it *is* erotica, largely along the lines of admittedly very unrealistic male fantasies. Soble could concede that if there were problems in particular cases about degrading pornography, then these could be dealt with. But, he would say, most pornography does not endorse the degradation of women anyway.

There is a difference of emphasis between Soble and Longino. Whereas Soble tends to concentrate on individuals, Longino tends to concentrate on society as a whole. Soble says that, for the most part, individuals do not have the sexist attitudes that Longino draws attention to. But Longino says that sexist attitudes—expressed in pornography—are the attitudes of society in general.

Further relevant sources are David Copp and Susan Wendell, eds., *Pornography and Censorship* (Prometheus, 1983); Catharine MacKinnon, "Pornography, Civil Rights, and Speech," *Harvard Civil Rights–Civil Liberties Law Review* (Winter 1985); Judith M. Hill, "Pornography and Degradation," *Hypatia* (Summer 1987); Gordon Hawkins, *Pornography in a Free Society* (Cambridge University Press, 1988); Linda Williams, *Hard Core: Power, Pleasure, and the "Frenzy of the Visible"* (University of California Press, 1989); Richard S. Randall, *Freedom and Taboo: Pornography and the Politics of a Self Divided* (University of California Press, 1989); Dolf Zillmann and Jennings Bryant, eds., *Pornography: Research Advances and Policy Considerations* (Lawrence Erlbaum, 1989); Donald Alexander Downs, *The New Politics of Pornography* (University of Chicago Press, 1989), which, among other things, deals with the Minneapolis and Indianapolis statutes (since declared invalid) that made pornography a legal offense against women; Susan Gubar and Joan Hoff, eds., *For Adult Users Only: The Dilemma of Violent Pornography* (Indiana University Press, 1989); Dorchen Leidholdt and Janice G. Raymond, eds., *The Sexual Liberals and the*

Attack on Feminism (Pergamon Press, 1990); Robert Emmet Long, ed., *Censorship* (H. W. Wilson, 1990); F. M. Christensen, *Pornography: The Other Side* (Praeger, 1990); Robert M. Baird and Stuart E. Rosenbaum, eds., *Pornography: Private Right or Public Menace?* (Prometheus, 1991); Robert J. Stoller, *Porn: Myths for the Twentieth Century* (Yale University Press, 1991); Bruce Russell, ed., *Freedom, Rights and Pornography: A Collection of Papers by Fred R. Berger* (Kluwer, 1991); Catharine MacKinnon, *Only Words* (Harvard University Press, 1993); Susan Easton, *The Problem of Pornography: Regulation and the Right to Free Speech* (Routledge, 1994); Nadine Strossen, *In Defense of Pornography: Free Speech and the Fight for Women's Rights* (Simon & Schuster, 1994); Chi Chi Sileo, "Pornographobia: Feminists Go to War," *Insight on the News* (February 27, 1995); Susan Dwyer, ed., *The Problem of Pornography* (Wadsworth, 1995); Harry M. Clor, *Public Morality and Liberal Society* (University of Notre Dame Press, 1996); Alix Nalezinski, "Acceptable and Unacceptable Levels of Risk: The Case of Pornography," *Social Theory and Practice* (Spring 1996); and Alan Soble, ed., *The Philosophy of Sex: Contemporary Readings*, 3rd ed. (Rowman & Littlefield, 1997).

ISSUE 11

Is Abortion Immoral?

YES: Don Marquis, from "Why Abortion Is Immoral," *The Journal of Philosophy* (April 1989)

NO: Jane English, from "Abortion and the Concept of a Person," *Canadian Journal of Philosophy* (October 1975)

ISSUE SUMMARY

YES: Professor of philosophy Don Marquis argues that abortion is generally wrong for the same reason that killing an innocent adult human being is generally wrong: it deprives the individual of a future that he or she would otherwise have.

NO: Philosopher Jane English (1947–1978) argues that there is no well-defined line dividing persons from nonpersons. She claims that both the conservative and the liberal positions are too extreme and that some abortions are morally justifiable and some are not.

Abortion is a divisive topic, and discussions can easily become polarized. Here we will briefly consider some of the biological facts associated with abortion and review some relevant historical and legal matters. The selections themselves will then look at the moral issues raised by abortion.

Conception occurs when the spermatozoon of a male unites with the ovum of a female. The single cell thus formed is called a zygote. In a normal pregnancy, this zygote will multiply into several cells, travel through the fallopian tube, enter the uterus, and implant itself in the uterine wall. When implantation is complete, one to two weeks after fertilization (as the original conception is also called), we can say that the pregnancy is established and that the zygote has become an embryo. Once the placenta and umbilical cord are established, the embryo takes nourishment by means of these from the blood of the pregnant woman and quickly grows primitive limbs and organs. At eight weeks from conception, the first brain waves can be detected and the embryo is now called a fetus. So-called quickening, the first felt spontaneous movement of the fetus, occurs at around 14 or 15 weeks. The threshhold of viability (the point at which the fetus can be kept alive outside the uterus) is dependent upon many factors, especially the development of the cardiopulmonary system. Depending on the level of available medical technology, viability can be reached sometime between 20 and 28 weeks. Birth generally takes place about 38 to 40 weeks after conception, although here too there is significant variation.

There are other possibilities once the spermatozoon and ovum unite. The fertilized ovum, for example, might never be implanted in the wall of the uterus and might be expelled uneventfully, and even without notice, from the body. Or the zygote might implant itself somewhere other than inside the uterus, resulting in an ectopic pregnancy. The embryo will not grow properly outside the uterus, and this kind of pregnancy can be dangerous to the mother. (In the case of an ectopic pregnancy, the Roman Catholic Church will permit an abortion to save the pregnant woman's life.) Another possibility is that the pregnancy will develop normally for a while but then end in miscarriage; this is sometimes called a spontaneous abortion.

The historic *Roe v. Wade* case, decided in 1973 by the U.S. Supreme Court in a split decision of 7–2, ruled that the nineteenth-century Texas statutes against abortion were unconstitutional. The Court divided the normal pregnancy into three trimesters and ruled as follows:

> For the stage prior to approximately the end of the first trimester, the abortion decision and its effectuation must be left to the medical judgment of the pregnant woman's attending physician. For the stage subsequent to approximately the end of the first trimester, the State, in promoting its interest in the health of the mother, may, if it chooses, regulate the abortion procedure in ways that are reasonably related to maternal health. For the stages subsequent to viability, the State, in promoting its interest in the potentiality of human life, may, if it chooses, regulate, and even proscribe, abortion except where it is necessary, in appropriate medical judgment, for the preservation of the life or health of the mother. (410 U.S. 113, 93 S. Ct. 705 [1973])

Before *Roe v. Wade*, some states permitted abortion only if a woman's life was in danger; abortion for any other reason or consideration was illegal and punishable by law. *Roe v. Wade* ruled that states do not have the right to regulate abortion procedures in any way during the first trimester of pregnancy. It is important to note that neither the Supreme Court nor the Texas statutes said anything about the relation of the woman to the fetus (or embryo) or about the reasons a woman might have for seeking an abortion.

In the following selections, Don Marquis constructs a secular argument to show that abortion is immoral. He addresses a question that is not considered by the Texas courts or the Supreme Court but is nevertheless thought by many people to be absolutely central here: When does the fetus become a human being (or person)? Jane English argues that this question is not decisive and in any case has no determinate answer. In her view, neither the standard conservative position nor the standard liberal position adequately addresses abortion.

YES

Don Marquis

WHY ABORTION IS IMMORAL

The view that abortion is, with rare exceptions, seriously immoral has received little support in the recent philosophical literature. No doubt most philosophers affiliated with secular institutions of higher education believe that the anti-abortion position is either a symptom of irrational religious dogma or a conclusion generated by seriously confused philosophical argument. The purpose of this essay is to undermine this general belief. This essay sets out an argument that purports to show, as well as any argument in ethics can show, that abortion is, except possibly in rare cases, seriously immoral, that it is in the same moral category as killing an innocent adult human being.

The argument is based on a major assumption. Many of the most insightful and careful writers on the ethics of abortion—such as Joel Feinberg, Michael Tooley, Mary Anne Warren, H. Tristram Engelhardt, Jr., L. W. Sumner, John T. Noonan, Jr., and Philip Devine[1]—believe that whether or not abortion is morally permissible stands or falls on whether or not a fetus is the sort of being whose life it is seriously wrong to end. The argument of this essay will assume, but not argue, that they are correct.

Also, this essay will neglect issues of great importance to a complete ethics of abortion. Some anti-abortionists will allow that certain abortions, such as abortion before implantation or abortion when the life of a woman is threatened by a pregnancy or abortion after rape, may be morally permissible. This essay will not explore the casuistry of these hard cases. The purpose of this essay is to develop a general argument for the claim that the overwhelming majority of deliberate abortions are seriously immoral.

* * *

A sketch of standard anti-abortion and pro-choice arguments exhibits how those arguments possess certain symmetries that explain why partisans of those positions are so convinced of the correctness of their own positions, why they are not successful in convincing their opponents, and why, to others, this issue seems to be unresolvable. An analysis of the nature of this standoff suggests a strategy for surmounting it.

Consider the way a typical anti-abortionist argues. She will argue or assert that life is present from the moment of conception or that fetuses look like babies or that fetuses possess a characteristic such as a genetic code that is both necessary and sufficient for being human. Anti-abortionists seem to believe that (1) the truth of all of these claims is quite obvious, and (2) establishing any of these claims is sufficient to show that abortion is morally akin to murder.

A standard pro-choice strategy exhibits similarities. The pro-choicer will argue or assert that fetuses are not persons or that fetuses are not rational agents or that fetuses are not social beings. Pro-choicers seem to believe that (1) the truth of any of these claims is quite obvious, and (2) establishing any of these claims is sufficient to show that an abortion is not a wrongful killing.

In fact, both the pro-choice and the anti-abortion claims do seem to be true, although the "it looks like a baby" claim is more difficult to establish the earlier the pregnancy. We seem to have a standoff. How can it be resolved?

As everyone who has taken a bit of logic knows, if any of these arguments concerning abortion is a good argument, it requires not only some claim characterizing fetuses, but also some general moral principle that ties a characteristic of fetuses to having or not having the right to life or to some other moral characteristic that will generate the obligation or the lack of obligation not to end the life of a fetus. Accordingly, the arguments of the anti-abortionist and the pro-choicer need a bit of filling in to be regarded as adequate.

Note what each partisan will say. The anti-abortionist will claim that her position is supported by such generally accepted moral principles as "It is always prima facie seriously wrong to take a human life" or "It is always prima facie seriously wrong to end the life of a baby." Since these are generally accepted moral principles, her position is certainly not obviously wrong. The pro-choicer will claim that her position is supported by such plausible moral principles as "Being a person is what gives an individual intrinsic moral worth" or "It is only seriously prima facie wrong to take the life of a member of the human community." Since these are generally accepted moral principles, the pro-choice position is certainly not obviously wrong. Unfortunately, we have again arrived at a standoff.

Now, how might one deal with this standoff? The standard approach is to try to show how the moral principles of one's opponent lose their plausibility under analysis. It is easy to see how this is possible. On the one hand, the anti-abortionist will defend a moral principle concerning the wrongness of killing which tends to be broad in scope in order that even fetuses at an early stage of pregnancy will fall under it. The problem with broad principles is that they often embrace too much. In this particular instance, the principle "It is always prima facie wrong to take a human life" seems to entail that it is wrong to end the existence of a living human cancer-cell culture, on the grounds that the culture is both living and human. Therefore, it seems that the anti-abortionist's favored principle is too broad.

On the other hand, the pro-choicer wants to find a moral principle concerning the wrongness of killing which tends to be narrow in scope in order that fetuses will *not* fall under it. The problem with narrow principles is that they often do not embrace enough. Hence, the needed principles such as "It is prima facie seriously wrong to kill only persons" or "It is prima facie wrong to kill only rational agents" do not explain why it is wrong to kill infants or young children or the severely retarded or even perhaps the severely mentally ill. Therefore, we seem again to have a standoff. The anti-abortionist charges, not unreasonably, that pro-choice principles concerning killing are too narrow to be acceptable; the pro-choicer charges, not unreasonably, that anti-abortionist principles concerning killing are too broad to be acceptable.

Attempts by both sides to patch up the difficulties in their positions run into further difficulties. The anti-abortionist will try to remove the problem in her position by reformulating her principle concerning killing in terms of human beings. Now we end up with: "It is always prima facie seriously wrong to end the life of a human being." This principle has the advantage of avoiding the problem of the human cancer-cell culture counterexample. But this advantage is purchased at a high price. For although it is clear that a fetus is both human and alive, it is not at all clear that a fetus is a human *being*. There is at least something to be said for the view that something becomes a human being only after a process of development, and that therefore first trimester fetuses and perhaps all fetuses are not yet human beings. Hence, the anti-abortionist, by this move, has merely exchanged one problem for another.[2]

The pro-choicer fares no better. She may attempt to find reasons why killing infants, young children, and the severely retarded is wrong which are independent of her major principle that is supposed to explain the wrongness of taking human life, but which will not also make abortion immoral. This is no easy task. Appeals to social utility will seem satisfactory only to those who resolve not to think of the enormous difficulties with a utilitarian account of the wrongness of killing and the significant social costs of preserving the lives of the unproductive.[3] A pro-choice strategy that extends the definition of 'person' to infants or even to young children seems just as arbitrary as an anti-abortion strategy that extends the definition of 'human being' to fetuses. Again, we find symmetries in the two positions and we arrive at a standoff.

There are even further problems that reflect symmetries in the two positions. In addition to counterexample problems, or the arbitrary application problems that can be exchanged for them, the standard anti-abortionist principle "It is prima facie seriously wrong to kill a human being," or one of its variants, can be objected to on the grounds of ambiguity. If 'human being' is taken to be a *biological* category, then the anti-abortionist is left with the problem of explaining why a merely biological category should make a moral difference. Why, it is asked, is it any more reasonable to base a moral conclusion on the number of chromosomes in one's cells than on the color of one's skin?[4] If 'human being', on the other hand, is taken to be a *moral* category, then the claim that a fetus is a human being cannot be taken to be a premise in the anti-abortion argument, for it is precisely what needs to be established. Hence, either the anti-abortionist's main category is a morally irrelevant, merely biological category, or it is of no use to the anti-abortionist in establishing (noncircularly, of course) that abortion is wrong.

Although this problem with the anti-abortionist position is often noticed, it is less often noticed that the pro-choice position suffers from an analogous problem. The principle "Only persons have the right to life" also suffers from an ambiguity. The term 'person' is typically defined in terms of psychological characteristics, although there will certainly be disagreement concerning which characteristics are most important. Supposing that this matter can be settled, the pro-choicer is left with the problem of explaining why *psychological* characteristics should make a *moral* difference. If the pro-choicer should attempt to deal with this problem by claiming that an explanation is not necessary, that in fact we do treat such a cluster of psychological properties as having moral significance, the sharp-witted anti-abortionist should have a ready response. We do treat being both living and human as having moral significance. If it is legitimate for the pro-choicer to demand that the anti-abortionist provide an explanation of the connection between the biological character of being a human being and the wrongness of being killed (even though people accept this connection), then it is legitimate for the anti-abortionist to demand that the pro-choicer provide an explanation of the connection between psychological criteria for being a person and the wrongness of being killed (even though that connection is accepted).[5] ...

[T]he pro-choicer cannot any more escape her problem by making person a purely moral category than the anti-abortionist could escape by the analogous move. For if person is a moral category, then the pro-choicer is left without the resources for establishing (noncircularly, of course) the claim that a fetus is not a person, which is an essential premise in her argument. Again, we have both a symmetry and a standoff between pro-choice and anti-abortion views.

Passions in the abortion debate run high. There are both plausibilities and difficulties with the standard positions. Accordingly, it is hardly surprising that partisans of either side embrace with fervor the moral generalizations that support the conclusions they preanalytically favor, and reject with disdain the moral generalizations of their opponents as being subject to inescapable difficulties. It is easy to believe that the counterexamples to one's own moral principles are merely temporary difficulties that will dissolve in the wake of further philosophical research, and that the counterexamples to the principles of one's opponents are... straightforward.... This might suggest to an impartial observer (if there are any) that the abortion issue is unresolvable.

There is a way out of this apparent dialectical quandary. The moral generalizations of both sides are not quite correct. The generalizations hold for the most part, for the usual cases. This suggests that they are all *accidental* generalizations, that the moral claims made by those on both sides of the dispute do not touch on the *essence* of the matter.

This use of the distinction between essence and accident is not meant to invoke obscure metaphysical categories. Rather, it is intended to reflect the rather atheoretical nature of the abortion discussion. If the generalization a partisan in the abortion dispute adopts were derived from the reason why ending the life of a human being is wrong, then there could not be exceptions to that generalization unless some special case obtains in which there are even more powerful countervailing reasons. Such generalizations would not be merely accidental generalizations; they would point to, or be based upon, the essence of the wrongness of killing, what it is that makes killing wrong. All this suggests that a necessary condition of resolving the abortion controversy is a more theoretical account of the wrongness of killing. After all, if we merely believe, but do not understand, why killing adult human beings such as ourselves is wrong, how could we conceivably show that abortion is either immoral or permissible?

* * *

In order to develop such an account, we can start from the following unproblematic assumption concerning our own case: it is wrong to kill *us*. Why is it wrong?...

What primarily makes killing wrong is neither its effect on the murderer nor its effect on the victim's friends and relatives, but its effect on the victim. The loss of one's life is one of the greatest losses one can suffer. The loss of one's life deprives one of all the experiences, activities, projects, and enjoyments that would otherwise have constituted one's future. Therefore, killing someone is wrong, primarily because the killing inflicts (one of) the greatest possible losses on the victim. To describe this as the loss of life can be misleading, however. The change in my biological state does not by itself make killing me wrong. The effect of the loss of my biological life is the loss to me of all those activities, projects, experiences, and enjoyments which would otherwise have constituted my future personal life. These activities, projects, experiences, and enjoyments are either valuable for their own sakes or are means to something else that is valuable for its own sake. Some parts of my future are not valued by me now, but will come to be valued by me as I grow older and as my values and capacities change. When I am killed, I am deprived both of what I now value which would have been part of my future personal life, but also what I would come to value. Therefore, when I die, I am deprived of all of the value of my future. Inflicting this loss on me is ultimately what makes killing me wrong. This being the case, it would seem that what makes killing *any* adult human being prima facie seriously wrong is the loss of his or her future.[6] ...

The claim that what makes killing wrong is the loss of the victim's future is directly supported by two considerations. In the first place, this theory explains why we regard killing as one of the worst of crimes. Killing is especially wrong, because it deprives the victim of more than perhaps any other crime. In the second place, people with AIDS or cancer who know they are dying believe, of course, that dying is a very bad thing for them. They believe that the loss of a future to them that they would otherwise have experienced is what makes their premature death a very bad thing for them. A better theory of the wrongness of killing would require a different natural property associated with killing which better fits with the attitudes of the dying. What could it be?

The view that what makes killing wrong is the loss to the victim of the value of the victim's future gains additional support when some of its implications are examined. In the first place, it is incompatible with the view that it is wrong to kill only beings who are biologically human. It is possible that there exists a different species from another planet whose members have a future like ours. Since having a future like that is what makes killing someone wrong, this theory entails that it would be wrong to kill members of such a species. Hence, this theory is opposed to the claim that only life that is biologically human has great moral worth, a claim which many anti-abortionists have seemed to adopt. This opposition, which this theory has in common with personhood theories, seems to be a merit of the theory.

In the second place, the claim that the loss of one's future is the wrong-making feature of one's being killed entails the possibility that the futures of some actual nonhuman mammals on our own planet are sufficiently like ours that it is seriously wrong to kill them also. Whether some animals do have the same right to life as human beings depends on adding to the account of the wrongness of killing some additional account of just what it is about my future or the futures of other adult human beings which makes it wrong to kill us. No such additional account will be offered in this essay. Undoubtedly, the provision of such an account would be a very difficult matter. Undoubtedly, any such account would be quite controversial. Hence, it surely should not reflect badly on this sketch of an elementary theory of the wrongness of killing that it is indeterminate with respect to some very difficult issues regarding animal rights.

In the third place, the claim that the loss of one's future is the wrong-making feature of one's being killed does not entail, as sanctity of human life theories do, that active euthanasia is wrong. Persons who are severely and incurably ill, who face a future of pain and despair, and who wish to die will not have suffered a loss if they are killed. It is, strictly speaking, the value of a human's future which makes killing wrong in this theory. This being so, killing does not necessarily wrong some persons who are sick and dying. Of course, there may be other reasons for a prohibition of active euthanasia, but that is another matter. Sanctity-of-human-life theories seem to hold that active euthanasia is seriously wrong even in an individual case where there seems to be good reason for it independently of public policy considerations. This consequence is most implausible, and it is a plus for the claim that the loss of a future of value is what makes killing wrong that it does not share this consequence.

In the fourth place, the account of the wrongness of killing defended in this essay does straightforwardly entail that it is prima facie seriously wrong to kill children and infants, for we do presume that they have futures of value. Since we do believe that it is wrong to kill defenseless little babies, it is important that a theory of the wrongness of killing easily account for this. Personhood theories of the wrongness of killing, on the other hand, cannot straightforwardly account for the wrongness of killing infants and young children.[7] Hence, such theories must add special ad hoc accounts of the wrongness of killing the young. The plausibility of such ad hoc theories seems to be a function of how desperately one wants such theories to work. The claim that the primary wrong-making feature of a killing is the loss to the victim of the value of its future accounts for the wrongness of killing young children and infants directly; it makes the wrongness of such acts as obvious as we actually think it is. This is a further merit of this theory. Accordingly, it seems that this value of a future-like-ours theory of the wrongness of killing shares strengths of both sanctity-of-life and personhood accounts while avoiding weaknesses of both. In addition, it meshes with a central intuition concerning what makes killing wrong.

The claim that the primary wrong-making feature of a killing is the loss to the victim of the value of its future has obvious consequences for the ethics of abortion. The future of a standard fetus includes a set of experiences, projects, activities, and such which are identical with the futures of adult human beings and are identical with the futures of young children. Since the reason that is sufficient to explain why it is wrong to kill human beings after the time of birth is a reason that also applies to fetuses, it follows that abortion is prima facie seriously morally wrong. . . .

* * *

How complete an account of the wrongness of killing does the value of a future-like-ours account have to be in order that the wrongness of abortion is a consequence? This account does not have to be an account of the necessary conditions for the wrongness of killing. Some persons in nursing homes may lack valuable human futures, yet it may be wrong to kill them for other reasons. Furthermore, this account does not obviously have to be the sole reason killing is wrong where the victim did have a valuable future. This analysis claims only that, for any killing where the victim did have a valuable future like ours, having that future by itself is sufficient to create the strong presumption that the killing is seriously wrong. . . .

* * *

In this essay, it has been argued that the correct ethic of the wrongness of killing can be extended to fetal life and

used to show that there is a strong presumption that any abortion is morally impermissible. If the ethic of killing adopted here entails, however, that contraception is also seriously immoral, then there would appear to be a difficulty with the analysis of this essay.

But this analysis does not entail that contraception is wrong. Of course, contraception prevents the actualization of a possible future of value. Hence, it follows from the claim that futures of value should be maximized that contraception is prima facie immoral. This obligation to maximize does not exist, however; furthermore, nothing in the ethics of killing in this paper entails that it does. The ethics of killing in this essay would entail that contraception is wrong only if something were denied a human future of value by contraception. Nothing at all is denied such a future by contraception, however. . . .

At the time of contraception, there are hundreds of millions of sperm, one (released) ovum and millions of possible combinations of all of these. There is no actual combination at all. Is the subject of the loss to be a merely possible combination? Which one? This alternative does not yield an actual subject of harm either. Accordingly, the immorality of contraception is not entailed by the loss of a future-like-ours argument simply because there is no nonarbitrarily identifiable subject of the loss in the case of contraception.

* * *

The purpose of this essay has been to set out an argument for the serious presumptive wrongness of abortion subject to the assumption that the moral permissibility of abortion stands or falls on the moral status of the fetus. Since a fetus possesses a property, the possession of which in adult human beings is sufficient to make killing an adult human being wrong, abortion is wrong. This way of dealing with the problem of abortion seems superior to other approaches to the ethics of abortion, because it rests on an ethics of killing which is close to self-evident, because the crucial morally relevant property clearly applies to fetuses, and because the argument avoids the usual equivocations on 'human life', 'human being', or 'person'. The argument rests neither on religious claims nor on Papal dogma. It is not subject to the objection of "speciesism." Its soundness is compatible with the moral permissibility of euthanasia and contraception. It deals with our intuitions concerning young children.

Finally, this analysis can be viewed as resolving a standard problem—indeed, *the* standard problem—concerning the ethics of abortion. Clearly, it is wrong to kill adult human beings. Clearly, it is not wrong to end the life of some arbitrarily chosen single human cell. Fetuses seem to be like arbitrarily chosen human cells in some respects and like adult humans in other respects. The problem of the ethics of abortion is the problem of determining the fetal property that settles this moral controversy. The thesis of this essay is that the problem of the ethics of abortion, so understood, is solvable.

NOTES

1. Feinberg, "Abortion," in *Matters of Life and Death: New Introductory Essays in Moral Philosophy*, Tom Regan, ed. (New York: Random House, 1986), pp. 256–293; Tooley, "Abortion and Infanticide," *Philosophy and Public Affairs*, II, 1 (1972): 37–65; Tooley, *Abortion and Infanticide* (New York: Oxford, 1984); Warren, "On the Moral and Legal Status of Abortion," *The Monist*, I.VII, 1 (1973): 43–61; Engelhardt, "The Ontology of Abortion," *Ethics*, I, XXXIV, 3 (1974):217–234; Sumner, *Abortion and Moral Theory* (Princeton: University Press, 1981); Noonan, "An Almost Absolute Value in History," in *The Morality of Abortion: Legal and Historical Perspectives*, Noonan, ed. (Cambridge: Harvard, 1970); and Devine, *The Ethics of Homicide* (Ithaca: Cornell, 1978).

2. For interesting discussions of this issue, see Warren Quinn, "Abortion: Identity and Loss," *Philosophy and Public Affairs*, XIII, 1 (1984):24–54; and Lawrence C. Becker, "Human Being: The Boundaries of the Concept," *Philosophy and Public Affairs*, IV, 4 (1975):334–359.

3. For example, see my "Ethics and the Elderly: Some Problems," in Stuart Spicker, Kathleen Woodward, and David Van Tassel, eds., *Aging and the Elderly: Humanistic Perspectives in Gerontology* (Atlantic Highlands, NJ: Humanities, 1978), pp. 341–355.

4. See Warren, *op. cit.*, and Tooley, "Abortion and Infanticide."

5. This seems to be the fatal flaw in Warren's treatment of this issue.

6. I have been most influenced on this matter by Jonathan Glover, *Causing Death and Saving Lives* (New York: Penguin, 1977), ch. 3; and Robert Young, "What Is So Wrong with Killing People?" *Philosophy*, LIV, 210 (1979):515–528.

7. Feinberg, Tooley, Warren, and Engelhardt have all dealt with this problem.

NO   Jane English

ABORTION AND THE
CONCEPT OF A PERSON

The abortion debate rages on. Yet the two most popular positions seem to be clearly mistaken. Conservatives maintain that a human life begins at conception and that therefore abortion must be wrong because it is murder. But not all killings of humans are murders. Most notably, self-defense may justify even the killing of an innocent person.

Liberals, on the other hand, are just as mistaken in their argument that since a fetus does not become a person until birth, a woman may do whatever she pleases in and to her own body. First, you cannot do to as you please with your own body if it affects other people adversely.[1] Second, if a fetus is not a person, that does not imply that you can do to it anything you wish. Animals, for example, are not persons, yet to kill or torture them for no reason at all is wrong.

At the center of the storm has been the issue of just when it is between ovulation and adulthood that a person appears on the scene. Conservatives draw the line at conception, liberals at birth. In this paper I first examine our concept of a person and conclude that no single criterion can capture the concept of a person and no sharp line can be drawn. Next I argue that if a fetus is a person, abortion is still justifiable in many cases; and if a fetus is not a person, killing it is still wrong in many cases. To a large extent, these two solutions are in agreement. I conclude that our concept of a person cannot and need not bear the weight that the abortion controversy has thrust upon it.

The several factions in the abortion argument have drawn battle lines around various proposed criteria for determining what is and what is not a person. For example, Mary Anne Warren[2] lists five features (capacities for reasoning, self-awareness, complex communication, etc.) as her criteria for personhood and argues for the permissibility of abortion because a fetus falls outside this concept. Baruch Brody[3] uses brain waves. Michael Tooley[4] picks having-a-concept-of-self as his criterion and concludes that

From Jane English, "Abortion and the Concept of a Person," *Canadian Journal of Philosophy*, vol. 5, no. 2 (October 1975), pp. 233–243. Copyright © 1975 by *Canadian Journal of Philosophy*. Reprinted by permission.

infanticide and abortion are justifiable, while the killing of adult animals is not. On the other side, Paul Ramsey[5] claims a certain gene structure is the defining characteristic. John Noonan[6] prefers conceived-of-humans and presents counterexamples to various other candidate criteria. For instance, he argues against viability as the criterion because the newborn and infirm would then be nonpersons, since they cannot live without the aid of others. He rejects any criterion that calls upon the sorts of sentiments a being can evoke in adults on the grounds that this would allow us to exclude other races as nonpersons if we could just view them sufficiently unsentimentally.

These approaches are typical: foes of abortion propose sufficient conditions for personhood which fetuses satisfy, while friends of abortion counter with necessary conditions for personhood which fetuses lack. But these both presuppose that the concept of a person can be captured in a strait jacket of necessary and/or sufficient conditions.[7] Rather, "person" is a cluster of features, of which rationality, having a self concept and being conceived of humans are only part.

What is typical of persons? Within our concept of a person we include, first, certain biological factors: descended from humans, having a certain genetic makeup, having a head, hands, arms, eyes, capable of locomotion, breathing, eating, sleeping. There are psychological factors: sentience, perception, having a concept of self and of one's own interests and desires, the ability to use tools, the ability to use language or symbol systems, the ability to joke, to be angry, to doubt. There are rationality factors: the ability to reason and draw conclusions, the ability to generalize and to learn from past experience, the ability to sacrifice present interests for greater gains in the future. There are social factors: the ability to work in groups and respond to peer pressure, the ability to recognize and consider as valuable the interests of others, seeing oneself as one among "other minds," the ability to sympathize, encourage, love, the ability to evoke from others the responses of sympathy, encouragement, love, the ability to work with others for mutual advantage. Then there are legal factors: being subject to the law and protected by it, having the ability to sue and enter contracts, being counted in the census, having a name and citizenship, the ability to own property, inherit, and so forth.

Now the point is not that this list is incomplete, or that you can find counterinstances to each of its points. People typically exhibit rationality, for instance, but someone who was irrational would not thereby fail to qualify as a person. On the other hand, something could exhibit the majority of these features and still fail to be a person, as an advanced robot might. There is no single core of necessary and sufficient features which we can draw upon with the assurance that they constitute what really makes a person; there are only features that are more or less typical.

This is not to say that no necessary or sufficient conditions can be given. Being alive is a necessary condition for being a person, and being a U.S. Senator is sufficient. But rather than falling inside a sufficient condition or outside a necessary one, a fetus lies in the penumbra region where our concept of a person is not so simple. For this reason I think a conclusive answer to the question whether a fetus is a person is unattainable.

Here we might note a family of simple fallacies that proceed by stating a necessary condition for personhood and showing that a fetus has that characteristic. This is a form of the fallacy of affirming the consequent. For example, some have mistakenly reasoned from the premise that a fetus is human (after all, it is a human fetus rather than, say, a canine fetus), to the conclusion that it is a human. Adding an equivocation on "being," we get the fallacious argument that since a fetus is something both living and human, it is a human being.

Nonetheless, it does seem clear that a fetus has very few of the above family of characteristics, whereas a newborn baby exhibits a much larger proportion of them —and a two-year-old has even more. Note that one traditional antiabortion argument has centered on pointing out the many ways in which a fetus resembles a baby. They emphasize its development ("It already has ten fingers...") without mentioning its dissimilarities to adults (it still has gills and a tail). They also try to evoke the sort of sympathy on our part that we only feel toward other persons ("Never to laugh... or feel the sunshine?"). This all seems to be a relevant way to argue, since its purpose is to persuade us that a fetus satisfies so many of the important features on the list that it ought to be treated as a person. Also note that a fetus near the time of birth satisfies many more of these factors than a fetus in the early months of development. This could provide reason for making distinctions among the different stages of pregnancy, as the U.S. Supreme Court has done.[8]

Historically, the time at which a person has been said to come into existence has varied widely. Muslims date personhood from fourteen days after conception. Some medievals followed Aristotle in placing ensoulment at forty days after conception for a male fetus and eighty days for a female fetus.[9] In European common law since the seventeenth century, abortion was considered the killing of a person only after quickening, the time when a pregnant woman first feels the fetus move on its own. Nor is this a variety of opinions surprising. Biologically, a human being develops gradually. We shouldn't expect there to be any specific time or sharp dividing point when a person appears on the scene.

For these reasons I believe our concept of a person is not sharp or decisive enough to bear the weight of a solution to the abortion controversy. To use it to solve that problem is to clarify *obscurum per obscurius* [to clarify what is obscure by what is more obscure].

Next let us consider what follows if a fetus is a person after all. Judith Jarvis Thomson's landmark article, "A Defense of Abortion,"[10] correctly points out that some additional argumentation is needed at this point in the conservative argument to bridge the gap between the premise that a fetus is an innocent person and the conclusion that killing it is always wrong. To arrive at this conclusion, we would need the additional premise that killing an innocent person is always wrong. But killing an innocent person is sometimes permissible, most notably in self-defense. Some examples may help draw out our intuitions or ordinary judgments about self-defense.

Suppose a mad scientist, for instance, hypnotized innocent people to jump out of the bushes and attack innocent passersby with knives. If you are so attacked, we agree you have a right to kill the attacker in self-defense, if killing him is the only way to protect your life or to save yourself from serious injury. It does not seem to matter here that the attacker is not malicious but himself an innocent pawn, for your killing of him is not done in a spirit of retribution but only in self-defense.

How severe an injury may you inflict in self-defense? In part this depends upon the severity of the injury to be avoided: you may not shoot someone merely to avoid having your clothes torn. This might lead one to the mistaken conclusion that the defense may only equal the threatened injury in severity; that to avoid death you may kill, but to avoid a black eye you may only inflict a black eye or the equivalent. Rather, our laws and customs seem to say that you may create an injury somewhat, but not enormously, greater than the injury to be avoided. To fend off an attack whose outcome would be as serious as rape, a severe beating or the loss of a finger, you may shoot; to avoid having your clothes torn, you may blacken an eye....

Some cases of pregnancy present a parallel situation. Though the fetus is itself innocent, it may pose a threat to the pregnant woman's well-being, life prospects or health, mental or physical. If the pregnancy presents a slight threat to her interests, it seems self-defense cannot justify abortion. But if the threat is on a par with a serious beating or the loss of a finger, she may kill the fetus that poses such a threat, even if it is an innocent person. If a lesser harm to the fetus could have the same defensive effect, killing it would not be justified. It is unfortunate that the only way to free the woman from the pregnancy entails the death of the fetus (except in very late stages of pregnancy). Thus a self-defense model supports Thomson's point that the woman has a right only to be freed from the fetus, not a right to demand its death.[11] ...

Thanks to modern technology, the cases are rare in which pregnancy poses as clear a threat to a woman's bodily health as an attacker brandishing a switchblade. How does self-defense fare when more subtle, complex and long-range harms are involved?

To consider a somewhat fanciful example, suppose you are a highly trained surgeon when you are kidnapped by the hypnotic attacker. He says he does not intend to harm you but to take you back to the mad scientist who, it turns out, plans to hypnotize you to have a permanent mental block against all your knowledge of medicine. This would automatically destroy your career which would in turn have a serious adverse impact on your family, your personal relationships and your happiness. It seems to me that if the only way you can avoid this outcome is to shoot the innocent attacker, you are justified in so doing. You are defending yourself from a drastic injury to your life prospects. I think it is no exaggeration to claim that unwanted pregnancies (most obviously among teenagers) often have such adverse life-long consequences as the surgeon's loss of livelihood.

Several parallels arise between various views on abortion and the self-defense model. Let's suppose further that these hypnotized attackers only operate at night, so that it is well known that they can be avoided completely by the considerable inconvenience of never leaving your house after dark. One view is that since you could stay home at night, therefore if you go out and are selected by one of these hypnotized people, you have no right to defend yourself. This parallels the view that abstinence is the only acceptable way to avoid pregnancy. Others might hold that you ought to take along some defense such as Mace which will deter the hypnotized person without killing him, but that if this defense fails, you are obliged to submit to the resulting injury, no matter how severe it is. This parallels the view that contraception is all right but abortion is always wrong, even in cases of contraceptive failure.

A third view is that you may kill the hypnotized person only if he will actually kill you, but not if he will only injure you. This is like the position that abortion is permissible only if it is required to save a woman's life. Finally we have the view that it is all right to kill the attacker, even if only to avoid a very slight inconvenience to yourself and even if you knowingly walked down the very street where all these incidents have been taking place without taking along any Mace or protective escort. If we assume that a fetus is a person, this is the analogue of the view that abortion is always justifiable, "on demand."

The self-defense model allows us to see an important difference that exists between abortion and infanticide, even if a fetus is a person from conception. Many have argued that the only way to justify abortion without justifying infanticide would be to find some characteristic of personhood that is acquired at birth. Michael Tooley, for one, claims infanticide is justifiable because the really significant characteristics of person[hood] are acquired some time after birth. But all such approaches look to characteristics of the developing human and ignore the relation between the fetus and the woman. What if, after birth, the presence of an infant or the need to support it posed a grave threat to the woman's sanity or life

prospects? She could escape this threat by the simple expedient of running away. So a solution that does not entail the death of the infant is available. Before birth, such solutions are not available because of the biological dependence of the fetus on the woman. Birth is the crucial point not because of any characteristics the fetus gains, but because after birth the woman can defend herself by a means less drastic than killing the infant. Hence self-defense can only be used to justify abortion without necessarily thereby justifying infanticide.

On the other hand, supposing a fetus is not after all a person, would abortion always be morally permissible? Some opponents of abortion seem worried that if a fetus is not a full-fledged person, then we are justified in treating it in any way at all. However, this does not follow. Nonpersons do get some consideration in our moral code, though of course they do not have the same rights as persons have (and in general they do not have moral responsibilities), and though their interests may be overridden by the interests of persons. Still, we cannot just treat them in any way at all.

Treatment of animals is a case in point. It is wrong to torture dogs for fun or to kill wild birds for no reason at all. It is wrong Period, even though dogs and birds do not have the same rights persons do. However, few people think it is wrong to use dogs as experimental animals, causing them considerable suffering in some cases, provided that the resulting research will probably bring discoveries of great benefit to people. And most of us think it all right to kill birds for food or to protect our crops. People's rights are different from the consideration we give to animals, then, for it is wrong to experiment on people, even if others might later benefit a great deal as a result of their suffering. You might volunteer to be a subject, but this would be supererogatory; you certainly have a right to refuse to be a medical guinea pig.

But how do we decide what you may or may not do to nonpersons? This is a difficult problem, one for which I believe no adequate account exists. You do not want to say, for instance, that torturing dogs is all right whenever the sum of its effects on people is good—when it doesn't warp the sensibilities of the torturer so much that he mistreats people. If that were the case, it would be all right to torture dogs if you did it in private, or if the torturer lived on a desert island or died soon afterward, so that his actions had no effect on people. This is an inadequate account, because whatever moral consideration animals get, it has to be indefeasible, too. It will have to be a general proscription of certain actions, not merely a weighing of the impact on people on a case-by-case basis....

An ethical theory must operate by generating a set of sympathies and attitudes toward others which reinforces the functioning of... moral principles. Our prohibition against killing people operates by means of certain moral sentiments including sympathy, compassion and guilt. But if these attitudes are to form a coherent set, they carry us further; we tend to perform supererogatory actions, and we tend to feel similar compassion toward person-like nonpersons.

It is crucial that psychological facts play a role here. Our psychological constitution makes it the case that for our ethical theory to work, it must prohibit certain treatment of nonpersons which are significantly person-like. If our moral rules allowed people to treat some person-like nonpersons in ways we do not want people to be treated, this would undermine the system of sympathies and attitudes that makes the ethical system work.... Thus it makes sense that it is those animals whose appearance and behavior are most like those people that get the most consideration in our moral scheme.

It is because of "coherence of attitudes," I think, that the similarity of a fetus to a baby is very significant. A fetus one week before birth is so much like a newborn baby in our psychological space that we cannot allow any cavalier treatment of the former while expecting full sympathy and nurturative support for the latter. Thus, I think that antiabortion forces are indeed giving their strongest arguments when they point to the similarities between a fetus and a baby, and when they try to evoke our emotional attachment to and sympathy for the fetus. An early horror story from New York about nurses who were expected to alternate between caring for six-week premature infants and disposing of viable 24-week aborted fetuses is just that—a horror story. These beings are so much alike that no one can be asked to draw a distinction and treat them so very differently.

Remember, however, that in the early weeks after conception, a fetus is very much unlike a person. It is hard to develop these feelings for a set of genes which doesn't yet have a head, hands, beating heart, response to touch or the ability to move by itself. Thus it seems to me that the alleged "slippery slope" between conception and birth is not so very slippery. In the early stages of pregnancy, abortion can hardly be compared to murder for psychological reasons, but in the latest stages it is psychologically akin to murder.

Another source of similarity is the bodily continuity between fetus and adult. Bodies play a surprisingly central role in our attitudes toward persons. One has only to think of the philosophical literature on how far physical identity suffices for personal identity or Wittgenstein's remark that the best picture of the human soul is the human body. Even after death, when all agree the body is no longer a person, we will observe elaborate customs of respect for the human body; like people who torture dogs, necrophiliacs are not to be trusted with people.[12] So it is appropriate that we show respect to a fetus as the body continuous with the body of the person. This is a degree of resemblance to persons that animals cannot rival. . . .

Even if a fetus is not a person, abortion is not always permissible, because of the resemblance of a fetus to a person. I agree with Thomson that it would be wrong for a woman who is seven months pregnant to have an abortion just to avoid having to postpone a trip to Europe. In the early months of pregnancy when the fetus hardly resembles a baby at all, then, abortion is permissible whenever it is in the interests of the pregnant woman or her family. The reasons would only need to outweigh the pain and inconvenience of the abortion itself. In the middle months, when the fetus comes to resemble a person, abortion would be justifiable only when the continuation of the pregnancy or the birth of the child would cause harms —physical, psychological, economic or social—to the woman. In the late months of pregnancy, even on our current assumption that a fetus is not a person, abortion seems to be wrong except to save a woman from significant injury or death.

The Supreme Court has recognized similar gradations in the alleged slippery slope stretching between conception and birth. To this point, the present paper has been a discussion of the moral status of abortion only, not its legal status. In view of the great physical, financial and sometimes psychological costs of abortion, perhaps the legal arrangement most compatible with the proposed moral solution would be the absence of restrictions, that is, so-called abortion "on demand."

So I conclude, first, that application of our concept of a person will not suffice to settle the abortion issue. After all, the biological development of a human being is gradual. Second, whether a fetus is a person or not, abortion is justifiable early in pregnancy to avoid modest harms and seldom justifiable late in pregnancy except to avoid significant injury or death.[13]

NOTES

1. We also have paternalistic laws which keep us from harming our own bodies even when no one else is affected. Ironically, antiabortion laws were originally designed to protect pregnant women from a dangerous but tempting procedure.

2. Mary Anne Warren, "On the Moral and Legal Status of Abortion," *Monist* 57 (1973), p. 55.

3. Baruch Brody, "Fetal Humanity and the Theory of Essentialism," in Robert Baker and Frederick Elliston, eds., *Philosophy and Sex* (Buffalo, N.Y., 1975).

4. Michael Tolley, "Abortion and Infanticide," *Philosophy and Public Affairs* 2 (1982).

5. Paul Ramsey, "The Morality of Abortion," in James Rachels, ed., *Moral Problems* (New York, 1971).

6. John Noonan, "Abortion and the Catholic Church: A Summary History," *Natural Law Forum* 12 (1967), pp. 125-131.

7. Wittgenstein has argued against the possibility of so capturing the concept of a game, *Philosophical Investigations* (New York, 1958), § 66.

8. Not because the fetus is partly a person and so has some of the rights of persons, but rather because of the rights of person-like nonpersons. This I discuss . . . below.

9. Aristotle himself was concerned, however, with the different question of when the soul takes form. For historical data, see Jimmye Kimmey, "How the Abortion Laws Happened," Ms. 1 (April 1973), pp. 48ff, and John Noonan, *loc. cit.*

10. J. J. Thomson, "A Defense of Abortion," *Philosophy and Public Affairs* 1 (1971).

11. *Ibid.*, p. 62.

12. On the other hand, if they can be trusted with people, then our moral customs are mistaken. It all depends on the facts of psychology.

13. I am deeply indebted to Larry Crocker and Arthur Kuflik for their constructive comments.

POSTSCRIPT

Is Abortion Immoral?

Whether or not a fetus can be considered a person is often at the center of the abortion issue. Marquis, however, does not find that a direct approach to this question breaks the deadlock that is characteristic of many discussions of the morality of abortion. Instead he argues that the effect of aborting a fetus, which is the loss of that fetus's future experiences, is the reason why abortion is immoral. Marquis considers this loss of future experiences to be the reason why killing adult human beings is wrong, and he carries the logic over to fetuses.

English also does not consider the question, Is a fetus a person? to be a key one, because, first, even if the fetus is *not* a person, this does not imply that we may do anything to it that we like. Second, even if it *is* a person, this does not mean that abortion may always be ruled out. Not only is the question not decisive, English claims, but it has no *right* answer. She does not mean that there really is a right answer but we do not know it; she means instead that our concepts (including the concept of a person) do not have clear boundaries. Likewise, we might ask, when does a baby become a child? Again, there is no right answer. The problem is not that babies turn into children without our being able to catch them in the act. There is no right answer because the concepts in our language (such as *baby* and *child*) do not have sharply defined boundaries. Thus, when we ask whether or not a fetus is a person, instead of finding out that it is or is not, we find out that it has some of the features of a person but that it lacks other features.

Judith Jarvis Thomson, in her ground-breaking article "In Defense of Abortion," *Philosophy and Public Affairs* (Fall 1971), argues that, from the premise that the fetus is a person with a right to life, it does not follow that a woman cannot disconnect herself from it and terminate an unwanted pregnancy. Suppose, she says, that you wake up one day to find yourself medically attached to a famous violinist who would die if you detached yourself. A violinist is a person and has a right to life. Does it then follow, asks Thomson, that you may not detach yourself from this unwanted arrangement?

Further readings on this issue are Joel Feinberg, *The Problem of Abortion*, 2d ed. (Wadsworth, 1984); Kristen Luker, *Abortion and the Politics of Motherhood* (University of California Press, 1984); Celeste Michelle Condit, *Decoding Abortion Rhetoric: Communicating Social Change* (University of Illinois Press, 1990); Janet Podell, ed., *Abortion* (H. W. Wilson, 1990); Laurence Tribe, *Abortion: The Clash of Absolutes* (W. W. Norton, 1990); "Abortion," in Lawrence C. Becker and Charlotte B. Becker, eds., *Encyclopedia of Ethics* (Garland, 1991); Bonnie Steinbock, *Life Before Birth: The Moral and Legal Status of Embryos and Fetuses*

(Oxford University Press, 1992); Frances Myrna Kamm, *Creation and Abortion: An Essay in Moral and Legal Philosophy* (Oxford University Press, 1992); Lewis M. Schwartz, *Arguing About Abortion* (Wadsworth, 1993); Ronald Dworkin, *Life's Dominion: An Argument about Abortion, Euthanasia, and Individual Freedom* (Alfred A. Knopf, 1993); Louis P. Pojman and Francis J. Beckwith, eds., *The Abortion Controversy: An Anthology* (Jones & Bartlett, 1994); Bhavani Sitaraman, *The Middleground: The American Public and the Abortion Debate* (Garland, 1994); David J. Garrow, *Liberty and Sexuality: The Right to Privacy and the Making of Roe v. Wade* (Macmillan, 1994); Laurie Shrage, *Moral Dilemmas of Feminism: Prostitution, Adultery, and Abortion* (Routledge, 1994); Ricky Solinger, *The Abortionist* (Free Press, 1994), which is the story of a woman abortionist in Oregon before *Roe v. Wade*; Miriam Claire, *The Abortion Dilemma: Personal Views on a Public Issue* (Insight Books, 1995); Ian Shapiro, ed., *Abortion: The Supreme Court Decisions* (Hackett, 1995); Mark A. Graber, *Rethinking Abortion: Equal Choice, the Constitution, and Reproductive Politics* (Princeton University Press, 1996); Peter Korn, *Lovejoy: A Year in the Life of an Abortion Clinic* (Atlantic Monthly Press, 1996); Marianne Githens and Dorothy McBride Stetson, eds., *Abortion Politics: Public Policy in Cross-Cultural Perspective* (Routledge, 1996); and Patrick Lee, *Abortion and Unborn Human Life* (Catholic University of America Press, 1996).

A related volume is Janice G. Raymond, Renate Klein, and Lynette J. Dumble, *RU 486: Misconceptions, Myths, and Morals* (Institute on Women and Technology, 1991).

On the Internet . . .

DRCNet Online Library of Drug Policy
The Drug Reform Coordination Network (DRCN) sponsors this site of links to drug policy organizations and studies. *http://druglibrary.org/*

Legalization of Drugs
This site is a comprehensive resource on the issue of legalizing narcotics. It provides access to a vast amount of research data and pro and con arguments in the debate over drug legalization.
http://www-mmc.library.wisc.edu/college/roadmaps/druglegalize.htm

Punishment and the Death Penalty
This site, sponsored by *Ethics Updates,* contains discussion forums, court decisions, statistical resources, and Internet resources on capital punishment.
http://ethics.acusd.edu/death_penalty.html

Euthanasia and End-of-Life Decisions
This site, sponsored by *Ethics Updates,* contains discussion questions, court decisions, statistical resources, and Internet resources on euthanasia.
http://ethics.acusd.edu/euthanasia.html

PART 4

Morality, Law, and Society

It is part of the social nature of human beings that we live in groups. And this requires that we have laws or rules that govern our relationships and interactions. Morality and shared values can be positive tools for social living. One presupposition in a democratic society is that social differences must be settled by open discussion and argument. The issues in this section include some of those that have strongly divided our own society and some that challenge existing social institutions and practices.

■ Should Drugs Be Legalized?

■ Should the Death Penalty Be Retained?

■ Is Euthanasia Immoral?

■ Is Affirmative Action Fair?

ISSUE 12

Should Drugs Be Legalized?

YES: Ethan A. Nadelmann, from "Should We Legalize Drugs? Yes," *American Heritage* (February/March 1993)

NO: David T. Courtwright, from "Should We Legalize Drugs? No," *American Heritage* (February/March 1993)

ISSUE SUMMARY

YES: Ethan A. Nadelmann, an assistant professor of politics and public affairs, argues that lessons from alcohol prohibition and the nature of the drug problem today show that much of this problem is due to drug prohibition. According to Nadelmann, current drug prohibition is not only costly and ineffective but counterproductive and immoral.

NO: Professor of history David T. Courtwright maintains that controlled legalization of drugs is unworkable. He argues that if people have easy access to drugs, there will be an increase in drug abuse and drug addiction.

No one can deny that the use of psychoactive substances has a great impact on society today—from the health effects of cigarettes to the criminal activity of street-corner crack dealers. In many ways, the greatest impact is from the smuggling, trafficking, and consumption of illegal drugs. These practices entail or lead to bribery, inner-city crime, babies born addicted to drugs such as crack, and a host of other social ills.

America has been waging a "war on drugs" that is supposed to address (if not solve) these problems. But the problems still exist, and the war on drugs has been going on for some time now. Critics wonder how effective the war is. Severe critics would say that the so-called war on drugs is not working at all and that it is time to try another approach.

Some have called for the legalization of drugs. If drugs were legal, advocates say, their sale and use could be regulated and controlled. The government would be able to raise revenue through taxation (instead of having huge drug profits go to organized crime), the quality and quantity of the drugs could be officially monitored, and much inner-city street crime could be eliminated. On the other hand, even after legalization, there would still be many drug addicts (perhaps even more of them), "crack babies," and other victims of drug use.

Proponents of drug legalization must offer a realistic plan for the legal market they propose. At least two elements should be addressed. First, what exactly is meant by *legalization*? Substances that are legal are not necessarily available at all times to everyone. Alcohol, for example, is a legal substance, but when and where and to whom it may be sold are all regulated by federal and local authorities. And some currently legal drugs are available only by prescription. Secondly, some further clarification is needed about what is meant by *drugs*. Much talk about drugs is very vague. Caffeine and nicotine are common drugs, but since they are already legal, we might say that we are considering here only illegal drugs. But why are some drugs legal and some illegal?

Prohibition (when the status of alcohol was changed from legal to illegal) is one of the useful test cases that people on both sides of this issue can appeal to. It is useful because although we cannot experiment with changing the legal status of some drugs for a limited time to see what would happen, Prohibition is a historical reality. Prohibition became effective on January 16, 1920, and was repealed December 5, 1933. During this time, the Constitution was amended to outlaw "the manufacture, sale, or transportation of intoxicating liquors within ... the United States." Also outlawed was all import and export of these items. During Prohibition, many of the problems that we now associate with the modern drug world existed: smuggling, official corruption, murder, large amounts of money being made by violent criminals, and organized criminal networks. The general public could, with a little effort— and in some cases with very little effort—buy and consume the very products that were against the law. And what was bought on the black market had no guarantees with respect to health or safety.

In the following selections, Ethan A. Nadelmann and David T. Courtwright use the historical experience with alcohol and other drugs as a source of lessons for today's drug problem, but they draw very different conclusions. Nadelmann argues that drugs should be legalized because this would eliminate much of what we now call the "drug problem." Courtwright, on the other hand, argues that drug legalization would be far more problematic than its proponents realize.

YES
Ethan A. Nadelmann

SHOULD WE LEGALIZE DRUGS? YES

The better title for this article, let me suggest at the outset, would be "Drug Prohibition: Con." Most opponents of "drug legalization" assume that it would involve making cocaine and heroin available the way alcohol and tobacco are today. But most legalization supporters favor nothing of the kind; in fact, we disagree widely as to which drugs should be legalized, how they should be controlled, and what the consequences are likely to be. Where drug-policy reformers do agree is in our critique of the drug-prohibition system that has evolved in the United States—a system, we contend, that has proved ineffective, costly, counterproductive, and immoral.

Efforts to reverse drug prohibition face formidable obstacles. Americans have grown accustomed to the status quo. Alcohol prohibition was overturned before most citizens had forgotten what a legal alcohol policy was like, but who today can recall a time before drug prohibition? Moreover, the United States has succeeded in promoting its drug-prohibition system throughout the world. Opponents of alcohol prohibition could look to successful foreign alcohol-control systems, in Canada and much of Europe, but contemporary drug anti-prohibitionists must look further—to history.

The principal evidence, not surprisingly, is Prohibition. The dry years offer many useful analogies, but their most important lesson is the need to distinguish between the harms that stem from drugs and the harms that arise from outlawing them. The Americans who voted in 1933 to repeal Prohibition differed greatly in their reasons for overturning the system. They almost all agreed, however, that the evils of alcohol consumption had been surpassed by those of trying to suppress it.

Some pointed to Al Capone and rising crime, violence, and corruption; others to the overflowing courts, jails, and prisons, the labeling of tens of millions of Americans as criminals and the consequent broadening disrespect for the law, the dangerous expansions of federal police powers and encroachments on individual liberties, the hundreds of thousands of Americans blinded, paralyzed, and killed by poisonous moonshine and industrial alcohol, and the increasing government expenditure devoted to enforcing the Prohibition laws and the billions in forgone tax revenues. Supporters of

Prohibition blamed the consumers, and some went so far as to argue that those who violated the laws deserved whatever ills befell them. But by 1933 most Americans blamed Prohibition.

If there is a single message that contemporary anti-prohibitionists seek to drive home, it is that drug prohibition is responsible for much of what Americans identify today as the "drug problem." It is not merely a matter of the direct costs—twenty billion dollars spent this year on arresting, prosecuting, and incarcerating drug-law violators. Choked courts and prisons, an incarceration rate higher than that of any other nation in the world, tax dollars diverted from education and health care, law-enforcement resources diverted from investigating everything from auto theft to savings-and-loan scams—all these are just a few of the costs our current prohibition imposes.

* * *

Consider also Capone's successors—the drug kingpins of Asia, Latin America, and the United States. Consider as well all the murders and assaults perpetrated by young drug dealers not just against one another but against police, witnesses, and bystanders. Consider the tremendous economic and social incentives generated by the illegality of the drug market—temptations so overwhelming that even "good kids" cannot resist them. Consider the violent drug dealers becoming the heroes of boys and young men, from Harlem to Medellín. And consider tens of millions of Americans being labeled criminals for doing nothing more than smoking a marijuana cigarette. In all these respects the consequences of drug prohibition imitate—and often exceed—those of alcohol prohibition.

Prohibition reminds us, too, of the health costs of drug prohibition. Sixty years ago some fifty thousand Americans were paralyzed after consuming an adulterated Jamaica ginger extract known as "jake." Today we have marijuana made more dangerous by government-sprayed paraquat and the chemicals added by drug dealers, heroin adulterated with poisonous powders, and assorted pills and capsules containing everything from antihistamines to strychnine. Indeed, virtually every illicit drug purchased at the retail level contains adulterants, at least some of which are far more dangerous than the drug itself. And restrictions on the sale of drug paraphernalia has, by encouraging intravenous drug addicts to share their equipment, severely handicapped efforts to stem the transmission of AIDS. As during Prohibition, many Americans view these ills as necessary and even desirable, but others, like their forebears sixty years ago, reject as perverse a system that degrades and destroys the very people it was designed to protect.

Prohibition's lessons extend in other directions as well. The current revisionist twist on that "Great Experiment" now claims that "Prohibition worked," by reducing alcohol consumption and alcohol-related ills ranging from cirrhosis to public drunkenness and employee absenteeism. There is some truth to this claim. But in fact, the most dramatic decline in American alcohol consumption occurred not between 1920 and 1933, while the Eighteenth Amendment was in effect, but rather between 1916 and 1922. During those years the temperance movement was highly active and successful in publicizing the dangers of alcohol. The First World War's spirit of self-sacrifice extended to temperance as a means of grain conservation, and there arose, as the historian David Kyvig puts it, "an atmosphere of hostility toward all things German, not the least of which was beer." In short, a great variety of factors coalesced in this brief time to substantially reduce alcohol consumption and its ills.

The very evidence on which proprohibition historians rely provides further proof of the importance of factors other than prohibition laws. One of these historians, John Burnham, has noted that the admission rate for alcohol psychoses to New York hospitals shrank from 10 percent between 1909 and 1912 to 1.9 percent in 1920—a decline that occurred largely before national prohibition and in a state that had not enacted its own prohibition law.

At best one can argue that Prohibition was most effective in its first years, when temperance norms remained strong and illicit sources of production had yet to be firmly established. By all accounts, alcohol consumption rose after those first years—despite increased resources devoted to enforcement. The pre-Prohibition decline in consumption, like the recent decline in cigarette consumption, had less to do with laws than with changing norms and the imposition of non-criminal-justice measures.

Perhaps the most telling indictment of Prohibition is provided by the British experience with alcohol control during a similar period. In the United States the death rate from cirrhosis of the liver dropped from as high as 15 per 100,000 population between 1910 and 1914 to 7 during the twenties only to climb back to pre-1910 levels by the 1960s, while in Britain the death rate from cirrhosis dropped from 10 in 1914 to 5 in 1920 and then gradually declined to a low of

2 in the 1940s before rising by a mere point by 1963. Other indicators of alcohol consumption and misuse dropped by similar magnitudes, even though the United Kingdom never enacted prohibition. Instead wartime Britain restricted the amount of alcohol available, taxed it, and drastically reduced the hours of sale. At war's end the government dropped restrictions on quantity but made taxes even higher and set hours of sale at only half the pre-war norm.

* * *

Britain thus not only reduced the negative consequences of alcohol consumption more effectively than did the United States, but did so in a manner that raised substantial government revenues. The British experience—as well as Australia's and most of continental Europe's—strongly suggests not only that our Prohibition was unsuccessful but that more effective post-Repeal controls might have prevented the return to high consumption levels.

But no matter how powerful the analogies between alcohol prohibition and contemporary drug prohibition, most Americans still balk at drawing the parallels. Alcohol, they insist, is fundamentally different from everything else. They are right, of course, insofar as their claims rest not on health or scientific grounds but are limited to political and cultural arguments. By most measures, alcohol is more dangerous to human health than any of the drugs now prohibited by law. No drug is as associated with violence in American culture—and even in illicit-drug-using subcultures—as is alcohol. One would be hard pressed to argue that its role in many Native American and other aboriginal communities has been any less destructive than that of illicit drugs in America's ghettos.

The dangers of all drugs vary greatly, of course, depending not just on their pharmacological properties and how they are consumed but also on the attitudes and beliefs of their users and the settings in which they use them. Alcohol by and large plays a benign role in Jewish and Asian-American cultures but a devastating one in some Native American societies, and by the same token the impact of cocaine among Yuppies during the early 1980s was relatively benign compared with its impact a few years later in impoverished ghettos.

*   *   *

The culture helps determine the setting of drug use, but so do the laws. Prohibitions enhance the dangers not just of drugs but of the settings in which they are used. The relationship between prohibition and dangerous adulterations is clear. So too is its impact on the potency and forms of drugs. For instance, Prohibition caused a striking drop in the production and sale of beer, while that of hard liquor increased as bootleggers from Al Capone on down sought to maximize their profits and minimize the risks of detection. Similarly, following the Second World War, the enactment of anti-opium laws in many parts of Asia in which opium use was traditional—India, Hong Kong, Thailand, Laos, Iran—effectively suppressed the availability of opium at the cost of stimulating the creation of domestic heroin industries and substantial increases in heroin use. The same transition had occurred in the United States following Congress's ban on opium imports in 1909. And when during the 1980s the U.S. government's domestic drug-

enforcement efforts significantly reduced the availability and raised the price of marijuana, they provided decisive incentives to producers, distributors, and consumers to switch to cocaine. In each case, prohibition forced switches from drugs that were bulky and relatively benign to drugs that were more compact, more lucrative, more potent, and more dangerous.

In the 1980s the retail purity of heroin and cocaine increased, and highly potent crack became cheaply available in American cities. At the same time, the average potency of most legal psychoactive substances declined: Americans began switching from hard liquor to beer and wine, from high-tar-and-nicotine to lower-tar-and-nicotine cigarettes, and even from caffeinated to decaffeinated coffee and soda. The relationship between prohibition and drug potency was, if not indisputable, still readily apparent.

In turn-of-the-century America, opium, morphine, heroin, cocaine, and marijuana were subject to few restrictions. Popular tonics such as Vin Mariani and Coca-Cola and its competitors were laced with cocaine, and hundreds of medicines —Mrs. Winslow's Soothing Syrup may have been the most famous—contained psychoactive drugs. Millions, perhaps tens of millions of Americans, took opiates and cocaine. David Courtwright estimates that during the 1890s as many as one-third of a million Americans were opiate addicts, but most of them were ordinary people who would today be described as occasional users.

Careful analysis of that era—when the very drugs that we most fear were widely and cheaply available throughout the country—provides a telling antidote to our nightmare legalization scenarios. For one thing, despite the virtual absence of any controls on availability, the proportion of Americans addicted to opiates was only two or three times greater than today. For another, the typical addict was not a young black ghetto resident but a middle-aged white Southern woman or a West Coast Chinese immigrant. The violence, death, disease, and crime that we today associate with drug use barely existed, and many medical authorities regarded opiate addiction as far less destructive than alcoholism (some doctors even prescribed the former as treatment for the latter). Many opiate addicts, perhaps most, managed to lead relatively normal lives and kept their addictions secret even from close friends and relatives. That they were able to do so was largely a function of the legal status of their drug use.

But even more reassuring is the fact that the major causes of opiate addiction then simply do not exist now. Late-nineteenth-century Americans became addicts principally at the hands of physicians who lacked modern medicines and were unaware of the addictive potential of the drugs they prescribed. Doctors in the 1860s and 1870s saw morphine injections as a virtual panacea, and many Americans turned to opiates to alleviate their aches and pains without going through doctors at all. But as medicine advanced, the levels of both doctor- and self-induced addiction declined markedly.

In 1906 the first Federal Pure Food and Drug Act required over-the-counter drug producers to disclose whether their products contained any opiates, cocaine, cannabis, alcohol, or other psychoactive ingredients. Sales of patent medicines containing opiates and cocaine decreased significantly thereafter—in good part because fewer Americans were interested in purchasing products that they now knew to contain those drugs.

Consider the lesson here. Ethical debates aside, the principal objection to all drug legalization proposals is that they invite higher levels of drug use and misuse by making drugs not just legal but more available and less expensive. Yet the late-nineteenth-century experience suggests the opposite: that in a legal market most consumers will prefer lower-potency coca and opiate products to the far more powerful concoctions that have virtually monopolized the market under prohibition. This reminds us that opiate addiction per se was not necessarily a serious problem so long as addicts had ready access to modestly priced opiates of reliable quality—indeed, that the opiate addicts of late-nineteenth-century America differed in no significant respects from the cigarette-addicted consumers of today. And it reassures us that the principal cause of addiction to opiates was not the desire to get high but rather ignorance —ignorance of their addictive qualities, ignorance of the alternative analgesics, and ignorance of what exactly patent medicines contained. The antidote to addiction in late-nineteenth-century America, the historical record shows, consisted primarily of education and regulation— not prohibition, drug wars, and jail.

Why, then, was drug prohibition instituted? And why did it quickly evolve into a fierce and highly punitive set of policies rather than follow the more modest and humane path pursued by the British? In part, the passage of the federal Harrison Narcotic Act, in 1914, and of state and local bans before and after that, reflected a belated response to the recognition that people could easily become addicted to opiates and cocaine. But it also was closely intertwined with the increasingly vigorous efforts of doctors and pharmacists to professionalize their disciplines and to monopolize the public's access to medicinal drugs. Most of all, though, the institution of drug prohibition reflected the changing nature of the opiate- and cocaine-using population. By 1914 the number of middle-class Americans blithely consuming narcotics had fallen sharply. At the same time, however, opiate and cocaine use had become increasingly popular among the lower classes and racial minorities. The total number of consumers did not approach that of earlier decades, but where popular opinion had once shied from the notion of criminalizing the habits of elderly white women, few such inhibitions impeded it where urban gamblers, prostitutes, and delinquents were concerned.

The first anti-opium laws were passed in California in the 1870s and directed at the Chinese immigrants and their opium dens, in which, it was feared, young white women were being seduced. A generation later reports of rising cocaine use among young black men in the South—who were said to rape white women while under the influence—prompted similar legislation. During the 1930s marijuana prohibitions were directed in good part at Mexican and Chicano workers who had lost their jobs in the Depression. And fifty years later draconian penalties were imposed for the possession of tiny amounts of crack cocaine—a drug associated principally with young Latinos and African-Americans.

But more than racist fears was at work during the early years of drug prohibition. In the aftermath of World War I, many Americans, stunned by the triumph of Bolshevism in Russia and fearful of domestic subversion, turned their backs on the liberalizing reforms of the preceding era. In such an atmosphere the very notion of tolerating drug use or maintaining addicts in the clinics that had arisen after 1914 struck most citizens as both immoral and unpatriotic. In 1919 the mayor of New York created the Committee on Public Safety to investigate two ostensibly related problems: revolutionary bombings and heroin use among youth. And in Washington that same year, the Supreme Court effectively foreclosed any possibility of a more humane policy toward drug addicts when it held, in *Webb et al.* v. *U.S.*, that doctors could not legally prescribe maintenance supplies of narcotics to addicts.

* * *

But perhaps most important, the imposition of drug prohibition cannot be understood without recalling that it occurred almost simultaneously with the advent of alcohol prohibition. Contemporary Americans tend to regard Prohibition as a strange quirk in American history—and drug prohibition as entirely natural and beneficial. Yet the prohibition against alcohol, like that against other drugs, was motivated in no small part by its association with feared and despised ethnic minorities, especially the masses of Eastern and Southern European immigrants.

Why was Prohibition repealed after just thirteen years while drug prohibition has lasted for more than seventy-five? Look at whom each disadvantaged. Alcohol prohibition struck directly at tens of millions of Americans of all ages, including many of society's most powerful members. Drug prohibition threatened far fewer Americans, and they had relatively little influence in the halls of power. Only the prohibition of marijuana, which some sixty million Americans have violated since 1965, has come close to approximating the Prohibition experience, but marijuana smokers consist mostly of young and relatively powerless Americans. In the final analysis alcohol prohibition was repealed, and opiate, cocaine, and marijuana prohibition retained, not because scientists had concluded that alcohol was the least dangerous of the various psychoactive drugs but because of the prejudices and preferences of most Americans.

There was, of course, one other important reason why Prohibition was repealed when it was. With the country four years into the Depression, Prohibition increasingly appeared not just foolish but costly. Fewer and fewer Americans were keen on paying the rising costs of enforcing its laws, and more and more recalled the substantial tax revenues that the legal alcohol business had generated. The potential analogy to the current recession is unfortunate but apt. During the late 1980s the cost of building and maintaining prisons emerged as the fastest-growing item in many state budgets, while other costs of the war on drugs also rose dramatically. One cannot help wondering how much longer Americans will be eager to foot the bills for all this.

Throughout history the legal and moral status of psychoactive drugs has kept changing. During the seventeenth century the sale and consumption of tobacco were punished by as much as death in much of Europe, Russia, China, and Japan. For centuries many of the same Muslim domains that forbade the sale and consumption of alcohol simultaneously tolerated and even regulated the sale of opium and cannabis.

Drug-related moralities have always been malleable, and their evolution can in no way be described as moral progress. Just as our moral perceptions of particular drugs have changed in the past, so will they in the future, and people will continue to circumvent the legal and moral barriers that remain. My confidence in this prediction stems from one other lesson of civilized human history. From the dawn of time humans have nearly universally shown a desire to alter their states of consciousness with psychoactive substances, and it is this fact that gives the lie to the declared objective of creating a "drug-free society" in the United States.

Another thing common to all societies, as the social theorist Thomas Szasz argued some years ago, is that they require scapegoats to embody their fears and take blame for whatever ails them. Today the role of bogeyman is applied to drug producers, dealers, and users. Just as anti-Communist propagandists once feared Moscow far beyond its actual influence and appeal, so today anti-drug proselytizers indict marijuana, cocaine, heroin, and assorted hallucinogens far beyond their actual psychoactive effects and psychological appeal. Never mind that the vast majority of Americans have expressed—in one public-opinion poll after another—little interest in trying these substances, even if they were legal, and never mind that most of those who have tried them have suffered few, if any, ill effects. The evidence of history and of science is drowned out by today's bogeymen. No rhetoric is too harsh, no penalty too severe.

* * *

Lest I be accused of exaggerating, consider the following. On June 27, 1991, the Supreme Court upheld, by a vote of five to four, a Michigan statute that imposed a mandatory sentence of life without possibility of parole for anyone convicted of possession of more than 650 grams (about 1.5 pounds) of cocaine. In other words, an activity that was entirely legal at the turn of the century, and that poses a danger to society roughly comparable to that posed by the sale of alcohol and tobacco, is today treated the same as first-degree murder.

The cumulative result of our prohibitionist war is that roughly 20 to 25 percent of the more than one million Americans now incarcerated in federal and state prisons and local jails, and almost half of those in federal penitentiaries, are serving time for having engaged in an activity that their great-grandparents could have pursued entirely legally.

Examples of less striking, but sometimes more deadly, penalties also abound. In many states anyone convicted of possession of a single marijuana joint can have his or her driver's license revoked for six months and be required to participate in a drug-treatment program. In many states anyone caught cultivating a marijuana plant may find all his or her property forfeited to the local police department. And in all but a few

cities needle-exchange programs to reduce the transmission of AIDS among drug addicts have been rejected because they would "send the wrong message" —as if the more moral message is that such addicts are better off contracting the deadly virus and spreading it. . . .

* * *

History holds one final lesson for those who cannot imagine any future beyond drug prohibition. Until well into the 1920s most Americans regarded Prohibition as a permanent fact of life. As late as 1930 Sen. Morris Shepard of Texas, who had coauthored the Prohibition Amendment, confidently asserted: "There is as much chance of repealing the Eighteenth Amendment as there is for a hummingbird to fly to the planet Mars with the Washington Monument tied to its tail."

History reminds us that things can and do change, that what seems inconceivable today can seem entirely normal, and even inevitable, a few years hence. So it was with Prohibition, and so it is—and will be—both with drug prohibition and the ever-changing nature of drug use in America.

NO   David T. Courtwright

SHOULD WE LEGALIZE DRUGS? NO

One thing that all parties in the American drug-policy debate agree on is that they want to eliminate the traffic in illicit drugs and the criminal syndicates that control it. There are two divergent strategies for achieving this end: the drug war and drug legalization, or, more precisely, controlled legalization, since few people want the government to simply abandon drug control and proclaim laissez faire.

The drug war was launched during the Reagan administration. It is actually the fourth such campaign, there having been sustained legislative and governmental efforts against drug abuse between 1909 and 1923, 1951 and 1956, and 1971 and 1973. What distinguishes the current war is that it is more concerned with stimulants like cocaine than with opiates, it is larger, and—no surprise in our age of many zeros—it is much more expensive.

The war against drugs has included the treatment of addicts and educational programs designed to discourage new users, but the emphasis has been on law enforcement, with interdiction, prosecution, imprisonment, and the seizure of assets at the heart of the campaign. The news from the front has been mixed. Price and purity levels, treatment and emergency-room admissions, urinalyses, and most other indices of drug availability showed a worsening of the problem during the 1980s, with some improvement in 1989 and 1990. The number of casual cocaine users has recently declined, but cocaine addiction remains widespread, affecting anywhere from about 650,000 to 2.4 million compulsive users, depending on whose definitions and estimates one chooses to accept. There has been some success in stopping marijuana imports—shipments of the drug are relatively bulky and thus easier to detect—but this has been offset by the increased domestic cultivation of high-quality marijuana, which has more than doubled since 1985. Heroin likewise has become both more available and more potent than it was in the late 1970s.

But cocaine has been the drug of greatest concern. Just how severe the crisis has become may be gauged by federal cocaine seizures. Fifty years ago the annual haul for the entire nation was 1 or 2 pounds, an amount that could easily be contained in the glove compartment of a car. As late as 1970 the total was under 500 pounds, which would fit in the car's trunk. In fiscal year

1990 it was 235,000 pounds—about the weight of 60 mid-size cars. And this represented a fraction, no more than 10 percent, of what went into the nostrils and lungs and veins of the approximately seven million Americans who used cocaine during 1990. Worse may be in store. Worldwide production of coca surged during 1989 to a level of 225,000 metric tons, despite U.S. efforts to eradicate cultivation. Global production of opium, marijuana, and hashish has likewise increased since President Reagan formally declared war on drugs in 1986.

* * *

The greatest obstacle to the supply-reduction strategy is the enormous amount of money generated by the illicit traffic. Drug profits have been used to buy off foreign and domestic officials and to secure protection for the most vulnerable stages of the drug-cultivation, -manufacturing, and -distribution process. These profits also hire various specialists, from assassins to money launderers to lawyers, needed to cope with interlopers; they pay for technological devices ranging from cellular phones to jet planes; and they ensure that should a trafficker die or land in jail, there will be no shortage of replacements.

It is hardly surprising that these stubborn economic realities, together with the drug war's uneven and often disappointing results, have led several commentators to question the wisdom of what they call the prohibition policy. What is unprecedented is that these disenchanted critics include mayors, prominent lawyers, federal judges, nationally syndicated columnists, a congressman, a Princeton professor, and a Nobel laureate in economics. They espouse variations of

a position that is often called controlled legalization, meaning that the sale of narcotics should be permitted under conditions that restrict and limit consumption, such as no sales to minors, no advertising, and substantial taxation. They cite the numerous advantages of this approach: several billion dollars per year would be realized from tax revenues and savings on law enforcement; crime would diminish because addicts would not have to hustle to keep themselves supplied with drugs; the murders associated with big-city drug trafficking would abate as lower-cost, legal drugs drive the traffickers out of business. Because these drugs would be of known quality and potency, and because they would not have to be injected with shared needles, the risk of overdose and infection would drop. The issue of foreign complicity in the drug traffic, which has complicated American diplomatic relations with many countries, would disappear. Under a policy of controlled legalization, it would be no more criminal or controversial to import coca from Colombia than to import coffee.

The more candid of the legalization proponents concede that these advantages would be purchased at the cost of increased drug abuse. Widespread availability, lower prices, and the elimination of the criminal sanction would result in more users, some of whom would inevitably become addicts. But how many more? Herbert Kleber, a treatment specialist and former deputy director of the Office of National Drug Control Policy, has argued that there would be between twelve and fifty-five million addicted users if cocaine and heroin were legally available. While it is impossible to anticipate the exact magnitude of the increase, history does support Kleber's argument. In countries like Iran or Thailand, where narcotics have long been cheap, potent, and readily available, the prevalence of addiction has been and continues to be quite high. Large quantities of opium sold by British and American merchants created a social disaster in nineteenth-century China; that Chinese sailors and immigrants subsequently introduced opium smoking to Britain and America is a kind of ironic justice. Doctors, who constantly work with and around narcotics, have historically had a very serious addiction problem: estimates of the extent of morphine addiction among American physicians at the turn of the century ran from 6 percent to an astonishing 23 percent. In a word, exposure matters.

Kleber has also attacked the crime-reduction rationale by pointing out that addicts will generally use much more of an illicit substance if the cost is low. They would spend most of their time using drugs and little of it working, thus continuing to resort to crime to acquire money. If the total number of addicts rose sharply as availability increased, total crime would also increase. There would be less crime committed by any single addict but more crime in the aggregate.

The debate over decriminalization is, in essence, an argument about a high-stakes gamble, and so far the opponents represent the majority view. At the close of the 1980s, four out of every five Americans were against the legalization of marijuana, let alone cocaine. But if the drug war produces another decade of indifferent results, growing disillusionment could conceivably prompt experiments in controlled legalization.

* * *

The controlled-legalization argument rests on the assumption that legal sales would largely eliminate the illicit traffic and its attendant evils. The history of drug use, regulation, and taxation in the United States suggests otherwise. The very phrase *controlled legalization* implies denying certain groups access to drugs. Minors are the most obvious example. No one advocates supplying narcotics to children, so presumably selling drugs to anyone under twenty-one would remain a criminal offense, since that is the cut-off point for sales of beverage alcohol. Unfortunately, illicit drug abuse in this century has become concentrated among the young—that is, among the very ones most likely to be made exceptions to the rule of legal sales.

Until about 1900 the most common pattern of drug dependence in the United States was opium or morphine addiction, brought about by the treatment of chronic diseases and painful symptoms. Addicts were mainly female, middle-class, and middle-aged or older; Eugene O'Neill's mother, fictionalized as Mary Tyrone in *Long Day's Journey into Night*, was one. Habitual users of morphine, laudanum, and other medicinal opiates in their adolescence were extremely rare, even in big cities like Chicago.

Another pattern of drug use was nonmedical and had its roots in marginal, deviant, and criminal subcultures. The "pleasure users," as they were sometimes called, smoked opium, sniffed cocaine, injected morphine and cocaine in combination, or, after 1910, sniffed or injected heroin. Nonmedical addicts began much younger than their medical counterparts. The average age of addiction (not first use, which would have been lower still) for urban heroin addicts studied in the 1910s was only nineteen or twenty years. They were also more likely to be male than those whose addiction was of medical origin, and more likely to have been involved in crime.

Initially the pleasure users were the smaller group, but during the first two decades of this century—the same period when the police approach to national drug control was formulated—the number of older, docile medical addicts steadily diminished. There were several reasons: doctors became better educated and more conservative in their use of narcotics; the population grew healthier; patent-medicine manufacturers were forced to reveal the contents of their products; and the numerous morphine addicts who had been created in the nineteenth century began to age and die off. Drug use and addiction became increasingly concentrated among young men in their teens and twenties, a pattern that continues to this day.

In 1980, 44 percent of drug arrests nationwide were of persons under the age of twenty-one. There were more arrests among teen-agers than among the entire population over the age of twenty-five; eighteen-year-olds had the highest arrest rate of any age group. By 1987 the proportion of those arrested under twenty-one had declined to 25 percent. This was partly due to the aging of the population and to the effects of drug education on students. But when large numbers of "echo boomers" —the children of the baby boomers— become adolescents during the 1990s, the percentage of under-twenty-one drug arrests will likely increase.

So, depending on timing and demographic circumstances, at least a quarter and perhaps more than a third of all drug buyers would be underage, and there would be a great deal of money to be made by selling to them. The primary source of supply would likely be di-

version—adults legally purchasing drugs and selling them to customers below the legal age. The sellers (or middlemen who collected and then resold the legal purchases) would make a profit through marking up or adulterating the drugs, and there might well be turf disputes and hence violence. Some of the dealers and their underage purchasers would be caught, prosecuted, and jailed, and the criminal-justice system would still be burdened with drug arrests. The black market would be altered and diminished, but it would scarcely disappear.

* * *

Potential for illegal sales and use extends far beyond minors. Pilots, police officers, fire fighters, drivers of buses, trains, taxis, and ambulances, surgeons, active-duty military personnel, and others whose drug use would jeopardize public safety would be denied access to at least some drugs, and those of them who did take narcotics would be liable to criminal prosecution, as would their suppliers. Pregnant women would also pose a problem. Drugs transmitted to fetuses can cause irreversible and enormously costly harm. Federal and local governments may soon be spending billions of dollars a year just to prepare the impaired children of addicts for kindergarten. Society has the right and the obligation to stop this neurological carnage, both because it cruelly handicaps innocents and because it harms everyone else through higher taxes and health-insurance premiums. Paradoxically, the arguments for controlled legalization might lead to denying alcohol and tobacco to pregnant women along with narcotics. Alcohol and tobacco can also harm fetal development, and several legalization proponents have observed that it is both inconsistent and unwise to treat them as if they were not dangerous because they are legal. If cocaine is denied to pregnant women, why not alcohol too? The point here is simply that every time one makes an exception for good and compelling reasons—every time one accents the "controlled" as opposed to the "legalization"—one creates the likelihood of continued illicit sales and use.

The supposition that this illegal market would be fueled by diversion is well founded historically. There has always been an undercurrent of diversion, especially in the late 1910s and 1920s, when black-market operators like Legs Diamond got their supplies not so much by smuggling as by purchases from legitimate drug companies. One possible solution is to require of all legal purchasers that which is required of newly enrolled methadone patients: consumption of the drug on the premises. Unfortunately, unlike methadone, heroin and cocaine are short-acting, and compulsive users must administer them every few hours or less.... Confining the use of heroin or cocaine or other street drugs to clinics would be a logistical nightmare. But the alternative, take-home supplies, invites illegal sales to excluded groups.

Another historical pattern of black-market activity has been the smuggling of drugs to prisoners. Contraband was one of the reasons the government built specialized narcotic hospitals in Lexington, Kentucky, and Fort Worth, Texas, in the 1930s. Federal wardens wanted to get addicts out of their prisons because they were constantly conniving to obtain smuggled drugs. But when drug-related arrests multiplied after 1965 and the Lexington and Fort Worth facilities were closed, the prisons again filled with inmates eager to obtain drugs. Birch Bayh, chairing a Senate investigation of the mat-

ter in 1975, observed that in some institutions young offenders had a more plentiful supply of drugs than they did on the outside.

Since then more jails have been crammed with more prisoners, and these prisoners are more likely than ever to have had a history of drug use. In 1989, 60 to 80 percent of male arrestees in twelve large American cities tested positive for drugs. It is hard to imagine a controlled-legalization system that would permit sales to prisoners. Alcohol, although a legal drug, is not sold licitly in prisons, and for good reason, as more than 40 percent of prisoners were under its influence when they committed their crimes. If drugs are similarly denied to inmates, then the contraband problem will persist. If, moreover, we insist that our nearly three million parolees and probationers remain clean on the theory that drug use aggravates recidivism, the market for illegal sales would be so much the larger.

By now the problem should be clear. If drugs are legalized, but not for those under twenty-one, or for public-safety officers, or transport workers, or military personnel, or pregnant women, or prisoners, or probationers, or parolees, or psychotics, or any of several other special groups one could plausibly name, then just exactly who is going to buy them? Noncriminal adults, whose drug use is comparatively low to begin with? Controlled legalization entails a dilemma. To the extent that its controls are enforced, some form of black-market activity will persist. If, on the other hand, its controls are not enforced and drugs are easily diverted to those who are underage or otherwise ineligible, then it is a disguised form of wholesale legalization and as such morally, politically, and economically unacceptable.

One of the selling points of controlled legalization was also one of the decisive arguments for the repeal of Prohibition: taxation. Instead of spending billions to suppress the illicit traffic, the government would reap billions by imposing duties on legitimate imports and taxes on domestically manufactured drugs. Not only could these revenues be earmarked for drug treatment and education programs, but they would also increase the prices paid by the consumer, thus discouraging consumption, especially among adolescents.

The United States government has had extensive historical experience with the taxation of legal narcotics. In the nineteenth and early twentieth centuries, opium was imported and subject to customs duties. The imports were assigned to one of three categories. The first was crude opium, used mainly for medicinal purposes and for the domestic manufacture of morphine. Foreign-manufactured morphine, codeine, and heroin made up the second class of imports, while the third was smoking opium, most of it prepared in Hong Kong and shipped to San Francisco.

* * *

The imposts [taxes] on these imported drugs fluctuated over the years, but they were generally quite stiff. From 1866 to 1914 the average ad valorem duty [calculated according to value] on crude opium was 33 percent; for morphine or its salts, 48 percent. From 1866 to 1908 the average duty on smoking opium was an extraordinarily high 97 percent. This last was in the nature of a sin tax; congressmen identified opium smoking with Chinese coolies, gamblers, pimps, and prostitutes and wished to discourage its importation and use.

These customs duties produced revenue; they also produced widespread smuggling, much of it organized by violent criminal societies like the Chinese tongs. The smugglers were as ingenious as their latter-day Mafia counterparts. They hid their shipments in everything from hollowed-out lumber to snake cages. Avoiding the customs collectors, they saved as much as three dollars a pound on crude opium, three dollars an ounce on morphine, and twelve dollars a pound on smoking opium. Twelve dollars seems a trifling sum by modern standards, hardly worth the risk of arrest, but in the nineteenth century it was more than most workers earned in a week. Someone who smuggled in fifty pounds of smoking opium in 1895 had gained the equivalent of a year's wages. One knowledgeable authority estimated that when the duty on smoking opium was near its peak, the amount smuggled into the United States was nearly twice that legally imported and taxed. Something similar happened with eighteenth-century tobacco imports to the British Isles. More than a third of the tobacco consumed in England and Scotland circa 1750 had been clandestinely imported in order to avoid a duty of more than five pence per pound. The principle is the same for domestically produced drugs: if taxes are sufficiently onerous, an illegal supply system will spring up. Moonshining existed before and after, as well as during, Prohibition.

The obvious solution is to set taxes at a sufficiently low level to discourage smuggling and illegal manufacturing. But again there is a dilemma. The most important illicit drugs are processed agricultural products that can be grown in several parts of the world by peasant labor. They are not, in other words, intrinsically expensive. Unless they are heavily taxed, legal consumers will be able to acquire them at little cost, less than ten dollars for a gram of cocaine. If drugs are that cheap, to say nothing of being 100 percent pure, the likelihood of a postlegalization epidemic of addiction will be substantially increased. But if taxes are given a stiff boost to enhance revenues and limit consumption, black marketeers will reenter the picture in numbers proportionate to the severity of the tax.

Tax revenues, like drugs themselves, can be addictive. In the twelve years after the repeal of Prohibition, federal liquor tax revenues ballooned from 259 million to 2.3 billion dollars. The government's dependence on this money was one important reason anti-liquor forces made so little progress in their attempts to restrict alcohol consumption during World War II. Controlled drug legalization would also bring about a windfall in tax dollars, which in an era of chronic deficits would surely be welcomed and quickly spent. Should addiction rates become too high, a conflict between public health and revenue concerns would inevitably ensue.

When both proponents and opponents of controlled legalization talk about drug taxes, they generally assume a single level of taxation. The assumption is wrong. The nature of the federal system permits state and local governments to levy their own taxes on drugs in addition to the uniform federal customs and excise taxes. This means that total drug taxes, and hence the prices paid by consumers, will vary from place to place. Variation invites interstate smuggling, and if the variation is large enough, the smuggling can be extensive and involve organized crime.

The history of cigarette taxation serves to illustrate this principle. In 1960 state taxes on cigarettes were low, between zero and eight cents per pack, but after 1965 a growing number of states sharply increased cigarette taxes in response to health concerns and as a politically painless way of increasing revenue. Some states, mainly in the Northeast, were considerably more aggressive than others in raising taxes. By 1975 North Carolina purchasers were paying thirty-six cents per pack while New Yorkers paid fifty-four cents. The price was higher still in New York City because of a local levy that reached eight cents per pack (as much as the entire federal tax) at the beginning of 1976.

Thus was born an opportunity to buy cheap and sell dear. Those who bought in volume at North Carolina prices and sold at New York (or Connecticut, or Massachusetts) prices realized a substantial profit, and by the mid-1970s net revenue losses stood at well over three hundred million dollars a year. Much of this went to organized crime, which at one point was bootlegging 25 percent of the cigarettes sold in New York State and *half* of those sold in New York City. The pioneer of the illegal traffic, Anthony Granata, established a trucking company with thirty employees operating vehicles on a six-days-a-week basis. Granata's methods—concealed cargoes, dummy corporations, forged documents, fortresslike warehouses, bribery, hijacking, assault, and homicide—were strikingly similar to those used by illicit drug traffickers and Prohibition bootleggers.

* * *

Although high-tax states like Florida or Illinois still lose millions annually to cigarette bootleggers, the 1978 federal

Contraband Cigarette Act and stricter law enforcement and accounting procedures have had some success in reducing over-the-road smuggling. But it is relatively easy to detect illegal shipments of cigarettes, which must be smuggled by the truckload to make a substantial amount of money. Cocaine and heroin are more compact, more profitable, and very easy to conceal. Smuggling these drugs to take advantage of state tax differentials would consequently be much more difficult to detect and deter. If, for example, taxed cocaine retailed in Vermont for ten dollars a gram and in New York for twelve dollars a gram, anyone who bought just five kilograms at Vermont prices, transported them, and sold them at New York prices would realize a profit of ten thousand dollars. Five kilograms of cocaine can be concealed in an attaché case.

* * *

Of course, if all states legalized drugs and taxed them at the same rate, this sort of illegal activity would not exist, but it is constitutionally and politically unfeasible to ensure uniform rates of state taxation. And federalism poses other challenges. Laws against drug use and trafficking have been enacted at the local, state, and federal levels. It is probable that if Congress repeals or modifies the national drug laws, some states will go along with controlled legalization while others will not. Nevada, long in the legalizing habit, might jettison its drug laws, but conservative Mormon-populated Utah might not. Alternately, governments could experiment with varying degrees of legalization. Congress might decide that anything was better than the current mayhem in the capital and legislate a broad legalization program for the District of Columbia. At the same time, Virginia and Maryland might experiment with the decriminalization of marijuana, the least risky legalization option, but retain prohibition of the nonmedical use of other drugs. The result would again be smuggling, whether from Nevada to Utah or, save for marijuana, from the District of Columbia to the surrounding states. It is hard to see how any state that chose to retain laws against drugs could possibly stanch the influx of prohibited drugs from adjacent states that did not. New York City's futile attempts to enforce its strict gun-control laws show how difficult it is to restrict locally that which is elsewhere freely available.

I referred earlier to the legalization debate as an argument about a colossal gamble, whether society should risk an unknown increase in drug abuse and addiction to eliminate the harms of drug prohibition, most of which stem from illicit trafficking. "Take the crime out of it" is the rallying cry of the legalization advocates. After reviewing the larger history of narcotic, alcohol, and tobacco use and regulation, it appears that this debate should be recast. It would be more accurate to ask whether society should risk an unknown but possibly substantial increase in drug abuse and addiction in order to bring about an unknown *reduction* in illicit trafficking and other costs of drug prohibition. Controlled legalization would take some, but by no means all, of the crime out of it. Just how much and what sort of crime would be eliminated would depend upon which groups were to be denied which drugs, the overall level of taxation, and differences in state tax and legalization policies. If the excluded groups were few *and* all states legalized all drugs *and* all governments taxed at uniformly low levels, then the black market would be largely eliminated. But these are precisely the conditions that would be most likely to bring about an unacceptably high level of drug abuse. The same variables that would determine how successful the controlled-legalization policy would be in eliminating the black market would also largely determine how unsuccessful it was in containing drug addiction.

POSTSCRIPT

Should Drugs Be Legalized?

Nadelmann makes a distinction between problems due to drug abuse and problems due to drug prohibition. The huge profits that are made by underground drug traffickers and organized crime, the overcrowded prisons filled with drug users and drug dealers, and drug-related crimes can be attributed to the drug prohibition side. But other problems—such as "crack babies" and drug-related accidents—are due to drug abuse itself. Even if legalization policies take care of the problems due to drug prohibition, how well do they take care of problems due to drug abuse? Moreover, with drugs of certifiable quality and quantity readily available, is it likely that there would be even more drug abuse than there is now?

The current debate concerns whether it is better to continue with the policy of drug prohibition or embrace a form of *controlled legalization*. Courtwright argues that policies of controlled legalization have a built-in difficulty. If the control is very tight—for example, no sales to those under 21, who are among the heaviest users of drugs—then these users will still participate in a black market for drugs. And most of the promised benefits of legalization will be lost. But if the control is very loose, then we are simply abandoning responsibility. It is also questionable whether or not educational and antidrug programs would be as effective as they are now if drugs were legal.

Nadelmann criticizes the so-called war on drugs. But even if the rhetoric of the war on drugs is inflated and, as Nadelmann says, if it is impossible anyway to have a "drug-free America," supporters of that war could still have as their goal a decrease in drug abuse, as opposed to absolute elimination. In this scenario, Courtwright could still maintain that the policy of drug prohibition is superior to any alternative policy.

Additional readings on drug legalization include Paul B. Stares, *Global Habit: The Drug Problem in a Borderless World* (Brookings Institution, 1996); William O. Walker III, ed., *Drugs in the Western Hemisphere: An Odyssey of Cultures in Conflict* (Scholarly Resources, 1996); Bruce L. Benson and David W. Rasmussen, *Illicit Drugs and Crime* (Independent Institute, 1996); Paul A. Winters, ed., *Teen Addiction* (Greenhaven, 1997); William J. Bennett, John J. DiIulio, Jr., and John P. Walters, *Body Count: Moral Poverty and How to Win America's War Against Crime and Drugs* (Simon & Schuster, 1997); Eva Bertram and Kenneth Sharpe, "War Ends, Drugs Win," *The Nation* (January 6, 1997); Michael Pollan, "Opium, Made Easy," *Harper's* (April 1997); Jann S. Wenner and Ethan A. Nadelmann, "Clinton's War on Drugs: Cruel, Wrong, Unwinnable," *Rolling Stone* (April 17, 1997); and Thomas W. Clark, "Keep Marijuana Illegal—for Teens," *The Humanist* (May/June 1997).

ISSUE 13

Should the Death Penalty Be Retained?

YES: Ernest van den Haag, from "The Death Penalty Once More," *U.C. Davis Law Review* (Summer 1985)

NO: Hugo Adam Bedau, from "A Reply to van den Haag," in Hugo Adam Bedau, ed., *The Death Penalty in America: Current Controversies* (Oxford University Press, 1997)

ISSUE SUMMARY

YES: Professor of law Ernest van den Haag argues that the death penalty is entirely in line with the U.S. Constitution and that although studies of its deterrent effect are inconclusive, the death penalty is morally justified and should be retained.

NO: Professor of philosophy Hugo Adam Bedau argues that the death penalty should be abolished because it is unconstitutionally applied, fails to have a deterrent effect, and is not morally justified.

Since punishment involves the intentional infliction of harm upon another person, and since the intentional infliction of harm is generally wrong, the idea of punishment itself is somewhat problematic. Punishment requires some strong rationale if it is not to be just another form of wrongdoing; capital punishment requires an especially strong rationale.

Consider some actual cases of capital punishment: Socrates was tried in ancient Athens and condemned to die (by drinking poison) for not believing in the gods of the state and for corrupting young people. In 1977 a princess and her lover were executed (by firing squad and beheading, respectively) in Saudi Arabia for adultery. Also in 1977 Gary Gilmore insisted that he receive the death penalty and was executed by a firing squad in Utah for murder.

Justification for capital punishment usually comes down to one of two different lines of reasoning. One is based on the idea of justice, the other on the idea of deterrence.

Justice, it is said, demands that certain criminal acts be paid for by death. The idea is that some people deserve death and have to pay for their criminal acts with their lives.

There are several objections to this view. One of the most important of these focuses on the idea of a person "paying" for a crime by death (or even in some other way). What concept of "paying" is being used here? It does not seem like an ordinary case of paying a debt. It seems to be a kind of vengeance, as when one person says to another "I'll make you pay for that," meaning "I'll make you suffer for that." Yet one of the ideas behind state-inflicted punishment is that it is supposed to be very official, even bureaucratic, and it is designed to eliminate private vendettas and personal vindictiveness. The state, in a civilized society, is not supposed to be motivated by revenge or vindictiveness. The state's only intent is to support law and order and to protect its citizens from coming to harm at the hands of wrongdoers.

The other major line of reasoning in support of capital punishment is based on the idea of deterrence. According to this view, capital punishment must be retained in order to deter criminals and potential criminals from committing capital crimes. An old joke reflects this view: A Texan tells a visitor that in the old days the local punishment for horse-stealing was hanging. The visitor is shocked. "You used to hang people just for taking horses?" "Nope," says the Texan, "horses never got stolen."

Unlike the argument about "paying," the logic behind deterrence is supposed to be intuitively easy to understand. However, claims about deterrence do not seem to be clearly borne out by actual statistics and empirical evidence.

Your intuition may support the judgment that the death penalty deters crime, but the empirical evidence is not similarly uniform and clear, and in some cases the evidence even points to the opposite conclusion. (For example, some people may be more likely to murder an innocent victim if they are reasonably certain of achieving their own death and perhaps some notoriety.) Or consider the example of the failure of deterrence that occurred in England when public hanging was the punishment for the crime of pickpocketing. Professional pickpockets, undeterred by the activity on the gallows, circulated among the crowd of spectators, aware that a good time to pick pockets was when everyone's attention was focused on something else—in this case, when the rope tightened around the neck of the convicted pickpocket.

Further thought about this matter of deterrence raises more questions. Consider this scenario: Two men get into an argument while drinking, and one pulls a gun and shoots the other, who dies. Do we suppose that this killer is even aware of the punishment for murder when he acts? Would he be deterred by the prospect of capital punishment but be willing to shoot if the punishment were only 20 years or life in prison?

In the following selections, Ernest van den Haag makes the case for the retention of capital punishment, while Hugo Adam Bedau argues for its abolition. Both authors discuss the constitutionality of the death penalty, its deterrent power, and its relation to justice and morality.

YES

Ernest van den Haag

THE DEATH PENALTY ONCE MORE

People concerned with capital punishment disagree on essentially three questions: (1) Is it constitutional? (2) Does the death penalty deter crime more than life imprisonment? (3) Is the death penalty morally justifiable?

IS THE DEATH PENALTY CONSTITUTIONAL?

The fifth amendment, passed in 1791, states that "no person shall be deprived of life, liberty, or property, without due process of law." Thus, with "due process of law," the Constitution authorizes depriving persons "of life, liberty or property." The fourteenth amendment, passed in 1868, applies an identical provision to the states. The Constitution, then, authorizes the death penalty. It is left to elected bodies to decide whether or not to retain it.

The eighth amendment, reproducing almost verbatim a passage from the English Bill of Rights of 1689, prohibits "cruel and unusual punishments." This prohibition was not meant to repeal the fifth amendment since the amendments were passed simultaneously. "Cruel" punishment is not prohibited unless "unusual" as well, that is, new, rare, not legislated, or disproportionate to the crime punished. Neither the English Bill of Rights, nor the eighth amendment, hitherto has been found inconsistent with capital punishment.

Evolving Standards

Some commentators argue that, in *Trop v. Dulles*, the Supreme Court indicated that "evolving standards of decency that mark the progress of a maturing society" allow courts to declare "cruel and unusual," punishments authorized by the Constitution. However, *Trop* was concerned with expatriation, a punishment that is not specifically authorized by the Constitution. The death penalty is. *Trop* did not suggest that "evolving standards" could de-authorize what the Constitution repeatedly authorizes. Indeed, Chief Justice Warren, writing for the majority in *Trop*, declared that "the death penalty... cannot be said to violate the constitutional concept of cruelty."[1] Furthermore, the argument based on "evolving standards" is paradoxical: the Constitution would be redundant if current views, enacted by judicial fiat, could supersede what it plainly says. If "standards of decency" currently invented or evolved could, without formal amendment, replace or repeal the standards authorized by the Constitution, the Constitution would be superfluous.

It must be remembered that the Constitution does not force capital punishment on the population but merely authorizes it. Elected bodies are left to decide whether to use the authorization. As for "evolving standards," how could courts detect them without popular consensus as a guide? Moral revelations accepted by judges, religious leaders, sociologists, or academic elites, but not by the majority of voters, cannot suffice. The opinions of the most organized, most articulate, or most vocal might receive unjustified deference. Surely the eighth amendment was meant to limit, but was not meant to replace, decisions by the legislative branch, or to enable the judiciary do what the voters won't do.[2] The general consensus on which the courts would have to rely could be registered only by elected bodies. They favor capital punishment. Indeed, at present, more than seventy percent of the voters approve of the death penalty. The state legislatures reflect as much. Wherefore, the Supreme Court, albeit reluctantly, rejected abolition of the death penalty by judicial *fiat*. This decision was subsequently qualified by a finding that the death penalty for rape is disproportionate to the crime,[3] and by rejecting all mandatory capital punishment.

Caprice
Laws that allowed courts too much latitude to decide, perhaps capriciously, whether to actually impose the death penalty in capital cases also were found unconstitutional. In response, more than two-thirds of the states have modified their death penalty statutes, listing aggravating and mitigating factors, and imposing capital punishment only when the former outweigh the latter. The Supreme Court is satisfied that this procedure meets the constitutional requirements of non-capriciousness. However, abolitionists are not.

In *Capital Punishment: The Inevitability of Caprice and Mistake*,[4] Professor Charles Black contends that the death penalty is necessarily imposed capriciously, for irremediable reasons. If he is right, he has proved too much, unless capital punishment is imposed more capriciously now than it was in 1791 or 1868, when the fifth and fourteenth amendments were enacted. He does not contend that it is. Professor Black also stresses that the elements of chance, unavoidable in all penalizations, are least tolerable when capital punishment is involved. But the irreducible chanciness inherent in human efforts does not constitutionally require the abolition of capital punishment, unless the framers were less aware of chance and human frailty than Professor Black is. (I shall turn to the moral as distinguished from the legal bearing of chanciness anon.)

Discrimination
Sociologists have demonstrated that the death penalty has been distributed in a discriminatory pattern in the past: black or poor defendants were more likely to be executed than equally guilty others. This argues for correction of the distributive process, but not for abolition of the penalty it distributes, unless constitutionally excessive maldistribution ineluctably inheres in the penalty. There is

no evidence to that effect. Actually, although we cannot be sure that it has disappeared altogether, discrimination has greatly decreased compared to the past.[5]

However, recently the debate on discrimination has taken a new turn. Statistical studies have found that, *ceteris paribus*, a black man who murders a white has a much greater chance to be executed than he would have had, had his victim been black.[6] This discriminates against black *victims* of murder: they are not as fully, or as often, vindicated as are white victims. However, although unjustified per se, discrimination against a class of victims need not, and here does not, amount to discrimination against their victimizers. The pattern discriminates *against* black murderers of whites and *for* black murderers of blacks. One may describe it as discrimination for, or discrimination against, just as one may describe a glass of water as half full or half empty. Discrimination against one group (here, blacks who kill whites) is necessarily discrimination in favor of another (here, blacks who kill blacks).

Most black victims are killed by black murderers, and a disproportionate number of murder victims is black. Wherefore the discrimination in favor of murderers of black victims more than offsets, numerically, any remaining discrimination against other black murderers.[7]

Comparative Excessiveness

Recently lawyers have argued that the death penalty is unconstitutionally disproportionate if defendants, elsewhere in the state, received lesser sentences for comparable crimes. But the Constitution only requires that penalties be appropriate to the gravity of the crime, not that they cannot exceed penalties imposed elsewhere. Although some states have adopted "comparative excessiveness" reviews, there is no constitutional requirement to do so.

Unavoidably, different courts, prosecutors, defense lawyers, judges and juries produce different penalties even when crimes seem comparable. Chance plays a great role in human affairs. Some offenders are never caught or convicted, while others are executed; some are punished more than others guilty of worse crimes. Thus, a guilty person, or group of persons, may get away with no punishment, or with a light punishment, while others receive the punishment they deserve. Should we let these others go too, or punish them less severely? Should we abolish the penalty applied unequally or discriminatorily?[8]

The late Justice Douglas suggested an answer to these questions:

> A law that . . . said that blacks, those who never went beyond the fifth grade in school, those who made less than $3,000 a year, or those who were unpopular or unstable should be the only people executed [would be wrong]. A law which in the overall view reaches that result in practice has no more sanctity than a law which in terms provides the same.[9]

Justice Douglas' answer here conflates an imagined discriminatory law with the discriminatory application of a non-discriminatory law. His imagined law would be inconsistent with the "equal protection of the laws" demanded by the fourteenth amendment, and the Court would have to invalidate it *ipso facto*. But discrimination caused by uneven application of non-discriminatory death penalty laws may be remedied by means other than abolition, as long as the discrimination is not intrinsic to the laws.

Consider now, albeit fleetingly, the moral as distinguished from the constitutional bearing of discrimination. Suppose guilty defendants are justly executed, but only if poor, or black and not otherwise. This unequal justice would be morally offensive for what may be called tautological reasons:[10] if any punishment for a given crime is just, then a greater or lesser punishment is not. Only one punishment can be just for all persons equally guilty of the same crime.[11] Therefore, different punishments for equally guilty persons or group members are unjust: some offenders are punished more than they deserve, or others less.

Still, equality and justice are not the same. "Equal justice" is not a redundant phrase. Rather, we strive for two distinct ideals, justice and equality. Neither can replace the other. We want to have justice and, having it, we want to extend it equally to all. We would not want equal injustice. Yet, sometimes, we must choose between equal injustice and unequal justice. What should we prefer? Unequal justice is justice still, even if only for some, whereas equal injustice is injustice for all. If not every equally guilty person is punished equally, we have unequal justice. It seems preferable to equal injustice—having no guilty person punished as deserved.[12] Since it is never possible to punish equally all equally guilty murderers, we should punish, as they deserve, as many of those we apprehend and convict as possible. Thus, even if the death penalty were inherently discriminatory—which is not the case —but deserved by those who receive it, it would be morally just to impose it on them. If, as I contend, capital punishment is just and not inherently discriminatory, it remains desirable to eliminate inequality in distribution, to apply the penalty to all who deserve it, sparing no racial or economic class. But if a guilty person or group escaped the penalty through our porous system, wherein is this an argument for sparing others?

If one does not believe capital punishment can be just, discrimination becomes a subordinate argument, since one would object to capital punishment even if it were distributed equally to all the guilty. If one does believe that capital punishment for murderers is deserved, discrimination against guilty black murderers and in favor of equally guilty white murderers is wrong, not because blacks receive the deserved punishment, but because whites escape it.

Consider a less emotionally charged analogy. Suppose traffic police ticketed all drivers who violated the rules, except drivers of luxury cars. Should we abolish tickets? Should we decide that the ticketed drivers of nonluxury cars were unjustly punished and ought not to pay their fines? Would they become innocent of the violation they are guilty of because others have not been ticketed? Surely the drivers of luxury cars should not be exempted. But the fact that they were is no reason to exempt drivers of nonluxury cars as well. Laws could never be applied if the escape of one person, or group, were accepted as ground for not punishing another. To do justice is primarily to punish as deserved, and only secondarily to punish equally.

Guilt is personal. No one becomes less guilty or less deserving of punishment because another was punished leniently or not at all. That justice does not catch up with all guilty persons understandably is resented by those caught. But it does not affect their guilt. If some, or all, white and rich murderers escape the death penalty, how does that reduce the guilt of black or poor murderers, or make them less deserving of punishment, or deserving of a lesser punishment?

Some lawyers have insisted that the death penalty is distributed among those guilty of murder as though by a lottery and that the worst may escape it.[13] They exaggerate, but suppose one grants the point. How do those among the guilty selected for execution by lottery become less deserving of punishment because others escaped it? What is wrong is that these others escaped, not that those among the guilty who were selected by the lottery did not.

Those among the guilty actually punished by a criminal justice system unavoidably are selected by chance, not because we want to so select them, but because the outcome of our efforts largely depends on chance. No murderer is punished unless he is unlucky enough both to be caught and to have convinced a court of his guilt. And courts consider evidence not truth. They find truth only when the evidence establishes it. Thus they may have reasonable doubts about the guilt of an actually guilty person. Although we may strive to make justice as equal as possible, unequal justice will remain our lot in this world. We should not give up justice, or the death penalty, because we cannot extend it as equally to all the guilty as we wish. If we were not to punish one offender because another got away because of caprice or discrimination, we would give up justice for the sake of equality. We would reverse the proper order of priorities.

IS THE DEATH PENALTY MORE DETERRENT THAN OTHER PUNISHMENTS?

Whether or not the death penalty deters the crimes it punishes more than alternative penalties—in this case life imprisonment with or without parole—has been widely debated since Isaac Ehrlich broke the abolitionist ranks by finding that from 1933–65 "an additional execution per year ... may have resulted on the average in seven or eight fewer murders."[14] Since his article appeared, a whole cottage industry devoted to refuting his findings has arisen.[15] Ehrlich, no slouch, has been refuting those who refuted him.[16] The result seems inconclusive.[17] Statistics have not proved conclusively that the death penalty does or does not deter murder more than other penalties.[18] Still, Ehrlich has the merit of being the first to use a sophisticated statistical analysis to tackle the problem, and of defending his analysis, although it showed deterrence. (Ehrlich started as an abolitionist.) His predecessors cannot be accused of mathematical sophistication. Yet the academic community uncritically accepted their abolitionist results. I myself have no contribution to make to the mathematical analyses of deterrent effects. Perhaps this is why I have come to believe that they may becloud the issue, leading us to rely on demonstrable deterrence as though decisive.

Most abolitionists believe that the death penalty does not deter more than other penalties. But most abolitionists would abolish it, even if it did.[19] I have discussed this matter with prominent abolitionists such as Charles Black, Henry Schwarzchild, Hugo Adam Bedau, Ramsey Clark, and many others. Each told me that, even if every execution were to deter a hundred murders, he would oppose it. I infer that, to these abolitionist leaders, the life of every murderer is more valuable than the lives of a hundred prospective victims, for these abolitionists would spare the murderer, even if doing so would cost a hundred future victims their lives.

Obviously, deterrence cannot be the decisive issue for these abolitionists. It is not necessarily for me either, since I would be for capital punishment on grounds of justice alone. On the other hand, I should favor the death penalty for murderers, if probably deterrent, or even just possibly deterrent. To me, the life of any innocent victim who might be spared has great value; the life of a convicted murderer does not. This is why I would not take the risk of sacrificing innocents by not executing murderers.

Even though statistical demonstrations are not conclusive, and perhaps cannot be, I believe that capital punishment is likely to deter more than anything else. They fear most death deliberately inflicted by law and scheduled by the courts. Whatever people fear most is likely to deter most. Hence, I believe that the threat of the death penalty may deter some murderers who otherwise might not have been deterred. And surely the death penalty is the only penalty that could deter prisoners already serving a life sentence and tempted to kill a guard, or offenders about to be arrested and facing a life sentence. Perhaps they will not be deterred. But they would certainly not be deterred by anything else. We owe all the protection we can give to law enforcers exposed to special risks.

Many murders are "crimes of passion" that, perhaps, cannot be deterred by any threat. Whether or not they can be would depend on the degree of passion; it is unlikely to be always so extreme as to make the person seized by it totally undeterrable. At any rate, offenders sentenced to death ordinarily are guilty of premediated murder, felony murder, or multiple murders. Some are rape murderers, or hit men, but, to my knowledge, no one convicted of a "crime of passion" is on death row. Whatever the motive, some prospective offenders are not deterrable at all, others are easily deterred, and most are in between. Even if only some murders were, or could be, deterred by capital punishment, it would be worthwhile....

Almost all convicted murderers try to avoid the death penalty by appeals for commutation to life imprisonment. However, a minuscule proportion of convicted murderers prefer execution. It is sometimes argued that they murdered for the sake of being executed, of committing suicide via execution. More likely, they prefer execution to life imprisonment. Although shared by few, this preference is not irrational per se. It is also possible that these convicts accept the verdict of the court, and feel that they deserve the death penalty for the crimes they committed, although the modern mind finds it hard to imagine such feelings. But not all murderers are ACLU humanists....

IS THE DEATH PENALTY MORAL?

Miscarriages

Miscarriages of justice are rare, but do occur. Over a long enough time they lead to the execution of some innocents.[20] Does this make irrevocable punishments morally wrong? Hardly. Our government employs trucks. They run over innocent bystanders more frequently than courts sentence innocents to death. We do not give up trucks because the benefits they produce outweigh the harm, including the death of innocents. Many human activities, even quite trivial ones, forseeably cause wrongful deaths. Courts may cause fewer wrongful deaths than golf. Whether one sees the benefit of doing justice by imposing capital punishment as moral, or as material, or both, it outweighs the loss of innocent lives through miscarriages, which are as unintended as traffic accidents.

Vengeance

Some abolitionists feel that the motive for the death penalty is an un-Christian and unacceptable desire for vengeance. But though vengeance be the motive, it is not the purpose of the death penalty. Doing justice and deterring crime are the purposes, whatever the motive. Purpose (let alone effect) and motive are not the same.

The Lord is often quoted as saying "Vengeance is mine." He did not condemn vengeance. He merely reserved it to Himself—and to the government. For, in the same epistle He is also quoted as saying that the ruler is "the minister of God, a revenger, to execute wrath upon him that doeth evil." The religious notion of hell indicates that the biblical God favored harsh and everlasting punishment for some. However, particularly in a secular society, we cannot wait for the day of judgment to see murderers consigned to hell. Our courts must "execute wrath upon him that doeth evil" here and now.

Charity and Justice

Today many religious leaders oppose capital punishment. This is surprising, because there is no biblical warrant for their opposition. The Roman Catholic Church and most Protestant denominations traditionally have supported capital punishment. Why have their moral views changed? When sharing secular power, the churches clearly distinguished between justice, including penalization as deserved, a function of the secular power, and charity, which, according to religious doctrine, we should feel for all those who suffer for whatever reasons. Currently, religious leaders seem to conflate justice and charity, to conclude that the death penalty and, perhaps, all punishment, is wrong because uncharitable. Churches no longer share secular power. Perhaps bystanders are more ready to replace justice with charity than are those responsible for governing.

Human Dignity

Let me return to the morality of execution. Many abolitoinists believe that capital punishment is "degrading to human dignity" and inconsistent with the "sanctity of life." Justice Brennan, concurring in *Furnam*, stressed these phrases repeatedly. [21] He did not explain what he meant.

Why would execution degrade human dignity more than life imprisonment? One may prefer the latter; but it seems at least as degrading as execution. Philosophers, such as Immanuel Kant and G. F. W. Hegel, thought capital punishment indispensable to redeem, or restore, the human dignity of the executed. Perhaps they were wrong. But they argued their case, whereas no one has explained why capital punishment degrades. Apparently those who argue that it does degrade dignity simply define the death penalty as degrading. If so, degradation (or dehumanization) merely is a disguised synonym for their disapproval. Assertion, reassertion, or definition, do not constitute evidence or argument, nor do they otherwise justify, or even explain, disapproval of capital punishment.

Writers, such as Albert Camus, have suggested that murderers have a miserable time waiting for execution and anticipating it.[22] I do not doubt that. But punishments are not meant to be pleasant. Other people suffer greatly waiting for the end, in hospitals, under circumstances that, I am afraid, are at least as degrading to their dignity as execution. These sufferers have not deserved their suffering by committing crimes, whereas murderers have. Yet, murderers suffer less on death row, unless their consciences bother them.

Lex Talionis

Some writers insist that the suffering the death penalty imposes on murderers exceeds the suffering of their victims. This is hard to determine, but probably true in some cases and not in other cases. However, the comparison is irrelevant. Murderers are punished, as are all offenders, not just for the suffering they caused their victims, but for the harm they do to society by making life insecure, by threatening everyone, and by requiring protective measures. Punishment, ultimately, is a vindication of the moral and legal order of society and not limited by the Lex Talionis, meant to limit private retaliation for harms originally regarded as private.

Sanctity of Life

We are enjoined by the Declaration of Independence to secure life. How can this best be achieved? The Constitution authorizes us to secure innocent life by taking the life of murderers, so that any one who deliberately wants to take an innocent life will know that he risks forfeiting his own. The framers did not think that taking the life of a murderer is inconsistent with the "sanctity of life" which Justice Brennan champions. He has not indicated why they were wrong.[23]

Legalized Murder?

Ever since Cesare Bonesana, Marchese di Beccaria, wrote Dei Delitti e Delle Pene, abolitionists have contended that executing murderers legitimizes murder by doing to the murderer what he did to his victim. Indeed, capital punishment retributes, or pays back the offender. Occasionally we do punish offenders by doing to them what they did to their victims. We may lock away a kidnapper who wrongfully locked away his victim, and we may kill the murderer who wrongfully killed his victim. To lawfully do to the offender what he unlawfully did to his victim in no way legitimizes his crime. It legitimizes (some) killing, and not murder. An act does not become a crime because of its physical character, which, indeed, it may share with the legal punishment, but because of its social, or, better, antisocial, character—because it is an unlawful act.

Severity

Is the death penalty too severe? It stands in a class by itself. But so does murder. Execution is irreparable. So is murder. In contrast, all other crimes and punishments are, at least partly or potentially, reparable. The death penalty thus is congruous with the moral and material gravity of the crime it punishes.[24]

Still, is it repulsive? Torture, however well deserved, now is repulsive to us. But torture is an artifact. Death is not, since nature has placed us all under sentence of death. Capital punishment, in John Stuart Mills' phrase, only "hastens death"

—which is what the murderer did to his victim. I find nothing repulsive in hastening the murderer's death, provided it be done in a nontorturous manner. Had he wished to be secure in his life, he could have avoided murder.

To believe that capital punishment is too severe for any act, one must believe that there can be no act horrible enough to deserve death.[25] I find this belief difficult to understand. I should readily impose the death penalty on a Hitler or a Stalin, or on anyone who does what they did, albeit on a smaller scale.

CONCLUSION

The death penalty has become a major issue in public debate. This is somewhat puzzling, because quantitatively it is insignificant. Still, capital punishment has separated the voters as a whole from a small, but influential, abolitionist elite. There are, I believe, two reasons that explain the prominence of the issue.

First, I think, there is a genuine ethical issue. Some philosophers believe that the right to life is equally imprescriptible for all, that the murderer has as much right to live as his victim. Others do not push egalitarianism that far. They believe that there is a vital difference, that one's right to live is lost when one intentionally takes an innocent life, that everyone has just the right to one life, his own. If he unlawfully takes that of another he, *eo ipso*, loses his own right to life.

Second, and perhaps as important, the death penalty has symbolic significance. Those who favor it believe that the major remedy for crime is punishment. Those who do not, in the main, believe that the remedy is anything but punishment. They look at the causes of crime and conflate them with compulsions, or with ex-cuses, and refuse to blame. The majority of the people are less sophisticated, but perhaps they have better judgment. They believe that everyone who can understand the nature and effects of his acts is responsible for them, and should be blamed and punished, if he could know that what he did was wrong. Human beings are human because they can be held responsible, as animals cannot be. In that Kantian sense the death penalty is a symbolic affirmation of the humanity of both victim and murderer.

NOTES

1. 356 U.S. 99 (1958).
2. The courts have sometimes confirmed the obsolescence of non-repealed laws or punishments. But here they are asked to invent it.
3. In Coker v. Georgia, 433 U.S. 584, 592 (1977), the Court concluded that the eighth amendment prohibits punishments that are " 'excessive' in relation to the crime committed." I am not sure about this disproportion. However, threatening execution would tempt rapists to murder their victims who, after all, are potential witnesses. By murdering their victims, rapists would increase their chances of escaping execution without adding to their risk. Therefore, I agree with the court's conclusion, though not with its argument.
4. C. BLACK, CAPITAL PUNISHMENT: THE INEVITABILITY OF CAPRICE AND MISTAKE (2d ed. 1981).
5. Most discrimination occurred in rape cases and was eliminated when the death penalty for rape was declared unconstitutional.
6. For a survey of the statistical literature, see, e.g., Bowers, *The Pervasiveness of Arbitrariness and Discrimination under Post-*Furman *Capital Statutes,* 74 J. CRIM. L. & CRIMINOLOGY 1067 (1983). His article is part of a "Symposium on Current Death Penalty Issues" compiled by death penalty opponents.
7. Those who demonstrated the pattern seem to have been under the impression that they had shown discrimination against black murderers. They were wrong. However, the discrimination against black victims is invidious and should be corrected.
8. The capriciousness argument is undermined when capriciousness is conceded to be unavoidable. But even when capriciousness is thought reducible, one wonders whether releasing or retrying one guilty defendant, because another equally guilty defendant was not punished as much, would help

reduce capriciousness. It does not seem a logical remedy.

9. Furman v. Georgia, 408 U.S. 238, 256 (1971) (Douglas, J., concurring).

10. I shall not consider here the actual psychological motives that power our unending thirst for equality.

11. If courts impose different punishments on different persons, we may not be able to establish in all cases whether the punishment is just, or (it amounts to the same) whether the different persons were equally guilty of the same crime, or whether their crimes were identical in all relevant respects. Thus, we may not be able to tell which of two unequal punishments is just. Both may be, or neither may be. Inequality may not entail more injustice than equality,and equality would entail justice only if we were sure that the punishment meted out was the just punishment.

12. Similarly, it is better that only some innocents suffer undeserved punishment than that all suffer it equally.

13. It would be desirable that all of the worst murderers be sentenced to death. However, since murderers are tried in different courts, this is unlikely. Further, sometimes the testimony of one murderer is needed to convict another, and cannot be obtained except by leniency. Morally, and legally it is enough that those sentenced to death deserve the penalty for their crimes, even if others, who may deserve it as much, or more, were not sentenced to death.

14. Ehrlich, *The Deterrent Effect of Capital Punishment: A Question of Life or Death*, 65 AM. ECON. REV. 397, 414 (1975).

15. *See, e.g.,* Baldus & Cole, *A Comparison of the Work of Thorsten Sellin and Isaac Ehrlich on the Deterrent Effect of Capital Punishment,* 85 YALE L.J. 170 (1975); Bowers & Pierce, *Deterrence or Brutalization: What is the Effect of Executions?,* 26 CRIME & DELINQ. 453 (1980); Bowers & Pierce, *The Illusion of Deterrence in Isaac Ehrlich's Research on Capital Punishment,* 85 YALE L.J. 187 (1975).

16. Ehrlich, *Fear of Deterrence,* 6 J. LEGAL STUD. 293 (1977); Ehrlich & Gibbons, *On the Measurement of the Deterrent Effect of Capital Punishment and the Theory of Deterrence,* 6 J. LEGAL STUD. 35 (1977).

17. At present there is no agreement even on whether the short run effects of executions delay or accelerate homicides. *See* Phillips, *The Deterrent Effect of Capital Punishment: New Evidence on an Old Controversy,* 86, AM. J. SOC. 139 (1980).

18. As stated in Gregg v. Georgia, 428 U.S. 153, 185 (1976), "Although some of the studies suggest that the death penalty may not function as a significantly greater deterrent than lesser penalties, there is no convincing empirical evidence either supporting or refuting this view."

19. Jeffrey Reiman is an honorable exception. *See* Reiman, *Justice, Civilization, and the Death Penalty: Answering van den Haag,* 14 PHIL. & PUB. AFF. 115 (1985).

20. Life imprisonment avoids the problem of executing innocent persons to some extent. It can be revoked. But the convict also may die in prison before his innocence is discovered.

21. "[T]he Cruel and Unusual Punishments Clause prohibits the infliction of uncivilized and inhuman punishments. The State, even as it punishes, must treat its members with respect for their intrinsic worth as human beings." Furman v. Georgia, 408 U.S. 238, 270 (1972) (Brennan, J., concurring). "When we consider why [certain punishments] have been condemned, . . . we realize that the pain involved is not the only reason. The true significance of these punishments [that have been condemned] is that they treat members of the human race a nonhumans, as objects to be toyed with and discarded." *Id.* at 272–73.

> In determining whether a punishment comports with human dignity, we are aided also by a second principle inherent in the Clause— that the State must not arbitrarily inflict a severe punishment. This principle derives from the notion that the State does not respect human dignity when, without reason, it inflicts upon some people a severe punishment that it does not inflict upon others.

Id. at 274. "Death is truly an awesome punishment. The calculated killing of a human being by the State involves, by its very nature, a denial of the executed person's humanity." *Id.* at 290. "In comparison to all other punishments today, then, the deliberate extinguishment of human life by the State is uniquely degrading to human dignity." *Id.* at 291.

22. In *Reflections on the Guillotine,* Camus stated that "[t]he parcel [the condemned person] is no longer subject to the laws of chance that hang over the living creature but to mechanical laws that allow him to foresee accurately the day of his beheading. . . . The Greeks, after all, were more humane with their hemlock." A. CAMUS, RESISTANCE, REBELLION AND DEATH 175, 202 (1960).

23. "Sanctity of life" may mean that we should not take, and should punish taking innocent life: *"homo homini res sacra."* In the past this meant that we should take the life of a murderer to secure innocent life, and stress its sacredness. Justice Brennan seems to mean that the life of the murderer should be sacred too—but no argument is given for this premise.

24. Capital punishment is not inconsistent with Weems v. United States, 217 U.S. 349 (1910), which merely held that punishment cannot be excessive, that is, out of proportion to the gravity of the crime.

Indeed, if life imprisonment suffices for anything else, it cannot be appropriate for murder.

25. The notion of deserving is strictly moral, depending exclusively on our sense of justice, unlike the notion of deterrence, which depends on the expected factual consequences of punishment.

Whilst deterrence along would justify most of the punishments we should impose, it may not suffice to justify all those punishments that our sense of justice demands. Wherefore criminal justice must rest on desert as well as deterrence, to be seen as morally justified.

NO

Hugo Adam Bedau

A REPLY TO VAN DEN HAAG

Ernest van den Haag divides his defense of the death penalty into three sections: its constitutionality, its preventive effects, and its moral status. It will be convenient to address his criticisms in the order in which he presents them....

* * *

Van den Haag argues five different issues on the constitutionality of the death penalty, the first of which rests on the text of the Fifth Amendment in the Bill of Rights (1791). Since "due process of law" is mentioned there in connection with lawful deprivation of "life, limb, or liberty," he concludes that "the Constitution... authorizes the death penalty." But this is triply wrong.

First, the text in question does not *authorize* the death penalty; instead, it presents us with a conditional proposition: If life is to be taken as a punishment, then it *must* be done with due process of law. In effect, this text presents the government with a choice: Either repeal the death penalty or carry it out according to the requirements of due process. As for any "authorization" of the death penalty, or any other punishment, that depends on the exercise of legislative power within the constraints of the Constitution....

Second, van den Haag passes over the crucial question whether our current procedures for imposing the death penalty really do satisfy the requirements of due process. I take his silence on the point to imply that he has no qualms here. Well, I do, and I invited him and others who would agree with him to read carefully the [1994] essay by Stephen Bright..., as well as other evidence in the same vein.[1]...

Finally, by parity of reasoning to van den Haag's own argument, if a state legislature were to enact corporal punishments of extreme cruelty, say cutting off the hand of a thief after his third felony conviction, the legislature could count on the reference to deprivation of "limb" in this clause of the Fifth Amendment to enable such a punishment to pass the Supreme Court's scrutiny—so long as the maiming were done with "due process of law." Are we seriously to believe that the Court would endorse such reasoning? I cannot; nothing in the Fifth Amendment precludes the Court from relying on the Eighth Amendment, prohibiting "cruel and unusual punishments," to rule out as unconstitutional any punishments that maim. The same is true of punishments that kill.

Van den Haag next attacks the argument that the Eighth Amendment prohibition against "cruel and unusual punishments" undermines the legitimacy of the death penalty in our day, even if it did not do so when the amendment was passed, because the clause must be interpreted (in the language of the Court's ruling in *Trop v. Dulles* [1958]) according to "evolving standards of decency." He dismisses this judicial language as "paradoxical" if used to interpret the Constitution in order to repeal punishments having statutory authority, since it would make the Constitution as written "superfluous." Van den Haag seems to think *Trop* was nonetheless correctly decided because the punishment ruled out by the Court in that case was "expatriation, a punishment not specifically authorized by the Constitution." But the Eighth Amendment nowhere mentions (and certainly doesn't "authorize") capital punishment, either.

The issue here is twofold: how to interpret the "cruel and unusual punishment" clause of that amendment, and how to apply that interpretation to the death penalty in light of the relevant facts. As the ratification discussions in 1789 show,[2] it was even then anticipated that at some future date this language might plausibly be used to strike down the death penalty. Nothing in either the Fifth or the Eighth Amendments prohibits the Supreme Court from concluding that two hundred years of experience with capital punishment reveals that it is, after all, cruel and unusual, that its administration makes a mockery of due process of law,

and that it also violates "the equal protection of the law" (Fourteenth Amendment).

In this regard it is important to notice that van den Haag mentions in passing (though without implying his approval) that the Supreme Court has declared the death penalty for rape (in *Coker v. Georgia* [1977]) and the mandatory death penalty for murder (in *Woodson v. North Carolina* [1976]) to be in violation of the Eighth Amendment. Consistent with his prior argument here, he must reject the legitimacy of these rulings. On his view, any legislature that wants to have the death penalty for rape is constitutionally "authorized" to do so, whether or not it is "disproportionate" to the crime. And the same is true of any other crime—armed robbery, kidnapping, treason, espionage, arson, train robbery, desecration of a grave—each of them punishable by death earlier in this century in one or another American jurisdiction. But by van den Haag's reasoning, since disproportionality is nowhere mentioned in the Eighth Amendment (having been invented by the Supreme Court in *Weems v. United States* [1910] as an appropriate interpretive principle to explain what a "cruel and unusual punishment" is), he must infer that courts have no authority to invoke disproportionality as a ground for declaring *any* penalties unconstitutional. Thus, he implicitly rejects the Supreme Court's authority to nullify the death penalty for murder by means of an argument that prevents the Court from applying the Eighth Amendment to invalidate *any* penalty, so long as that penalty is carried out by "due process of law" and was tolerated by the Framers.

Van den Haag next addresses the objection that the death penalty as administered is too capricious to be tolerated on constitutional grounds. (As his essay preceded the Court's decision in *McCleskey v. Kemp* by two years, he had no opportunity to mention that this decision supports his own views.) He replies in two steps: First, he endorses the Supreme Court's decision in *Gregg* that the post-*Furman* statutory reforms have eliminated whatever caprice infected the administration of pre-*Furman* death penalties. This judgment simply will not withstand scrutiny. The good-faith hopes of the *Gregg* majority in 1976 (especially evident in the concurring opinion by Justice White) have simply not been borne out in practice in the two decades since then. No serious and informed student of the administration of the death penalty believes these statutes have so far accomplished more than cosmetic reforms, however well-intentioned they may have been when enacted.[3]

The next objection van den Haag raises is that unless we are to believe the administration of the death penalty today is *more* capricious than it was in the previous century, its capriciousness today fails to show any constitutionally relevant defect. This is a bad argument because it ignores the holding in *Furman*, which ... was based above all on the capricious, arbitrary, and discriminatory administration of the death penalty of that day. Unless there is *less*—indeed, little or no—caprice in the death penalty as administered today, in contrast to what there was when *Furman* was decided, the post-*Furman* statutes ought to be invalidated by the reasoning that prevailed in *Furman*. ...

Van den Haag devotes two paragraphs to attacking the claim that racial discrimination in administering the death penalty establishes that penalty's unconstitutionality. (Subsequent to his essay,

David Baldus and his two coauthors published *Equal Justice and the Death Penalty: A Legal and Empirical Analysis* [1990], amply establishing just such discrimination.) Van den Haag concedes that there is some racial discrimination in the way this penalty is administered. The importance of this concession is not to be underestimated; few defenders of the death penalty today are willing to concede as much. Van den Haag probably attaches little weight to it because he probably would also concede that the whole criminal justice system is tilted slightly against nonwhites, thus reducing to relative insignificance whatever racial discrimination the death penalty involves. He insists that the remedy is not to abolish the death penalty but to abolish the discrimination (which, he adds, favor[s] murderers of blacks and therefore favors blacks over whites, since most black murder victims are killed by blacks). When this is taken as an abstract proposition, one must agree with van den Haag: Since capital statutes as they are written do not discriminate on racial grounds, they ought not to be repealed just because they are administered with discriminatory results.

But this remedy of nondiscrimination, which van den Haag so easily proposes, simply flies in the face of everything we know about the history of the death penalty in this nation, and especially in the South. Are we seriously to think that in Texas or Alabama or South Carolina (or even outside the South, in California, Illinois, or New York) prosecutors and trial juries will remedy their history of racial discrimination by meting out death penalties regardless of the race of the victim or the offender? No, we are not. (See the sobering story told at length by James W. Marquart and his two coauthors in their book, *The Rope, The Chair, and the*

Needle: Capital Punishment in Texas, 1923–1990 [1994].)[4] Van den Haag's argument is simply beside the point; it is a frivolous appeal to an abstract possibility that two centuries of experience tell us will not be put into practice, not in our lifetimes and not in those of our children or their children. If we really want to improve on the rough justice of our current practices involving the death penalty, the only way to do so is to abolish it and sentence *all* convicted murderers to prison, whatever their race and the race of their victim(s). No doubt inequities will remain, but their magnitude will have been dramatically reduced.

Van den Haag's final and lengthiest constitutional consideration takes up proportionality review. A year after his essay was published, the Supreme Court ruled in *Pulley v. Harris* (1984) as he would have wished, rejecting the argument to make proportionality review a constitutional requirement in capital cases. However, nowhere in his discussion does he address the equal protection clause of the Fourteenth Amendment and what relevance it may have, although that ought to be his chief, if not his sole, concern here. Instead, he invites us to consider which is worse—giving some murderers their just deserts (a death penalty) even when we do not give it to all murderers, or giving it to none because we cannot give it to all. Van den Haag favors, he says, justice over equality if we cannot have both. Again, taken abstractly, his position here is plausible.

But, also once again, why take the matter so abstractly? We have ample empirical evidence, based on actual research... on prosecutorial decision making, the deliberations of capital juries, and the conduct of clemency hearings in capital cases, to believe that the disproportional-ity in sentencing is *not* the result of a random "lottery" or of mere "chance" (van den Haag's favorite explanatory factors). Rather, it is due to illegitimate factors of race, class, and social policy. (Stephen Nathanson has discussed this point with some care; see Nathanson 1987.) This is why the decision to execute a given capital offender is vulnerable to criticism on equal protection grounds.

In another place, van den Haag and I debated the question, Can any legal punishments of the guilty be unjust to them? As might be expected, he argued the negative and I argued the affirmative. Since part of what I said there is relevant to the present issue, I will quote from that essay:

> Once it is known that the jurisdiction's sentencing practices are producing disparities, and these disparities are based on irrelevant factors such as gender or race, then it is known that a social practice (i.e., discretionary sentencing) is producing inequities owing to impermissible causes—factors that sentencers are not entitled to consider in justifying the disparate exercise of their sentencing discretion. Whatever the mechanisims through which these causes (e.g., unconscious racism) affect social practices, the result is not unlike the paradigm of injustice in which guilty parties are victimized by punishments determined by factors irrelevant either to their culpability or to the unlawful harm they have caused. In the case of unconscious racism, as in the previous cases, the offender has a right that irrelevant factors not determine his sentence. But, the sentencing practice that imposes the heavier sentence on Smith demonstrably violates this right, quite apart from whether there is any evidence that the sentencer intentionally discriminated against Smith. Such sentencing practices do not violate

Smith's right to the lesser sentence, for he has no such right. Instead, these practices violate Smith's right not to be sentenced one way rather than another owing to adventitious factors that bear no relation to his guilt. This is why the heavier sentence is an injustice *to* him.

The point underlying this conclusion is simple. Injustice in punishment, which for our purposes is injustice in sentencing, is an injustice to the guilty offender only when the sentencing disparities are explained by factors that have nothing to do with the desert of the offender. Clearly, sentence disparities based on the gender, race, color, or nationality of the offender, as well as the arbitrary outcomes of a fair lottery, are irrelevant to the offender's desert. Every guilty offender has a right that his sentence not be determined by factors irrelevant to his desert. The fact that some sentences are based on such criteria is merely another variation of the general theme that arbitrary or unfair procedures, which produce irrelevant grounds for exercising sentencing discretion, yield an unjust result, quite apart from whatever may be said about the justice of the result from some other perspective. (Bedau 1987c: 1429–30)

* * *

With constitutional issues disposed of, van den Haag addresses deterrence and the empirical research on which judgments of deterrence are and ought to be made. Oddly, he says nothing explicit about incapacitation, although the special incapacitative effects of the death penalty are usually touted by those of its defenders who attach importance to deterrence.... He concludes that the results of all the empirical research are "inconclusive," and so he is inclined to advise partisans on each side of the death penalty debate to distrust reliance on research of this sort. This is a minimalist interpretation of the evidence if ever there was one, since it wrongly encourages the inexperienced student of this subject to think that the empirical pros and cons about the special deterrent effects of the death penalty are at a standoff. Van den Haag and others who support the death penalty on deterrent grounds need to ponder the essay... by William C. Bailey and Ruth D. Peterson [1994] to see just how completely without foundation is any belief in the deterrent efficacy of the death penalty in the United States during the past half century.

Van den Haag then insists that despite the lack of empirical evidence he still believes the death penalty is a better deterrent. Why? "[B]ecause people fear death more than anything else." Perhaps they would say they do, if they were asked to answer the question, Which do you fear more, a death penalty or life in prison? But armed robbers, gangland hit men, kids in cars hell-bent on drive-by shootings, and other persons really interested in murdering someone are not thinking about that question. They are thinking instead about this question: "What's the best way for me to commit the crime and not get caught?" Van den Haag also argues that the death penalty must be a better deterrent because death row convicts would rather have their sentences commuted to life in prison. This preference tends to show that life imprisonment is believed to be a less *severe* punishment than death. It does not show that death is a better *deterrent*—unless you accept as an axiom that the more severe a punishment is thought to be, the better a deterrent it is. The truth of that belief matters not at all if rational people will be deterred from murder as well by a long prison sentence as by a death sentence.

Van den Haag concedes that many murderers are undeterrable but adds: "Even if only some murders were, or could be, deterred by capital punishment, it would be worthwhile." Many agree with him (though they might not, if they were to read the critique by David Conway; see Conway 1974). But one must ask, What cost are you prepared to pay to gain this elusive extra deterrence? The dollar costs ... are mounting rapidly, with no end in sight. Quite apart from these costs are the moral costs, chief of which is the great risk of executing the innocent (I will return to this later)....

Throughout his discussion of deterrence, van den Haag fails to address a crucial question: If the death penalty is to be defended on grounds of its superior deterrence (or incapacitation), what stops us from defending even more savage penalties if they prove (or seem likely to prove) to be an even better deterrent than the death penalty as currently used? Later in his essay, he dismisses torture on the subjective ground that it is "repulsive to us." Well, it is not repulsive to torturers, and to them van den Haag evidently has nothing to say except to express his personal disapproval. It's of no use to his argument that everyone agrees the Constitution prohibits such "cruel and unusual punishments" as boiling in oil or crucifixion or burning at the stake. He has to explain, consistent with his endorsement of the importance of extra deterrence, how and why he respects the moral basis of the constitutional prohibition. He fails to do that; his ethical subjectivism prevents him from doing so. Like every other defender of the death penalty on deterrent grounds, van den Haag has nursed an asp to his bosom that will destroy whatever

limits he thinks might be morally appropriate on cruel punishments—limits that in any case he can treat as nothing more than collective subjective preferences.

I complete my criticism of van den Haag's view on deterrence by responding to his claim that I and other abolitionists who oppose the death penalty on principle would evidently tolerate the murder of hundreds rather than execute any convicted murderers even if we knew that by doing so we could have prevented those murders by the extra deterrence the death penalty provides.... I would point out two things.

First, my unwillingness to execute (or to have the state hire someone to execute) a convicted murderer is not the same as someone else's decision to commit murder. Neither is it in any sense the cause of such a decision. My refusal to authorize killing the guilty is not equivalent to my authorizing the death of the innocent. So my refusal to authorize executions does not make me responsible for murder, even if those executions would have deterred murderers that imprisonment would not.

Second, ... [w]here the death penalty today is concerned, ... any version of this dilemma is so conjectural that worrying about it is as implausible as worrying about sharks on dry land. Van den Haag is right that I oppose the death penalty in principle and without exceptions; he is wrong in implying that I would tolerate with equanimity the deaths of innocents simply to avoid lawful execution of one who is guilty. I favor abolition, not least because I am confident that zero deterrence would be lost.

* * *

In the final and most important (but briefest and least coherent) part of his argument, van den Haag raises eight scattered issues collected under the heading of the morality of the death penalty. On the first of these, miscarriages of justice, he concedes that in the long run the death penalty "lead[s] to the execution of some innocents." This is another important concession, and he repeated it a few years later (1986:1664). But these losses are rare and worth it, he argues, because of the offsetting advantages that *only* the death penalty provides—at which point he recycles his belief in the deterrent superiority of the death penalty. As for his analogy (we tolerate high-speed highways despite our knowledge that they increase traffic deaths), all one can say is that there is *no* analogy between a morally defensible practice in which lethal accidents do occur that take statistical lives and a morally dubious practice in which lethal events are designed for particular individuals in the mistaken belief that they deserve it. . . .

Van den Haag rebukes Christian religious leaders who oppose the death penalty, reminding them that "there is no biblical warrant for their opposition." . . . However, even if van den Haag is right about how to read and interpret the Bible, all he has done is put in question the legitimacy of professing Christians opposing the death penalty on narrowly biblical (constructing "biblical" to mean "literally textual") grounds. This does nothing to undermine any nonreligious moral arguments against the death penalty, which Jews and Christians are as entitled to advance as well as anyone else.

Van den Haag next tackles the concept and role of "human dignity" and denies that there is any mileage for abolitionists to be gained by invoking this value. He adds that "no one has explained why

capital punishment degrades" human dignity, and he implies that no one can. In an essay published some years after his and designed to explain the idea of the death penalty as a violation of human dignity, I began by using the four principles Justice Brennan introduced in his concurring opinion in *Furman* in order to explain why the death penalty was an affront to human dignity and thus in violation of the Eighth Amendment's prohibition of "cruel and unusual punishments." The essential part of my argument, taken out of the context of a rather long discussion, was this:

Let us reformulate Brennan's four principles in a more uniform manner that emphasizes their connection to human dignity. Taking them in the order in which he mentions them, this is what we get: First, it is an affront to the dignity of a person to be forced to undergo catastrophic harm at the hands of another when, before the harm is imposed, the former is entirely at the mercy of the latter, as is always the case with legal punishment. Second, it offends the dignity of a person who is punished according to the will of a punisher free to pick and choose arbitrarily among offenders so that only a few are punished very severely when all deserve the same severe punishment if any do. Third, it offends the dignity of a person to be subjected to a severe punishment when society shows by its actual conduct in sentencing that it no longer regards this severe punishment as appropriate. Finally, it is an affront to human dignity to impose a very severe punishment on an offender when it is known that a less severe punishment will achieve all the purposes it is appropriate to try to achieve by punishing anyone in any manner whatsoever.

These reformulations link the concept of human dignity explicitly with the concept of "cruel and unusual punishments" via the notion of appropriate limits to the permissible severity of punishments. This is easily seen if we recall several of the constitutive elements of human dignity discussed earlier: Respect for the autonomy of rational creatures forbids its needless curtailment in the course of deserved punishment. Respect for the equal worth of persons forbids inequitable punishments of convicted offenders equally guilty. The fundamental equal rights of persons, including convicted offenders, precludes treating some offenders as if they had ceased to be persons. (Bedau 1992:160–61)

Van den Haag turns to the law of retaliation, *lex talionis*, only to reject its authority. This is another important concession because it deprives him of arguing from this general principle of retaliatory punishments to the special case of the death penalty for murder, in which we take "a life for a life." (Of course, his disavowal of *lex talionis* also spares him the embarrassment of trying to cope with the inapplicability and absurdity of this law for a wide range of crimes, just as it frees him to defend the death penalty, should he wish to, for crimes that include no murder.) Instead, he argues that "[p]unishment, ultimately, is a vindication of the moral and legal order of society." No doubt it ought to be, although it behooves those who would defend punishment in these terms to convince us that the current moral and legal order is sufficiently just to warrant our punitive practices (Jeffrey Reiman's retributive argument against the death penalty rests primarily on the structural injustices in our society; see Reiman 1985 and 1988). But of course one can grant van den Haag's claim about the nature or ultimate purpose of state punishment

without for one moment suggesting that law and moral order can be vindicated *only* or *best* by the use of death penalties or any other unnecessary punishment. This is precisely what I would deny and what van den Haag apparently believes and ought to defend. But he doesn't....

The next target of his critique is the ideal of "the sanctity of life," which some abolitionists (notably, Justice Brennan) insist the death penalty violates. He does not try to explain this ideal or why one might think it is inconsistant with the death penalty. Instead, he recycles constitutional considerations, purporting to show that the Framers, who accepted this ideal, did so in a manner that did not rule out capital punishment. But none of this really speaks to the moral issues involved. For my part, I would put this ideal to one side in the present discussion because the *sanctity* of life (all life? only human life? only innocent human life?) is not a secular concept but a religious one —unlike the *right* to life, which is a secular concept. For some reason, van den Haag has virtually nothing to say about this idea (but see my penultimate paragraph below). Whatever role the sanctity of life properly plays in a religiously based morality, it really cannot be used as a building block for a secular morality. Nor can it be properly used to evaluate from a secular perspective such controversial issues as suicide, euthanasia, abortion, war—or the death penalty. Since van den Haag does not discuss the bearing of our right to life on the morality of the death penalty, I will excuse myself from doing so here.[5]

Van den Haag's penultimate barb is directed at those abolitionists who think that executing murderers "legitimizes murder by doing to the murderer what he did to his victim." He rejects this objection because it confuses the legitimate killing of convicted murderers with the illegitimate killing by murderers. This strikes me as completely begging the question. The point of the objection he wishes to refute is that where the legitimacy of killing lies in the eye of the killer, we must be very careful what killings we are prepared to permit.

... The reason abolitionists believe the death penalty legitimates murder in the eyes of some is that the grounds on which the government acts in deciding whom to prosecute for a death sentence, whom to convict of capital murder, whom to sentence to death, whom to refuse clemency, looks suspiciously vindictive, arbitrary, and illegitimate. This invites some to reason as follows: "If the government is permitted to kill for its reasons, then I should be permitted to kill for mine." Van den Haag's argument is not with abolitionists, who do not endorse this reasoning, but with whoever does reason in this manner. Simply declaring that murder is wrong and the death penalty legitimate is hardly sufficient.

Finally, van den Haag turns to the question whether the death penalty is "too severe" and concludes that it is not. Yes, it is "irreparable"—but so is murder. No, it is not "repulsive"—since we all must die someday. And he ends by informing us how readily he would put to death a Hitler, a Stalin, or "anyone who does what they did, albeit on a smaller scale." But whether the death penalty is too severe depends on what one thinks the purpose and rationale of its severity is. Whatever that purpose or rationale, I think it is unnecessary for deterrence or incapacitation, arbitrary and discriminatory in the retribution it inflicts, and therefore an affront to our civilized sensibilities.

As to whether the death penalty is repulsive, I suggest that van den Haag inform himself more vividly about what happens during a typical electrocution —a pretty ugly affair at best, as Deborah Denno has shown in considerable detail (Denno 1994, 1996) and as demonstrated by the repulsive 1990 electrocution of Jesse Tafero in Florida (von Drehle 1995:409). I would grant ... that the physical act of execution by lethal injection is not repulsive typically or necessarily—no doubt, a widely shared belief and a significant factor in explaining the popularity of lethal injection with American legislatures during the past twenty years. But this emphasis on the details of particular executions or on techniques for carrying out the death penalty obscures what is arguably repulsive about executions as such: It is not only that the prisoner dies, or dies in agony, or dies with ugly disfigurement, but that the lethal act itself is the result of calculated planning by the impersonal state in which the state's overwhelming power is on display against the helplessness of the prisoner. ...

When van den Haag reminds us that death is inevitable in the nature of things, he does not make a very persuasive point. Human disappointment, pain, loneliness, bereavement, and other forms of misery and suffering are part of the human condition and virtually inevitable for each of us. Yet is that a good reason for complacency in their face if it is within our power to remedy or mitigate, even if only briefly or slightly, these inevitabilities? Van den Haag does not address this question.

As for Hitler and Stalin, they are often the trump card used by modern defenders of the death penalty who cannot believe that anyone really would oppose *all* executions. The trouble is that appealing to Hitler and Stalin sheds no light on whether to execute all or some or none of the more than three thousand prisoners on American death rows today. For myself, I would be glad to make an exception to my absolute rejection of the death penalty by permitting van den Haag to destroy tyrants such as these if he would give me the lives of those actually under sentence of death today, whose crimes are pathetically insignificant if measured against genocide, aggressive warfare, and the other crimes against humanity of which these dictators and their henchmen were guilty.

Van den Haag ends his essay by making two points with which abolitionists ought to agree—in part. First, he insists that the national debate over the death penalty is important because it involves "a genuine ethical issue." He is right, but what is this issue as he sees it? It is whether "the right to life" extends to all humans and cannot ever be forfeited. He thinks it can be; I think it cannot, and elsewhere I have tried to explain why (Bedau 1987b:55–59). Even if I am right, I suggest that this is not the important ethical issue in the debate. The paramount ethical issue posed by the death penalty is this: Whether or not everyone has an unforfeitable right to life, do *we* do the right thing in authorizing killing some criminals when we know there is an adequate alternative punishment (imprisonment), or do we do the right thing when we refuse to kill any, no matter how guilty they are? The issue, in short, is not the right to life; it is the right to *kill*.

Second, van den Haag insists that we are rightly concerned about the death penalty because it has important "symbolic significance," a significance far beyond its practical import. Again, this is correct. For him, however, this symbolic significance lies in its "affirmation of the humanity of both victim and murderer." Van den Haag here has the support of no less a philosopher than Immanuel Kant, though he does not mention this. I, on the other hand, think the whole idea is bizarre. The very thought that I affirm the humanity of a murderer by treating him more or less as he treated his innocent and undeserving victim would be funny were it not so momentous. For me, the death penalty symbolizes *unlimited impersonal power* over the individual, with dramatically final and irreversible results whenever it is expressed. As long as we choose to hang this moral albatross around our necks, I see no way for us to enjoy, much less help the rest of the world to enjoy, the benefits of a truly human community.

NOTES

1. See, e.g., Greenberg 1982, 1986; Weisberg 1984; Radelet and Pierce 1985; Goodpaster 1983; Brennan 1986; Marshall 1986; Amsterdam 1988; V. Berger 1988.

2. See R. Berger 1982; 45–46 and my review of his book, Bedau 1983:1159–60.

3. Justice White supported the decision in *Gregg v. Georgia* by arguing that the Georgia legislature "has made an effort" to identify appropriate aggravating and mitigating circumstances relevant to the choice of sentence in capital cases (pp. 221, 222); he added that "[t]here is reason to expect that Georgia's current system would escape the infirmities which invalidated its previous system" (p.222); and so on regarding prosecutorial discretion in indictments (pp. 224–25) and proportionality review by the Georgia Supreme Court (pp. 223–24). What Justice White has not done since he wrote these words in 1976 is to revisit in appropriate detail the administration of the death penalty in Georgia and elsewhere, to see how the promise of compliance with the mandate of *Furman*—which he supported—has not been kept.

4. See also my review of this book, Bedau 1997.

5. The contemporary philosophical discussion of the right to life leaves much to be desired. My own discussions, beginning with Bedau 1968, are at best a starting point.

REFERENCES

Amsterdam, Anthony. 1988. "Race and the Death Penalty." *Criminal Justice Ethics* 7(winter/spring): 2, 84, 86.

Bailey, William C., and Ruth D. Peterson. 1994. "Murder, Capital Punishment, and Deterrence: A Review of the Evidence and an Examination of Police Killings." *Journal of Social Issues* 50(summer): 53–74.

Baldus, David, Charles Pulaski Jr., and George G. Woodworth. 1990. *Equal Justice and the Death Penalty: A Legal and Empirical Analysis.* Boston: Northeastern University Press.

Bedau, H. A. 1968. "The Right to Life." *The Monist* 52(October): 550–72.

Bedau, H. A. 1983. "Berger's Defense of the Death Penalty: How Not to Read the Constitution." *Michigan Law Review* 81(March): 1152–65.

Bedau, H. A. 1987a. *Death Is Different: Studies in the Morality, Law, and Politics of Capital Punishment.* Boston: Northeastern University Press.

Bedau, H. A. 1987b. "Objections to the Death Penalty from the Moral Point of View." *Revue internationale de droit penal* 58(3e et 4e trimstres): 557–65.

Bedau, H. A. 1987c. "Justice in Punishment and Assumption of Risks: Some Comments in Response to van den Haag." *Wayne State Law Review* 33(summer): 1423–34.

Bedau, H. A. 1992. *The Case Against the Death Penalty.* 4th ed. New York: American Civil Liberties Union.

Bedau, H. A. 1997. "Book review [of Marquart, Ekland-Olson, and Sorenson 1994]." In Schabas ed. 1997, forthcoming.

Berger, Raoul. 1982. *Death Penalties: The Supreme Court's Obstacle Course.* Cambridge: Harvard University Press.

Berger, Vivian. 1988. "Rolling the Dice to Decide Who Dies." *New York State Bar Journal* (October): 32–37.

Brennan, William J., Jr. 1986. "Constitutional Adjudication and the Death Penalty: A View from the Court." *Harvard Law Review* 100(December): 313–31.

Brennan, William J., Jr. 1994. "Counsel for the Poor: The Death Sentence Not for the Worst Crime but for the Worst Lawyer." *Yale Law Journal* 103(May): 1835–83.

Conway, David A. 1974. "Capital Punishment and Deterrence: Some Considerations in Dialogue Form." *Philosophy & Public Affairs* 3(summer): 431–33.

Davis, Michael. 1996. *Justice in the Shadow of Death: Rethinking Capital and Lesser Punishments.* Lanham, MD.: Rowman & Littlefield.

Denno, Deborah. 1994a. "Is Electrocution an Unconstitutional Method of Execution? The Engineering of Death over the Century." *William and Mary Law Review* 35(winter): 551–692.

Denno, Deborah. 1996. "Are Executions Constitutional?" *Iowa Law Review* 82: forthcoming.

Glover, Jonathan. 1977. *Causing Death and Saving Lives.* Harmondsworth, Eng.: Penguin Books.

Goodpaster, Gary. 1983. "The Trial for Life: Effective Assistance of Counsel in Death Penalty Cases," *New York University Law Review* 58(May): 299–362.

Greenberg, Jack. 1982. "Capital Punishment as a System." *Yale Law Journal* 91(April): 908–36.

Greenberg, Jack. 1986. "Against the American System of Capital Punishment." *Harvard Law Review* 99(May): 1670–80.

Marquart, James W., Sheldon Ekland-Olson, and Jonathan R. Sorensen. 1994. *The Rope, the Chair, and the Needle: Capital Punishment in Texas, 1923–1990.* Austin: University of Texas Press.

Marshall, Thurgood. 1986. "Remarks on the Death Penalty Made at the Judicial Conference of the Second Circuit." *Columbia Law Review* 86(January): 1–8.

Murphy, Jeffrie G. 1979. "Cruel and Unusual Punishment." In Murphy, *Retribution, Justice, and Therapy: Essays in the Philosophy of Law.* Dordrecht, Holland: D. Reidel, pp. 223–49.

Nathanson, Stephen. 1987. *An Eye for an Eye? The Morality of Punishing by Death.* Boston: Northeastern University Press.

Radelet, Michael L., and Glenn L. Pierce. 1985. "Race and Prosecutorial Discretion in Homicide Cases." *Law & Society Review* 19:587–621.

Reiman, Jeffrey. 1985. "Justice, Civilization, and the Death Penalty: Answering van den Haag." *Philosphy & Public Affairs* 14(spring): 115–48.

Reiman, Jeffrey. 1988. "The Justice of the Death Penalty in an Unjust World." In Haas and Inciardi 1988:29–48.

Saunders, John T. 1988. "Why the Numbers Should Sometimes Count." *Philosophy & Public Affairs* 17(winter): 3–14.

Sorell, Tom. 1987. *Moral Theory and Capital Punishment.* Oxford: Blackwells.

Taurek, John M. 1977. "Should the Numbers Count?" *Philosophy & Public Affairs* 6(summer): 293–316.

Van den Haag, Ernest. 1986. "The Ultimate Punishment: A Defense." *Harvard Law Review* 99(May): 1662–69.

von Drehle, David. 1995. *Among the Lowest of the Dead: The Culture of Death Row.* New York: Random House.

Weisberg, Robert. 1984. "Deregulating Death." *Supreme Court Review 1983:* 305–95.

TABLE OF CASES

Coker v. Georgia, 433 U.S. 584 (1977)

Furman v. Georgia, 408 U.S. 238 (1972)

Gregg v. Georgia, 428 U.S. 153 (1976)

McCleskey v. Kemp, 481 U.S. 279 (1987)

Pulley v. Harris, 465 U.S. 37 (1984)

Trop v. Dulles, 356 U.S. 86 (1958)

Weems v. United States, 217 U.S. 349 (1910)

Woodson v. North Carolina, 428 U.S. 280 (1976)

POSTSCRIPT

Should the Death Penalty Be Retained?

The argument is sometimes made that even if capital punishment is not a deterrent (or, more radically, even if capital punishment actually encourages crime), justice demands that certain criminals be executed. For example, former Nazis who killed many innocent people are today tracked down and brought to trial. Usually, these are elderly men who have lived many years without killing anyone. If the death penalty is demanded for these people, would this demand receive support from the deterrence line of reasoning? Probably not. First, these people have already stopped killing and so do not need to be deterred. Second, should we suppose that executing them will deter potential future Nazis, Aryan supremacists, and other racists from murder? More likely, in these cases, the argument is that these former Nazis should die for what they have done as a matter of justice.

A special issue for Americans is whether or not the death penalty is constitutional—in particular, whether or not it is cruel and unusual punishment. In a series of important legal cases (including *Furman v. Georgia*, 1972, and *Gregg v. Georgia*, 1976), the U.S. Supreme Court found that capital punishment *as then applied* was indeed unconstitutional. The main problem was that a lack of explicit standards in applying the death penalty gave much room for discretion, which in turn allowed prejudice and racism to hide behind legality. But the Court allowed the development of procedures of administering capital punishment that did not violate the Constitution.

Relevant literature includes Wendy Lesser, *Pictures at an Execution* (Harvard University Press, 1993); Victor Streib, ed., *A Capital Punishment Anthology* (Anderson Publishing, 1993); Randall Coyne and Lyn Entzeroth, *Capital Punishment and the Judicial Process* (Carolina Academic Press, 1994); Jeffrie G. Murphy, *Punishment and Rehabilitation*, 3rd ed. (Wadsworth, 1995); Robert M. Baird and Stuart E. Rosenbaum, eds., *Punishment and the Death Penalty: The Current Debate* (Prometheus, 1995); Martin Perlmutter, "Desert and Capital Punishment," in John Arthur, ed., *Morality and Moral Controversies*, 4th ed. (Prentice Hall, 1996); Michael Davis, *Justice in the Shadow of Death: Rethinking Capital and Lesser Punishments* (Rowman & Littlefield, 1996); Margery B. Koosed, ed., *Capital Punishment*, 3 vols. (Garland, 1996), particularly volume 1; Paul A. Winters, ed., *Death Penalty* (Greenhaven Press, 1997); Louis Pojman and Jeffrey Reiman, *Capital Punishment* (Rowman & Littlefield, 1997); and William A. Schabas, ed., *The International Sourcebook on Capital Punishment* (Northeastern University Press, 1997).

In addition, an entire issue of *Focus on Law Studies: Teaching About Law in the Liberal Arts* (Spring 1997) is devoted to consideration of the death penalty.

ISSUE 14

Is Euthanasia Immoral?

YES: J. Gay-Williams, from "The Wrongfulness of Euthanasia," in Ronald Munson, ed., *Intervention and Reflection: Basic Issues in Medical Ethics*, 5th ed. (Wadsworth, 1995)

NO: Richard Brandt, from "A Moral Principle About Killing," in Marvin Kohl, ed., *Beneficent Euthanasia* (Prometheus Books, 1975)

ISSUE SUMMARY

YES: J. Gay-Williams believes that euthanasia is immoral because it violates one's natural personal will to survive. He argues that a public policy allowing euthanasia would have severe negative practical effects.

NO: Moral philosopher Richard Brandt argues that killing human beings ordinarily injures them and violates their preferences. But in cases of euthanasia, when both of these conditions are lacking, he asserts that the killing could be allowable.

The word *euthanasia* comes from two Greek elements: the prefix *eu* (meaning good, easy, or fortunate) and the word *thanatos* (meaning death). The root idea is that in euthanasia one undergoes a good death, or an easy or fortunate one.

Euthanasia means more than this, however. We do not use the term unless we are referring to a case in which someone kills another person in order to give that person an easy death. Suppose your grandmother lives to a great age and, having put all her personal affairs in order, dies a painless death while asleep. However good or easy a death this might have been—and however much we might hope that when we or our loved ones die this will be the way —such a case is *not* one of euthanasia. The key element of a person killing a person is absent. It is precisely this element that makes euthanasia morally controversial.

Now the fact that any one person kills another does not automatically make euthanasia wrong. There are killings in a "just" war, in self-defense, and in state executions. Although some might well claim that any one of these three is wrong, it would be difficult indeed to maintain that all three of these are always wrong.

One difference between euthanasia and the three cases mentioned above is that in those cases the person who is killed is regarded by the killer as an enemy, an attacker, or a criminally guilty person. But the person who dies in euthanasia is not regarded as such. Often the person killed is a relative, a friend, or a medical patient of the killer. A common phrase used for euthanasia that recognizes this feature is "mercy killing."

Proponents of euthanasia generally do perceive euthanasia as a merciful practice, one that offers a way out—perhaps the only way out—of a painful existence. For example, consider the following true story. A physicist who had worked with X rays for many years developed skin cancer. As a result of this disease, he lost part of his jaw, his upper lip, his nose, his left hand, two fingers from his right hand, and his sight. Blind and in great pain, he was given about a year to live by his doctors, who could neither cure the cancer nor eliminate the pain. He begged for death. He wanted one of his three brothers to kill him. Two refused, but the third, to whom he had always felt the closest, reluctantly shot him to death.

Opponents of euthanasia, on the other hand, point out that euthanasia—far from resembling justified killing—fits the standard definition of murder: the killing of an innocent person. Moreover, if this killing is tolerated, where will it stop? The possibilities are many. Suppose the physicist in the previous case had become mentally incapacitated before expressing a wish to die. Would his brothers or his doctors then make a judgment about euthanasia? Suppose the patient has no relatives and no money and lives on public funds. Would taxpayers then decide? Perhaps various groups—the old, the infirm, those with incurable diseases, the insane, or even those with undesirable character traits—would be killed in this way. Opponents of euthanasia ask, Where will the line be drawn once the killing of the innocent is condoned? They rule out *all* euthanasia, thus eliminating the need to draw such a line.

In the following selections, J. Gay-Williams argues that euthanasia is intrinsically wrong and also likely to lead to disagreeable consequences. Support for euthanasia, he suspects, is the result of an unthinking sentimentalism. Richard Brandt presents what he believes is a rational analysis of what is wrong with killing human beings. He argues that euthanasia, which is free of these elements, is not wrong.

YES

J. Gay-Williams

THE WRONGFULNESS OF EUTHANASIA

My impression is that euthanasia—the idea, if not the practice—is slowly gaining acceptance within our society. Cynics might attribute this to an increasing tendency to devalue human life, but I do not believe this is the major factor. Well-publicized, tragic stories like that of Karen Quinlan elicit from us deep feelings of compassion. We think to ourselves, "She and her family would be better off if she were dead." It is an easy step from this very human response to the view that if someone (and others) would be better off dead, then it must be all right to kill that person.[1] Although I respect the compassion that leads to this conclusion, I believe the conclusion is wrong. I want to show that euthanasia is wrong. It is inherently wrong, but it is also wrong judged from the standpoints of self-interest and of practical effects.

Before presenting my arguments to support this claim, it would be well to define "euthanasia." An essential aspect of euthanasia is that it involves taking a human life, either one's own or that of another. Also, the person whose life is taken must be someone who is believed to be suffering from some disease or injury from which recovery cannot reasonably be expected. Finally, the action must be deliberate and intentional. Thus, euthanasia is intentionally taking the life of a presumably hopeless person. Whether the life is one's own or that of another, the taking of it is still euthanasia.

It is important to be clear about the deliberate and intentional aspect of the killing. If a hopeless person is given an injection of the wrong drug by mistake and this causes his death, this is wrongful killing but not euthanasia. The killing cannot be the result of accident. Furthermore, if the person is given an injection of a drug that is believed to be necessary to treat his disease or better his condition and the person dies as a result, then this is neither wrongful killing nor euthanasia. The intention was to make the patient well, not kill him. Similarly, when a patient's condition is such that it is not reasonable to hope that any medical procedures or treatments will save his life, a failure to implement the procedures or treatments is not euthanasia. If the person dies, this will be as a result of his injuries or disease and not because of his failure to receive treatment.

From J. Gay-Williams, "The Wrongfulness of Euthanasia," in Ronald Munson, ed., *Intervention and Reflection: Basic Issues in Medical Ethics*, 5th ed. (Wadsworth, 1995). Copyright © 1979 by Ronald Munson. Reprinted by permission.

The failure to continue treatment after it has been realized that the patient has little chance of benefitting from it has been characterized by some as "passive euthanasia." This phrase is misleading and mistaken.[2] In such cases, the person involved is not killed (the first essential aspect of euthanasia), nor is the death of the person intended by the withholding of additional treatment (the third essential aspect of euthanasia). The aim may be to spare the person additional and unjustifiable pain, to save him from the indignities of hopeless manipulations, and to avoid increasing the financial and emotional burden of the family. When I buy a pencil it is so that I can use it to write, not to contribute to an increase in the gross national product. This may be the unintended consequence of my action, but it is not the aim of my action. So it is with failing to continue the treatment of a dying person. I intend his death no more than I intend to reduce the GNP by not using medical supplies. His is an unintended dying, and so-called "passive euthanasia" is not euthanasia at all.

1. THE ARGUMENT FROM NATURE

Every human being has a natural inclination to continue living. Our reflexes and responses fit us to fight attackers, flee wild animals, and dodge out of the way of trucks. In our daily lives we exercise the caution and care necessary to protect ourselves. Our bodies are similarly structured for survival right down to the molecular level. When we are cut, our capillaries seal shut, our blood clots, and fibrogen is produced to start the process of healing the wound. When we are invaded by bacteria, antibodies are produced to fight against the alien organisms, and their remains are swept out of the body by special cells designed for clean-up work.

Euthanasia does violence to this natural goal of survival. It is literally acting against nature because all the processes of nature are bent towards the end of bodily survival. Euthanasia defeats these subtle mechanisms in a way that, in a particular case, disease and injury might not.

It is possible, but not necessary, to make an appeal to revealed religion in this connection.[3] Man as trustee of his body acts against God, its rightful possessor, when he takes his own life. He also violates the commandment to hold life sacred and never to take it without just and compelling cause. But since this appeal will persuade only those who are prepared to accept that religion has access to revealed truths, I shall not employ this line of argument.

It is enough, I believe, to recognize that the organization of the human body and our patterns of behavioral responses make the continuation of life a natural goal. By reason alone, then, we can recognize that euthanasia sets us against our own nature.[4] Furthermore, in doing so, euthanasia does violence to our dignity. Our dignity comes from seeking our ends. When one of our goals is survival, and actions are taken that eliminate the goal, then our natural dignity suffers. Unlike animals, we are conscious through reason of our nature and our ends. Euthanasia involves acting as if this dual nature—inclination towards survival and awareness of this as an end—did not exist. Thus, euthanasia denies our basic human character and requires that we regard ourselves or others as something less than fully human.

2. THE ARGUMENT FROM SELF-INTEREST

The above arguments are, I believe, sufficient to show that euthanasia is inherently wrong. But there are reasons for considering it wrong when judged by standards other than reason. Because death is final and irreversible, euthanasia contains within it the possibility that we will work against our own interest if we practice it or allow it to be practiced on us.

Contemporary medicine has high standards of excellence and a proven record of accomplishment, but it does not possess perfect and complete knowledge. A mistaken diagnosis is possible, and so is a mistaken prognosis. Consequently, we may believe that we are dying of a disease when, as a matter of fact, we may not be. We may think that we have no hope of recovery when, as a matter of fact, our chances are quite good. In such circumstances, if euthanasia were permitted, we would die needlessly. Death is final and the chance of error too great to approve the practice of euthanasia.

Also, there is always the possibility that an experimental procedure or a hitherto untried technique will pull us through. We should at least keep this option open, but euthanasia closes it off. Furthermore, spontaneous remission does occur in many cases. For no apparent reason, a patient simply recovers when those all around him, including his physicians, expected him to die. Euthanasia would just guarantee their expectations and leave no room for the "miraculous" recoveries that frequently occur.

Finally, knowing that we can take our life at any time (or ask another to take it) might well incline us to give up too easily. The will to live is strong in all of us, but it can be weakened by pain and suffering and feelings of hopelessness. If during a bad time we allow ourselves to be killed, we never have a chance to reconsider. Recovery from a serious illness requires that we fight for it, and anything that weakens our determination by suggesting that there is an easy way out is ultimately against our own interest. Also, we may be inclined towards euthanasia because of our concern for others. If we see our sickness and suffering as an emotional and financial burden on our family, we may feel that to leave our life is to make their lives easier.[5] The very presence of the possibility of euthanasia may keep us from surviving when we might.

3. THE ARGUMENT FROM PRACTICAL EFFECTS

Doctors and nurses are, for the most part, totally committed to saving lives. A life lost is, for them, almost a personal failure, an insult to their skills and knowledge. Euthanasia as a practice might well alter this. It could have a corrupting influence so that in any case that is severe doctors and nurses might not try hard enough to save the patient. They might decide that the patient would simply be "better off dead" and take the steps necessary to make that come about. This attitude could then carry over to their dealings with patients less seriously ill. The result would be an overall decline in the quality of medical care.

Finally, euthanasia as a policy is a slippery slope. A person apparently hopelessly ill may be allowed to take his own life. Then he may be permitted to deputize others to do it for him should he no longer be able to act. The judgment of others then becomes the ruling factor.

Already at this point euthanasia is not personal and voluntary, for others are acting "on behalf of" the patient as they see fit. This may well incline them to act on behalf of other patients who have not authorized them to exercise their judgment. It is only a short step, then, from voluntary euthanasia (self-inflicted or authorized), to directed euthanasia administered to a patient who has given no authorization, to involuntary euthanasia conducted as part of a social policy.[6] Recently many psychiatrists and sociologists have argued that we define as "mental illness" those forms of behavior that we disapprove of.[7] This gives us license then to lock up those who display the behavior. The category of the "hopelessly ill" provides the possibility of even worse abuse. Embedded in a social policy, it would give society or its representatives the authority to eliminate all those who might be considered too "ill" to function normally any longer. The dangers of euthanasia are too great to all to run the risk of approving it in any form. The first slippery step may well lead to a serious and harmful fall.

I hope that I have succeeded in showing why the benevolence that inclines us to give approval of euthanasia is misplaced. Euthanasia is inherently wrong because it violates the nature and dignity of human beings. But even those who are not convinced by this must be persuaded that the potential personal and social dangers inherent in euthanasia are sufficient to forbid our approving it either as a personal practice or as a public policy.

Suffering is surely a terrible thing, and we have a clear duty to comfort those in need and to ease their suffering when we can. But suffering is also a natural part of life with values for the individual and for others that we should not overlook. We may legitimately seek for others and for ourselves an easeful death, as Arthur Dyck has pointed out.[8] Euthanasia, however, is not just an easeful death. It is a wrongful death. Euthanasia is not just dying. It is killing.

NOTES

1. For a sophisticated defense of this position see Philippa Foot, "Euthanasia," *Philosophy and Public Affairs*, vol. 6 (1977), pp. 85–112. Foot does not endorse the radical conclusion that euthanasia, voluntary and involuntary, is always right.

2. James Rachels rejects the distinction between active and passive euthanasia as morally irrelevant in his "Active and Passive Euthanasia," *New England Journal of Medicine*, vol. 292, pp. 78–80. But see the criticism by Foot, pp. 100–103.

3. For a defense of this view see J.V. Sullivan, "The Immorality of Euthanasia," in Marvin Kohl, ed., *Beneficent Euthanasia* (Buffalo, New York: Prometheus Books, 1975), pp. 34–44.

4. This point is made by Ray V. McIntyre in "Voluntary Euthanasia: The Ultimate Perversion," *Medical Counterpoint*, vol. 2, pp. 26–29.

5. See McIntyre, p. 28.

6. See Sullivan, "The Immorality of Euthanasia," pp. 34–44, for a fuller argument in support of this view.

7. See, for example, Thomas S. Szasz, *The Myth of Mental Illness*, rev. ed. (New York: Harper & Row, 1974).

8. Arthur Dyck, "Beneficent Euthanasia and Benemortasia," Kohl; *op. cit.*, pp. 117–129.

NO

Richard Brandt

A MORAL PRINCIPLE ABOUT KILLING

One of the Ten Commandments states: "Thou shalt not kill." The commandment does not supply an object for the verb, but the traditional Catholic view has been that the proper object of the verb is "innocent human beings" (except in cases of extreme necessity), where "innocent" is taken to exclude persons convicted of a capital crime or engaged in an unjust assault aimed at killing, such as members of the armed forces of a country prosecuting an unjust war. Thus construed, the prohibition is taken to extend to suicide and abortion. (There is a qualification: that we are not to count cases in which the death is not wanted for itself or intended as a *means* to a goal that is wanted for itself, provided that in either case the aim of the act is the avoidance of some evil greater than the death of the person.) Can this view that all killing of innocent human beings is morally wrong be defended, and if not, what alternative principle can be?

This question is one the ground rules for answering which are far from a matter of agreement. I should myself be content if a principle were identified that could be shown to be one that would be included in any moral system that rational and benevolent persons would support for a society in which they expected to live. Apparently others would not be so content; so in what follows I shall simply aim to make some observations that I hope will identify a principle with which the consciences of intelligent people will be comfortable. I believe the rough principle I will suggest is also one that would belong to the moral system rational and benevolent people would want for their society.

Let us begin by reflecting on what it is to kill. The first thing to notice is that *kill* is a biological term. For example, a weed may be killed by being sprayed with a chemical. The verb *kill* involves essentially the broad notion of death —the change from the state of being biologically alive to the state of being dead. It is beyond my powers to give any general characterization of this transition, and it may be impossible to give one. If there is one, it is one that human beings, flies, and ferns all share; and to kill is in some sense to bring that transition about. The next thing to notice is that at least human beings do not live forever, and hence killing a human being at a given time must

From Richard Brandt, "A Moral Principle About Killing," in Marvin Kohl, ed., *Beneficent Euthanasia* (Prometheus Books, 1975). Copyright © 1975 by Prometheus Books, Inc. Reprinted by permission.

be construed as *advancing the date* of its death, or as *shortening its life*. Thus it may be brought about that the termination of the life of a person occurs at the time *t* instead of at the time *t* + *k*. Killing is thus shortening the span of organic life of something.

There is a third thing to notice about *kill*. It is a term of causal agency and has roots in the legal tradition. As such, it involves complications. For instance, suppose I push a boulder down a mountainside, aiming it at a person X and it indeed strikes X, and he is dead after impact and not before (and not from a coincidental heart attack); in that case we would say that I killed X. On the other hand, suppose I tell Y that X is in bed with Y's wife, and Y hurries to the scene, discovers them, and shoots X to death; in that case, although the unfolding of events from my action may be as much a matter of causal law as the path of the boulder, we should *not* say that I killed X. Fortunately, for the purpose of principles of the morally right, we can sidestep such complications. For suppose I am choosing whether to do *A* or *B* (where one or the other of these "acts" may be construed as essentially *in*action—for example, *not* doing what I know is the one thing that will *prevent* someone's death); then it is enough if I know, or have reason to think it highly probable, that were I to do *A*, a state of the world including the death of some person or persons would ensue, whereas were I to do *B*, a state of the world of some specified different sort would ensue. If a moral principle will tell me in this case whether I am to do *A* or *B*, that is all I need. It could be that a moral principle would tell me that I am absolutely never to perform any action *A*, such that were I to do it the death of some innocent human being would

ensue, provided there is some alternative action I might perform, such that were I to do it no such death would ensue.

It is helpful, I think, to reformulate the traditional Catholic view in a way that preserves the spirit and intent of that view (although some philosophers would disagree with this assessment) and at the same time avoids some conceptions that are both vague and more appropriate to a principle about when a person is morally blameworthy for doing something than to a principle about what a person ought morally to do. The terminology I use goes back, in philosophical literature, to a phrase introduced by W. D. Ross, but the conception is quite familiar. The alternative proposal is that there is a *strong prima facie obligation* not to kill any human being except in justifiable self-defense; in the sense (of prima facie) that it is morally *wrong* to kill any human being except in justifiable self-defense *unless* there is an even stronger prima facie moral obligation to do something that cannot be done without killing. (The term *innocent* can now be omitted, since if a person is not innocent, there may be a stronger moral obligation that can only be discharged by killing him; and this change is to the good since it is not obvious that we have no prima facie obligation to avoid killing people even if they are not innocent.) This formulation has the result that sometimes, to decide what is morally right, we have to compare the stringencies of conflicting moral obligations—and that is an elusive business; but the other formulation either conceals the same problem by putting it in another place, or else leads to objectionable implications. (Consider one implication of the traditional formulation, for a party of spelunkers in a cave by the oceanside. It is found that a rising tide is bringing water into the cave and all will be drowned unless they escape at once. Unfortunately, the first man to try to squeeze through the exit is fat and gets wedged inextricably in the opening, with his head inside the cave. Somebody in the party has a stick of dynamite. Either they blast the fat man out, killing him, or all of them, including him, will drown. The traditional formulation leads to the conclusion that all must drown.)

Let us then consider the principle: "There is a strong prima facie moral obligation not to kill any human being except in justifiable self-defense." I do not believe we want to accept this principle without further qualification; indeed, its status seems not to be that of a basic principle at all, but derivative from some more-basic principles. W. D. Ross listed what he thought were the main basic prima facie moral obligations; it is noteworthy that he listed a prima facie duty not to *cause injury*, but he did not include an obligation not to kill. Presumably this was no oversight. He might have thought that killing a human being is always an injury, so that the additional listing of an obligation not to kill would be redundant; but he might also have thought that killing is sometimes *not* an injury and that it is prima facie obligatory not to kill only when, and because, so doing would injure a sentient being.

What might be a noninjurious killing? If I come upon a cat that has been mangled but not quite killed by several dogs and is writhing in pain, and I pull myself together and put it out of its misery, I have killed the cat but surely not *injured* it. I do not injure something by relieving its pain. If someone is being tortured and roasted to death and I know he wishes nothing more than a merciful

termination of life, I have not injured him if I shoot him; I have done him a favor. In general, it seems I have not injured a person if I treat him in a way in which he would want me to treat him if he were fully rational, or in a way to which he would be indifferent if he were fully rational. (I do not think that terminating the life of a human fetus in the third month is an injury; I admit this view requires discussion.[1])

Consider another type of killing that is not an injury. Consider the case of a human being who has become unconscious and will not, it is known, regain consciousness. He is in a hospital and is being kept alive only through expensive supportive measures. Is there a strong prima facie moral obligation not to withdraw these measures and not to take positive steps to terminate his life? It seems obvious that if he is on the only kidney machine and its use could *save* the life of another person, who would lead a normal life after temporary use, it would be wrong not to take him off. Is there an obligation to continue, or not to terminate, if there is no countering obligation? I would think not, with an exception to be mentioned; and this coincides with the fact that he is *beyond* injury. There is also not an obligation *not* to preserve his life, say, in order to have his organs available for use when they are needed.

There seems, however, to be another morally relevant consideration in such a case—knowledge of the patient's own wishes when he was conscious and in possession of his faculties. Suppose he had feared such an eventuality and prepared a sworn statement requesting his doctor to terminate his life at once in such circumstances. Now, if it is morally obligatory to some degree to carry out a person's wishes for disposal of his body and possessions after his death, it would seem to be equally morally obligatory to respect his wishes in case he becomes a "vegetable." In the event of the existence of such a document, I would think that if he can no longer be injured we are free to withdraw life-sustaining measures and also to take positive steps to terminate life—and are even morally bound, prima facie, to do so. (If, however, the patient had prepared a document directing that his body be preserved alive as long as possible in such circumstances, then there would be a prima facie obligation *not* to cease life-sustaining measures and not to terminate. It would seem obvious, however, that such an obligation would fall far short of giving the patient the right to continued use of a kidney machine when its use by another could save that person's life.) Some persons would not hesitate to discontinue life-sustaining procedures in such a situation, but would balk at more positive measures. But the hesitation to use more positive procedures, which veterinarians employ frequently with animals, is surely nothing but squeamishness; if a person is in the state described, there can be no injury to him in positive termination more than or less than that in allowing him to wither by withdrawing life-supportive procedures.

If I am right in my analysis of this case, we must phrase our basic principle about killing in such a way as to take into account (1) whether the killing would be an injury and (2) the person's own wishes and directives. And perhaps, more important, any moral principle about killing must be viewed simply as an implicate of more basic principles about these matters.

Let us look for corroboration of this proposal to how we feel about another type of case, one in which termination would be of positive benefit to the agent. Let us suppose that a patient has a terminal illness and is in severe pain, subject only to brief remissions, with no prospect of any event that could make his life good, either in the short or long term. It might seem that here, with the patient in severe pain, at least life-supportive measures should be discontinued, or positive termination adopted. But I do not think we would accept this inference, for in this situation the patient, let us suppose, has his preferences and is able to express them. The patient may have strong religious convictions and prefer to go on living despite the pain; if so, surely there is a prima facie moral obligation not positively to terminate his life. Even if, as seemingly in this case, the situation is one in which it would be *rational* for the agent, from the point of view of his own welfare, to direct termination of his life,[2] it seems that if he (irrationally) does the opposite, there is a prima facie moral obligation not to terminate and some prima facie obligation to sustain it. Evidently a person's own expressed wishes have moral force. (I believe, however, that we think a person's expressed wishes have *less* moral force when we think the wishes are irrational.)

What is the effect, in this case, if the patient himself expresses a preference for termination and would, if he were given the means, terminate his own existence? Is there a prima facie obligation to sustain his life—and pain—against his will? Surely not. Or is there an obligation *not* to take positive measures to terminate his life immediately, thereby saving the patient much discomfort? Again, surely not. What possible reason could be offered to justify the claim that the answer is affirmative, beyond theological ones about God's will and our being bound to stay alive at His pleasure? The only argument I can think of is that there is some consideration of public policy, to the effect that a recognition of such moral permission might lead to abuses or to some other detriment to society in the long run. Such an argument does seem weak.

It might be questioned whether a patient's request should be honored, if made at a time when he is in pain, on the grounds that it is not rational. (The physician may be in a position to see, however, that the patient is quite right about his prospects and that his personal welfare would be maximized by termination.) It might also be questioned whether a patient's formal declaration, written earlier, requesting termination if he were ever in his present circumstances, should be honored, on the grounds that at the earlier time he did not know what it would be like to be in his present situation. It would seem odd, however, if *no* circumstances are identifiable in which a patient's request for termination is deemed to have moral force, when his request *not* to terminate is thought morally weighty in the same circumstances, even when this request is clearly irrational. I think we may ignore such arguments and hold that, in a situation in which it is rational for a person to choose termination of his life, his expressed wish is morally definitive and removes both the obligation to sustain life and the obligation not to terminate.

Indeed, there is a question whether or not in these circumstances a physician has not a moral obligation at least to withdraw life-supporting measures, and perhaps positively to terminate life. At least there seems to be a general moral obligation to render assistance when a person is in need, when it can be given at small cost to oneself, and when it is requested. The obligation is the stronger when one happens to be the only person in a position to receive such a request or to know about the situation. Furthermore, the physician has acquired a special obligation if there has been a long-standing personal relationship with the patient—just as a friend or relative has special obligations. But since we are discussing not the possible obligation to terminate but the obligation *not* to terminate, I shall not pursue this issue.

The patient's own expression of preference or consent, then, seems to be weighty. But suppose he is unable to express his preference; suppose that his terminal disease not only causes him great pain but has attacked his brain in such a way that he is incapable of thought and of rational speech. May the physician, then, after consultation, take matters into his own hands? We often think we know what is best for another, but we think one person should not make decisions for another. Just as we must respect the decision of a person who has decided after careful reflection that he wants to commit suicide, so we must not take the liberty of deciding to bring another's life to a close contrary to his wishes. So what may be done? Must a person suffer simply because he cannot express consent? There is evidence that can be gathered about what conclusions a person would draw if he were in a state to draw and express them. The patient's friends will have some recollection of things he has said in the past, of his values and general ethical views. Just as we can have good reason to think, for example, that he would vote Democratic if voting for president in a certain year, so we can have good reason to think he would take a certain stand about the termination of his own life in various circumstances. We can know of some persons who because of their religious views would want to keep on living until natural processes bring their lives to a close. About others we can know that they decidedly would not take this view. We can also know what would be the *rational* choice for them to make, and our knowledge of this can be *evidence* about what they would request if they were able. There are, of course, practical complications in the mechanics of a review board of some kind making a determination of this sort, but they are hardly insurmountable.

I wish to consider one other type of case, that of a person who, say, has had a stroke and is leading, and for some time can continue to lead, a life that is comfortable but one on a very low level, *and* who has antecedently requested that his life be terminated if he comes, incurably, into such a situation. May he then be terminated? In this case unlike the others, there are probably ongoing pleasant experiences, perhaps on the level of some animals, that seem to be a good thing. One can hardly say that *injury* is being done such a person by keeping him alive; and one might say that some slight injury is being done him by terminating his existence. There is a real problem here. Can the (slight) goodness of these experiences stand against the weight of an earlier firm declaration requesting that life be terminated in a situation of hopeless senility? There is no *injury* in keeping the person alive despite his request, but there seems something *indecent* about keeping a mind alive after a severe stroke, when we know quite well that, could he have anticipated it, his own action would have been to terminate

his life. I think that the person's own request should be honored; it should be if a person's expressed preferences have as much moral weight as I think they should have.

What general conclusions are warranted by the preceding discussion? I shall emphasize two. First, there is a prima facie obligation *not* to terminate a person's existence when this would injure him (except in cases of self-defense or of senility of a person whose known wish is to be terminated in such a condition) *or* if he wishes not to be terminated. Second, there is *not* a prima facie obligation not to terminate when there would be *no* injury, or when there would be a positive benefit (release from pain) in so doing, provided the patient has not declared himself otherwise or there is evidence that his wishes are to that effect. Obviously there are two things that are decisive for the morality of terminating a person's life: whether so doing would be *injury* and whether it conforms to what is known of his *preferences*.

I remarked at the outset that I would be content with some moral principles if it could be made out that rational persons would want those principles incorporated in the consciences of a group among whom they were to live. It is obvious why rational persons would want these principles. They would want injury avoided both because they would not wish others to injure them and because, if they are benevolent, they would not wish others injured. Moreover, they would want weight given to a person's own known preferences. Rational people do want the decision about the termination of their lives, where that is possible; for they would be uncomfortable if they thought it possible that others would be free to terminate their lives without consent. The threat of serious illness is bad enough without that prospect. On the other hand, this discomfort would be removed if they know that termination would not be undertaken on their behalf without their explicit consent, except after a careful inquiry had been made, both into whether termination would constitute an injury and whether they would request termination under the circumstances if they were in a position to do so.

If I am right in all this, then it appears that killing a person is not something that is just prima facie wrong *in itself*; it is wrong roughly only if and because it is an *injury* of someone, or if and because it is contrary to the *known preferences* of someone. It would seem that a principle about the prima facie wrongness of killing is *derivative* from principles about when we are prima facie obligated not to injure and when we are prima facie obligated to respect a person's wishes, at least about what happens to his own body. I do not, however, have any suggestions for a general statement of principles of this latter sort.

NOTES

1. See my "The Morality of Abortion" in *The Monist*, 56 (1972), pp. 503–26; and, in revised form, in a forthcoming volume edited by R. L. Perkins.

2. See my "The Morality and Rationality of Suicide," in James Rachels, ed., *Moral Problems* (in press); and, in revised form, in E. S. Shneidman, ed., *Suicidology: Current Developments* (forthcoming).

POSTSCRIPT

Is Euthanasia Immoral?

One of the puzzles in the euthanasia debate is whether or not there is a morally significant difference between active euthanasia and passive euthanasia. The difference between these two is that in the first case one takes active measures in order to bring about death, while in the latter case one passively allows death to happen (although it is possible that one could prevent the death). An example of the first case would be the shooting of the physicist that was mentioned in the introduction to this issue. An example of the latter case would be the failure to operate on a patient when the operation could be lifesaving. Take the example of a baby born with several physical and mental problems who is allowed to die because a relatively routine operation that would make food digestion possible is not performed. Parents may withhold permission for surgery in such cases because, although alive after the surgery, the baby would remain disabled.

Much of the popular discussion about euthanasia refers to "pulling the plug" on life-support systems. Is this passive euthanasia because the patient is then allowed to die of natural causes, or is it active euthanasia because if the action of pulling the plug were not taken, the patient would still be alive? James Rachels has challenged the supposition that active euthanasia is morally worse than passive euthanasia in an important article, "Active and Passive Euthanasia," *The New England Journal of Medicine* (January 9, 1975). See also Bonnie Steinbock and Alastair Norcross, eds., *Killing and Letting Die*, 2d ed. (Fordham University Press, 1994).

Moral, legal, and social questions concerning euthanasia are discussed in Carol Wekesser, ed., *Euthanasia: Opposing Viewpoints* (Greenhaven Press, 1995); Melvin I. Urofsky and Philip E. Urofsky, eds., *The Right to Die: A Two-Volume Anthology of Scholarly Articles*, 2 vols. (Garland, 1995); John Keown, ed., *Euthanasia Examined: Ethical, Clinical and Legal Perspectives* (Cambridge University Press, 1995); and Tom L. Beauchamp and Robert M. Veatch, eds., *Ethical Issues in Death and Dying*, 2d ed. (Prentice Hall, 1996).

See also James M. Humber, Robert F. Almeder, and Gregg A. Kasting, eds., *Physician-Assisted Death* (Humana Press, 1994); Tom Beauchamp, ed., *Intending Death: The Ethics of Assisted Suicide and Euthanasia* (Prentice Hall, 1996); Steve Hallock, "Physician-Assisted Suicide: 'Slippery Slope' or Civil Right?" *The Humanist* (July/August 1996); and Leon R. Kass and Nelson Lund, "Courting Death: Assisted Suicide, Doctors, and the Law," *Commentary* (December 1996). Margaret Pabst Battin's *The Least Worst Death: Essays in Bioethics on the End of Life* (Oxford University Press, 1994) includes discussions of suicide, physician-assisted suicide, and euthanasia in the Netherlands.

ISSUE 15

Is Affirmative Action Fair?

YES: Albert G. Mosley, from "Affirmative Action: Pro," in Albert G. Mosley and Nicholas Capaldi, *Affirmative Action: Social Justice or Unfair Preference?* (Rowman & Littlefield, 1996)

NO: Nicholas Capaldi, from "Affirmative Action: Con," in Albert G. Mosley and Nicholas Capaldi, *Affirmative Action: Social Justice or Unfair Preference?* (Rowman & Littlefield, 1996)

ISSUE SUMMARY

YES: Professor of philosophy Albert G. Mosley argues that affirmative action is a continuation of the history of black progress since the *Brown v. Board of Education* desegregation decision of 1954 and the Civil Rights Bill of 1964. He defends affirmative action as a "benign use of race."

NO: Professor of philosophy Nicholas Capaldi argues that affirmative action is a vague notion but when suitably defined, it is illegal and without moral justification. Moreover, affirmative action policies lead to reverse discrimination and violate the fundamental norm of individualism.

Throughout history, women and minority groups have been discriminated against in the United States. However, it might be difficult for many of us today to appreciate the extent of past discrimination and the ways in which social, legal, and political institutions were discriminatory.

Slavery is probably the most blatant form of past racism. We know that people were bought and sold, but the words are so familiar that the realities they stand for may never rise to consciousness. Many particular events and experiences lie behind a simple word like *slavery*. For example, the importation of slaves to this country was illegal before slaveholding itself became so. When ships at sea bringing African slaves to America found themselves in danger of being confronted by the law, it was easy to do what smugglers on the high seas always do with their contraband: the blacks, chained together and weighted down, were dropped overboard. Even after the Civil War, blacks were denied the right to vote, to testify in court, to own land, or to make contracts. In many states, laws restricted blacks in every conceivable aspect of their lives, including education, employment, and housing.

With respect to discrimination against women, consider the following, written by U.S. Supreme Court justice Joseph Bradley in concurring with the Court's decision in *Bradwell v. Illinois* (1873) that the state of Illinois was justified in denying Myra Bradwell a license to practice law on the grounds that she was a woman:

> [T]he civil law, as well as nature herself, has always recognized a wide difference in the respective spheres and destinies of man and woman. Man is, or should be, woman's protector and defender. The natural and proper timidity and delicacy which belongs to the female sex evidently unfits it for many of the occupations of civil life. The constitution of the family organization, which is founded in the divine ordinance, as well as in the nature of things, indicates the domestic sphere as that which properly belongs to the domain and functions of womanhood. The harmony ... of interests and views which belong ... to the family institution is repugnant to the idea of a woman adopting a distinct and independent career from that of her husband.... The paramount destiny and mission of woman are to fulfill the noble and benign offices of wife and mother.

Such thoughts are rarely openly expressed these days, and segregation and discrimination do not have legal support. One wonders, though, how much attitudes have actually changed. The law can change, but old attitudes can persist, and they can even be preserved and passed down from generation to generation. Moreover, the results of past social injustices are with us today.

Some of the consequences of past discrimination are systemic rather than individual-based. However much *individuals* might reject certain attitudes and practices of the past, there will usually be some *systemic* problems that are not so easily eliminated. There are systemic consequences of racist and sexist practices in the professions, in housing, in education, in the distribution of wealth, etc. For example, even if previously "white only" schools take down their "white only" signs, and the individuals involved agree to accept applicants of any race, the school system itself would be left virtually unchanged from its segregationist days. The situation of white-only schools would systematically perpetuate itself. This is where many feel that affirmative action can step in and change the system.

Albert G. Mosley places controversies surrounding affirmative action in a historical context and considers the justification of affirmative action both from the "backward-looking" perspective of corrective justice and from the "forward-looking" perspective of the social distribution of harms and benefits. Nicholas Capaldi seriously questions the meaning of the phrase "affirmative action" and argues that in any but the most innocuous sense, affirmative action is illegal and immoral.

YES

Albert G. Mosley

AFFIRMATIVE ACTION: PRO

LEGISLATIVE AND JUDICIAL BACKGROUND

In 1941, Franklin Roosevelt issued Executive Order 8802 banning discrimination in employment by the federal government and defense contractors. Subsequently, many bills were introduced in Congress mandating equal employment opportunity but none were passed until the Civil Rights Act of 1964. The penalty for discrimination in Executive Order 8802 and the bills subsequently proposed was that the specific victim of discrimination be "made whole," that is, put in the position he or she would have held were it not for the discriminatory act, including damages for lost pay and legal expenses.

The contemporary debate concerning affirmative action can be traced to the landmark decision of *Brown v. Board of Education* (1954), whereby local, state, and federal ordinances enforcing segregation by race were ruled unconstitutional. In subsequent opinions, the Court ruled that state-mandated segregation in libraries, swimming pools, and other publicly funded facilities was also unconstitutional. In *Swann v. Charlotte-Mecklenburg* (1971), the Court declared that "in order to prepare students to live in a pluralistic society" school authorities might implement their desegregation order by deciding that "each school should have a prescribed ratio of Negro to White students reflecting the proportion for the district as a whole."[1] The ratio was not to be an inflexible one, but should reflect local variations in the ratio of Whites to Blacks. But any predominantly one-race school in a district with a mixed population and a history of segregation was subject to "close scrutiny." This requirement was attacked by conservatives as imposing a "racial quota," a charge that reverberates in the contemporary debate concerning affirmative action.

With the Montgomery bus boycotts of the mid-1950s, Blacks initiated an era of nonviolent direct action to publicly protest unjust laws and practices that supported racial discrimination. The graphic portrayals of repression and violence produced by the civil rights movement precipitated a national revulsion against the unequal treatment of African Americans. Blacks demanded their constitutional right to participate in the political process and share equal access to public accommodations, government-supported programs, and employment opportunities. But as John F. Kennedy stated in an address to Congress: "There is little value in a Negro's obtaining the right to be admitted to hotels and restaurants if he has no cash in his pocket and no job."[2]

Kennedy stressed that the issue was not merely eliminating discrimination, but eliminating as well the oppressive economic and social burdens imposed on Blacks by racial discrimination.[3] To this end, he advocated a weak form of affirmative action, involving eliminating discrimination and expanding educational and employment opportunities (including apprenticeships and on-the-job training). The liberal vision was that, given such opportunities, Blacks would move up the economic ladder to a degree relative to their own merit. Thus, a principal aim of the Civil Rights Act of 1964 was to effect a redistribution of social, political, and economic benefits and to provide legal remedies for the denial of individual rights.

THE CIVIL RIGHTS ACT OF 1964

The first use of the phrase "affirmative action" is found in Executive Order 10952, issued by President John F. Kennedy in 1961. This order established the Equal Employment Opportunity Commission (EEOC) and directed that contractors on projects funded, in whole or in part, with federal funds "take affirmative action to ensure that applicants are employed, and employees are treated during their employment, without regard to the race, creed, color, or national origin."

As a result of continuing public outrage at the level of violence and animosity shown toward Blacks, a stronger version of the Civil Rights Bill was presented to the Congress than Kennedy had originally recommended. Advocates pointed out that Blacks suffered an unemployment rate that was twice that of Whites and that Black employment was concentrated in semiskilled and unskilled jobs. They emphasized that national prosperity would be improved by eliminating discrimination and integrating Black talent into its skilled and professional workforce.[4]

Fewer Blacks were employed in professional positions than had the requisite skills, and those Blacks who did occupy positions commensurate with their skill level had half the lifetime earnings of Whites. Such facts were introduced during legislative hearings to show the need to more fully utilize and reward qualified Blacks throughout the labor force, and not merely in the unskilled and semiskilled sectors....

CONCEPTUAL ISSUES

There are many interests that governments pursue—maximization of social production; equitable distribution of rights, opportunities, and services; social safety and cohesion; restitution—and those interests may conflict in various situations. In particular, governments as well as their constituents have a prima facie obligation to satisfy the liabilities they incur. One such liability derives from past and present unjust exclusionary acts depriving minorities and women of opportunities and amenities made available to other groups.

"Backward looking" arguments defend affirmative action as a matter of *corrective justice,* where paradigmatically the harm-doer is to make restitution to the harmed so as to put the harmed in the position

the harmed most likely would have occupied had the harm not occurred. An important part of making restitution is the acknowledgment it provides that the actions causing injury were unjust and such actions will be curtailed and corrected. In this regard Bernard Boxill writes:

> Without the acknowledgement of error, the injurer implies that the injured has been treated in a manner that befits him.... In such a case, even if the unjust party repairs the damage he has caused... nothing can be demanded on legal or moral grounds, and the repairs made are gratuitous.... justice requires that we acknowledge that this treatment of others can be required of us; thus, where an unjust injury has occurred, the injurer reaffirms his belief in the other's equality by conceding that repair can be demanded of him, and the injured rejects the allegation of his inferiority... by demanding reparation.[5]

This view is based on the idea that restitution is a basic moral principle that creates obligations that are just as strong as the obligations to maximize wealth and distribute it fairly.[6] If x has deprived y of opportunities y had a right not to be deprived of in this manner, then x is obligated to return y to the position y would have occupied had x not intervened; x has this obligation irrespective of other obligations x may have....

[An] application of this principle involves the case where x is not a person but an entity, like a government or a business. If y was unjustly deprived of employment when firm F hired z instead of y because z was White and y Black, then y has a right to be made whole, that is, brought to the position he/she would have achieved had that deprivation not occurred. Typically, this involves giving y a position at least as good as the one he/she would have acquired originally and issuing back pay in the amount that y would have received had he/she been hired at the time of the initial attempt.

Most critics of preferential treatment acknowledge the applicability of principles of restitution to individuals in specific instances of discrimination. The strongest case is where y was as or more qualified than z in the initial competition, but the position was given to z because y was Black and z was White.[7] Subsequently, y may not be as qualified for an equivalent position as some new candidate z', but is given preference because of the past act of discrimination by F that deprived y of the position he or she otherwise would have received.

Some critics have suggested that, in such cases, z' is being treated unfairly. For z', as the most qualified applicant, has a right not to be excluded from the position in question purely on the basis of race; and y has a right to restitution for having unjustly been denied the position in the past. But the dilemma is one in appearance only. For having unjustly excluded y in the past, the current position that z' has applied for is not one that F is free to offer to the public. It is a position that is already owed to y, and is not available for open competition. Judith Jarvis Thompson makes a similar point:

> suppose two candidates [A and B] for a civil service job have equally good test scores, but there is only one job available. We could decide between them by coin-tossing. But in fact we do allow for declaring for A straightway, where A is a veteran, and B is not. It may be that B is a non-veteran through no fault of his own... Yet the fact is that B is not a veteran and A is. On the assumption

that the veteran has served his country, the country owes him something. And it is plain that giving him preference is not an unjust way in which part of that debt of gratitude can be paid.[8]

In a similar way, individual Blacks who have suffered from acts of unjust discrimination are owed something by the perpetrator(s) of such acts, and this debt takes precedence over the perpetrator's right to use his or her options to hire the most qualified person for the position in question.

Many White males have developed expectations about the likelihood of their being selected for educational, employment, and entrepreneurial opportunities that are realistic only because of the general exclusion of women and non-Whites as competitors for such positions. Individuals enjoying inflated odds of obtaining such opportunities because of racist and sexist practices are recipients of an "unjust enrichment."

Redistributing opportunities would clearly curtail benefits that many have come to expect. And given the frustration of their traditional expectations, it is understandable that they would feel resentment. But blocking traditional expectations is not unjust if those expectations conflict with the equally important moral duties of restitution and just distribution. It is a question, not of "is," but of "ought": not "Do those with decreased opportunities as a result of affirmative action feel resentment?" but "Should those with decreased opportunities as a result of affirmative action feel resentment?" ...

Since Title VII [of the Civil Rights Act of 1964] protects bona fide seniority plans, it forces the burden of rectification to be borne by Whites who are entering the labor force rather than Whites who are the direct beneficiaries of past discriminatory practices. Given this limitation placed on affirmative action remedies, the burden of social restitution may, in many cases, be borne by those who were not directly involved in past discriminatory practices. But it is generally not true that those burdened have not benefited at all from past discriminatory practices. For the latent effects of acts of invidious racial discrimination have plausibly bolstered and encouraged the efforts of Whites in roughly the same proportion as it inhibited and discouraged the efforts of Blacks. Such considerations are also applicable to cases where F discriminated against y in favor of z, but the make-whole remedy involves providing compensation to y' rather than y. This suggests that y' is an *undeserving beneficiary* of the preferential treatment meant to compensate for the unjust discrimination against y, just as z' above appeared to be the innocent victim forced to bear the burden that z benefited from. Many critics have argued that this misappropriation of benefits and burdens demonstrates the unfairness of compensation to groups rather than individuals. But it is important that the context and rationale for such remedies be appreciated.

In cases of "egregious" racial discrimination, not only is it true that F discriminated against a particular Black person y, but F's discrimination advertised a general disposition to discriminate against any other Black person who might seek such positions. The specific effect of F's unjust discrimination was that y was refused a position he or she would otherwise have received. The latent (or dispositional) effect of F's unjust discrimination was that many Blacks who otherwise would have sought such positions were discouraged from doing so. Thus, even if the specific y actually discriminated against can no longer be compensated, F has an obligation to take affirmative action to communicate to Blacks as a group that such positions are indeed open to them. After being found in violation of laws prohibiting racial discrimination, many agencies have disclaimed further discrimination while in fact continuing to do so.[9] In such cases, the courts have required the discriminating agencies to actually hire and/or promote Blacks who may not be as qualified as some current White applicants until Blacks approach the proportion in F's labor force they in all likelihood would have achieved had F's unjust discriminatory acts not deterred them.

Of course, what this proportion would have been is a matter of speculation. It may have been less than the proportion of Blacks available in the relevant labor pool from which applicants are drawn if factors other than racial discrimination act to depress the merit of such applicants. This point is made again and again by critics. Some, such as Thomas Sowell, argue that cultural factors often mitigate against Blacks meriting representation in a particular labor force in proportion to their presence in the pool of candidates looking for jobs or seeking promotions.[10] Others, such as Michael Levin, argue that cognitive deficits limit Blacks from being hired and promoted at a rate proportionate to their presence in the relevant labor pool.[11] What such critics reject is the assumption that, were it not for pervasive discrimination and overexploitation, Blacks would be equally represented in the positions in question. What is scarcely considered is the possibility that, were it not for racist exclusions, Blacks might be over rather than under represented in competitive positions.

Establishing Blacks' presence at a level commensurate with their proportion in the relevant labor market need not be seen as an attempt to actualize some valid prediction. Rather, given the impossibility of determining what level of representation Blacks would have achieved were it not for racist discrimination, the assumption of proportional representation is the only *fair* assumption to make. This is not to argue that Blacks should be maintained in such positions, but their contrived exclusion merits an equally contrived rectification.[12]

Racist acts excluding Blacks affected particular individuals, but were directed at affecting the behavior of the group of all those similar to the victim. Likewise, the benefits of affirmative action policies should not be conceived as limited in their effects to the specific individuals receiving them. Rather, those benefits should be conceived as extending to all those identified with the recipient, sending the message that opportunities are indeed available to qualified Black candidates who would have been excluded in the past.…

FORWARD-LOOKING JUSTIFICATIONS OF AFFIRMATIVE ACTION

… [Some] have defended preferential treatment but denied that it should be viewed as a form of reparation. This latter group rejects "backward looking" justifications of affirmative action and defends it instead on "forward-looking" grounds that include distributive justice, minimizing subordination, and maximizing social utility.

Thus, Ronald Fiscus argues that backward-looking arguments have distorted the proper justification for affirmative action policies.[13] Backward-looking arguments depend on the paradigm of traditional tort cases, where a specific individual x has deprived another individual y of a specific good t through an identifiable act a, and x is required to restore y to the position y would have had, had a not occurred. But typically, preferential treatment requires that x' (rather than x) restore y' (instead of y) with a good t' that y' supposedly would have achieved had y not been deprived of t by x. The displacement of perpetrator (x' for x) and victim (y' for y) gives rise to the problem of (1) White males who are innocent of acts having caused harm nonetheless being forced to provide restitution for such acts; and (2) Blacks who were not directly harmed by those acts nonetheless becoming the principal beneficiaries of restitution for those acts....

Fiscus argues that the backward-looking argument reinforces the perception that preferential treatment is unfair to innocent White males, and so long as this is the case, both the courts and the public are likely to oppose strong affirmative action policies such as quotas, set-asides, and other preferential treatment policies.

In contrast, Fiscus recommends that preferential treatment be justified in terms of distributive justice, which as a matter of equal protection, "requires that individuals be awarded the positions, advantages, or benefits they would have been awarded under fair conditions," that is, conditions under which racist exclusion would not have precluded Blacks from attaining "their deserved proportion of the society's important benefits." Conversely, "distributive justice also holds that individuals or groups may not claim positions, advantages, or benefits that they would not have been awarded under fair conditions."[14] These conditions jointly prohibit White males from claiming an unreasonable share of social benefits and protects White males from having to bear an unreasonable share of the redistributive burden.

Fiscus takes the position that any deviation between Blacks and Whites from strict proportionality in the distribution of current goods is evidence of racism. Thus, if Blacks were 20 percent of a particular population but held no positions in the police or fire departments, that is indicative of past and present racial discrimination....

Because the Equal Protection Clause of the Fourteenth Amendment protects citizens from statistical discrimination on the basis of race, the use of race as the principal reason for excluding certain citizens from benefits made available to other citizens is a violation of that person's constitutional rights. This was one basis for [Alan] Bakke's suit against the UC-Davis medical school's 16 percent minority set-aside for medical school admission. There were eighty-four seats out of the one hundred admission slots that he was eligible to fill, and he was excluded from competing for the other sixteen slots because of his race. On the basis of the standard criteria (GPA, MCAT scores, etc.), Bakke argued that he would have been admitted before any of the Black applicants admitted under the minority set-aside. He therefore claimed that he was being excluded from the additional places available because he was White.

Currently, Blacks have approximately 3.25 times fewer physicians than would be expected given their numbers in the population. Native Americans have 7 times fewer physicians than what would have been expected if intelligent, well-trained, and motivated Native Americans had tried to become physicians at the same rate as did European Americans.

For Fiscus, the underrepresentation of African and Native Americans among physicians and the maldistribution of medical resources to minority communities is clearly the effect of generations of racist exclusions.... Not only are qualified members of the oppressed group harmed by ... prejudice, but even more harmed are the many who would have been qualified but for injuries induced by racial prejudice.

For Fiscus, individuals of different races would have been as equally distributed in the social body as the molecules of a gas in a container and he identifies the belief in the inherent equality of races with the Equal Protection Clause of the Fourteenth Amendment.[15] In a world without racism, minorities would be represented among the top one hundred medical school applicants at UC-Davis in the same proportion as they were in the general population. Accordingly, because Bakke did not score among the top eighty-four Whites, he would not have qualified for admission. Thus, he had no right to the position he was contesting, and indeed if he were given such a position in lieu of awarding it to a minority, Bakke would be much like a person who had received stolen goods. "Individuals who have not personally harmed minorities may nevertheless be prevented from reaping the benefits of the harm inflicted by the society at large."[16]

Justice O'Connor has voiced skepticism toward the assumption that members of different races would "gravitate with mathematical exactitude to each employer or union absent unlawful discrimination."[17] She considers it

sheer speculation as to "how many minority students would have been admitted to the medical school at Davis absent past discrimination in educational opportunities."[18] I likewise consider it speculative to assume that races would be represented in every area in proportion to their proportion of the general population. But because it is impossible to reasonably predict what that distribution would have been absent racial discrimination, it is not mere speculation but morally fair practice to assume that it would have been the same as the proportion in the general population. Given the fact of legally sanctioned invidious racism against Blacks in U.S. history, the burden of proof should not be on the oppressed group to prove that it would be represented at a level proportionate to its presence in the general population. Rather, the burden of proof should be on the majority to show why its overrepresentation among the most well off is not the result of unfair competition imposed by racism. We are morally obligated to assume proportional representation until there are more plausible reasons than racism for assuming otherwise....

Thus, it should be the responsibility of the Alabama Department of Public Safety to show why no Blacks were members of its highway patrol as of 1970, even though Blacks were 25 percent of the relevant workforce in Alabama. It should be the responsibility of the company and the union to explain why there were no Blacks with seniority in the union at the Kaiser plant in Louisiana, although Blacks made up 39 percent of the surrounding population. Likewise, it should be the responsibility of the union to explain why no Blacks had been admitted to the Sheet Metal Workers' Union in New York City although minorities were 29 percent of the available workforce. If no alternative explanations are more plausible, then the assumption that the disparity in representation is the result of racism should stand.

The question should not be whether White males are innocent or guilty of racism or sexism, but whether they have a right to inflated odds of obtaining benefits relative to minorities and women. A White male is innocent only up to the point where he takes advantage of "a benefit he would not qualify for without the accumulated effects of racism. At that point he becomes an accomplice in, and a beneficiary of, society's racism. He becomes the recipient of stolen goods.[19] ...

Cass Sunstein also argues that the traditional compensation model based on the model of a discrete injury caused by one individual (the tort-feasor or defendant) and suffered by another individual (the plaintiff) is inadequate to capture the situation arising from racial and sexual discrimination.[20] With the traditional tortlike model, the situation existing prior to the injury is assumed to be noncontestable, and the purpose of restitution is to restore the injured party to the position that party would have occupied if the injury had not occurred. But in cases where the injury is not well defined, where neither defendant nor plaintiff are individuals connected by a discrete event, and where the position the injured party would have occupied but for the injury is unspecifiable, then in such cases dependence on the traditional model of compensatory justice is questionable.[21]

In contrast to the position taken by Fiscus, Sunstein argues that the claim that affirmative action and preferential treatment is meant to put individuals in the position they would have occupied

had their groups not been subject to racial and sexual discrimination is nonsensical: "What would the world look like if it had been unaffected by past discrimination on the basis of race and sex?... the question is unanswerable, not because of the absence of good social science, but because of the obscure epistemological status of the question itself."[22]

Affirmative action must be justified in terms of alternative conceptions of the purpose of legal intervention, and Sunstein recommends instead the notion of "risk management" (intended to offset increased risks faced by a group rather than compensate the injuries suffered by a particular individual) and the "principle of nousubordination" (whereby measures are taken to reverse a situation in which an irrelevant difference has been transformed by legally sanctioned acts of the state into a social disadvantage). The notion of risk management is meant to apply to cases where injuries are "individually small but collectively large" so that pursuing each case individually would be too costly both in terms of time and effort.[23] In such cases, those harmed may be unable to establish a direct causal link between their injuries and the plaintiff's actions. Thus, a person who develops a certain type of cancer associated with a toxin produced by a particular company might have developed that condition even in the absence of the company's negligent behavior. At most, they can argue that the company's actions caused an increased risk of injury, rather than any specific instance of that injury.

Harms suffered in this way systematically affect certain groups with higher frequency than other groups, without it being possible to establish causal links between the injuries of specific plaintiffs and the actions of the defendant.

Regulatory agencies should be designed to address harms that are the result of increased risks rather than of a discrete action.[24] One of their principle aims should be not to compensate each injured party (and only injured parties), "but instead to deter and punish the risk-creating behavior" by redistributing social goods.[25] ...

The principle of nonsubordination is meant to apply to cases where the existing distribution of wealth and opportunities between groups are the result of law rather than natural attributes.[26] The purpose of affirmative action from a forward-looking perspective should be to end social subordination and reverse the situation in which irrelevant differences have been, through social and legal structures, turned into systematic disadvantages operative in multiple spheres that diminish participation in democratic forms of life.[27] ...

> affirmative action does not appear an impermissible 'taking' of an antecedent entitlement. Because the existing distribution of benefits and burdens between Blacks and Whites and men and women is not natural ... and because it is in part a product of current laws and practices having discriminatory effects, it is not decisive if some Whites and men are disadvantaged as a result.[28]

A central question in the debate over affirmative action is the extent to which racial classifications are important in accomplishing the goal of relieving the subordinate status of minorities and women. Given the aim of improving safety in transportation, classifying people in terms of their race is rationally irrelevant, while classifying them in terms of their driving competency, visual acuity, and maturity is essential. On the other hand, given the aim of improving health care in Black neighborhoods, classifying applicants for medical school in terms of their race is, in addition to their academic and clinical abilities, a very relevant factor.

To illustrate, African Americans, Hispanics, and Native Americans make up 22 percent of the population but represent only 10 percent of entering medical students and 7 percent of practicing physicians. A number of studies have shown that underrepresented minority physicians are more likely than their majority counterparts to care for poor patients and patients of similar ethnicity. Indeed, "each ethnic group of patients was more likely to be cared for by a physician of their own ethnic background than by a physician of another ethnic background."[29] This suggests that sociocultural factors such as language, physical identity, personal background, and experiences are relevant factors in determining the kinds of communities in which a physician will establish a practice. If this is the case, then the race of a medical school applicant would be an important factor in providing medical services to certain underrepresented communities. Thus, while there might be some purposes for which race is irrelevant, there might be other purposes in which race is important (though perhaps not necessary) for achieving the end in view.[30] The remedy targets Blacks as a group because racially discriminatory practices were directed against Blacks as a group.[31]

... Preferential treatment programs are meant to offset the disadvantages imposed by racism so that Blacks are not forced to bear the principal costs of that error.

... To condemn polices meant to correct for racial barriers as themselves erecting barriers is to ignore the difference between action and reaction, cause and effect, aggression and self-defense. ...

CONCLUSION

Racism was directed against Blacks whether they were talented, average, or mediocre, and attenuating the effects of racism requires distributing remedies similarly. Affirmative action policies compensate for the harms of racism (overt and institutional) through antidiscrimination laws and preferential policies. Prohibiting the benign use of race as a factor in the award of educational, employment and business opportunities would eliminate compensation for past and present racism and reinforce the moral validity of the status quo, with Blacks overrepresented among the least well off and underrepresented among the most well off.

It has become popular to use affirmative action as a scapegoat for the increased vulnerability of the White working class. But it should be recognized that the civil rights revolution (in general) and affirmative action (in particular) has been beneficial, not just to Blacks, but also to Whites (e.g., women, the disabled, the elderly) who otherwise would be substantially more vulnerable than they are now.

Affirmative action is directed toward empowering those groups that have been adversely affected by past and present exclusionary practices. Initiatives to abolish preferential treatment would inflict a grave injustice on African Americans, for they signal a reluctance to acknowledge that the plight of African Americans is the result of institutional practices that require institutional responses.

NOTES

1. Kent Greenawalt, *Discrimination and Reverse Discrimination* (New York: Alfred A. Knopf, 1983), 129 ff.

2. Kathanne W. Greene, *Affirmative Action and Principles of Justice* (New York: Greenwood Press, 1989), 22.

3. Kennedy stated: "Even the complete elimination of racial discrimination in employment—a goal toward which this nation must strive—will not put a single unemployed Negro to work unless he has the skills required." Greene, *Affirmative Action*, 23.

4. Greene, *Affirmative Action*, 31.

5. Bernard Boxill, "The Morality of Reparation" in *Social Theory and Practice*, 2, no. 1, Spring 1972: 118–119. It is for such reasons that welfare programs are not sufficient to satisfy the claims of Blacks for restitution. Welfare programs contain no admission of the unjust violation of rights and seek merely to provide the basic means for all to pursue opportunities in the future.

6. I am presuming that most of us would recognize certain primae facie duties such as truth telling, promise keeping, restitution, benevolence, justice, nonmalficence as generally obligatory. See W. D. Ross, *The Right and the Good* (Oxford: Clarendon Press, 1930).

7. Even in the case where y was only as qualified as z, a fair method of choice between candidates should produce an equitable distribution of such positions between Blacks and Whites in the long run if not in the short.

8. Judith Jarvis Thompson, *Philosophy and Public Affairs* 2 (Summer 1973): 379–380.

9. *Sheet Metal Workers v. EEOC* (1986); *United States v. Paradise* (1987).

10. Thomas Sowell, *Ethnic America* (New York: Basic Books, 1981); *Preferential Policies: An International Perspective* (New York: William Morrow, 1990); For a recent critique of Sowell's position, see Christopher Jencks, *Rethinking Social Policy: Race, Poverty, and the Underclass* (New York: Harper, 1993) chap. 1.

11. Michael Levin, "Race, Biology, and Justice" in *Public Affairs Quarterly*, 8, no. 3 (July 1994). There are many good reasons for skepticism regarding the validity of using IQ as a measure of cognitive ability. See *The Bell Curve Wars* ed. Steven Fraser (New York: Basic Books, 1995); *The Bell Curve Debate* ed. by Russell Jacoby and Naomi Glauberman (New York: Times Books, 1995); Allan Chase, *The Legacy of Malthus* (Urbana: University of Illinois Press, 1980); Steven J. Gould, *The Mismeasure of Man* (New York: Norton, 1981); R. C. Lewontin, S. Rose, L. J. Kamin, *Not In Our Genes* (New York: Pantheon Books, 1984).

12. See Robert Fullinwider, *The Reverse Discrimination Controversy: A Moral and Legal Analysis* (Totowa, N.J.: Rowman & Littlefield, 1980), 117. Ronald

Fiscus, *The Constitutional Logic of Affirmative Action* (Durham, N.C.: Duke University Press, 1992).

13. Ronald J. Fiscus, *The Constitutional Logic of Affirmative Action* (Durham, N.C.: Duke University Press, 1992).

14. Fiscus, *Constitutional Logic*, 13.

15. Fiscus, *Constitutional Logic*, 20–26.

16. Fiscus, *Constitutional Logic*, 38.

17. *Sheet Metal Workers v. EEOC*, 478 US 421, 494 (1986); Fiscus, *Constitutional Logic*, 42.

18. *City of Richmond v. J. A. Croson Co.*, 109 S.Ct. at 724 (1989); Fiscus, *Constitutional Logic*, 42.

19. Fiscus, *Constitutional Logic*, 47. With regard to the problem of so-called "undeserving beneficiaries" of affirmative action Fiscus writes: "When the rightful owner of stolen goods cannot be found, the law ... may or may not award possession to the original but wrongful claimant; but if it does not, if it awards possession to a third party whose claim is arguable, the original claimant cannot justifiably feel morally harmed. And the government's action cannot be said to be arbitrary unless it awards the goods to an individual whose claim is even less plausible than that of the original claimant." (49).

20. Cass Sunstein, "Limits of Compensatory Justice" in *Nomos* 33, *Compensatory Justice*, ed. John Chapman (New York: New York University Press, 1991), 281–310.

21. "It is not controlling and perhaps not even relevant that the harms that affirmative action attempts to redress cannot be understood in the usual compensatory terms.... the nature of the problem guarantees that the legal response cannot take the form of discrete remedies for discrete harms" (Sunstein, "Limits," 297).

22. Sunstein, "Limits," 303.

23. The orientation of the EEOC toward investigating individual cases of alleged discrimination is one explanation of its extraordinary backlog of over 80,000 cases. This orientation precludes it from focusing on systemic practices that affect many individuals, and instead forces it to expend resources dealing with particular instances. See "The EEOC: Pattern and Practice Imperfect" by Maurice Munroe in *Yale Law and Policy Review*, 13, no. 2, (1995):219–80.

24. Sunstein, "Limits," 292.

25. Sunstein, "Limits," 289.

26. "The current distribution of benefits and burdens as between blacks and whites and women and men is not part of the state of nature but a consequence of past and present social practices" (Sunstein, "Limits," 294).

27. See also Thomas H. Simon, *Democracy and Social Justice* (Lanham, Md.: Rowman & Littlefield, 1995), chap. 5.

28. Sunstein, "Limits," 306.

29. Gang Xu, Sylvia Fields, et al., "The Relationship between the Ethnicity of Generalist Physicians and Their Care for Underserved Populations," Ohio University College of Osteopathic Medicine, Athens, Ohio, 10.

30. Of course, we may ask whether the use of race is necessary for the achievement of the end in view or whether it is one among alternative ways of achieving that end. For instance, it might be possible to induce doctors to practice in Black neighborhoods by providing doctors, irrespective of their race, with suitable monetary incentives. But given the importance of nonmonetary factors in physician-patient relationships, it is doubtful that purely monetary rewards would be sufficient to meet the needs of underserved populations.

31. Remedial action based on the imbalance between blacks in the available work force and their presence in skilled jobs categories presumes that imbalance is caused by racial discrimination. This assumption has been challenged by many who cite cultural and cognitive factors that might equally be the cause of such imbalances. See Thomas Sowell, *Markets and Minorities* (New York: Basic Books, 1981); Richard Herrenstein and Charles Murray, *The Bell Curve* (New York: The Free Press, 1994). This literature has itself been subject to critique: for Sowell, see Christopher Jencks, *Rethinking Social Policy* (New York: Harper, 1993); for Herrenstein and Murray, see *The Bell Curve Wars*, ed. Steven Fraser (New York: Basic Books, 1995).

NO

Nicholas Capaldi

AFFIRMATIVE ACTION: CON

WHAT IS AT ISSUE?

Affirmative action is a set of policies designed to address a problem. I begin by identifying that problem as the failure of African Americans to participate fully in American life. Affirmative action, however, is not a simple or coherent set of policies, as indicated by the existence of different versions of it. I shall single out five different definitions of "affirmative action" and identify the two most important and interesting ones as compensation (definition 4) and preference (definition 5). Affirmative action in these senses is illegal, immoral, impractical, and illogical when put into practice. Ultimately it undermines U.S. society by leading to cynicism and nihilism....

There are those who will maintain that affirmative action as a policy is also intended to apply to women, Hispanics, and other allegedly oppressed groups. I maintain, however, that of all the groups routinely mentioned, African Americans are the ones having the most difficulty. Affirmative action is then an issue almost exclusively for African Americans.

What is meant by participating fully? To participate fully in our society means to be an autonomous and responsible individual—to be law-abiding, self-supporting, self-defining, and constructively active in one or more institutions. Any statistical survey will confirm that with regard to unemployment, welfare, crime, family breakdown, and other social problems, African Americans are *"overrepresented"* remarkably out of proportion to their percentage in the population. What these statistics show is that not only are African Americans as a group not participating fully but far too many of them are socially dysfunctional.

There are those who will define participation differently, who will maintain that African Americans are "underrepresented" in leadership positions. They conceptualize the issue in terms of statistics that show that African Americans as a group are not as successful as others.[1] This conceptualization confuses full participation with success,[2] and it presumes some monolithic conception of "success." It also automatically defines the solution of the problem in terms of proportional representation.

The relevant statistic is that of being "overrepresented" in prison populations, in welfare recipiency, and in other categories of social pathology. That is, it is the presence of a vast socially dysfunctional group that is the problem. Overcoming this dysfunction does not entail proportional representation because... being functional entails thinking of oneself as an individual.

Some will maintain that "underrepresentation" and "overrepresentation" are two sides of the same coin, so that in eliminating one, the other is eliminated as well. This construal is false for four reasons. First, participating fully has no direct logical connection with a specified degree of achievement; second, autonomous individuals do not construe either their own achievement or that of others as symbols of group membership, hence even to define the problem in this fashion is to show oneself to be not fully autonomous; third, stressing "underrepresentation" becomes a self-serving vehicle through which any self-styled elite can advance its own interest as an elite; finally, the belief that overcoming "underrepresentation" will automatically lead to overcoming "overrepresentation" is empirically false.

Prior to the civil rights movement, it was widely maintained that social dysfunction among African Americans was the result of a previous history of slavery (which ended with the Civil War), *de jure* segregation, pervasive racism, and inferior social services—such as schooling. What the civil rights movement inaugurated was the elimination of *de jure* segregation and a move to improve social services. Racism itself would disappear, it was widely believed via school integration. This activity encompassed equalizing access to resources and bringing people together so as to overcome stereotypes. However, despite all of these changes, too many African Americans remain dysfunctional. In fact, there is some evidence that many if not most of the programs inaugurated with the Civil Rights Act of 1964 have actually exacerbated the dysfunction.[3]

Affirmative action is the name of a series of initiatives introduced by the civil rights movement and intended to do what previous public policies had not done, that is, allow African Americans to participate more fully in American life.

WHAT IS AFFIRMATIVE ACTION?

There is no generally accepted definition of affirmative action. This tells us a number of things. First, any discussion of whether it is a good or a bad thing will turn on what one understands this expression to mean.

Let us take one example of a definition. "Affirmative action is the name given to a number of policies designed to overcome past and present discrimination and provide opportunity for those traditionally denied it."[4] In this sample definition we can distinguish among (1) the policy or set of practices to be instituted—none of which are specifically mentioned; (2) the intention behind the policy—the quite laudable one of expanding opportunities for those who have not had them; and (3) the explicit diagnosis of why those opportunities were not there—the presumption that discrimination is the exclusive or major reason for the lack of opportunity.

Any debate about whether one is for or against affirmative action must specify whether one agrees or disagrees with (2) the intention or goal, (1) policies designed to achieve that goal, and (3) the definition and diagnosis of the problem to which one is applying both the goal and the policies. There are at least three major responses to the foregoing definition:

One might approve of the intention but believe that the policies will not achieve the intention. This becomes a debate about the best means of achieving a commonly agreed upon goal.

One might approve of the intention but believe that although the policies will achieve their goal, the policies will also conflict with and undermine other socially important goals. This becomes a debate about prioritizing our goals in a world where it is not possible to have everything.

One might approve of the intention but disapprove of the policies because we disagree with the diagnosis. This becomes a debate about what is the nature and source of the problem to which affirmative action as a policy is addressed.

Lack of a generally agreed upon definition also reflects a lack of consensus on the legal and moral status of the concept. The use of the expression is now so widespread that many are apt to presume that there is some firm foundation in law, in morality, or in public policy for it. Among the things that the ongoing debate about affirmative action has revealed are both the ignorance of and the disagreement about the moral, legal, and political principles that inform or should inform public policy. Perhaps the most useful thing that will come out of a debate about affirmative action is that it will require us, as a society, to refocus on our fundamental principles.

Five major definitions of affirmative action exist:

Definition 1 (open-search): Affirmative action consists of those policies de-signed to advertise all openings as widely as possible and to monitor appointments and promotions processes in order to insure that the process is open, nondiscriminatory, and promotes excellence.

Definition 2 (punitive): Affirmative action consists of any policy, private or public, *ordered by the court* to redress proven cases of individual discrimination. The remedy may involve a specific *numerical objective,* but the numerical objective is limited to a specific time and place.

Definition 3 (minority set asides): Affirmative action refers to congressionally mandated rules concerning federal contracts and involving a specific percentage of contracts to be set aside for minority contractors.

Definition 4 (backward-compensation): Affirmative action covers any policy designed to redress alleged cases of discrimination against a group by placing members of the group in the positions they would have allegedly held if the alleged discrimination had not taken place. This is a *contrary-to-fact conditional:* it claims to identify what would happen *if* something else had *not* happened.

Definition 5 (forward-preferential): Affirmative action designates any policy in social planning, without any causal claim of what would have been, designed to produce a society or institution that reflects some stated goal and invokes *quotas* of group representation.[5]

AFFIRMATIVE ACTION IS ILLEGAL

Affirmative action in anything other than the most innocuous sense is illegal. Affirmative action in the senses of definitions 1, 2, and 3 (in a highly limited version) is legal. Affirmative action in the senses of definitions 4 and 5 is illegal. ...

[A]ccording to the Fourteenth Amendment to the United States Constitution, no state can "deprive any person of life, liberty, or property, without due process of law; nor deny to any person within its jurisdiction the equal protection of the laws." This amendment makes clear that it is individuals, not groups, who have rights.

The first relevant use of the expression "affirmative action" appears in an executive order issued in September 1965 by then President Lyndon B. Johnson requiring federal contractors to take "affirmative action to ensure that applicants are employed, and that employees are treated during employment, without regard to their race, creed, color, or national origin." This is an executive order, not a legislative decision and not a decision of the United States Supreme Court; what it makes explicit is the anti-discrimination principles that are already in the law (thereby encompassing definition 1); curiously, sex and gender are not mentioned.

... Titles VI and VII of the Civil Rights Act of 1964 unequivocally outlaw preference (definition 5). Two provisions spell this out:

> 703 (h) it shall not be unlawful employment practice... for an employer to give and act upon the results of any professionally developed ability test provided that such test, its administration or action upon the results is not designed, intended or used to discriminate because of race, color, religion, sex or national origin....
>
> 703 (j) Nothing contained in this title shall be interpreted to require any employer... to grant preferential treatment to any individual or to any group because of the race, color, religion, sex, or national origin of such individual or group on account of an imbalance which may exist with respect to the total number of percentage of persons of any race, color, religion, sex or national origin employed by any employer.

Lest there be any misunderstanding about these provisions, it is useful to cite the legislative record concerning them. As then Senator Hubert H. Humphrey put it, "Title VII does not require an employer to achieve any sort of racial balance in his work force by giving preferential treatment to any individual or group."[6] Senator Harrison Williams noted that Title VII "specifically prohibits the Attorney General or any agency of the government, from requiring employment to be on the basis of racial or religious quotas. Under this provision an employer with only white employees could continue to have only the best qualified persons even if they were all white."[7] Senator Joseph Clark stated, "Quotas are themselves discriminatory."[8] If anyone still has any doubts, then recall the words of Representative Emanuel Celler, Chairman of the House Judiciary Committee and the congressman responsible for introducing the legislation:

> it is likewise not true that the Equal Employment Opportunity Commission would have power to rectify existing 'racial or religious imbalance' in employment by requiring the hiring of certain people without regard to their qualifications simply because they are of a given race or religion. Only actual discrimination could be stopped.[9]

... [I]n *Griggs v. Duke Power Co.* (1971), the U.S. Supreme Court went out of its way to disclaim preference.

Congress did not intend ... to guarantee a job to every person regardless of qualifications... [Title VII] does not command that any person be hired simply because he was formerly the subject of discrimination, or because he is a member of a minority group. Discriminatory preference for any group, minority or majority, is precisely and only what Congress has proscribed.... Congress has not commanded that the less qualified be preferred over the better qualified simply because of minority origins. Far from disparaging job qualifications as such, Congress has made such qualifications the controlling factor, so that race, religion, nationality, and sex become irrelevant."[10]

... The final and most important case to substantiate the claim that affirmative action in any interesting sense is illegal is *Adarand Constructors, Inc. v. Pena* (1995). Congress had, in the Minority Business Enterprise provision of the Public Works Employment Act of 1977, required that 10 percent of the federal funds allocated to state and local governments for public works projects must be used to purchase goods and services from minority-owned businesses even if nonminority-owned firms offered a lower bid. The reasoning behind this legislation was that minorities had been discriminated against in the past and were due redress. This is a case of punitive action (definition 2). Some had suggested that it constituted legislative endorsement of either compensation (definition 4) or preference (definition 5).

The Adarand decision effectively reduced this policy to the punitive version (definition 2). One reason this decision is so important is that it clarified a somewhat bewildering series of previous decisions.[11]

As Justice O'Connor expressed it in *Adarand:*

The Court's failure to produce a majority opinion in Bakke, Fullilove, and Wygant left unresolved the proper analysis for remedial race-based governmental action.... The Court resolved the issue, at least in part, in 1989.... A majority of the court in *Croson* held that 'the standard of review under the Equal Protection Clause is not dependent on the race of those burdened or benefitted by a particular classification,' and that the single standard of review for racial classifications should be 'strict scrutiny.'

"Strict scrutiny" means that previous discrimination must be established, that is, we are dealing with definition 2, and that the redress must be carefully limited in time and place.

Justice O'Connor continues:

Accordingly, we hold today that all racial classifications, imposed by whatever federal, state, or local government actor, must be analyzed by a reviewing court under strict scrutiny. In other words, such classifications are constitutional only if they are narrowly tailored measures that further compelling governmental interests.

Our action today makes explicit what Justice Powell thought implicit in the Fullilove lead opinion: federal racial classifications, like those of a State, must serve a compelling governmental interest, and must be narrowly tailored to further that interest.[12]

Affirmative action as either compensation or preference is illegal. If such policies are so pervasive, this reflects the illegal and unauthorized activities of government bureaucracies (a widespread problem that goes way beyond affirmative action); it reflects those activist judges who confuse the judicial process with the legislative process and who confuse their own values with the true moral foundations of the United States; it reflects the ideological agenda of many academics; it reflects the unscrupulous activities of politicians whose careers are predicated on maintaining voting blocks based upon racial clientage; and it reflects fear in the business community of endless litigation.

AFFIRMATIVE ACTION IS IMMORAL

As a society the United States is committed to six major normative premises:

1. We are committed to the belief in a *cosmic order* ("In God We Trust").
2. We are committed to the belief in the sanctity of the *individual.*

The *Declaration of Independence* declares:

> We hold these truths to he self-evident, that all men are created equal, that they are endowed by their Creator with certain unalienable Rights, that among these are Life, Liberty, and the pursuit of Happiness. That to secure these rights, Governments are instituted among Men, deriving their just powers from the consent of the governed.

In his dissent in the *Plessy v. Ferguson* case (1896), Justice Harlan enunciated the fundamental principle of individuality in a specific way, namely that the U.S. Constitution is and ought to be *color-blind.*[13] This reiterates the point that it is the individual as such and not membership in a group that defines who we are. "Our constitution is color-blind, and neither knows nor tolerates classes among citizens.... The law regards man as man, and takes no account of his surroundings or of his color."[14]

In arguing against the then majority view, Harlan warned that the separate but equal doctrine "will, in time prove to be quite as pernicious as the decision made by this tribunal in the Dred Scott case."[15] The point of Harlan's observation is that invidious comparisons or classifications deny individuals the equal protection of the laws. Finally, Harlan reiterated that "the destinies of the two races, in this country, are indissolubly linked together, and the interests of both require that the common government of all shall not permit the seeds of race hate to be planted under the sanction of law."[16]

In his famous "I have a dream" speech on the steps of the Lincoln Memorial in 1964, Dr. Martin Luther King, Jr., looked forward to when his children would "live in a nation where they will not be judged by the color of their skin but by the content of their character."

Harlan's view has also been echoed in a recent statement by Justice Scalia:

> government can never have a "compelling interest" in discriminating on the basis of race in order to 'make up' for past racial discrimination in the opposite direction.... Individuals who have been wronged by unlawful racial discrimination should be made whole; but under our constitution there can be no such thing as either a creditor or debtor race. That concept is alien to the constitution's focus upon the individual... To pursue the concept of racial entitlement—even for the most admirable and benign of purposes—is to reinforce and preserve for future mischief the way of thinking that produced race slavery, race privilege, and race hatred. In the eyes of government, we are just one race here. It is American.[17]

The sanctity of the individual has to be understood in a special moral way.

The sanctity of the individual means:

a. that human beings possess the rational capacity to recognize a universal cosmic order;
b. that human beings have the internal capacity to be unconstrained in their decision to act in accordance with the cosmic order, that is, *free will;*
c. that true freedom and dignity consist in the inner or self-discipline that comes with the exercise of these capacities; and
d. that these capacities can only be discovered retrospectively by their exercise; limited government and a free market economy are the only political and economic institutions compatible with individual dignity; the justification of such institutions is not their efficiency but their efficacy for the exercise of personal autonomy.

The continuous Western meaning of freedom is self-government; the modern version of freedom is the self-government of the individual (not the classical notion of a self-governing polis).

This special moral understanding of individuality has most recently been enunciated by Justice Clarence Thomas in his condemnation of affirmative action (understood in the preferential sense).

I believe that there is a moral [and] constitutional equivalence... between laws designed to subjugate a race and those that distribute benefits on the basis of race in order to foster some current notion of equality. Government cannot make us equal; it can only recognize, respect, and protect us as equal before the law. That these programs may have been motivated, in part, by good intentions cannot provide refuge from the principles that under our Constitution, the government may not make distinctions on the basis of race. As far as the Constitution is concerned, it is irrelevant whether a government's racial classifications are drawn by those who wish to oppress a race or by those who have a sincere desire to help those thought to be disadvantaged. There can be no doubt that the paternalism that appears to lie at the heart of this program is at war with the principle of inherent equality that underlies and infuses our Constitution.... These programs not only raise grave constitutional questions, they also undermine the moral basis of the equal protection principle. Purchased at the price of immeasurable human suffering, the equal protection principle reflects our Nation's understanding that such classifications ultimately have a destructive impact on the individual and our society... there can be no doubt that racial paternalism and its unintended consequences can be as poisonous and pernicious as any other form of discrimination.[18]

3. We are committed to the belief that the communal good is not something over and above the good of the individuals who make up the community.
4. We are committed to the belief that the *rule of law* means due process and equality before the law (i.e., equality of opportunity and not equality of result).

The popular understanding of these principles is reflected in a poll conducted by *USA Today* (24 March, 1995, 3A). In this survey, 73 percent favor "special efforts to find qualified minorities and women and then encouraging them to apply for jobs with that company," and at the same time 84 percent of the public oppose "favoring a minority who is less qualified than a white applicant, when filling a job in a business that has few minority workers."

5. We subscribe to a *republican* or limited form of government and not a democracy. It is a system in which liberty is established by restraining government through checks and balances of power.
6. We embrace *a free market economy*. The only real good is the good of the individual. Free market economies are especially important because they combine efficiency and morality.

The wealth created in a free market economy is a good thing because: (a) It enhances the human condition. Income is not merely a means to consumer satisfaction, nor merely an incentive. Rather, income is *a means to accomplishment*. (b) Wealth liberates us from the culture of poverty. Whereas in the medieval world it was wealth that created a scandal, the scandal of the modern world is the existence of poverty. (c) Private wealth provides a check on the power of the government, and leads to the expansion of individual liberties. (d) Finally, wealth provides the dynamic of social reform. . . .

Most of the participants in the affirmative action debate subscribe to these fundamental moral principles. Even those who have actively supported the implementation of preferential programs agree that these are the fundamental principles. What they have urged is that the programs of preference are a temporary means to achieve the fundamental values. Joseph Califano, former Secretary of Health, Education, and Welfare under President Carter, wrote in 1989 that affirmative action was intended "only as a temporary expedient to speed blacks' entry into the social and economic mainstream. . . . it was never conceived as a permanent program and its time is running out."[19] Even in his dissent in Bakke [1978], Justice Blackmun stated that "in order to get beyond racism, we must first take account of race," thereby acknowledging that affirmative action at best is a temporary expedient. What is at issue is whether we can temporarily suspend these principles for a desirable end, that is, whether the end justifies the means. . . .

One last thing we want to note about our fundamental moral principles is their logical status. In calling these our fundamental norms, we are not describing how people actually behave but how they ought to behave. Having these as norms permits us to identify those cases where we have failed to live up to them. Too many proponents of affirmative action fail to understand the logical status of norms, thinking that they have either invalidated the norms (e.g., color-blindness) or they have invalidated our claim to have identified the norm as norm because of our failure to live up to it. In practice, the United States has failed in part and continues to fail to live up to the ideal of a color-blind society—but these are grounds for trying harder, not for adopting race consciousness as a norm.

There are two moral arguments routinely presented in favor of affirmative action. One reflects definition 4 (compensation) and one reflects definition 5 (preference). We turn now to those arguments and my rebuttal of them.

The compensation argument maintains that slavery and discrimination practiced over a long period of time have disadvantaged the present generations of African Americans so that they (1) cannot compete effectively, and (2) therefore, should be awarded positions and promotions in a manner consistent with the punitive principles as enunciated in definition 2. This is not a strictly legal argument because the law demands that overt and provable practices of discrimination against specific individuals must be the basis of redress and remediation.

The argument makes two assumptions. The first is the statistical assumption that every group possesses the same talents and interests in the same proportion as their percentage in the population. The second assumption is that it is possible to construct a contrary-to-fact conditional argument of an historical-causal kind to substantiate this claim of what might have been.

The compensation argument can be rebutted on the following grounds:

1. It misconstrues the legal nature of compensation.[20] In order for "compensation" to be invoked, we must (a) show that the injury—in this case failure to achieve—was caused by discrimination (or analogous phenomenon), (b) identify the party at fault, and (c) calculate a relevant benefit to be paid by the parry at fault. Item (a) is never established in a direct causal fashion; with regard to item (b) the perpetrating parties are either long dead or identified in a hopelessly amorphous fashion as "society at large"; with regard to item (c), there is no way to extract a benefit given what we have said about item (b), and any relevant benefit would be monetary, not a position that the alleged injured party is unable to hold if injured.

2. The punitive redress that the courts have imposed never involve giving positions to people who cannot compete effectively but to people who can compete but were never given the opportunity to compete.

3. There is absolutely no evidence for the extraordinary statistical assumption; moreover, if you believe that some groups are under-represented then it follows as a matter of logical truth that some groups are overrepresented. Who is willing to point the finger at allegedly overrepresented groups?

4. To put such a policy into action leads to *reverse discrimination*, that is, penalizing innocent individuals by denying them opportunities; this amounts to believing that the end justifies the means.

5. There is no way to substantiate the contrary-to-fact conditional argument (Justice Powell's point in *Bakke*): (a) That a significant number of African Americans fully participate is counterevidence—why were they, unlike their brethren, not harmed to the point of being unable to compete effectively? (b) We can construct equally plausible (or implausible) contrary-to-fact scenarios, for example, the African American descendants of slaves are beneficiaries of slavery in that they have better lives (or even are alive in greater numbers) than they would have been if slavery had not existed. (c) We can reverse the reverse-discrimination with the following equally plausible (or implausible) scenario—African Americans actually owe compensation to the United States! The failure of present generations of African Americans to participate fully is not the result of slavery and discrimination but of other factors, for some of which they bear responsibility.... Moreover, this failure to participate fully has actually harmed non-African Amer-

icans more than helped them because it has wasted enormous resources and thereby limited the number of opportunities available to everybody else....

Let us now turn to the preference argument. This argument maintains that because of the history of slavery and discrimination, African Americans have never been made to feel that they belong. This is especially problematic in a democratic society. Affirmative action is a way to help African Americans realize the basic values of the United States.

This argument rests upon a number of misconceptions. First of all, it is conceptualizing the problem in terms of the notion of a "democratic society." This is incorrect for two reasons. The United States is not a democracy but a republic. In a republic, government is limited to serving other interests because those interests reflect the basic rights of individuals. That is, political institutions are subordinate to moral preconceptions. James Madison argued that it was a utopian delusion to expect unanimity; factions were inevitable; the instrument for avoiding factional strife was checks and balances. Democracy is not an intrinsic end but a quite limited institutional arrangement that reflects more fundamental values. There is a serious confusion here of normative priority. Politicizing U.S. society and politicizing the issue of why African Americans do not participate as much as we would all wish is the wrong way to approach this issue.

Second, conceptualizing the problem from the point of view of groups (that is, African Americans conceived of as a voting block) is symptomatic of the failure to develop a sense of individuality.

The question is not whether my group participates fully, the question is whether "I" or "you" participate fully.

Third, part of the reason that so many African Americans feel that they do not belong is that they have failed to embrace, much less understand, the fundamental values that animate our society.

NOTES

1. There are always interesting anomalies in statistical evidence. For example, African-American women college graduates on average earn more than White women college graduates (*The Economic Status of Black Women: An Exploratory Investigation.* [Washington, D.C.: U.S. Commission on Civil Rights, 1990], 12).

2. An obsession with 'success' understood in terms of prestige is symptomatic of the academic world, a world in which most of the literature on affirmative action is produced. See N. Capaldi, *Out of Order: Affirmative Action and the Crisis of Doctrinaire Liberalism.* Buffalo: Prometheus Books, 1985.

3. Charles Murray, *Losing Ground: Amen Social Policy, 1950–1980.* New York: Basic Books, 1984.

4. G. Horne, *Reversing Discrimination: The Case for Affirmative Action.* New York: International Publishers, 1992, 1.

5. See M. Rosenfeld, *Affirmative Action and Justice: A Philosophical and Constitutional Inquiry.* New Haven: Yale University Press, 1991, 47–48: "Affirmative action shall be assumed henceforth to include some kind of preferential treatment. Specifically, affirmative action shall refer to the preferential hiring, promotion, and laying off of minorities and women, to the preferential admission of minorities or women to universities, or to the preferential selection of businesses owned by minorities or women to perform government public contracting work for purposes of remedying a wrong or of increasing the proportion of minorities or women in the relevant labor force, entrepreneurial class, or university student population. Moreover, such preferential treatment may be required in order, among other things, to achieve a defined goal or to fill a set quota."

6. Humphrey (110 Cong. Rec. 12723).

7. Williams (110 Cong. Rec. 1433).

8. Clark (110 Cong. Rec. 7218).

9. Celler (110 Cong. Rec. 1518).

10. *Griggs v. Duke Power Co.*, 401 U.S. 424 (1971).

11. Controversial intervening cases included: (a) *United Steelworkers of America v. Weber* (1979). Under pressure from the Labor Department, Kaiser Alu-

minum and the United Steelworkers agreed to a training program which imposed a 50 percent quota for African Americans. The agreement was temporary; there was no commitment to maintaining racial balance; and no decision on defining what is permissible affirmative action. Most notable in this case is Justice Rehnquist's dissent in which he argued that even the "voluntary" policy is inconsistent with Title VII, and his critique of Justice Brennan in which Rehnquist denounced the idea that Title VII does not require but permits preference as an "Orwellian" interpretation of the law. (b) *Fullilove v. Klutznick* (1980). Here, the majority upheld minority set-asides as a version of our definition 2. (c) *Wygant v. Jackson Board of Education* (1986). The Board of Education of Jackson, Michigan, and the local teacher's union had entered into an agreement whereby layoffs were determined not simply by seniority but in order to maintain racial balance. The majority's view, as expressed by Justice Powell, reasserted that group classifications are suspect and justified only if they serve a compelling state interest and must be tailored so as not to burden innocent parties. (d) *Richmond v. Croson* (1989). The City of Richmond, Virginia, itself had adopted a 30 percent set-aside provision for minority contractors. Here the majority held that racial classifications are suspect categories.

12. O'Connor (1995, *Adarand*), 1839–41.

13. See L. D. Weeden, "Just Say No to Race Exclusive College Scholarships: From an Afrocentric Perspective," *Thurgood Marshall Law Review*, xx, 1995, 205–241.

14. Harlan, 163 U.S. 537, 16 S. Ct. 1146. See Charles A. Lofgren, *The Plessy Case: A Legal-Historical Interpretation*, New York: Oxford University Press, 1987.

15. 163 U.S. 537, 559 (1896) (Harlan, J., dissenting).

16. 163 U.S. 537, 1147.

17. Scalia (1995, *Adarand*) 1844.

18. Thomas (1995, *Adarand*) 1845.

19. Califano quoted in P. C. Roberts and L. M. Stratton, "Proliferation of Privilege," *National Review* (November 6, 1995), 41. See L. Pojman, "The Moral Status of Affirmative Action," *Public Affairs Quarterly*, vi, 1992, 181–206.

20. Randy E. Barnett, "Compensation and Rights in the Liberal Conception of Justice," *Nomos*, xxxiii, 1991, 311–329, has made an even stronger case by pointing out that compensation in Anglo-American common law is tied to a liberal conception of justice that is rights-based not injury based. "In fact, the liberal conception of justice also requires that a right be violated before the legal system may justly rectify even a sharply defined injury produced by a discrete and unitary event clearly caused by a defendant's conduct." (315).

POSTSCRIPT

Is Affirmative Action Fair?

That racial discrimination and sexual discrimination have existed in the United States is a matter of historical record and beyond dispute. But the question remains, What follows for us here and now?

Opponents of affirmative action say that nothing at all follows, except perhaps that we might be more careful and vigilant about allowing any form of discrimination, including modern forms of reverse discrimination.

Proponents of strong affirmative action say that although these views might *look* fair and aim to *be* fair, they are not fair. Just preventing discrimination without taking positive action to improve minorities' positions in society would simply freeze an unfairly established status quo. As American society is now, blacks are not represented in professions, in graduate schools, in business boardrooms, or in positions of social and political leadership in a way that is consistent with their numbers in the population. This is not for lack of interest or ability; it is a legacy of social injustice. To insist that we now freeze this status quo and proceed "fairly," on a case-by-case basis, will guarantee that the white-biased social momentum will continue for at least the foreseeable future. Advocates of affirmative action want to eradicate the effects of past discrimination and to put an end to the bias in momentum as soon as possible. They call for active measures to achieve this.

Sources that are relevant to this issue include Frederick R. Lynch, *Invisible Victims: White Males and the Crisis of Affirmative Action* (Greenwood Press, 1989); Shelby Steele, *The Content of Our Character: A New Vision of Race in America* (St. Martin's Press, 1990); Gertrude Ezorsky, *Racism and Justice: The Case for Affirmative Action* (Cornell University Press, 1991); Thomas Hill, Jr., "The Message of Affirmative Action," *Social Philosophy and Policy* (vol. 8, 1991); Michel Rosenfeld, *Affirmative Action and Justice: A Philosophical and Constitutional Inquiry* (Yale University Press, 1991); Ellen Frankel Paul, ed., *Reassessing Civil Rights* (Basil Blackwell, 1991); Stephen L. Wasby, ed., *The Constitutional Logic of Affirmative Action* (Duke University Press, 1992); Andrew Kull, *The Colorblind Constitution* (Harvard University Press, 1992); Studs Terkel, *Race: How Blacks and Whites Think and Feel About the American Obsession* (New Press, 1992); Hared Taylor, *Paved With Good Intentions: The Failure of Race Relations in Contemporary America* (Carol & Graf, 1992); Bernard R. Boxhill, *Blacks and Social Justice*, rev. ed. (Rowman & Littlefield, 1992); Andrew Hacker, *Two Nations: Black and White, Separate, Hostile, Unequal* (Scribner, 1992); Ronald J. Fiscus, *The Constitutional Logic of Affirmative Action* (Duke University Press, 1992); Stanley Fish, "Reverse Racism, or How the Pot Got to Call the Kettle Black," *The Atlantic Monthly* (November 1993); Christopher Jencks, *Rethinking*

Social Policy: Race, Poverty, and the Underclass (Harper Perennial, 1993); Steven M. Cahn, ed., *Affirmative Action and the University* (Temple University Press, 1993); Ruth Sidel, *Battling Bias: The Struggle for Identity and Community on College Campuses* (Penguin, 1994); Noel Ignatiev and John Garvey, eds., *Race Traitor* (Routledge, 1994); Carl Cohen, *Naked Racial Preference: The Case Against Affirmative Action* (Madison Books, 1995); Ralph R. Reiland, "Affirmative Action or Equal Opportunity?" *Regulation* (vol. 18, 1995), pp. 19–23; Michael Kinsley, "The Spoils of Victimhood," *The New Yorker* (March 27, 1995); and Steven M. Cahn, ed., *The Affirmative Action Debate* (Routledge, 1995).

Other sources on this controversial policy are W. Avon Drake and Robert D. Holsworth, eds., *Affirmative Action and the Stalled Quest for Black Progress* (University of Illinois Press, 1996); George E. Curry, ed., *The Affirmative Action Debate* (Addison-Wesley, 1996); Christopher Edley, Jr., *Not All Black and White: Affirmative Action, Race, and American Values* (Hill & Wang, 1996); Carol M. Swain, ed., *Race Versus Class: The New Affirmative Action Debate* (University Press of America, 1996); Richard F. Thomasson, Faye J. Crosby, and Sharon D. Herzberger, *Affirmative Action: The Pros and Cons of Policy and Practice* (University Press of America, 1996); John David Skrentny, *The Ironies of Affirmative Action: Politics, Culture, and Justice in America* (University of Chicago Press, 1996); Robert Emmett Long, ed., *Affirmative Action* (H. W. Wilson, 1996); Barbara Bergmann, *In Defense of Affirmative Action* (Basic Books, 1996); Terry Eastland, *Ending Affirmative Action: The Case for Colorblind Justice* (Basic Books, 1996); Jewelle Taylor Gibbs, *Color of Justice: Rodney King, O. J. Simpson, and Race in America* (Jossey-Bass, 1996); K. Anthony Appiah and Amy Gutmann, *Color Conscious: The Political Morality of Race* (Princeton University Press, 1996); Clarence Page, *Showing My Color: Impolite Essays on Race in America* (Harper-Collins, 1996); "Racism and the Law: The Legacy and Lessons of Plessy," a special issue of *Law and Philosophy* (May 1997); "The Affirmative Action Debate," a special issue of *Report from the Institute for Philosophy and Public Policy* (Winter–Spring 1997); Bryan K. Fair, *Notes of a Racial Caste Baby: Color Blindness and the End of Affirmative Action* (New York University Press, 1997); and Celia Wolfe-Devine, *Diversity and Community in the Academy: Affirmative Action in Faculty Appointments* (Rowman & Littlefield, 1997).

A concise account of civil rights history (including the birth of the phrase "affirmative action") is Hugh Davis Graham, *Civil Rights and the Presidency: Race and Gender in American Politics, 1960–1972* (Oxford University Press, 1992). The position that affirmative action policies are necessary for women is defended by Susan D. Clayton and Faye J. Crosby, *Justice, Gender and Affirmative Action* (University of Michigan Press, 1992).

On the Internet . . .

Ethics on The World Wide Web

This site provides links to associations, organizations, and institutes dedicated to teaching about ethics and to promoting higher standards of behavior both in individuals and globally.
http://www5.fullerton.edu/les/associations.html

World Hunger

This site, sponsored by *Ethics Updates,* contains discussion questions, court decisions, statistical resources, and Internet resources on world hunger.
http://ethics.acusd.edu/world_hunger.html

Ethics Connection Home Page

The Ethics Connection home page is sponsored by the Markula Center for Applied Ethics at Santa Clara University in California. It includes electronic versions of the center's quarterly publication *Issues in Ethics* and a forum for discussing contemporary ethical issues.
http://www.scu.edu/Ethics/homepage.shtml

PART 5

Morality and the
International Scene

Moral issues do not generally recognize political and geographical boundaries. Those who take opposing sides on questions of abortion and capital punishment will generally divide up in exactly the same ways regardless of where the question is localized. What makes the issues in this section international is not that they raise questions that transcend political boundaries and established legal jurisdictions—moral issues generally do that anyway—but that they specifically recognize problems that might arise from those political and legal boundaries and the divisions of people into various national groups.

■ Are Human Rights Basic to Justice?

■ Do Rich Nations Have an Obligation to Help Poor Nations?

ISSUE 16

Are Human Rights Basic to Justice?

YES: Rhoda E. Howard, from "Human Rights and the Necessity for Cultural Change," *Focus on Law Studies* (Fall 1992)

NO: Vinay Lal, from "The Imperialism of Human Rights," *Focus on Law Studies* (Fall 1992)

ISSUE SUMMARY

YES: Rhoda E. Howard, a Canadian sociologist, argues that universal human rights are so basic and so important that sometimes cultures have to change in order to accommodate them.

NO: Vinay Lal, a professor of humanities, argues that the idea of human rights is fundamentally a Western concept that is alien to most cultural traditions in the Third World. To impose human rights policies on these cultures is a form of Western imperialism.

Suppose we learn of some foreign culture's practice that initially strikes us as unfair to some of the individuals involved. Initially, we will want to make sure that we really do understand the situation, that we see things from the standpoint of those of the foreign culture. Otherwise, we will have a very ethnocentric point of view. But once we achieve some insight into the local interpretation or understanding of the culture's practice, is it still possible that the practice will seem to violate individual rights? Does an accurate and proper understanding of a foreign practice always vindicate it against such a charge? Does our concept of individual human rights fail to apply to those in other cultures?

Some have claimed that it is difficult to judge another culture's practices, that it is difficult to see things from the other's point of view. It has also been said that cultural practices form a network of interconnections, so it is complicated to try to isolate any one practice for examination. But so far, these are only practical difficulties. With great care, they might be overcome.

But there is a more fundamental challenge to our ability to judge a given cultural practice as unfair, unjust, or in violation of human rights. Suppose we say, for example, that a woman has a right to speak her mind in public and that the culture that does not allow this is in violation of her human rights. Or we might say that a culture that condemns people born into a certain caste or lineage to a lifetime of misery is in violation of the basic human rights of these people. The fundamental challenge to such judgments comes out in the following questions: Is the concept of individual human rights that is defined by these examples applicable to *all* cultures (whether they recognize it or not)? Or is it part of a peculiarly Western way of interpreting or judging cultures?

If we answer the first question affirmatively, then we have a reference point for making judgments. But we must back that answer up with some account of human rights and how it is that individuals have them, which rights they have, and so on. On the other hand, an affirmative answer to the second question would seem easier to support. An examination of the history of individual human rights shows that this concept grew out of Western history. An examination of the practices and cultures of many Third World countries shows that the idea of individual human rights is often alien to them or is understood quite differently than it is in the West.

Indeed, a Third World criticism of the West is that it is altogether too preoccupied with individuals and their rights and not appreciative enough of the role of community in human life. A Western view, it is said, often pits the individual *against* the community in defense of that individual's rights.

If we were to simply give up the idea of basic human rights, then we would seem to give up the idea that a culture could ever violate these rights. This would allow an "anything goes" attitude toward cultures and traditions, which seems simply irresponsible.

In the following selections, Rhoda E. Howard argues that even though the concept of individual human rights is derived from Western experience, this by no means rules out its applicability in the Third World. In fact, in some settings, human rights can be tools of positive cultural development. Vinay Lal argues that the idea of human rights may be a noble one, but the political reality is that such notions are only tools of Western interests in the Third World.

YES

Rhoda E. Howard

HUMAN RIGHTS AND THE NECESSITY FOR CULTURAL CHANGE

Many critics of the concept of human rights argue that it undermines indigenous cultures, especially in the underdeveloped world (Cobbah, 1987; Pollis and Schwab, 1980; Renteln, 1990). I agree that the concept of human rights often undermines cultures. Cultural rupture is often a necessary aspect of the entrenchment of respect for human rights. Culture is not of absolute ethical value; if certain aspects of particular cultures change because citizens prefer to focus on human rights, then that is a perfectly acceptable price to pay.

Human rights are rights held by the individual merely because she or he is human, without regard to status or position. In principle, all human beings hold human rights equally. These rights are claims against the state that do not depend on duties to the state, although they do depend on duties to other citizens, e.g., not to commit crimes. They are also claims that the individual can make against society as a whole. Society, however, may have cultural preconceptions that certain types of individuals ought not to be entitled to such rights. Thus, culture and human rights come into conflict. The concept of cultural relativism recognizes this, but does not consider the possibility that, in such instances, perhaps the better path to choose is to change the culture in order to promote human rights.

Cultural relativism is a method of social analysis that stresses the importance of regarding social and cultural phenomena from the "perspective of participants in or adherents of a given culture" (Bidney, 1968). Relativism assumes that there is no one culture whose customs and beliefs dominate all others in a moral sense. Relativism is a necessary corrective to ethical ethnocentrism. But it is now sometimes taken to such an extreme that any outsider's discussions of local violations of human rights are criticized as forms of ideological imperialism.

In effect, this extreme position advocates not cultural relativism but cultural absolutism. Cultural absolutists posit particular cultures as of absolute moral value, more valuable than any universal principle of justice. In the left-right/North-South debate that permeates today's ideological exchanges,

From Rhoda E. Howard, "Human Rights and the Necessity for Cultural Change," *Focus on Law Studies*, vol. 8, no. 1 (Fall 1992). Copyright © 1992 by The American Bar Association. Reprinted by permission.

cultural absolutists specifically argue that culture is of more importance than the internationally accepted principles of human rights.

Cultural absolutists argue that human rights violate indigenous cultures because they are Western in origin. But the origins of any idea, including human rights, do not limit its applicability. The concept of human rights arose in the West largely in reaction to the overwhelming power of the absolutist state; in the Third World today, states also possess enormous power against which citizens need to be protected. As societies change, so ideals of social justice change.

Cultures are not immutable aspects of social life, ordained forever to be static. Cultures change as a result of structural change: secularism, urbanization and industrialism are among the chief causes of cultural change both in the West since the eighteenth century and in the underdeveloped world today (Howard, 1986, chapter 2). Cultures can also be manipulated by political or social spokespersons in their own interest. Culturalism is frequently an argument that is used to "cover" political repression, as when Kenyan President Daniel arap Moi told a female environmental activist not to criticize his policies because it is "against African tradition" for women to speak up in public. This does not mean that all aspects of culture must necessarily be ruptured in order that human rights can be entrenched. Many aspects of culture, such as kinship patterns, art or ritual, have nothing to do with human rights and can safely be preserved, even enhanced, when other rights-abusive practices are corrected. Many aspects of public morality are similarly not matters of human rights. The existence or abolition of polygamous marriage, for example, is not an international human rights issue, despite objections to it in the West. Nor is the proper degree of respect one should show to one's elders, or the proper norms of generosity and hospitality. The apparent Western overemphasis on work at the expense of family is a cultural practice that Third World societies can avoid without violating human rights. Many other such matters, such as whether criminal punishment should be by restitution or imprisonment, can be resolved without violating international human rights norms.

Jack Donnelly argues that "weak" cultural relativism is sometimes an appropriate response to human rights violations. Weak cultural relativism would "allow occasional and strictly limited local variations and exceptions to human rights," while recognizing "a comprehensive set of prima facie universal human rights" (Donnelly, 1989, p. 110). This is an appropriate position if the violation of a human right is truly a cultural practice that no political authority and no socially dominant group initiates or defends. Consider the case of female genital operations in Africa and elsewhere. Governments do not promote these violations; indeed, through education about their detrimental health consequences, they try to stop them. Nevertheless there is strong popular sentiment in favour of the operations, among women as well as (if not more so than) men (Slack, 1988). Similarly, child betrothal, officially a violation of international human rights norms, is popularly accepted in some cultures (Howard, 1986, chapter 8). And certain forms of freedom of speech, such as blasphemy and pornography, are deeply offensive to popular sentiment in many cultures, whether or not the government permits or prohibits them.

Although a weak cultural relativist stance is appropriate in some instances as a protection of custom against international human rights norms, to implement human rights does mean that certain cultural practices must be ruptured. One obvious example is the universal subordination of women as a group to men as a group, backed up by men's collective economic, political and physical power over women. If women have achieved greater access to human rights in North America since the second wave of feminism began about 1970, it is largely because they have challenged cultural stereotypes of how they ought to behave. Feminist activists no longer believe that women ought to be deferential to men or wives subordinate to their husbands. Nor do they any longer hold to the almost universal cultural belief that women's divinely ordained purpose in life is to bear children. Feminists in other parts of the world such as India or Africa are making similar challenges to their cultures in the process of asserting their rights (on women's rights as human rights, see Bunch, 1990, and Eisler, 1987.)

Many critics of human rights find them overly individualistic; they point to the selfish materialism they see in Western (North American) society. But the individualism of Western society reflects not protection but neglect of human rights, especially economic rights (Howard, "Ideologies of Social Exclusion," unpublished). In the United States, certain economic rights are regarded as culturally inappropriate. A deeply ingrained belief exists that everyone ought to be able to care for himself and his family. Since the U.S. is or was the land of opportunity (at least for white people), anyone who lives in poverty is personally responsible for his being in that state. Thus the U.S. has the worst record of provision of economic rights of any major Western democratic state. The right to health is not acknowledged, nor is the right to housing or food. Before such rights are acknowledged and provided in the U.S., the cultural belief in the virtues of hard work and pulling oneself up by one's bootstraps will have to be replaced by a more collectivist vision of social responsibility. The culturally ingrained belief that blacks are inferior people not deserving of the respect and concern of whites will also need to be ruptured.

Critics of human rights sometimes argue that cultures are so different that there is no possibility of shared meanings about social justice evolving across cultural barriers. The multivocality of talk about rights precludes any kind of consensus. The very possibility of debate is rejected. Indeed, debate, the idea that people holding initially opposing views can persuade each other through logic and reason of their position, is rejected as a form of thought typical of rationalist and competitive Western society. Western thought, it is argued, silences the oppressed.

Yet it is precisely the central human rights premises of freedom of speech, press and assembly that all over the world permit the silenced to gain a social voice. Human rights undermine constricting status-based categorizations of human beings: they permit people from degraded social groups to demand social change. Rational discourse about human rights permits degraded workers, peasants, untouchables, women and members of minority groups to articulate and consider alternate social arrangements than those that currently oppress them (see also Teson, 1985).

Human rights are "inauthentic" in many cultures because they challenge the ingrained privileges of the ruling classes, the wealthy, the Brahmin, the patriarch, or the member of a privileged ethnic or religious group. The purpose of human rights is precisely to change many culturally ingrained habits and customs that violate the dignity of the individual. Rather than apologizing that human rights challenge cultural norms in many societies, including our own, we should celebrate that fact.

This article is based in large part on my Human Rights and the Search for Community *(in progress). Unpublished papers from this project, available on request, include* "Cultural Absolutism and the Nostalgia for Community," *and* "Ideologies of Social Exclusion in North American Society."

REFERENCES

Bidney, David. 1968. "Cultural Relativism," in *International Encyclopedia of the Social Sciences,* Volume III. New York: Macmillan.

Bunch, Charlotte. 1990. "Women's Rights as Human Rights: Toward a Re-Vision of Human Rights." *Human Rights Quarterly* 12: 486–98.

Cobbah, Josiah A. M. 1987. "African Values and the Human Rights Debate: An African Perspective." *Human Rights Quarterly* 9: 309–31.

Donnelly, Jack. 1989. *Universal Human Rights in Theory and Practice.* Ithaca, N.Y.: Cornell University Press.

Eisler, Riane. 1987. "Human Rights: Toward an Integrated Theory for Action." *Human Rights Quarterly* 9: 287–308.

Howard, Rhoda E. 1986. *Human Rights in Commonwealth Africa.* Totowa, NJ.: Rowman and Littlefield.

Pollis, Adamantia, and Peter Schwab, "Human Rights: A Western Concept with Limited Applicability," in Pollis and Schwab, eds. 1980. *Human Rights: Cultural and Ideological Perspectives.* New York: Praeger.

Renteln, Alison Dundes. 1990. *International Human Rights: Universalism versus Relativism.* Newbury Park, CA.: Sage.

Slack, Alison T. 1988. "Female Circumcision: A Critical Appraisal." *Human Rights Quarterly* 10: 437–86.

Teson, Fernando R. 1985. "International Human Rights and Cultural Relativism." *Virginia Journal of International Law* 25: 869–98.

NO
Vinay Lal

THE IMPERIALISM
OF HUMAN RIGHTS

The notion of human rights is deeply embedded in modern legal and political thought and could well be considered one of the most significant achievements of contemporary culture and civilization. Certain classes of people in all societies have, from the beginning of time, been endowed with "rights" which others could not claim. The immunity that emissaries (now diplomats) from one state to another have always received constitutes one of the norms of conduct that has guided relations between states. Likewise, most cultures have had, in principle at least, intricate rules to govern the conduct of warfare. Civilians were not to be taken hostage as a military strategy; a soldier was not to be shot as he was surrendering; and so on.

Some of these customary modes of conduct are now enshrined in the law, transmitted on the one hand into "rights" that the citizen can claim against the state, and on the other hand into restraints on the state's agenda to produce conformity and contain dissent. The individual has been given a great many more rights, and—what is unique to modern times—never before have such rights been placed under the protection of the law. States are bound in their relations to their subjects by a myriad of international agreements and laws, including the Geneva Conventions, the International Covenant on Civil and Political Rights, the United Nations Charter, the Universal Declaration of Human Rights, and the U.N. Body of Principles for the Protection of All Persons Under Any Form of Detention or Punishment.

Moreover, it is only in our times that the "international community" seems prepared to enforce sanctions against a state for alleged violations of such rights. With the demise of communism, the principal foes of human rights appear to have been crushed, and the very notion of "human rights" seems sovereign. Should we then unreservedly endorse the culture of "human rights" as it has developed in the liberal-democratic framework of the modern West, indeed even as a signifier of the "end of history" and of the emergence of the New World Order? On the contrary, I would like to suggest several compelling reasons why, far from acquiescing in the suggestion that the notion of

From Vinay Lal, "The Imperialism of Human Rights," *Focus on Law Studies*, vol. 8, no. 1 (Fall 1992). Copyright © 1992 by The American Bar Association. Reprinted by permission.

human rights is the most promising avenue to a new era in human relations, we should consider the discourse of human rights as the most evolved form of Western imperialism. Indeed, human rights can be viewed as the latest masquerade of the West—particularly America, the torchbearer since the end of World War II of "Western" values— to appear to the world as the epitome of civilization and as the only legitimate arbiter of human values.

To understand the roots of the modern discourse of "human rights," we need to isolate the two central notions from which it is derived, namely the "individual" and the "rule of law." It has been a staple of Western thought since at least the Renaissance that—while the West recognizes the individual as the true unit of being and the building block of society, non-Western cultures have been built around collectivities, conceived as religious, linguistic, ethnic, tribal or racial groups. As the *Economist*—and one could multiply such examples a thousand-fold —was to boldly declare in its issue of 27 February 1909, "whatever may be the political atom in India, it is certainly not the individual of Western democratic theory, but the community of some sort." In the West the individual stands in singular and splendid isolation, the promise of the inherent perfectibility of man; in the non-West, the individual is nothing, always a part of a collectivity in relation to which his or her existence is defined, never a being unto himself or herself. Where the "individual" does not exist, one cannot speak of his or her rights; and where there are no rights, it is perfectly absurd to speak of their denial or abrogation.

On the Western view, moreover, if the atomistic conception of the "individual" is a prerequisite for a concern with human

rights, so is the "rule of law" under which alone can such rights be respected. In a society which lives by the "rule of law," such laws as the government might formulate are done so in accordance with certain normative criteria—for example, they shall be non-discriminatory, blind to considerations of race, gender, class, and linguistic background; these laws are then made public, so that no person might plead ignorance of the law; and the judicial process under which the person charged for the infringement of such laws is tried must hold out the promise of being fair and equitable. As in the case of "individual," the "rule of law" is held to be a uniquely Western contribution to civilization, on the two-fold assumption that democracy is an idea and institution of purely Western origins, and that the only form of government known to non-Western societies was absolutism. In conditions of "Oriental Despotism," the only law was the law of the despot, and the life and limb of each of his subjects was hostage to the tyranny of his pleasures and whims. In the despotic state, there was perhaps only one "individual," the absolute ruler; under him were the masses, particles of dust on the distant horizon. What rights were there to speak of then?

Having briefly outlined how the notions of the "individual" and the "rule of law" came to intersect in the formulation of the discourse of human rights, we can proceed to unravel some of the more disturbing and unacceptable aspects of this discourse. Where once the language of liberation was religion, today the language of emancipation is law. Indeed, the very notion of "human rights," as it is commonly understood in the international forum today, is legalistic. Proponents of the "rule of law," convinced of the uniqueness of the West, are not prepared to concede that customs and traditional usages in most "Third World" countries have functioned for centuries in place of "law," and that even without the "rule of law" there were conventions and traditions which bound one person to respect the rights of another. We expect rights to be protected under the law and the conformity of states to the "rule of law." Many obvious and commonplace objections to such a state of affairs come to mind. By what right, with what authority, and with what consequences do certain states brand other states as "outlaw" or "renegade" states, living outside the pale of the "rule of law," allegedly oblivious to the rights of their subjects, and therefore subject to sanctions from the "international community?"

There is, as has been argued, one "rule of law" for the powerful, and an altogether different one for those states that do not speak the "rational," "diplomatic," and "sane" language that the West has decreed to be the universal form of linguistic exchange. It is not only the case that when Americans retaliate against their foes, they are engaged in "just war" or purely "defensive" measures in the interest of national security, but also that when Libyans or Syrians do so, they are transformed into "terrorists" or ruthless and self-aggrandizing despots in the pursuit of international dominance. The problem is more acute: who is to police the police? The United States claims adherence to international law, but summarily rejected the authority of the World Court when it condemned the United States for waging undeclared war against Nicaragua. More recently, the U.S. Supreme Court, in an astounding judgment barely noticed in the American press, upheld the constitutionality of a decision of a circuit court in Texas which, by allowing American law enforcement officers to kidnap nationals of a foreign state for alleged offenses under American law to be brought to the United States for trial, effectively proclaims the global jurisdiction of American law. As a noted Indian commentator has written, "We are thus back in the 15th, 16th, and 17th century world of piracy and pillage" (Ashok Mitra, "No Holds Barred for the U.S.," *Deccan Herald*, 3 July 1992). Were not the Libyans and Sandinistas supposed to be the pirates?

There are, however, less obvious and more significant problems with the legalistic conception of a world order where "human rights" will be safeguarded. The present conception of "human rights" largely rests on a distinction between state and civil society, a distinction here fraught with hazardous consequences. The rights which are claimed are rights held against the state or, to put it another way, with the blessing of the state: the right to freedom of speech and expression, the right to gather in public, the right to express one's grievances within the limits of the constitution, and so forth. The state becomes the guarantor of these rights, when in fact it is everywhere the state which is the most flagrant violator of human rights.

Not only does the discourse of "human rights" privilege the state, but the very conception of "rights" must of necessity remain circumscribed. The right to a fair hearing upon arrest, or to take part in the government of one's country, is acknowledged as an unqualified political and civil right, but the right to housing, food, clean air, an ecologically-sound environment, free primary and secondary education, public transportation, a high standard of health, the preservation of one's ethnic identity and culture, and security in the event of unemployment or impairment due to disease and old age is not accorded parity. When, as in the United States, certain communities are in a systematic and calculated fashion deprived of the basic amenities required to sustain a reasonable standard of living, when an entire economy is designed on a war footing, does not that constitute a gross and inexcusable infringement of the "human rights" of those who are most disempowered in our society? Is it not ironic that in the very week this year when rebellious demonstrators in Thailand were being hailed in the Western media as champions of human rights, martyrs to freedom, and foes of tyranny, the insurrectionists in Los Angeles were contemptuously dismissed by the same media as "rioters," "hooligans," "arsonists," and "murderers?" No doubt some were just exactly that, but that admission cannot allow us to obfuscate the recognition that the action of the insurrectionists was fueled by a deep-seated resentment at the violation of their social, economic, and cultural rights.

Certainly there are organizations, such as the Minority Rights Group (London) and Cultural Survival (Boston), which have adopted a broader conception of "human rights," and whose discourse is as concerned with the numerous rights of "collectivities," whether conceived in terms of race, gender, class, ethnic or linguistic background, as it is with the rights of "individuals." But this is not the discourse of "human rights" in the main, and it is emphatically not the discourse of Western powers, which have seldom adhered to the standards that they expect others to abide by, and would use even food and medicine, as the contin-

uing embargo against Iraq so vividly demonstrates, to retain their political and cultural hegemony even as they continue to deploy the rhetoric of "human rights." Never mind that state formation in the West was forged over the last few centuries by brutally coercive techniques—colonialism, genocide, eugenics, the machinery of "law and order"—to create homogeneous groups. One could point randomly to the complete elimination of the Tasmanian Aboriginals, the extermination of many Native American tribes, the Highland Clearances in Scotland, even the very processes by which a largely Breton-speaking France became, in less than a hundred years, French-speaking. We should be emphatically clear that what are called "Third World" countries should not be allowed the luxury, the right if you will, of pointing to the excesses of state formation in the West to argue, in a parody of the ludicrous evolutionary model where the non-Western world is destined to become progressively free and democratic, that they too must ruthlessly forge ahead with "development" and "progress" before their subjects can be allowed "human rights."

The idea of "human rights" is noble and its denial an effrontery to humankind. But it is only as an imagined idea that we can embrace it, and our fascination with this idea must not deflect us from the understanding that, as an ideological and political tool of the West, and particularly of the only remaining superpower, "human rights" is contaminated. Perhaps, before "human rights" is flaunted by the United States as what most of the rest of the world must learn to respect, the movement for "human rights" should first come home to roost. As Noam Chomsky has written, people in the Third World "have never understood the deep totalitarian strain in Western culture, nor have they ever understood the savagery and cynicism of Western culture." Could there be greater testimony to this hypocrisy than the fact that inscribed on the marble wall of the main lobby at CIA headquarters in Virginia is this quotation from John (VIII: 32): "And Ye Shall Know the Truth/And the Truth Shall Make You Free?"

POSTSCRIPT

Are Human Rights Basic to Justice?

Howard makes clear that in her view the issue here is not simply a matter of one cultural group imposing its ways on another. She acknowledges a certain amount of variation and relativity in cultural practices. The example of marriage is useful in this regard. Marriage arrangements and social institutions are quite different in different cultures—e.g., polygamy is widespread in Western Africa. Howard's point is that however various cultures arrange matters, they must recognize basic human rights or else they are simply unjust. Yet even this stand is somewhat softened by Howard's acknowledgment of what she calls "weak cultural relativism." She seems willing to allow that a particular culture or "popular sentiment" may violate human rights but that an official government may never do so.

A defender of Lal's viewpoint, however, could take Howard's distinction between what is culturally relative and what is not and affirm that human rights fall on the relative side. Like marriage arrangements, human rights vary. As strong as the concept of rights is in the West, to apply it to various cultures outside the West is to practice a new form of Western imperialism.

Is an appeal to rights an appeal to something universal, something that ought to be recognized by all cultures? Is it only a rhetorical appeal, one that may or may not have meaning or use in a given cultural environment? Or is it part of the West's systematic domination of the world?

The full text of the Universal Declaration of Human Rights, the International Covenant on Civil and Political Rights, relevant portions of the Charter of the United Nations, and other documents, as well as useful historical background, can be found in Paul Williams, ed., *The International Bill of Rights* (Entwhistle Books, 1981). Peter G. Brown and Douglas MacClean, eds., *Human Rights and U.S. Foreign Policy: Principles and Applications* (Lexington Books, 1979) nicely brings together questions about abstract ideas and real political practice. Also useful are Jack Donnelly, *Universal Human Rights in Theory and Practice* (Cornell University Press, 1989), the *Yearbook on Human Rights* (published biennially by the United Nations), and *Human Rights Quarterly*. Sources that are relevant to female genital mutilation (referred to by Howard as "female genital operations")—a particular topic of controversy in this context—are Sandra D. Lane and Robert A. Rubinstine, "Judging the Other: Responding to Traditional Female Genital Surgeries," *Hastings Center Report* (May–June 1996); Memuna M. Sillah and Asha Samad, "Bundu Trap," *Natural History* (August 1996); Alan Cooperman "No End in Sight to a Gruesome and Widespread Ritual," *U.S. News and World Report* (July 7, 1997); and "Female Genital and Sexual Mutilation," *WIN News* (Winter 1997).

ISSUE 17

Do Rich Nations Have an Obligation to Help Poor Nations?

YES: Peter Singer, from *Practical Ethics,* 2d ed. (Cambridge University Press, 1993)

NO: Garrett Hardin, from "Lifeboat Ethics: The Case Against Helping the Poor," *Psychology Today* (vol. 8, 1974)

ISSUE SUMMARY

YES: Professor of philosophy Peter Singer argues that citizens of rich nations can help those in poor nations without great harm to themselves and that, therefore, they *should* help.

NO: Biologist Garrett Hardin argues that since birthrates in poorer nations are high and the earth can provide only finite resources, future generations of all nations will be hurt if wealthy nations help poor nations.

If the wealth of a community were concentrated in the hands of a few people while many other people were so poor that they would likely die of exposure or starve to death, it would be reasonable to say that the wealthy had an obligation to help their neighbors. If the wealth of a nation were concentrated in the hands of a relatively small number of people while the majority were in dire need, again it would be reasonable to say that the wealthy had an obligation to help their countrymen.

Other questions are worth exploring in order to understand the relationship between rich and poor. For instance, do wealthy people acquire their wealth at the expense of the needy? If so, then the wealthy have an obligation to help the needy, since they are to some extent responsible for the others' condition. How great is the discrepancy between the rich and the poor? The greater the discrepancy, the stronger the case for obligation. How poor are the poor? There may be no limit to the riches that one can acquire, but there is an absolute bottom limit to the level of poverty to which one can descend; at some point one dies. The greater the absolute need of the needy, the better the case for obligation on the part of the wealthy.

How great a burden will fall on the "haves" if they come to the assistance of the "have nots"? If the discrepancy between the two groups is very large, and if the needy are very poor indeed, then the wealthy can help the poor without falling too many rungs on the ladder of wealth.

These questions all concern the distribution of wealth among the members of a community and among the members of a nation. Should we also ask these questions with respect to the entire human race? Our world is divided into countries, some of which are quite wealthy, including the United States, other industrial nations, and oil-rich Arab countries. These countries, although in the minority, control most of the world's wealth. It is also true that the discrepancy between the rich nations and the poor nations is great and that the level of existence in many poor nations is abysmally low. The outlook for inhabitants of poor countries is even worse during times of war, drought, political oppression, flood, famine, and epidemic disease.

Is the community of nations different from a community of individuals? Does the same reasoning apply to both cases? We probably would not let someone die of exposure or starvation on our own doorstep, but should this concern extend over vast distances?

In the following selections, Peter Singer argues that needy nations are quite needy, that wealthy nations are quite wealthy, and that the wealthy nations can help the distant needy at a relatively low cost. Therefore, he says, rich nations *should* help poor ones. Singer also dismisses the idea that moral obligations to others vary according to geographical location. Garrett Hardin argues that although the people in question may be very bad off, wealthy nations are not in a position to help them. If aid were rendered to poor nations, he contends, future generations of all countries would be hurt because such aid would support high birthrates in poor countries, thereby depleting the earth's finite resources and making life worse for large numbers of people

YES

Peter Singer

RICH AND POOR

SOME FACTS ABOUT POVERTY

Consider these facts: by the most cautious estimates, 400 million people lack the calories, protein, vitamins and minerals needed to sustain their bodies and minds in a healthy state. Millions are constantly hungry; others suffer from deficiency diseases and from infections they would be able to resist on a better diet. Children are the worst affected. According to one study, 14 million children under five die every year from the combined effects of malnutrition and infection. In some districts half the children born can be expected to die before their fifth birthday.

Nor is lack of food the only hardship of the poor. To give a broader picture, Robert McNamara, when president of the World Bank, suggested the term 'absolute poverty'. The poverty we are familiar with in industrialised nations is relative poverty—meaning that some citizens are poor, relative to the wealth enjoyed by their neighbours. People living in relative poverty in Australia might be quite comfortably off by comparison with pensioners in Britain, and British pensioners are not poor in comparison with the poverty that exists in Mali or Ethiopia. Absolute poverty, on the other hand, is poverty by any standard. In McNamara's words:

> Poverty at the absolute level ... is life at the very margin of existence. The absolute poor are severely deprived human beings struggling to survive in a set of squalid and degraded circumstances almost beyond the power of our sophisticated imaginations and privileged circumstances to conceive.
>
> Compared to those fortunate enough to live in developed countries, individuals in the poorest nations have:

- An infant mortality rate eight times higher
- A life expectancy one-third lower
- An adult literacy rate 60 per cent less
- A nutritional level, for one out of every two in the population, below acceptable standards;
- And for millions of infants, less protein than is sufficient to permit optimum development of the brain.

McNamara has summed up absolute poverty as 'a condition of life so characterised by malnutrition, illiteracy, disease, squalid surroundings, high infant mortality and low life expectancy as to be beneath any reasonable definition of human decency'.

Absolute poverty is, as McNamara has said, responsible for the loss of countless lives, especially among infants and young children. When absolute poverty does not cause death, it still causes misery of a kind not often seen in the affluent nations. Malnutrition in young children stunts both physical and mental development. According to the United Nations Development Programme, 180 million children under the age of five suffer from serious malnutrition. Millions of people on poor diets suffer from deficiency diseases, like goitre, or blindness caused by a lack of vitamin A. The food value of what the poor eat is further reduced by parasites such as hookworm and ringworm, which are endemic in conditions of poor sanitation and health education.

Death and disease apart, absolute poverty remains a miserable condition of life, with inadequate food, shelter, clothing, sanitation, health services and education. The Worldwatch Institute estimates that as many as 1.2 billion people—or 23 per cent of the world's population—live in absolute poverty. For the purposes of this estimate, absolute poverty is defined as "the lack of sufficient income in cash or kind to meet the most basic biological needs for food, clothing, and shelter." Absolute poverty is probably the principal cause of human misery today.

SOME FACTS ABOUT WEALTH

This is the background situation, the situation that prevails on our planet all the time. It does not make headlines. People died from malnutrition and related diseases yesterday, and more will die tomorrow. The occasional droughts, cyclones, earthquakes, and floods that take the lives of tens of thousands in one place and at one time are more newsworthy. They add greatly to the total amount of human suffering; but it is wrong to assume that when there are no major calamities reported, all is well.

The problem is not that the world cannot produce enough to feed and shelter its people. People in the poor countries consume, on average, 180 kilos of grain a year, while North Americans average around 900 kilos. The difference is caused by the fact that in the rich countries we feed most of our grain to animals, converting it into meat, milk, and eggs. Because this is a highly inefficient process, people in rich countries are responsible for the consumption of far more food than those in poor countries who eat few animal products. If we stopped feeding animals on grains and soybeans, the amount of food saved would—if distributed to those who need it—be more than enough to end hunger throughout the world.

These facts about animal food do not mean that we can easily solve the world food problem by cutting down on animal products, but they show that the problem is essentially one of distribution rather than production. The world does produce enough food. Moreover, the poorer nations themselves could produce far more if they made more use of improved agricultural techniques.

So why are people hungry? Poor people cannot afford to buy grain grown by farmers in the richer nations. Poor farmers cannot afford to buy improved seeds, or fertilisers, or the machinery needed for drilling wells and pumping water. Only by transferring some of the wealth of the rich nations to the poor can the situation be changed.

That this wealth exists is clear. Against the picture of absolute poverty that McNamara has painted, one might pose a picture of 'absolute affluence'. Those who are absolutely affluent are not necessarily affluent by comparison with their neighbours, but they are affluent by any reasonable definition of human needs. This means that they have more income than they need to provide themselves adequately with all the basic necessities of life. After buying (either directly or through their taxes) food, shelter, clothing, basic health services, and education, the absolutely affluent are still able to spend money on luxuries. The absolutely affluent choose their food for the pleasures of the palate, not to stop hunger; they buy new clothes to look good, not to keep warm; they move house to be in a better neighbourhood or have a playroom for the children, not to keep out the rain; and after all this there is still money to spend on stereo systems, video-cameras, and overseas holidays.

At this stage I am making no ethical judgments about absolute affluence, merely pointing out that it exists. Its defining characteristic is a significant amount of income above the level necessary to provide for the basic human needs of oneself and one's dependents. By this standard, the majority of citizens of Western Europe, North America, Japan, Australia, New Zealand, and the oil-rich Middle Eastern states are all absolutely affluent. To quote McNamara once more:

> 'The average citizen of a developed country enjoys wealth beyond the wildest dreams of the one billion people in countries with per capita incomes under $200.'

These, therefore, are the countries—and individuals—who have wealth that they could, without threatening their own basic welfare, transfer to the absolutely poor.

At present, very little is being transferred. Only Sweden, the Netherlands, Norway, and some of the oil-exporting Arab states have reached the modest target, set by the United Nations, of 0.7 per cent of gross national (GNP). Britain gives 0.31 per cent of its GNP in official development assistance and a small additional amount in unofficial aid from voluntary organisations. The total comes to about £2 per month per person, and compares with 5.5 per cent of GNP spent on alcohol, and 3 per cent on tobacco. Other, even wealthier nations, give little more: Germany gives 0.41 per cent and Japan 0.32 per cent. The United States gives a mere 0.15 per cent of its GNP.

THE MORAL EQUIVALENT OF MURDER?

If these are the facts, we cannot avoid concluding that by not giving more than we do, people in rich countries are allowing those in poor countries to suffer from absolute poverty, with consequent malnutrition, ill health, and death. This is not a conclusion that applies only to governments. It applies to each absolutely affluent individual, for each of us has the opportunity to do something about the situation; for instance, to give our time or money to voluntary organisations like Oxfam, Care, War on Want, Freedom from Hunger, Community Aid Abroad, and so on. If, then, allowing someone to die is not intrinsically different from killing someone, it would seem that we are all murderers. . . .

Here is a summary of . . . five differences that normally exist between killing and allowing to die, in the context of absolute poverty and overseas aid. The lack of an identifiable victim is of no moral significance, though it may play an important role in explaining our attitudes. The idea that we are directly responsible for those we kill, but not for those we do not help, depends on a questionable notion of responsibility and may need to be based on a controversial theory of rights. Differences in certainty and motivation are ethically significant, and show that not aiding the poor is not to be condemned as murdering them; it could, however, be on a par with killing someone as a result of reckless driving, which is serious enough. Finally the difficulty of completely discharging the duty of saving all one possibly can makes it inappropriate to blame those who fall short of this target as we blame those who kill; but this does not show that the act itself is less serious. Nor does it indicate anything about those who, far from saving all they possibly can, make no effort to save anyone.

These conclusions suggest a new approach. Instead of attempting to deal with the contrast between affluence and poverty by comparing not saving with deliberate killing, let us consider afresh whether we have an obligation to assist those whose lives are in danger, and if so, how this obligation applies to the present world situation.

THE OBLIGATION TO ASSIST

The Argument for an Obligation to Assist

The path from the library at my university to the humanities lecture theatre passes a shallow ornamental pond. Suppose that on my way to give a lecture I notice that a small child has fallen in and is in danger of drowning. Would anyone deny that I ought to wade in and pull the child out? This will mean getting my clothes muddy and either cancelling my lecture or delaying it until I can find something dry to change into; but compared with the avoidable death of a child this is insignificant.

A plausible principle that would support the judgment that I ought to pull the child out is this: if it is in our power to prevent something very bad from happening, without thereby sacrificing anything of comparable moral significance, we ought to do it. This principle seems uncontroversial. . . .

Nevertheless the uncontroversial appearance of the principle that we ought to prevent what is bad when we can do so without sacrificing anything of comparable moral significance is deceptive. If it were taken seriously and acted upon, our lives and our world would be fundamentally changed. For the principle applies, not just to rare situations in which one can save a child from a pond, but to the everyday situation in which we can assist those living in absolute poverty. In saying this I assume that absolute poverty, with its hunger and malnutrition, lack of shelter, illiteracy, disease, high infant mortality, and low life expectancy, is a bad thing. And I assume that it is within the power of the affluent to reduce absolute poverty, without sacrificing anything of comparable moral significance. If these two assumptions and the principle we have been discussing are correct, we have an obligation to help those in absolute poverty that is no less strong than our obligation to rescue a drowning child from a pond. Not to help would be wrong, whether or not it is intrinsically equivalent to killing. Helping is not, as conventionally thought, a charitable act that it is praiseworthy to do, but not wrong to omit; it is something that everyone ought to do.

This is the argument for an obligation to assist. Set out more formally, it would look like this.

First premise: If we can prevent something bad without sacrificing anything of comparable significance, we ought to do it.

Second premise: Absolute poverty is bad.

Third premise: There is some absolute poverty we can prevent without sacrificing anything of comparable moral significance.

Conclusion: We ought to prevent some absolute poverty.

The first premise is the substantive moral premise on which the argument rests, and I have tried to show that it can be accepted by people who hold a variety of ethical positions.

The second premise is unlikely to be challenged. Absolute poverty is, as Mc-Namara put it, 'beneath any reasonable definition of human decency' and it would be hard to find a plausible ethical view that did not regard it as a bad thing.

The third premise is more controversial, even though it is cautiously framed. It claims only that some absolute poverty can be prevented without the sacrifice of anything of comparable moral significance. It thus avoids the objection that

any aid I can give is just 'drops in the ocean' for the point is not whether my personal contribution will make any noticeable impression on world poverty as a whole (of course it won't) but whether it will prevent some poverty. This is all the argument needs to sustain its conclusion, since the second premise says that any absolute poverty is bad, and not merely the total amount of absolute poverty. If without sacrificing anything of comparable moral significance we can provide just one family with the means to raise itself out of absolute poverty, the third premise is vindicated.

I have left the notion of moral significance unexamined in order to show that the argument does not depend on any specific values or ethical principles. I think the third premise is true for most people living in industrialised nations, on any defensible view of what is morally significant. Our affluence means that we have income we can dispose of without giving up the basic necessities of life, and we can use this income to reduce absolute poverty. Just how much we will think ourselves obliged to give up will depend on what we consider to be of comparable moral significance to the poverty we could prevent: stylish clothes, expensive dinners, a sophisticated stereo system, overseas holidays, a (second?) car, a larger house, private schools for our children, and so on. . . .

Objections to the Argument

Taking care of our own. Anyone who has worked to increase overseas aid will have come across the argument that we should look after those near us, our families, and then the poor in our own country, before we think about poverty in distant places.

No doubt we do instinctively prefer to help those who are close to us. Few could stand by and watch a child drown; many can ignore a famine in Africa. But the question is not what we usually do, but what we ought to do, and it is difficult to see any sound moral justification for the view that distance, or community membership, makes a crucial difference to our obligations.

Consider, for instance, racial affinities. Should people of European origin help poor Europeans before helping poor Africans? Most of us would reject such a suggestion out of hand.... [because] people's need for food has nothing to do with their race, and if Africans need food more than Europeans, it would be a violation of the principle of equal consideration to give preference to Europeans.

The same point applies to citizenship or nationhood. Every affluent nation has some relatively poor citizens, but absolute poverty is limited largely to the poor nations. Those living on the streets of Calcutta, or in the drought-prone Sahel region of Africa, are experiencing poverty unknown in the West. Under these circumstances it would be wrong to decide that only those fortunate enough to be citizens of our own community will share our abundance.

We feel obligations of kinship more strongly than those of citizenship. Which parents could give away their last bowl of rice if their own children were starving? To do so would seem unnatural, contrary to our nature as biologically evolved beings—although whether it would be wrong is another question altogether. In any case, we are not faced with that situation, but with one in which our own children are well-fed, well-clothed, well-educated, and would now like new bikes, a stereo set, or their own car. In these circumstances any special obligations we might have to our children have been fulfilled, and the needs of strangers make a stronger claim upon us.

The element of truth in the view that we should first take care of our own, lies in the advantage of a recognised system of responsibilities. When families and local communities look after their own poorer members, ties of affection and personal relationships achieve ends that would otherwise require a large, impersonal bureaucracy. Hence it would be absurd to propose that from now on we all regard ourselves as equally responsible for the welfare of everyone in the world; but the argument for an obligation to assist does not propose that. It applies only when some are in absolute poverty, and others can help without sacrificing anything of comparable moral significance. To allow one's own kin to sink into absolute poverty would be to sacrifice something of comparable significance; and before that point had been reached, the breakdown of the system of family and community responsibility would be a factor to weigh the balance in favour of a small degree of preference for family and community. This small degree of preference is, however, decisively outweighed by existing discrepancies in wealth and property.

Property rights. Do people have a right to private property, a right that contradicts the view that they are under an obligation to give some of their wealth away to those in absolute poverty? According to some theories of rights (for instance, Robert Nozick's), provided one has acquired one's property without the use of unjust means like force and fraud, one may be entitled to enormous wealth while others starve. This individualistic conception of rights is in contrast to other views, like the early Christian doctrine to be found in the works of Thomas Aquinas, which holds that since property exists for the satisfaction of human needs, 'whatever a man has in superabundance is owed, of natural right, to the poor for their sustenance'. A socialist would also, of course, see wealth as belonging to the community rather than the individual, while utilitarians, whether socialist or not, would be prepared to override property rights to prevent great evils.

Does the argument for an obligation to assist others therefore presuppose one of these other theories of property rights, and not an individualistic theory like Nozick's? Not necessarily. A theory of property rights can insist on our *right* to retain wealth without pronouncing on whether the rich *ought* to give to the poor. Nozick, for example, rejects the use of compulsory means like taxation to redistribute income, but suggests that we can achieve the ends we deem morally desirable by voluntary means. So Nozick would reject the claim that rich people have an 'obligation' to give to the poor, in so far as this implies that the poor have a right to our aid, but might accept that giving is something we ought to do and failing to give, though within one's rights, is wrong—for there is more to an ethical life than respecting the rights of others.

The argument for an obligation to assist can survive, with only minor modifications, even if we accept an individualistic theory of property rights. In any case, however, I do not think we should accept such a theory. It leaves too much to chance to be an acceptable ethical view. For instance, those whose forefathers happened to inhabit some sandy wastes around the Persian Gulf are now fabulously wealthy, because oil lay under those sands; while those whose forefathers settled on better land south of the Sahara live in absolute poverty, because of drought and bad harvests. Can this distribution be acceptable from an impartial point of view? If we imagine ourselves about to begin life as a citizen of either Bahrein or Chad—but we do not know which—would we accept the principle that citizens of Bahrein are under no obligation to assist people living in Chad?

Population and the ethics of triage. Perhaps the most serious objection to the argument that we have an obligation to assist is that since the major cause of absolute poverty is overpopulation, helping those now in poverty will only ensure that yet more people are born to live in poverty in the future.

In its most extreme form, this objection is taken to show that we should adopt a policy of 'triage'. The term comes from medical policies adopted in wartime. With too few doctors to cope with all the casualties, the wounded were divided into three categories: those who would probably survive without medical assistance, those who might survive if they received assistance, but otherwise probably would not, and those who even with medical assistance probably would not survive. Only those in the middle category were given medical assistance. The idea, of course, was to use limited medical resources as effectively as possible. For those in the first category, medical treatment was not strictly necessary; for those in the third category, it was likely to be useless. It has been suggested that we should apply the same policies to countries, according to their prospects of becoming self-sustaining. We would not aid countries that even without our help will soon help to feed their populations. We would not aid countries that, even with our help, will not be able to limit their population to a level they can feed. We would aid those countries where our help might make the difference between success and failure in bringing food and population into balance.

Advocates of this theory are understandably reluctant to give a complete list of the countries they would place into the 'hopeless' category; Bangladesh has been cited as an example, and so have some of the countries of the Sahel region of Africa. Adopting the policy of triage would, then, mean cutting off assistance to these countries and allowing famine, disease, and natural disasters to reduce the population of those countries to the level at which they can provide adequately for all.

In support of this view Garrett Hardin has offered a metaphor: we in the rich nations are like the occupants of a crowded lifeboat adrift in a sea full of drowning people. If we try to save the drowning by bringing them aboard, our boat will be overloaded and we shall all drown. Since it is better that some survive than none, we should leave the others to drown. In the world today, according to Hardin, 'lifeboat ethics' apply. The rich should leave the poor to starve, for otherwise the poor will drag the rich down with them....

Putting aside the controversial issue of the extent to which food production might one day be increased, it is true, as we have already seen, that the world now produces enough to feed its inhabitants—the amount lost by being fed to animals itself being enough to meet existing grain shortages. Nevertheless population

growth cannot be ignored. Bangladesh could, with land reform and using better techniques, feed its present population of 115 million; but by the year 2000, according to United Nations Population Division estimates, its population will be 150 million. The enormous effort that will have to go into feeding an extra 35 million people, all added to the population within a decade, means that Bangladesh must develop at full speed to stay where it is. Other low-income countries are in similar situations. By the end of the century, Ethiopia's population is expected to rise from 49 to 66 million; Somalia's from 7 to 9 million, India's from 853 to 1041 million, Zaire's from 35 to 49 million.[1]

What will happen if the world population continues to grow? It cannot do so indefinitely. It will be checked by a decline in birth rates or a rise in death rates. Those who advocate triage are proposing that we allow the population growth of some countries to be checked by a rise in death rates—that is, by increased malnutrition, and related diseases; by widespread famines; by increased infant mortality; and by epidemics of infectious diseases.

The consequences of triage on this scale are so horrible that we are inclined to reject it without further argument. How could we sit by our television sets, watching millions starve while we do nothing? Would not that be the end of all notions of human equality and respect for human life?... Don't people have a right to our assistance, irrespective of the consequences?

Anyone whose initial reaction to triage was not one of repugnance would be an unpleasant sort of person. Yet initial reactions based on strong feelings are not always reliable guides. Advocates of triage are rightly concerned with the long-term consequences of our actions. They say that helping the poor and starving now merely ensures more poor and starving in the future. When our capacity to help is finally unable to cope —as one day it must be—the suffering will be greater than it would be if we stopped helping now. If this is correct, there is nothing we can do to prevent absolute starvation and poverty, in the long run, and so we have no obligation to assist. Nor does it seem reasonable to hold that under these circumstances people have a right to our assistance. If we do accept such a right, irrespective of the consequences, we are saying that, in Hardin's metaphor, we should continue to haul the drowning into our lifeboat until the boat sinks and we all drown.

... The question is: how probable is this forecast that continued assistance now will lead to greater disasters in the future?

Forecasts of population growth are notoriously fallible, and theories about the factors that affect it remain speculative. One theory, at least as plausible as any other, is that countries pass through a 'demographic transition' as their standard of living rises. When people are very poor and have no access to modern medicine their fertility is high, but population is kept in check by high death rates. The introduction of sanitation, modern medical techniques, and other improvements reduces the death rate, but initially has little effect on the birth rate. Then population grows rapidly. Some poor countries, especially in sub-Saharan Africa, are now in this phase. If standards of living continue to rise, however, couples begin to realise that to have the same number of children surviving to maturity as in the past, they do not need to give birth to as many children as their parents did. The need for

children to provide economic support in old age diminishes. Improved education and the emancipation and employment of women also reduce the birth-rate, and so population growth begins to level off. Most rich nations have reached this stage, and their populations are growing only very slowly, if at all.

If this theory is right, there is an alternative to the disasters accepted as inevitable by supporters of triage. We can assist poor countries to raise the living standards of the poorest members of their population. We can encourage the governments of these countries to enact land reform measures, improve education, and liberate women from a purely child-bearing role. We can also help other countries to make contraception and sterilisation widely available. There is a fair chance that these measures will hasten the onset of the demographic transition and bring population growth down to a manageable level. According to United Nations estimates, in 1965 the average woman in the third world gave birth to six children, and only 8 per cent were using some form of contraception; by 1991 the average number of children had dropped to just below four, and more than half the women in the third world were taking contraceptive measures. Notable successes in encouraging the use of contraception had occurred in Thailand, Indonesia, Mexico, Colombia, Brazil, and Bangladesh. This achievement reflected a relatively low expenditure in developing countries—considering the size and significance of the problem—of $3 billion annually, with only 20 per cent of this sum coming from developed nations. So expenditure in this area seems likely to be highly cost-effective. Success cannot be guaranteed; but the evidence suggests that we can reduce population growth by improving economic security and education, and making contraceptives more widely available. This prospect makes triage ethically unacceptable. We cannot allow millions to die from starvation and disease when there is a reasonable probability that population can be brought under control without such horrors.

Population growth is therefore not a reason against giving overseas aid, although it should make us think about the kind of aid to give. Instead of food handouts, it may be better to give aid that leads to a slowing of population growth. This may mean agricultural assistance for the rural poor, or assistance with education, or the provision of contraceptive services. Whatever kind of aid proves most effective in specific circumstances, the obligation to assist is not reduced.

NOTES

1. Ominously, in the twelve years [1981–1993] that have passed between editions of this book, the signs are that the situation is becoming even worse than was then predicted. In 1979 Bangladesh had a population of 80 million and it was predicted that by 2000 its population would reach 146 million; Ethiopia's was only 29 million, and was predicted to reach 54 million; and India's was 620 million and predicted to reach 958 million.

NO
Garrett Hardin

LIFEBOAT ETHICS: THE CASE AGAINST HELPING THE POOR

Environmentalists use the metaphor of the earth as a "spaceship" in trying to persuade countries, industries and people to stop wasting and polluting our natural resources. Since we all share life on this planet, they argue, no single person or institution has the right to destroy, waste, or use more than a fair share of its resources.

But does everyone on earth have an equal right to an equal share of its resources? The spaceship metaphor can be dangerous when used by misguided idealists to justify suicidal policies for sharing our resources through uncontrolled immigration and foreign aid. In their enthusiastic but unrealistic generosity, they confuse the ethics of a spaceship with those of a lifeboat.

A true spaceship would have to be under the control of a captain, since no ship could possibly survive if its course were determined by committee. Spaceship Earth certainly has no captain; the United Nations is merely a toothless tiger, with little power to enforce any policy upon its bickering members.

If we divide the world crudely into rich nations and poor nations, two thirds of them are desperately poor, and only one third comparatively rich, with the United States the wealthiest of all. Metaphorically each rich nation can be seen as a lifeboat full of comparatively rich people. In the ocean outside each lifeboat swim the poor of the world, who would like to get in, or at least to share some of the wealth. What should the lifeboat passengers do?

First, we must recognize the limited capacity of any lifeboat. For example, a nation's land has a limited capacity to support a population and as the current energy crisis has shown us, in some ways we have already exceeded the carrying capacity of our land.

ADRIFT IN A MORAL SEA

So here we sit, say fifty people in our lifeboat. To be generous, let us assume it has room for ten more, making a total capacity of sixty. Suppose the fifty of us in the lifeboat see 100 others swimming in the water outside, begging for admission to our boat or for handouts. We have several options: we may be tempted to try to live by the Christian ideal of being "our brother's keeper," or by the Marxist ideal of "to each according to his needs." Since the needs of all in the water are the same, and since they can all be seen as "our brothers," we could take them all into our boat, making a total of 150 in a boat designed for sixty. The boat swamps, everyone drowns. Complete justice, complete catastrophe.

Since the boat has an unused excess capacity of ten more passengers, we could admit just ten more to it. But which ten do we let in? How do we choose? Do we pick the best ten, the neediest ten, "first come, first served"? And what do we say to the ninety we exclude? If we do let an extra ten into our lifeboat, we will have lost our "safety factor," an engineering principle of critical importance. For example, if we don't leave room for excess capacity as a safety factor in our country's agriculture, a new plant disease or a bad change in the weather could have disastrous consequences.

Suppose we decide to preserve our small safety factor and admit no more to the lifeboat. Our survival is then possible, although we shall have to be constantly on guard against boarding parties.

While this last solution clearly offers the only means of our survival, it is morally abhorrent to many people. Some say they feel guilty about their good luck. My reply is simple: "Get out and yield your place to others." This may solve the problem of the guilt-ridden person's conscience, but it does not change the ethics of the lifeboat. The needy person to whom the guilt-ridden person yields his place will not himself feel guilty about his good luck. If he did, he would not climb aboard. The net result of conscience-stricken people giving up their unjustly held seats is the elimination of that sort of conscience from the lifeboat.

This is the basic metaphor within which we must work out our solutions. Let us now enrich the image, step by step, with substantive additions from the real world, a world that must solve real and pressing problems of overpopulation and hunger.

The harsh ethics of the lifeboat become even harsher when we consider the reproductive differences between the rich nations and the poor nations. The people inside the lifeboats are doubling in numbers every eighty-seven years; those swimming around outside are doubling, on the average, every thirty-five years, more than twice as fast as the rich. And since the world's resources are dwindling, the difference in prosperity between the rich and the poor can only increase.

As of 1973, the U.S. had a population of 210 million people, who were increasing by 0.8 percent per year. Outside our lifeboat, let us imagine another 210 million people, (say the combined populations of Columbia, Ecuador, Venezuela, Morocco, Pakistan, Thailand, and the Philippines) who are increasing at a rate of 3.3 percent per year. Put differently, the doubling time for this aggregate population is twenty-one years, compared to eighty-seven years for the U.S.

MULTIPLYING THE RICH AND THE POOR

Now suppose the U.S. agreed to pool its resources with those seven countries, with everyone receiving an equal share. Initially the ratio of Americans to non-Americans in this model would be one-to-one. But consider what the ratio would be after eighty-seven years, by which time the Americans would have doubled to a population of 420 million. By then, doubling every twenty-one years, the other group would have swollen to 3.54 billion. Each American would have to share the available resources with more than eight people.

But, one could argue, this discussion assumes that current population trends will continue, and they may not. Quite so. Most likely the rate of population increase will decline much faster in the U.S. than it will in the other countries, and there does not seem to be much we can do about it. In sharing with "each according to his needs," we must recognize that needs are determined by population size, which is determined by the rate of reproduction, which at present is regarded as a sovereign right of every nation, poor or not. This being so, the philanthropic load created by the sharing ethic of the spaceship can only increase.

THE TRAGEDY OF THE COMMONS

The fundamental error of spaceship ethics, and the sharing it requires, is that it leads to what I call "tragedy of the commons." Under a system of private property, the men who own property recognize their responsibility to care for it, for if they don't they will eventually suffer. A farmer, for instance, will allow no more cattle in a pasture than its carrying capacity justifies. If he overloads it, erosion sets in, weeds take over, and he loses the use of the pasture.

If a pasture becomes a commons open to all, the right of each to use it may not be matched by a corresponding responsibility to protect it. Asking everyone to use it with discretion will hardly do, for the considerate herdsman who refrains from overloading the commons suffers more than a selfish one who says his needs are greater. If everyone would restrain himself, all would be well; but it takes only one less than everyone to ruin a system of voluntary restraint. In a crowded world of less than perfect human beings, mutual ruin is inevitable if there are no controls. This is the tragedy of the commons.

One of the major tasks of education today should be the creation of such an acute awareness of the dangers of the commons that people will recognize its many varieties. For example, the air and water have become polluted because they are treated as commons. Further growth in the population or per capita conversion of natural resources into pollutants will only make the problem worse. The same holds true for the fish of the oceans. Fishing fleets have nearly disappeared in many parts of the world, technological improvements in the art of fishing are hastening the day of complete ruin. Only the replacement of the system of the commons with a responsible system of control will save the land, air, water and oceanic fisheries.

THE WORLD FOOD BANK

In recent years there has been a push to create a new commons called a World Food Bank, an international depository of food reserves to which nations would contribute according to their abilities and from which they would draw according to their needs. This humanitarian proposal has received support from many liberal international groups, and from such prominent citizens as Margaret Mead, U.N. Secretary General Kurt Waldheim, and Senators Edward Kennedy and George McGovern.

A world food bank appeals powerfully to our humanitarian impulses. But before we rush ahead with such a plan, let us recognize where the greatest political push comes from, lest we be disillusioned later. Our experience with the "Food for Peace program," or Public Law 480, gives us the answer. This program moved billions of dollars worth of U.S. surplus grain to food-short, population-long countries during the past two decades. But when P.L. 480 first became law, a headline in the business magazine *Forbes* revealed the real power behind it: "Feeding the World's Hungry Millions: How It Will Mean Billions for U.S. Business."

And indeed it did. In the years 1960 to 1970, U.S. taxpayers spent a total of $7.9 billion on the Food for Peace Program. Between 1948 and 1970, they also paid an additional $50 billion for other economic-aid programs, some of which went for food and food-producing machinery and technology. Though all U.S. taxpayers were forced to contribute to the cost of P.L. 480, certain special interest groups gained handsomely under the program. Farmers did not have to contribute the grain; the Government, or rather the taxpayers, bought it from them at full market prices. The increased demand raised prices of farm products generally. The manufacturers of farm machinery, fertilizers and pesticides benefited by the farmers' extra efforts to grow more food. Grain elevators profited from storing the surplus until it could be shipped. Railroads made money hauling it to ports, and shipping lines profited from carrying it overseas. The implementation of P.L. 480 required the creation of a vast Government bureaucracy, which then acquired its own vested interest in continuing the program regardless of its merits.

EXTRACTING DOLLARS

Those who proposed and defended the Food for Peace program in public rarely mentioned its importance to any of these special interests. The public emphasis was always on its humanitarian effects. The combination of silent selfish interests and highly vocal humanitarian apologists made a powerful and successful lobby for extracting money from taxpayers. We can expect the same lobby to push now for the creation of a World Food Bank.

However great the potential benefit to selfish interests, it should not be a decisive argument against a truly humanitarian program. We must ask if such a program would actually do more good than harm, not only momentarily but also in the long run. Those who propose the food bank usually refer to a current "emergency" or "crisis" in terms of world food supply. But what is an emergency? Although they may be infrequent and sudden, everyone knows that emergencies will occur from time to time. A well-run family, company, organization or country prepares for the likelihood of accidents and emergencies. It expects them, budgets for them, it saves for them.

LEARNING THE HARD WAY

What happens if some organizations or countries budget for accidents and others do not? If each country is solely responsible for its own well-being, poorly managed ones will suffer. But they can learn from experience. They may mend their ways, and learn to budget for infrequent but certain emergencies. For example, the weather varies from year to year, and periodic crop failures are certain. A wise and competent government saves out of the production of the good years in anticipation of bad years to come. Joseph taught this policy to Pharaoh in Egypt more than 2,000 years ago. Yet the great majority of the governments in the world today do not follow such a policy. They lack either the wisdom or the competence, or both. Should those nations that do manage to put something aside be forced to come to the rescue each time an emergency occurs among the poor nations?

"But it isn't their fault!" some kind-hearted liberals argue. "How can we blame the poor people who are caught in an emergency? Why must they suffer for the sins of their governments?" The concept of blame is simply not relevant here. The real question is, what are the operational consequences of establishing a world food bank? If it is open to every country every time a need develops, slovenly rulers will not be motivated to take Joseph's advice. Someone will always come to their aid. Some countries will deposit food in the world food bank, and others will withdraw it. There will be almost no overlap. As a result of such solutions to food shortage emergencies, the poor countries will not learn to mend their ways, and will suffer progressively greater emergencies as their populations grow.

POPULATION CONTROL THE CRUDE WAY

On the average, poor countries undergo a 2.5 percent increase in population each year; rich countries, about 0.8 percent. Only rich countries have anything in the way of food reserves set aside, and even they do not have as much as they should. Poor countries have none. If poor countries received no food from the outside, the rate of their population growth would be periodically checked by crop failures and famines. But if they can always draw on a world food bank in time of need, their population can continue to grow unchecked, and so will their "need" for aid. In the short run, a world food bank may diminish that need, but in the long run it actually increases the need without limit.

Without some system of worldwide food sharing, the proportion of people in the rich and poor nations might eventually stabilize. The overpopulated poor countries would decrease in numbers, while the rich countries that had room for more people would increase. But with a well-meaning system of sharing, such as a world food bank, the growth differential between the rich and the poor countries will not only persist, it will increase. Because of the higher rate of population growth in the poor countries of the world, 88 percent of today's children are born poor, and only 12 percent rich. Year by year the ratio becomes worse, as the fast-reproducing poor outnumber the slow-reproducing rich.

A world food bank is thus a commons in disguise. People will have more motivation to draw from it than to add to any common store. The less provident and less able will multiply at the expense of the abler and more provident, bringing eventual ruin upon all who share in the commons. Besides, any system of "sharing" that amounts to foreign aid from the rich nations to the poor nations will carry the taint of charity, which will contribute little to the world peace so devoutly desired by those who support the idea of a world food bank. . . .

CHINESE FISH AND MIRACLE RICE

The modern approach to foreign aid stresses the export of technology and advice, rather than money and food. As an ancient Chinese proverb goes: "Give a man a fish and he will eat for a day, teach him how to fish and he will eat for the rest of his days." Acting on this advice, the Rockefeller and Ford Foundations have financed a number of programs for improving agriculture in the hungry nations. Known as the "Green Revolution," these programs have led to the development of "miracle rice" and "miracle wheat," new strains that offer bigger harvests and greater resistance to crop damage. Norman Borlaug, the Nobel Prize winning agronomist who, supported by the Rockefeller Foundation, developed "miracle wheat," is one of the most prominent advocates of a world food bank.

Whether or not the Green Revolution can increase food production as much as its champions claim is a debatable but possibly irrelevant point. Those who support this well-intended humanitarian effort should first consider some of the fundamentals of human ecology. Ironically, one man who did was the late Alan Gregg, a vice president of the Rockefeller Foundation. Two decades ago he expressed strong doubts about the wisdom of such attempts to increase food production. He likened the growth and spread of humanity over the surface of the earth to the spread of cancer in the human body, remarking that "cancerous growths demand food; but, as far as I know, they have never been cured by getting it."

OVERLOADING THE ENVIRONMENT

Every human born constitutes a draft on all aspects of the environment: food, air, water, forests, beaches, wildlife, scenery and solitude. Food can, perhaps, be significantly increased to meet a growing demand. But what about clean beaches, unspoiled forests, and solitude? If we satisfy a growing population's need for food, we necessarily decrease its per capita supply of the other resources needed by men.

India, for example, now has a population of 600 million, which increases by 15 million each year. This population already puts a huge load on a relatively impoverished environment. The country's forests are now only a small fraction of what they were three centuries ago, and floods and erosion continually destroy the insufficient farmland that remains. Every one of the 15 million new lives added to India's population puts an additional burden on the environment, and increases the economic and social costs of crowding. However humanitarian our intent, every Indian life saved through medical or nutritional assistance from abroad diminishes the quality of life for those who remain, and for subsequent generations. If rich countries make it possible, through foreign aid, for 600 million Indians to swell to 1.2 billion in a mere twenty-eight years, as their current growth rate threatens, will future generations of Indians thank us for hastening the destruction of their environment? Will our good intentions be sufficient excuse for the consequences of our actions?

My final example of a commons in action is one for which the public has the least desire for rational discussion—immigration. Anyone who publicly questions the wisdom of current U.S. immigration policy is promptly charged with bigotry, prejudice, ethnocentrism, chauvinism, isolationism or selfishness....

IMMIGRATION VS. FOOD SUPPLY

World food banks *move food to the people*, hastening the exhaustion of the environment of the poor countries. Unrestricted immigration, on the other hand, *move people to the food*, thus speeding up the destruction of the environment of the rich countries. We can easily understand why poor people should want to make this latter transfer, but why should rich hosts encourage it?

As in the case of foreign-aid programs, immigration receives support from selfish interests and humanitarian impulses. The primary selfish interest in unimpeded immigration is the desire of employers for cheap labor, particularly in industries and trades that offer degrading work. In the past, one wave of foreigners after another was brought into the U.S. to work at wretched jobs for wretched wages. In recent years the Cubans, Puerto Ricans and Mexicans have had this dubious honor. The interests of the employers of cheap labor mesh well with the guilty silence of the country's liberal intelligentsia. White Anglo-Saxon Protestants are particularly reluctant to call for a closing of the doors to immigration for fear of being called bigots.

But not all countries have such reluctant leadership. Most educated Hawaiians, for example, are keenly aware of the limits of their environment, particularly in terms of population growth. There is only so much room on the islands, and the islanders know it. To Hawaiians, immigrants from the other forty-nine states present as great a threat to those from other nations. At a recent meeting of Hawaiian government officials in Honolulu, I had the ironic delight of hearing a speaker, who like most of his audience was of Japanese ancestry, ask how the country might practically and constitutionally close its doors to further immigration. One member of the audience countered: "How can we shut the door now! We have many friends and relatives in Japan that we'd like to bring here some day so that they can enjoy Hawaii too." The Japanese-American speaker smiled sympathetically and answered: "Yes, but we have children now, and someday we'll have grandchildren too. We can bring more people here from Japan only by giving away some of the land that we hope to pass on to our grandchildren some day. What right do we have to do that?"

At this point, I can hear U. S. liberals asking: "How can you justify slamming the door once you're inside? You say that immigrants should be kept out. But aren't we all immigrants, or the descendants of immigrants? If we insist on staying, must we not admit all others?" Our craving for intellectual order leads us to seek and prefer symmetrical rules and morals: a single rule for me and everybody else; the same rule yesterday, today, and tomorrow. Justice, we feel, should not change with time and place.

We Americans of non-Indian ancestry can look upon ourselves as the descendants of thieves who are guilty morally, if not legally, of stealing this land from its Indian owners. Should we then give back the land to the now living American descendants of those Indians? However morally or logically sound this proposal may be, I, for one, am unwilling to live by it and I know no one else who is. Besides, the logical consequence would be absurd. Suppose that, intoxicated with a sense of pure justice, we should decide to turn our land over to the Indians. Since all our wealth has also been derived from the land, wouldn't we be morally obliged to give that back to the Indians too?

PURE JUSTICE VS. REALITY

Clearly, the concept of pure justice produces an infinite regression to absurdity. Centuries ago, wise men invented statutes of limitations to justify the rejection of such pure justice, in the interest of preventing continual disorder. The law zealously defends property rights, but only relatively recent property rights. Drawing a line after an arbitrary time has elapsed may be unjust, but the alternatives are worse.

We are all the descendants of thieves, and the world's resources are inequitably distributed. But we must begin the journey to tomorrow from the point where we are today. We cannot remake the past. We cannot safely divide the wealth equitably among all peoples so long as people reproduce at different rates. To do so would guarantee that our grandchildren, and everyone else's grandchildren, would have only a ruined world to inherit.

To be generous with one's own possessions is quite different from being generous with those of posterity. We should call this point to the attention of those who, from a commendable love of justice and equality, would institute a system of the commons, either in the form of a world food bank, or of unrestricted immigration. We must convince them if we wish to save at least some parts of the world from environmental ruin.

Without a true world government to control reproduction and the use of available resources, the sharing ethic of the spaceship is impossible. For the foreseeable future, our survival demands that we govern our actions by the ethics of a lifeboat, harsh though they may be. Posterity will be satisfied with nothing else.

POSTSCRIPT

Do Rich Nations Have an Obligation to Help Poor Nations?

The wealth of the earth is unevenly distributed. Some nations find oil in their deserts, and others only sand. Some are hit by severe droughts or floods, and others are not. Some countries benefit from the foresight of their politicians, while others suffer from revolution or political corruption. All of these factors have an impact on the life prospects of an individual. But to what extent, if any, do these matters affect a rich nation's responsibility to a poor one?

Singer argues that the need in poor countries is indeed great and that wealthy nations have the ability to help. By cutting back on luxuries, he says, the well-to-do can prevent people from starving to death. Moreover, because great good can be accomplished at a relatively low cost, wealthy nations have an obligation to do so.

Hardin does not believe that the cost is really so low. He agrees that good can be done, suffering can be relieved, and lives can be saved, but he warns that the populations of poor countries will rise at faster rates than will the populations of rich countries. Consequently, in the end, the suffering will only be postponed, and more lives will be devastated.

Singer can accommodate some of this criticism. If Hardin is right that the countries in question have population problems and extremely high rates of population growth, then *these* are problems that rich nations should address. Singer's overseas aid would include contraceptive devices, information, and programs, in addition to food and medicine.

Of course, there is always the possibility that a given nation will be opposed to contraception or population control and that its population will grow unchecked. In such a case, Hardin would be on stronger ground. The sovereignty of nations comes into play here. No nation has the legal power to diagnose a problem in another country and to prescribe and apply a remedy for it. What is often sad in these cases is that the inhabitants of the poor country themselves may lack political power; they are then at the mercy of those who do have control.

Robert N. Van Wyk, in "Perspectives on World Hunger and the Extent of Our Positive Duties," *Public Affairs Quarterly* (April 1988), specifically discusses Singer and Hardin. Sources for background information, empirical data, and bibliographic references on this issue are Arline T. Golkin, *Famine: A Heritage of Hunger* (Regina Books, 1987) and Patricia L. Kutzner, *World Hunger: A Reference Handbook* (ABC-CLIO, 1991).

Other sources are William Aiken and Hugh LaFollette, eds., *World Hunger and Moral Obligation* (Prentice Hall, 1977); Peter G. Brown and Henry Shue, eds., *Food Policy: The Responsibility of the United States in the Life and Death Choices* (Free Press, 1977); Susan George, *How the Other Half Dies: The Real Reasons for World Hunger* (Allanheld, 1977); Library of Congress, Congressional Research Service, *Feeding the World's Population: Developments in the Decade Following the World Food Conference of 1974* (Government Printing Office, 1984); The Hunger Project, *Ending Hunger: An Idea Whose Time Has Come* (Praeger, 1985); Onora O'Neill, *Faces of Hunger* (Allen & Unwin, 1985); Gary E. McCuen, ed., *World Hunger and Social Justice* (GEM Publications, 1986); Frances M. Lappé and Joseph Collins, *World Hunger: Twelve Myths* (Institute for Food & Development Policy, 1986); Brian W. J. LeMay, ed., *Science, Ethics, and Food* (Smithsonian Institution Press, 1988); Jean Dreze and Amartya Sen, *Hunger and Public Action* (Clarendon Press, 1989); Lehman B. Fletcher, ed., *World Food in the 1990s: Production, Trade, and Aid* (Westview Press, 1992); Phillips Foster, *The World Food Problem: Tackling the Causes of Undernutrition in the Third World* (Lynne Rienner, 1992); and Henry Shue, *Basic Rights: Subsistence, Affluence and U.S. Foreign Policy*, 2d ed. (Princeton University Press, 1996).

CONTRIBUTORS TO THIS VOLUME

EDITOR

STEPHEN SATRIS was born in New York City. He received a BA in philosophy from the University of California, Los Angeles, an MA in philosophy from the University of Hawaii at Manoa, and a Ph.D. in philosophy from Cambridge University, England. He has written on moral and philosophical issues for professional journals, and he is the author of *Ethical Emotivism* (Martinus Nijhoff, 1987). He has taught at several American universities, and he currently teaches philosophy at Clemson University in Clemson, South Carolina. Professor Satris is a former president of the South Carolina Society for Philosophy.

STAFF

David Dean   List Manager
David Brackley   Developmental Editor
Ava Suntoke   Developmental Editor
Tammy Ward   Administrative Assistant
Brenda S. Filley   Production Manager
Juliana Arbo   Typesetting Supervisor
Diane Barker   Proofreader
Lara Johnson   Graphics
Richard Tietjen   Publishing Systems Manager

AUTHORS

JOHN ARTHUR is a philosopher at the State University of New York at Binghamton. He has published on social, political, and legal philosophy.

HUGO ADAM BEDAU is a professor of philosophy at Tufts University in Medford, Massachusetts. He has written widely on social, political, and legal topics, especially on the death penalty, and he is the author of *Death Is Different: Studies in the Morality, Law, and Politics of Capital Punishment* (Northeastern University Press, 1987).

TOM BETHELL is a contributing editor to the *National Review* and a visiting media fellow at the Hoover Institution.

RICHARD BRANDT taught philosophy for many years at Swarthmore College and the University of Michigan. He has written books on moral issues and on the philosophy of Friedrich Schleiermacher, including *A Theory of the Right and the Good* (Oxford University Press, 1979).

NICHOLAS CAPALDI is the McFarlin Professor of Philosophy at the University of Tulsa in Tulsa, Oklahoma. Among his books is *Out of Order: Affirmative Action and the Crisis of Doctrinaire Liberalism* (Prometheus Books, 1985).

DAVID T. COURTWRIGHT is a professor of history in and chair of the Department of History and Philosophy at the University of North Florida in Jacksonville, Florida. A member of the American Historical Association, his research interests focus on history and on drug abuse and alcoholism. His publications include *Dark Paradise: Opiate Addiction in America Before 1940* (Harvard University Press, 1982).

ROBERT DAWIDOFF teaches history at the Claremont Graduate School. A 1996–1997 Getty Scholar, he is writing a history of gay men in American culture.

JANE ENGLISH (1947–1978) was a philosopher whose published work was primarily on feminism and social philosophy.

J. GAY-WILLIAMS, a very private individual, does not wish to have any biographical information included on him in any publication.

TRUDY GOVIER spends her time lecturing at the University of Calgary in Calgary, Alberta, Canada, writing on a variety of philosophical topics, and taking care of family responsibilities. She is a former professor of philosophy at Trent University in Peterborough, Ontario, Canada.

GARRETT HARDIN, an ecologist and microbiologist, is best known for his 1968 essay "The Tragedy of the Commons," which is widely accepted as a fundamental contribution to ecology, population theory, economics, and political science. He was a professor of human ecology at the University of California, Santa Barbara, for more than 30 years. Since his retirement in 1978, he has devoted himself to writing and public speaking.

MELVILLE J. HERSKOVITS (1895–1963) was a prominent American anthropologist who conducted field research in West Africa, sub-Saharan Africa, the Caribbean, and South America. He was the founding president of the African Studies Association.

CARL F. HOROWITZ is a policy analyst at the Heritage Foundation in Washington, D.C., a public policy research and education institute whose programs are intended to apply a conservative philosophy to current policy questions. He has also held an academic appointment at Virginia Polytechnic Institute and State University.

RHODA E. HOWARD is a professor of sociology at McMaster University in Hamilton, Ontario, Canada.

VINAY LAL is the William R. Kenan Fellow in the Society of Fellows in the Humanities at Columbia University in New York City.

C. STEPHEN LAYMAN is a professor of the philosophy of religion and ethics in the Department of Philosophy at Seattle Pacific University in Seattle, Washington.

MICHAEL P. T. LEAHY is a British philosopher at the University of Kent in England.

HELEN E. LONGINO is a professor in the Center for Advanced Feminist Studies at the University of Minnesota in Minneapolis, Minnesota, where she teaches and writes on feminist theory and the philosophy of science. She is the author of *Science as Social Knowledge: Value and Objectivity in Scientific Inquiry* (Princeton University Press, 1990).

DON MARQUIS is a professor of philosophy at the University of Kansas in Lawrence, Kansas. He has written on issues in medical ethics.

JOHN S. MAYO is president emeritus of Lucent Technologies Bell Laboratories, formerly AT&T Bell Laboratories.

ALBERT G. MOSLEY is a professor of philosophy at Ohio University in Athens, Ohio. He is the editor of *African Philosophy: Selected Readings* (Prentice Hall, 1995) and the author of numerous articles on affirmative action.

ETHAN A. NADELMANN is director of the Lindesmith Center, a drug-policy research institute in New York, and an assistant professor of politics and public affairs at Princeton University in Princeton, New Jersey. He was the founding coordinator of the Harvard Study Group on Organized Crime, and he has been a consultant to the Department of State's Bureau of International Narcotics Matters. He is also an assistant editor of the *Journal of Drug Issues*.

MICHAEL NAVA is the author of five mystery novels featuring gay Latino attorney Henry Rios, four of which have earned him Lambda Literary Awards. He earned his law degree at the Stanford University School of Law. He has been a Los Angeles deputy city attorney and a research attorney for the California Court of Appeals. He currently has a private practice in San Francisco.

THOMAS W. PEARD is an assistant professor of philosophy at Baker University in Baldwin City, Kansas. He earned his Ph.D. in philosophy and his J.D. from the University of Colorado at Boulder. He has several years of experience as a practicing attorney, and he specializes in philosophy of law, philosophy of language, and related areas.

LOUIS P. POJMAN is a professor of philosophy at the United States Military Academy. He is the author or editor of more than 20 books, including *Ethics: Discovering Right and Wrong*, 2d ed. (Wadsworth, 1995) and *What Can We Know?* (Wadsworth, 1995). He earned his Ph.D. from Oxford University, and he has been a Fulbright Fellow to the University of Copenhagen.

ELIZABETH POWERS teaches in the German department at Drew University in Madison, New Jersey, and writes for national publications on literary and feminist subjects. She is the author of two novels and coeditor of *Pilgrim Souls: An Anthology of Spiritual Autobiography* (Simon & Schuster, 1998).

JAMES RACHELS, a philosopher, is the University Professor of Philosophy at the University of Alabama, Birmingham. He has written on issues in morality and method ethics, and he is the author of many books, including *Created from Animals: The Moral Implications of Darwinism* (Oxford University Press, 1990).

JONATHAN RAUCH is a writer for the *Economist* in London and the author of *Kindly Inquisitors: The New Attacks on Free Thought* (University of Chicago Press, 1993).

BERTRAND RUSSELL (1872–1970) was a philosopher and logician whose most notable contributions have been to the philosophy of logic and mathematical logic. He is the author or coauthor of over 50 books, including *Principia Mathematica* (Cambridge University Press, 1910), with Alfred North Whitehead, and *A History of Western Philosophy* (Allen & Unwin, 1945).

RUTH SIDEL is a professor of sociology at Hunter College in New York City. She received an M.S.W. at the Boston University School of Social Work and a Ph.D. at Union Graduate School. Her publications include *Women and Children Last: The Plight of Poor Women in Affluent America* (Viking Penguin, 1987).

PETER SINGER is a professor of philosophy and deputy director of the Centre for Human Bioethics at Monash University in Clayton, Victoria, Australia, where he has been teaching since 1977. He is coeditor of the journal *Bioethics*, and his publications include *The Reproduction Revolution* (Charles Scribner, 1984) and *Should the Baby Live? The Problem of Handicapped Infants* (Oxford University Press, 1985), with Helga Kuhse.

JAMES H. SNIDER is a university fellow in the political science department at Northwestern University in Evanston, Illinois. A former school board member, he is coauthor, with Terra Ziporyn, of *Future Shop: How New Technologies Will Change the Way We Shop and What We Buy* (St. Martin's Press, 1992).

ALAN SOBLE is a professor of philosophy and University Research Professor at the University of New Orleans. He founded the Society for the Philosophy of Sex and Love in 1977 and served as its director until 1992. He is the author of many works, including *The Philosophy of Sex and Love: An Introduction* (Paragon House, 1997) and *Sexual Investigations* (New York University Press, 1996).

ERNEST VAN DEN HAAG is a distinguished scholar at the Heritage Foundation, in Washington, D.C., a public policy research and education institute whose programs are intended to apply a conservative philosophy to current policy questions. A regular lecturer at Columbia University, Yale University, and Harvard University, he is also a contributing editor to *National Review* magazine, and he is coauthor, with John P. Conrad, of *The Death Penalty: A Debate* (Plenum, 1983).

INDEX